KV-012-749

A Sense of Place:

Multidisciplinary Essays in Honour of Malachy McEldowney

Malachy McEldowney

A Sense of Place: Multidisciplinary Essays in Honour of Malachy McEldowney

Edited by Frank Gaffikin, Stephen McKay, Michael Murray, Brendan Murtagh and Ken Sterrett

Institute of Spatial and Environmental Planning
Queen's University Belfast

Published in 2015
by the Institute of Spatial and Environmental Planning
Queen's University Belfast

British Library Cataloguing in Publication Data
A Catalogue record for this book
is available from the British Library

ISBN
978-0-9551347-2-2

Cover design by Jonathan McHugh (www.beepencil.com)
Layout and printing by CDS, Print & Repro Centre,
Queen's University Belfast

Contents

List of Illustrations

List of Tables

List of Photographs

Notes on Contributors

Michael Bannon is Professor Emeritus of Planning at the School of Geography, Planning and Environmental Policy, University College Dublin.

Jayne Bassett is Lecturer in Planning at the School of Planning, Architecture and Civil Engineering, Queen's University Belfast.

Jonathan Bell is a PhD graduate in Planning from the School of Planning, Architecture and Civil Engineering, Queen's University Belfast.

Elaine Bennett was a Research Assistant on the Housing and Asset Transfer research project (funded by the BRIC Programme) at the School of Planning, Architecture and Civil Engineering, Queen's University Belfast.

Philip Boland is Lecturer in Planning at the School of Planning, Architecture and Civil Engineering, Queen's University Belfast.

Pat Braniff is Director of Braniff Associates, Chartered Town Planners, Belfast.

John Brontë is a PhD student in Planning at the School of Planning, Architecture and Civil Engineering, Queen's University Belfast.

Rachel Conn is a MSc graduate in Sustainable Rural Development from the Gibson Institute, Queen's University Belfast.

Lisa Copeland is Lecturer in Planning at the School of Planning, Architecture and Civil Engineering, Queen's University Belfast.

Michael Donnelly is Research Assistant at the School of Planning, Architecture and Civil Engineering, Queen's University Belfast.

Geraint Ellis is Professor of Planning at the School of Planning, Architecture and Civil Engineering, Queen's University Belfast.

Douglas Ferguson was, until retirement, Senior Lecturer in Civil Engineering at the School of Planning, Architecture and Civil Engineering, Queen's University Belfast.

Wesley Flannery is Lecturer in Planning at the School of Planning, Architecture and Civil Engineering, Queen's University Belfast.

Frank Gaffikin is Professor of Planning at the School of Planning, Architecture and Civil Engineering, Queen's University Belfast.

Mark Hackett is an Architect and Co-Director of The Forum for Alternative Belfast.

John Hendry is Professor Emeritus of Planning at the School of Planning, Architecture and Civil Engineering, Queen's University Belfast.

David Houston is Programmer in Planning at the School of Planning, Architecture and Civil Engineering, Queen's University Belfast.

Ruth Hunter is Lecturer at the UKCRC Centre of Excellence for Public Health (Northern Ireland), Queen's University Belfast.

Frank Kee is Clinical Professor at the UKCRC Centre of Excellence for Public Health (Northern Ireland), Queen's University Belfast.

Luke Kelleher is Research Assistant at the School of Planning, Architecture and Civil Engineering, Queen's University Belfast.

Karen Latimer is Medical & HSC Librarian at Library Services, Queen's University Belfast.

Michael Lennon is Lecturer in Spatial Planning at the School of Planning and Geography, Cardiff University.

Adrian Long is Professor Emeritus of Civil Engineering at the School of Planning, Architecture and Civil Engineering, Queen's University Belfast.

Ruth McAreavey is Lecturer in Planning at the School of Planning, Architecture and Civil Engineering, Queen's University Belfast.

Stephen McKay is Senior Lecturer in Planning at the School of Planning, Architecture and Civil Engineering, Queen's University Belfast.

Jenny Muir is Lecturer in Planning at the School of Planning, Architecture and Civil Engineering, Queen's University Belfast.

Michael Murray is Reader in Planning at the School of Planning, Architecture and Civil Engineering, Queen's University Belfast.

Brendan Murtagh is Reader in Planning at the School of Planning, Architecture and Civil Engineering, Queen's University Belfast.

William J V Neill is Professor Emeritus of Spatial Planning at the Department of Geography and Environment in the School of Geosciences, University of Aberdeen.

Eoin O'Neill is Lecturer in Environmental Policy at the School of Geography, Planning and Environmental Policy, University College Dublin.

Linda Price is Lecturer in Planning at the School of Planning, Architecture and Civil Engineering, Queen's University Belfast.

Anthony Quinn is Director of Braniff Associates, Chartered Town Planners, Belfast.

Mark Scott is Professor of Planning and Head of School at the School of Geography, Planning and Environmental Policy, University College Dublin.

Urmi Sengupta is Lecturer in Planning at the School of Planning, Architecture and Civil Engineering, Queen's University Belfast.

Ken Sterrett is Senior Lecturer in Planning at the School of Planning, Architecture and Civil Engineering, Queen's University Belfast.

Aileen Stockdale is Professor of Planning at the School of Planning, Architecture and Civil Engineering, Queen's University Belfast.

Mark Tully is Lecturer at the UKCRC Centre of Excellence for Public Health (Northern Ireland), Queen's University Belfast.

Rick Wilford is Professor Emeritus of Politics at the School of Politics, International Studies and Philosophy, Queen's University Belfast.

Malachy McEldowney

This book is dedicated not to Malachy's career, but instead to him as a person. This is more than semantic quibble. In his professional life, Malachy has disavowed narrow careerism. Rather, his work reflects his life and values. While the term 'holistic' is much in vogue at present, that mode has always been central to Malachy's protocol. Quite simply, he walks the talk and is very much the unassuming person of merit and accomplishment. His easy charm, modesty, and kindness, paired with his incisive intellectual rigour, denote a disposition that is indispensable to planning places with people in mind. In short, he is both a scholar and a gentleman, and sensible enough to appreciate that the latter is ultimately more important than the former.

The contemporary academy emphasises virtues of inter-disciplinarity and international networking. Over many decades, Malachy has exemplified both. Indeed, he has been a border-crosser in the geographical and figurative sense. Though rooted in the island of Ireland, his love of travel and diversity has ensured against any parochial perspective that would privilege the ethnic over the civic. His qualification and practice in both planning and architecture serve him well in bridging this unfortunate divide in the built environment, and in understanding the difference between grand plans and their actual delivery. Despite his rural origin and affinity, his studies have focussed largely on the urban and regional. An unrepentant modernist, he holds preeminent architectural styles of all traditions in deep esteem. While concerned about design and conservation of the best heritage, he operates under no delusion that there are design solutions to present-day spatial problems that have to be contextualised in all their complex social derivation. Moreover, in the milieu of this contested society, as a person from a Catholic background, he enjoyed a long and happy marriage to Sally, a person from a Protestant background. Though devoted to their own children in a closely knit family, they showed generous spirit to be open to extending their family through regular fostering.

In all these ways and more, Malachy demonstrates through deeds over words what it means to be both human and humane - no better attributes for the good academic in an applied scholarship. Since today's world is one of an intriguing assortment of both people and place, his inherent talent for hybridity - for crossing borders - positions him favourably for rounded and grounded analysis of modern times. For all who work with him, he makes for a stimulating and amiable colleague. In no small part, that is because he remains collegial. So, for example, when Malachy was Head of Environmental Planning at Queen's between 1993 and 2002, he was responsible for the growth and development of the discipline through a visionary and judicious appointment of people, in whom he invested faith and trust. These are the qualities that make for good human relations, and productive collective endeavour.

A brief excursion through Malachy's biography illustrates the foundations for these varied aptitudes. Born in Kilrea, he was a good example of that post-war generation that benefited from the new Welfare State's 1947 Education Act, with his schooling ultimately leading to St Columb's College in Derry/Londonderry, an establishment dating back to 1879, and including in its alumni, two Nobel laureates, Seamus Heaney and John Hume. From there, his study of Architecture at Queen's was followed by a course in Civic Design at Liverpool University, and subsequent practice in urban design and planning with Leicester City Council between 1973 and 1979, an interesting place of increasing ethnic diversity in Britain. Malachy's academic career at Queen's began in 1981 having moved from De Montford University and leading to his subsequent appointment as Professor of Planning.

Indicative of his global networking were the periods he spent as Visiting Professor at the University of Kansas in the US (1984) and the University of Niteroi in Brazil (1988). Further international linkages reflect themselves in the European studies he has undertaken. For instance, just regarding the last decade, he played a prominent part in the European Cooperation in the field of Scientific and Technical (COST) research into *European Cities: Insights into Outskirts*, which explored the varied patterns of urban agglomerations, home to 80% of European residents. Another such study, traversing 13 European countries, involved investigation into the *Contemporary Discourses in European Academy*, addressing the impact of multiculturalism, neo-liberalism, and globalism on the changing structure and culture of European universities, and the related shifting impact of these important anchor institutions on their city-regions. Such comparative work demonstrates again the intellectual and geographical reach of his scholarship. Worthy of note is the similarity between his pedagogy and writing. Both epitomise a deceptively conversational tone, which while appealing and engaging, retains a very structured and insightful narrative and analysis. Once more, this style reflects his distinctive ability to convey complexity in an unpretentious manner.

Recognition of Malachy's contribution to the field has taken many forms, from the many students who can testify to his inspirational influence to well-deserved honours, such as the RTPI Northern Ireland President's Planning Leaders Award in 2012. As editors of this *festschrift* we are delighted on behalf of all our contributors to celebrate and honour Malachy McEldowney as scholar and friend.

The editors

Appreciation

My first encounter with Planning was in late 1968 when I was appointed Assistant Professor (Structural Engineering) at Queen's University, Kingston, Ottawa, Canada. The former Head of Department, Professor Stanley Lash, had just returned from a year in London where he had attended an MSc course on Planning. Stanley had helped plan a few sub-divisions in Kingston and realised that his background in Civil Engineering had been highly beneficial. Thus, he set about introducing a Masters course in Planning in 1970 which ran in parallel with other MSc courses in Structures, Hydraulics and Soil Sciences. Unfortunately, few Civil Engineering graduates shared his enthusiasm for the subject and, as is the case throughout the world, the course tended to attract Geographers and Economists. Thus some 40 years later the two years Master of Planning (MPL) is now offered at the School of Urban and Regional Planning. It is highly regarded internationally and it has established strong links with China.

In 1989 the disciplines of Civil Engineering, Architecture and Planning were re-structured into a School in the Faculty of Engineering at Queen's University Belfast. I became Director of the School of the Built Environment which was made up of two Departments; one was Architecture and Planning (with John Hendry as Head of Department), and the other was Civil Engineering (with Alan Jennings as Head of Department). It quickly became apparent that without an undergraduate course in Planning, this important discipline in the School would be vulnerable. Thus, after much heart searching and debate, it was agreed at the School Board that an undergraduate course in Planning would be launched in the 1990s. Malachy McEldowney was appointed Head of a new Department of Environmental Planning and we became a School with three Departments. In hindsight this was a wise decision as the undergraduate course in Planning at Queen's is now well established and attracts excellent, well qualified students.

In 2002-2003 I was privileged to become the 138th President of the Institution of Civil Engineers (ICE), a first for a resident of Northern Ireland. This is the oldest professional body for Engineers in the world and was established in 1818 (the first President was none other than the great Thomas Telford). Because of my interest in Planning, I became aware of the links between our professions and I will quote a paragraph (based on Council minutes) from a history of the Institution of Civil Engineers which places this in context:

> In the immediate post war period, when reconstruction of war-torn cities and the need for rehousing people on a large scale had the highest priority, a new breed

> of experts, the town planners, evolved. The appointment of a Minister of Town and Country Planning for England and Wales supported this development, and he and the Secretary of State for Scotland invited the Institution's views on the problems which were presented. A conference was held by the Institution in 1947 with representatives of the Royal Institute of British Architects, the Royal Institution of Chartered Surveyors, and the Institution of Municipal Engineers, and its conclusion was work in this field should properly be entrusted to engineers, architects and surveyors with the necessary technical qualifications and experience. The Council saw no reason for the creation of a separate profession covering town planning. (Watson, 1988, pp.84-85)

Clearly their "advice" was not accepted as the government of the day decided to liaise with the Town Planning Institute.

During a hectic but most challenging year in office, I travelled extensively to visit some of our 80,000 members, as far West as Vancouver, South as Capetown and East as Tokyo. One of the highlights of the year was a visit to Shanghai to attend a Bridge Engineering Conference and award Professor Xu Kwang Di an Honorary Fellowship of the ICE – the select group of thirty Honorary Fellows includes the Senior Fellow, the Duke of Edinburgh, and the King of Thailand. In the 1990s, Xu had been Mayor of the city of Shanghai (it now has a population of over 20 million) but he had great respect for the UK education system, having lectured at Imperial College earlier in his career. As a consequence, whilst Mayor, he sent three or four of his senior staff in Shanghai to study Planning in London. He repeated this for a number of years and the benefits of a consistent approach to Planning in Shanghai are evident in that most impressive city. For example, a ring road around Shanghai was built in less than 18 months whilst the much less impressive M25 around London took many decades. During our visit we joined Xu and his team for lunch with the British Consul in Shanghai and the travel time from our hotel to the Consulate took us one and a half hours by taxi. After lunch, Xu insisted that we travel with him to the conference hotel where I was to award him with the Honorary Fellowship. We travelled in a motorcade of black Buicks along traffic free streets and got to the hotel in 15 minutes.

The conclusion I have reached is that Planners have an extremely important role to play across the world and it has been a privilege to contribute to this. I have always found Malachy McEldowney to be a wonderful friend and colleague. I knew that Planning was in safe hands when he was Head of Department.

Reference

Watson, J.G. (1988) *The Civils.* London: ICE Publishing, Thomas Telford Ltd.

Adrian Long

In his personal life, Malachy has been a long time proponent of sustainable transport, having selected one of the early battery/petrol, hybrid powered, saloon cars for his personal use – the Toyota Prius. He also makes use of local public transport and is an enthusiastic social touring (but not racing style) cyclist. In his professional life at Queen's, Malachy was an integral part of the Joint Universities Land Use Transportation Unit (JULUTU) set up between the two Northern Ireland universities in the early 1990s. This Unit was spearheaded by Professor John Hendry from Queen's and Professor Austin Smyth from UUJ. This was a multi-disciplinary academic team linking strategic planning, engineering infrastructure and economic forecasting/ evaluation. One of the Unit's early projects was commissioned by the Northern Ireland Transport Holding Company (NITHC) to investigate alternative urban transport strategies for Greater Belfast.

As part of this commission, a study tour for members of the JULUTU and NITHC / Translink was organised in May 1992 involving travel to Belgium and Germany to view a variety of urban transport systems that might have future application for Belfast. The group was 15-20 strong and overland travel was arranged from Belfast via Cairnryan and onward by coach to the P&O Hull to Zeebrugge overnight ferry. On arrival in Belgium visits were made to Ghent to view articulated single-decker trolleybuses, to Brussels to view different traditional tram systems and to Rochefort to view the experimental test track of the Bombardier Guided Light Transit (GLT) vehicle. This three-car articulated rubber tyred vehicle was able to negotiate 10m radius curves on unguided sections by independent computerised steering of its four axles and could be both guided (centre single track) or unguided for added flexibility.

A visit was also made to cities in Germany including Cologne and Essen. The latter was one of the few cities at that time to have adopted a Guided Bus system and our group was invited to take a trip on one of the adapted vehicles. Whilst on board, an emergency stop was advertised to the passengers but some of the academics were not listening and did not return to their seats as requested. The brakes were suddenly applied and the sight of one or two heavyweight academics hurtling up the central aisle towards the driver is not to be forgotten, but alas is not recorded for posterity!

With Manchester getting its Metrolink LRT system in 1992 and Sheffield opening its LRT in 1994, interest in tracked urban systems in UK and Ireland continued. Unfortunately, unlike Dublin, Belfast did not take the plunge and 20 plus years later, after a plethora of consultancy reports, it is still developing its first Bus Rapid Transit system.

Members of this team, that included Malachy McEldowney, continued to work with Northern Ireland government bodies on other sustainable transport projects over the next twenty years. Assignments included developing and monitoring Park and Ride schemes, alternative rapid transit technologies, the school journey, Quality Bus Corridors and priority for buses at traffic signal controlled intersections. Much of this research activity was undertaken jointly with Austin Smyth and his transport research unit at Napier University. This interdisciplinary research helped to cement professional and academic links within the then School of the Built Environment at Queen's and latterly within the School of Planning, Architecture and Civil Engineering at this university.

Douglas Ferguson

Chapter 1

Patrick Abercrombie's Dublin of the Future

Michael J. Bannon

Introduction

In June 1915 Patrick Abercrombie was appointed as the second Lever Chair in Civic Design and Town Planning at Liverpool University. The Department of Civic Design, founded in 1909 as the world's first school of Town Planning, had a new leader that "possessed an exceptional capacity to bring together a number of leading ideas and express them in an accessible and liberating way".[1] His approach to town planning was interdisciplinary, deeply empirical and focussed on marrying urban transformation with environmental sensitivities. His first major plan, *Dublin of the Future: The New Town Plan*, was entered to the Dublin Town Planning Competition in 1914 and succeeded in bringing him wide recognition.[2] This chapter is concerned with that event and the proposals brought forward by Abercrombie and his team for the restructuring of Dublin. Interestingly, many of the issues and ideas explored a century ago have resonance with the contemporary city. But the chapter has added meaning for this book of essays in that Malachy McEldowney is a graduate of the Department of Civic Design at Liverpool University and who, as a friend of the Planning School at University College Dublin, has been bringing students at Queen's on fieldtrips to Dublin over many years.

The Dublin Town Planning Competition

A number of major planning figures appeared on the Dublin scene during the first two decades of the twentieth century that included William Lever, Raymond Unwin and Patrick Geddes.[3] At that time there was an awakening of concern about the bad condition of housing, unemployment, ill health and above all the scourge of tuberculosis. From about 1906 the wife of the Lord Lieutenant, Lady Aberdeen, had taken a lead role in a social reform campaign, especially against tuberculosis, culminating in the convening of the Royal Institute of Public Health 1911 Annual Congress in Dublin. To this she invited Patrick Geddes and his City and Town Planning Exhibition as a backcloth to the Congress and as a platform for environmental reform. The Exhibition embraced a programme of lectures that included an address on "The need for Town Planning" by Professor Stanley Adshead who had been appointed head of the new Department of Civic Design at Liverpool University in 1909. By 1913 Geddes was back in Dublin giving evidence to an inquiry into Dublin housing conditions. It may have been during this visit that he persuaded Lord Aberdeen, as well as Her Ladyship, about the educational benefit of a Dublin Town Planning Competition, alongside a staging of his enlarged City and Town Planning Exhibition. The idea of a town planning competition had been common-place in Germany and Austria for the best part of fifty years and Geddes saw in such competitions an excellent means of stimulating new ideas.[4] Under pressure from Geddes, Lord Aberdeen agreed to offer a prize of £500 for the winning entry in the competition. The competition was to be seen in relation to a forthcoming Civic Exhibition and Summer School designed to help educate citizens about their own environment:

> It is in connection with this Exhibition that a prize of £500 has been offered for the best survey and scheme of building improvement in this city, and a (sic) claim that the money may justly be regarded as being not less directed to the ultimate benefit of its inhabitants, and especially the poorest of the inhabitants than if it were expended on gifts of meat and clothing. Probably the latter form of benefit would be less desirable than the other, certainly in the long run.[5]

Notice of the competition was widely circulated[6] and by 31st March 1914 the Housing and Town Planning Association of Ireland (HTPAI) Technical Committee had finalised detailed particulars and conditions of the competition. The designs, to be completed and submitted before 1 September 1914,[7] were to consist of a written report, containing a summary of main conclusions, recommendations and estimates, together with drawings mounted on linen and on stretchers at scales of 12" or 6" to one mile, 25" to one mile and street sections at 1 inch to 20 feet.[8]

The planning proposals were to relate to a Greater Dublin area taking in Howth, Glasnevin, Ashtown, Dundrum, and Dalkey. The submissions should have regard to the following main headings:

1. Communications: road, rail and canal systems; existing and proposed industrial locations and main existing and proposed streets and thoroughfares.
2. Housing: existing tenements, number, location and types of dwellings required, housing densities, phasing of developments, open space in every area using the American standard of 10 per cent Open Space and the relocation of institutions from centre city to suburbs.
3. Metropolitan improvements: better use of the city's situation including

the rivers and bay, preservation or expansion needs of public buildings – for example, Administration Buildings, New Art Gallery, Cathedral etc., provision of parkways and park system.

The submitted plans were to be assessed by Geddes, Dr John Nolen (Professor of City Planning at Cambridge, Massachusetts) and Charles McCarthy, the Dublin city architect. The winning submission was to become the property of the HTPAI which was also prepared to preserve for reference any submissions receiving honourable mention. The guidelines emphasised that too much remained unknown about Dublin's needs as yet to allow any definite commitment to implement any of the schemes. Rather the objective was to "elicit Plans and Reports of a preliminary and suggestive character, and thus obtain contributions and alternatives which may be of value towards the guidance of the future development of the City in its various directions".[9]

A total of eight entries were received, of which four were by Irish contestants, two from Liverpool and one from both London and Illinois, USA. Unfortunately, as a result of Geddes's absence in India[10] and the problems of transatlantic navigation, the three assessors were unable to meet to assess the Competition entries and a decision was deferred until August 1916, by which time Geddes had returned to Europe preparing for the Exposition de la Reconstituee in Paris.[11] The entries were examined and after "prolonged and repeated scrutiny, day by day, and by each of the Adjudicators independently"[12] an outright winner was announced and four other submissions received "Honourable Mention".

So good were some of the entries that one of the adjudicators regretted that they were legally bound to give the prize of £500 to the outright winner.[13] Nolen had earlier expressed the hope that "some public spirited gentlemen would supplement the Lord Lieutenant's generous prize for plans by at least two more prizes of £200 and £100."[14]

Having considered all the entries, the prize of £500 was awarded to Patrick Abercrombie, who in association with Sydney and Arthur Kelly, Liverpool surveyors, had compiled the winning entry. The prize was awarded to Abercrombie and his colleagues having regard to the "magnitude and comprehensiveness of exhibit, evidencing corresponding thought and labour" as well as "skill and beauty of execution".[15] The winning entry which was outlined to the public by the *Irish Builder*[16] was ultimately published, together with survey notes and additional material, by the Civics Institute of Ireland in 1922.[17] The competition entry by Abercrombie was the beginning of a lasting association by him with the development and planning of Dublin.[18]

The adjudicators were delighted with the mass of designs and "the many proposals of practical value and suggestive interest" brought forward by the various submissions and "each and all of the Competitors have their particular excellences".[19] Given the detailed terms of reference, the advance material made available to the contestants[20] and the common backcloth of the Civic Exhibition and Summer School, it is hardly surprising that many aspects of the various submissions concur both in respect of the analysis of the existing situation and the resolution of problems. Recurring features in many of the eight submissions include a central passenger station, replacement of the "metal bridge", the erection of a civic centre, the location of a new cathedral and the laying out of new and improved thoroughfares particular a north-south route from Broadstone to St Patrick's Cathedral and the opening up of east-west routes from St. Stephen's Green to Newmarket. The westward continuation of Abbey St was favoured by six of the eight authors.[21] The most extensive report was submitted by Cushing Smith of Illinois and he was complimented "for giving a clear and succinct expression of what is meant and aimed at by Town Planning in general".[22] His proposals included electrification of railways, elimination of the river viaduct, suburbanisation of freight yards, expansion of the port area, development of parks along the rivercourses, location of industry near workers and rail lines, an elaborate subway system, development of playgrounds and the encouragement of functional segregation into special "tracts"[23].

Not surprisingly the entry by Irish architects Kaye-Parry and Ross exercised restraint in regard to the demolition proposals. They had just completed a major vacant and derelict sites survey for the Dublin housing inquiry and thus were especially well informed. The authors emphasised the south western development of the city including industrial expansion in that area as well as in the port area. They proposed a new street from Dame St to Dominic St.[24] They were complimented on "an excellent contribution to the needed City Survey".

But, apart from the winning entry, it was the plans and proposals of London-based Ashbee and Chettle[25] which were most favourably received and it was said "no other Report expresses a fuller and more comprehensive grasp of civic problems".[26] The adjudicators were especially keen that this report be published and, apparently, had circumstances not prevented the full completion of their plans, "the author of the premiated Design might have found in this (submission) a more serious competitor".[27] The less applauded submissions were characterised by bold solutions such as elevated railways, major road developments and the ensuing disruption of the city's fabric.

While the various submitted proposals generated a range of welcome ideas, the adjudicators stated bluntly that "we are not thereby endorsing, all or any of the particular proposals of this series of Plans as solving the problems of Greater Dublin; nor are we recommending their being put into execution to the exclusion of all other alternatives".[28] Years later, Abercrombie reflected that the "competitive circumstances made it impossible to avoid the spectacular".[29] Indeed even Abercrombie's winning entry was criticised by Geddes as impractical since "I told Abercrombie privately his survey was less adequate than it should have been".[30] To Geddes the main value of all the competition entries, including that of Abercrombie, was as tools to educate the public about the nature of town planning.

Abercrombie's plan for Dublin

Unlike Geddes, Patrick Abercrombie was something of an aristocrat, the son of a professional house, educated at Uppingham, and a man who cherished the best things in life. As an architect planner, he widened the dimensions of the planning debate in Dublin as the emphasis shifted away from social policy in town planning. Coming from the University of Liverpool, as noted above, Abercrombie was a member of a department which looked for inspiration to the Ecole des Beaux Arts and Abercrombie himself was clearly influenced by Henard, the French architect and disciple of Haussmann.[31] In addition, Abercrombie had travelled widely in Europe and written widely on European city planning,[32] though he was clearly much impressed with Paris. Abercrombie's Dublin competition entry, which was his first applied planning work, was clearly influenced by the hope and confidence engendered by the Irish Home Rule movement: "The re-establishment of a National Parliament should give the necessary impetus to set a great Town Plan in motion, and the access of material prosperity which will ensue will provide the means to carry it out."[33] Just as Paris under Napoleon III had emerged from a period of darkness which followed the splendour of the eighteenth century, so too, Dublin was about to embark on a second phase of grandeur after the nineteenth century depression. Just as Napoleon III had led the revival and the re-planning of Paris, Dublin was to be refashioned in a manner befitting its new role as a national capital. Dublin, however, was 'coming on stream' in a new age of enlightenment:

> But more fortunate than Paris, Dublin is to be remodelled during a period of greater town planning enlightenment, when Architectural Effect and Traffic Convenience are not alone regarded as the chief essentials: Hygiene Housing and adequate Park Provision, those two aspects partly neglected by Haussmann, are now given their proper place, and these four elements will compose a city that is worthy to be the capital of a modern country.[34]

The plan (Figure 1.1), based on examination of the 1922 published report[35], can be assessed in terms of the three headings laid down by the organisers: Communications, Housing and Metropolitan Improvements.

The central issue for Abercrombie was the finding of the 1913 Dublin Housing Inquiry that 64,000 persons were in immediate need of re-housing

Figure 1.1: City of Dublin New Town Plan

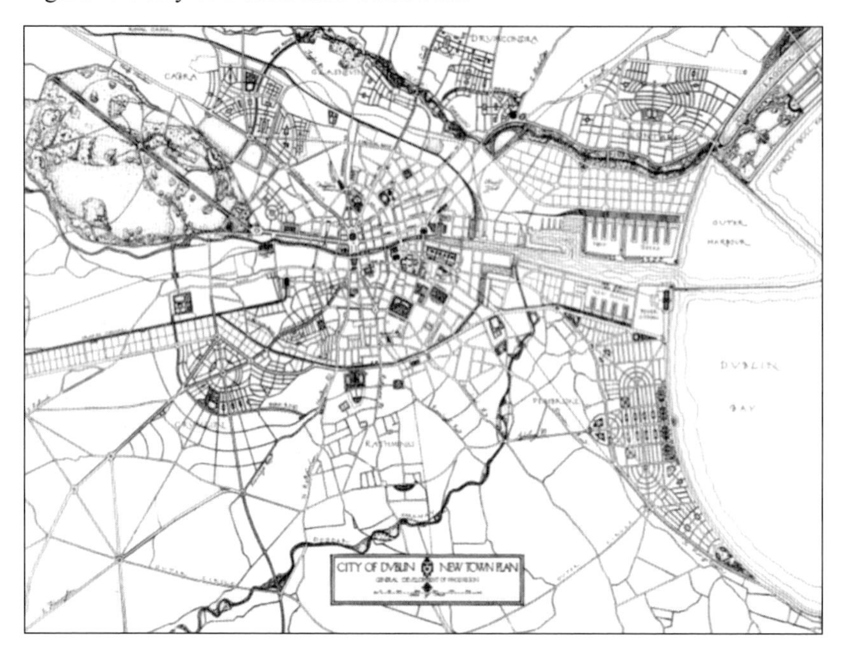

Source: Abercrombie, P. *et al* (1922) *Dublin of the Future*. Dublin: Civics Institute of Ireland.

and that 14,000 new dwellings were required.[36] Abercrombie accepted the recommended density of the campaign group, Citizen's Housing League, of not more than 75 persons per "normal urban acre", and to obtain this the existing built-up area would have to be thinned of 59,750 inhabitants. While an ultimate population "of one or two million inhabitants" in Dublin was deemed easily attainable in the near future[37], sketch plans were prepared only for those areas scheduled to re-house the required number moving out of the overcrowded centre. He argued against re-housing people in the centre since "this would be the old fashioned way", it would keep densities too high and it would also inhibit the commercial expansion and physical remodelling of the old centre to befit its new capital city role.

The over-crowded population was to be re-housed at 12 houses to the acre on 996 acres in Crumlin, Cabra and Drumcondra.[38] These areas were to be laid out on broad neighbourhood lines with a neighbourhood centre "just off, but close by, a main traffic route".[39] Major roads would surround residential districts and housing layouts were recommended on the lines of Bourneville and Port Sunlight, but avoiding the 'fussy picturesqueness' of the early garden suburbs. Some of the smallest housing was set at right angles to the traffic streets and accessible by narrow walks leading to a central children's playground.[40] Allotments would account for the same area as parks - one acre in ten. Where housing was to be provided in the centre, it was proposed to remodel some of the better existing tenements by knocking three houses into one, retaining the central staircase and converting the other two stair wells into sanitary blocks. A further 3,698 persons would be housed in flats on the redeveloped part of City Quay with a further 1,000 on the redeveloped site of the Royal Barracks.

The proposed enlargement of the metropolitan area footprint, in addition to suburban housing, allowed for large areas of industrial development along the Grand Canal at Crumlin and a major reclamation of Dublin Bay.[41] The city would be served by an integrated transport system focussed upon a new Traffic Centre located on both sides of the Liffey immediately east of the Four Courts and stretching from the Ormond Market to Christ Church Cathedral. Upon this centre would converge a new system of rail, tramcar and road transportation. A new underground rail link running mainly along Abbey St would interconnect Amiens St, Westland Row and Kingsbridge Stations, while Broadstone would be linked to Harcourt St Station with an interchange at the underground Central Station. The overhead rail crossing at the Custom House would be undergrounded, thus bringing about "the much desired removal of this bridge, which is a blot on the architectural beauty of the city".[42] There would also be a freight rail link from the docks to the Crumlin industrial area, following the line of the G.S. & O. line under the Phoenix Park. An elaborate tram system and bus network would serve all suburban areas and convey passengers along a largely new system of roads to the Central Station.

The published plan envisaged improved routes - main radials - leading from Drumcondra, Cabra, Lucan, Crumlin, Harold's Cross, Donnybrook and the south-east coast. Of the thirteen radials ten would have an average width of 60ft while the Crumlin, Phoenix Park and Cabra routes were to be 120ft wide; they were described as "super-normal radials" and modelled on the lines of the Champs Elysees in Paris or the Charlottenburg Avenue in Berlin. In the outer parts of the city there would be two circular routes. The outer route would be about 3.5 miles from the centre while the existing Circular Roads would be connected east of the Custom House by an opening bridge at Erne St - Lime St. The Cabra Avenue would come into the Traffic Centre through the grounds of Grangegorman[43] while the Crumlin Avenue would cross the Grand Canal and follow Cork St into the Coombe. The industrial areas of Crumlin and the docks would be interlinked by a 120ft wide road following the south bank of the Grand Canal. The infilled parts of the bay would be used to create new docks, provide industrial land and a location for the "Power Citadel" a huge coal-fired power station. The infill area of Sandymount would be used for residential purposes.[44]

The existence of 1,360 derelict sites[45], the clearance of unsound tenements, the removal of institutions and the impact of new radial routes on the existing structure and fabric of the city gave Abercrombie ample scope to propose "Metropolitan Improvements", thereby providing an opportunity to engage in the spectacular and to propose a new Beaux-Arts type centre in which much of the eastern part of central Dublin would be redeveloped in "La Grande Manner". The overall similarity of approach to Haussmann in Paris is striking[46] even to the extent of providing a site for a Bourse (stock exchange). The broad aim of the redevelopment proposals was to move the central focus of the city westwards,[47] thereby leaving O'Connell St as a monumental route, and creating a new focus around a Traffic Centre at the Four Courts, similar to Place de la Concorde in Paris. This Traffic Centre would be the convergence point of fifteen routes and, together with an inner circular route (along Dominick St, South William St, Kevin St, New Market, Pimlico, Bridgefoot St, Queen St to Broadstone), it would have required wholesale clearance and redevelopment of the area.[48] A new cathedral was to be erected on a cleared site nearby the Linenhall to the north of Capel St (Figure 1.2), while a new national theatre, on the lines of the Paris Opera, would be situated alongside Parnell Square and dominating O'Connell St. Abercrombie proposed that the Houses of Parliament should be suitably enlarged and extended northwards to Aston's Quay.[49] Smithfield Market would become the new retail market area. The Liffey Quays were to be landscaped; the crescent around to the north of the Custom House would be completed and a new bridge was to be erected across the Liffey directly in front of the Custom House. The other major metropolitan improvement related to the provision of parks. In gross terms Dublin had an average of approximately one acre of open space for every 100 persons but this was largely due to the existence of the Phoenix Park and the Bull Island. These few large spaces masked the total need figures and thus local spaces and recreation facilities were severely underprovided.[50] Abercrombie envisaged an increase of park provision from 1,712 acres to 3,312 acres. Parks and open spaces would be provided in a hierarchical manner from small playgrounds (for which derelict sites might be used) and neighbourhood parks (made possible by relocation of institutions) to great town parks and elaborately designed parkways along the Tolka and Dodder rivers. There were also proposals for "park highways" and nature reserves in the Howth and Dublin Mountain areas. As with most of the competition entries, land vacated by institutions would be used mostly for local parks and open space provision.[51]

Finally, the Abercrombie planning proposals introduced the concepts of zoning and phasing of development. The zoning map introduced six land use zones and also four grades of residential use development,[52] decreasing in density outwards from the neighbourhood centres. The phasing map related to

Figure 1.2: Diagrammatic sketch showing suggested Cathedral site.

Source: Abercrombie, P. *et al* (1922) *Dublin of the Future*. Dublin: Civics Institute of Ireland.

the programme of road development with priority being given to immediate work on the construction of the Cabra and Crumlin Avenues and also part of the Traffic Centre. Outer suburban roads were indicated as long-term proposals.[53]

Even though these proposals formed part of a competition, any discussion of implementation called for both planning legislation and planning machinery. While the Housing and Town Planning Association of Ireland had already emphasised that much better use could be made of existing legislation,[54] the Association did actively promote the enactment of new Irish planning legislation. While there were many demands that the English 1909 Housing and Town Planning Act should be extended to Ireland, many were also doubtful as to its applicability believing that even if it were extended to Ireland,[55] "nothing could come of it owing to the financial difficulties involved in its application".[56] Indeed Geddes wished for an extension 'of planning powers and, while he considered the 1909 Act to be "a great advance on its predecessors", he was clearly unsure of its relevance to Ireland and he encouraged Ireland to look to the Continent rather than to English manufacturing towns for its inspiration.[57]

Like Geddes, Abercrombie argued that developments carried out without reference to planning principles could frustrate progress and that "enormous results can be obtained if only everything that is done, however small, is part of a thought-out organic scheme".[58] The lack of a plan could equally discourage investment - "a waterlogged bog with no prospect of drainage will not attract an enterprising farmer".[59] In other words, if Ireland were to be prosperous and if that prosperity were to be reflected in the capital city - "the capital of a country ought to be a national asset" - planning legislation was required.

Abercrombie called for an Act of Parliament, not following the English Act since "the relative conditions are not the same",[60] but an Act setting up a central Commission on Town Planning[61] with subsidiary local boards comprised of the mayor or chairman of the local authority, a number of ratepayers' representatives, the engineer, surveyor and architect of the municipality, in addition to a town planning and housing expert. Local Boards in country places could have jurisdiction over several municipalities with it being "taken for granted that Town Planning is a necessity for every town and village".[62] Local and county boards would prepare schemes, district plans and even a regional plan. Proposals from local and county Boards would have to be approved by the Central Board[63] and ratified by Parliament.

In the absence of a proper survey[64] Abercrombie saw his *Dublin of the Future* report as a symbol of the comprehensive plan required for Dublin - "a starting point and possibly as a quarry of ideas from which the final plan may be built."[65] The report would serve to educate people as to the magnitude of the task before them and it should be regarded as a local textbook on town planning.[66] But comprehensive planning was needed to ensure that Dublin was a national asset and that the expected prosperity of a new Ireland was reflected in the restored grandeur and civic splendour of its capital city.

Concluding comments

Reaction to both the competition results generally and to the Abercrombie proposals in particular was muted and mixed. The contents of Abercrombie's report was first outlined to the general public in the *Irish Builder*, which praised the clarity of the text but was dubious of the various major redevelopment proposals for the centre.[67] The Civics Institute, which formally took over the functions of the HTPAI from 30 June 1916 and remained active for almost thirty years, organised a public display of the competition entries in November 1916 and these again featured prominently in the 1917 Dublin Civic Week exhibition in the Chamber of Commerce when Abercrombie addressed the Dublin Rotary Club on "The Interdependence of Housing and Transport" with reference to his proposals.[68] However at that time, the advent of a war of independence was an inauspicious time for planning progress. While there was little prospect of ever implementing the Abercrombie proposals,[69] they did generate considerable discussion. The award drew institutional attention to Abercrombie[70] and also initiated his lifelong association with planning in Dublin; many years later Abercrombie still believed that "in the main, the general outline of the plan of 1914 could yet be followed, subject to certain modifications".[71] In the end the winning entry was eventually published in 1922, some five years after the announcement of the award - as a result of the work of the Civics Institute. Nonetheless, the Competition entry as published is hard to square with his later work on Dublin which limits the size of the city and introduces a London-like arrangement of greenbelt and growth villages;[72] it is very different to his 1922 report which clearly influenced Horace T. O'Rourke (author of the 1925 Dublin Civic Survey) and the architectural profession in Dublin. While the need for planning at local, regional and national level was recognised and encouraged by a wide spectrum of opinion in the new state, concrete results were to be limited and long delayed. For the most part, another forty years were to pass before the emergence of workable planning legislation, an active planning profession and the beginnings of effective planning.

Acknowledgement
This chapter draws on research previously published in Bannon, M. (1985) The genesis of modern Irish planning, in Bannon, M. (ed.) *The emergence of Irish planning 1880-1920*. Dublin: Turoe Press, pp. 189-261.

Endnotes

1 Dehaene, M. (2004) Urban lessons for the modern planner: Patrick Abercrombie and the study of urban development, *Town Planning Review*, 75(1), pp.1-30.

2 Wright, M. (1982) *Lord Leverhulme's unknown venture: the Lever Chair and the beginnings of town and regional planning 1908-48.* London: Hutchinson Benham.

3 Aalen, F.H.A. (1985) "The Working Class housing movement in Dublin, 1850-1920", in M.J. Bannon (ed) *The emergence of Irish planning 1880-1920*. Dublin: Turoe Press, pp131-188.

4 Breitling, P. (1980) "The role of the competition in the genesis of urban planning: Germany and Austria in the Nineteenth Century" in A. Sutcliffe (ed) *The rise of modern urban planning, 1800-1914*. London: Mansell, pp.31-54.

5 Quoted from speech by Lord Aberdeen to Burns Club - See *Irish Architect & Craftsman*, Vol. VI, (1914), p. 645.

6 "Civics Exhibition, Ireland, 1914: Competition for Designs for The Improvement and extension of Dublin", *Journal R.I.B.A.*, Vol. 21 (1914), p. 409 - also *Town Planning Review*, Vol. V (1914), p. 68.

7 *The Irish Builder & Engineer*, Vol. LVI (1914), pp. 256-9, called for six to twelve months for preparation of submissions.

8 See *Irish Architect & Craftsman*, Vol. VI (1914), pp. 774-5.

9 P. Abercrombie, *Town & Country Planning*, (Thornton & Butterworth, London, 1933), p. 137.

10 The reasons for the lengthy delay in the adjudication were outlined in *Irish Builder & Engineer*, Vol. LVIII (1916), p. 302.

11 Kitchen, P. (1975) *A most unsettling person: an introduction to the ideas and life of Patrick Geddes*. London: Victor Gollancz.

12 *Competitive Designs for Town Plan of Dublin: Report of The Adjudicators*, (Civics Institute of Ireland, 17 October 1916), 12 pp. The author wishes to thank Dr Cuthbert, of Heriot Watt University, who brought to his attention the existence of an independent nine page assessment of the Competition entries by Thomas Adams, who was then Town Planning Adviser to the Canadian Commission on Conservation. The report is dated September 6,1916 and reaches broadly similar recommendations to the adjudicators.

13 J. Nolen, "Greater Dublin: Competitive Designs for the Town Plan of Dublin, Ireland," *Landscape Arch.*, Vol. VII (1917), p. 75.

14 *Irish Architect & Craftsman*, Vol. VII (1917),p. 747.

15 *Adjudicators' Report*, op. cit., p. 2.

16 *Irish Builder & Engineer*, Vol. LVIII (1916), pp. 463-4.

17 P. Abercrombie et. al., *Dublin of The Future* (Civics Institute of Ireland, Dublin, 1922), 55 pp.

18 For an overview of the life and work of Abercrombie see G. Dix (1981) , "Patrick Abercrombie" in G.E. Cherry (ed) *Pioneers in British planning*. London: The Architectural Press, pp. 103-30.

19 *Adjudicators' Report, op. cit.*, p. 3. The most complete record of the various submissions is held in the Archives Department, Cornell University, New York.

20 Amongst the available material was the *Report and Evidence of the 1913 Housing Inquiry* as well as a detailed survey of dereliction in Dublin prepared for the Local Government Board by Kaye-Parry and Ross in 1914.

21 Simultaneously Geddes and Unwin had proposed the westward development of Henry St. while others were later to propose the westward development of Princess St. to relieve congestion around Nelson's Pillar. See "Town Planning and Traffic Organisation In Dublin" *Irish Builder & Engineer*, Vol. LXIX (1927), p.880.

22 *Adjudicators' Report, op. cit.*, p. 5.

23 Details of scheme in *Dublin Civic Survey* (Civics Institute of Ireland, Dublin, 1925), pp. 132-7. See also report on competition in *The Builder*, Vol. CXII, (5 July 1917), pp. 14-16.

24 See *Civic Survey, op, cit.*, pp. 138-9.

25 Two manuscript copies of the Ashbee and Chettle Competition entry are known to exist, one of which is in the UCD Planning Library in Richview.

26 *Adjudicators' Report*, p. 3.

27 Ibid., p. 4.

28 Ibid., p.3.

29 Abercrombie, et. al., *op. cit.*, Preface, p. ix.

30 Letter from Geddes to his daughter Nora, 1922, *Geddes Papers*, MS 10502, National Library of Scotland, Edinburgh.

31 Many examples of Henard's work can be seen in N. Evanson (1979) *Paris: A Century of Change, 1878-1978*, London: Yale Univ. Press, 382 pp.

32 These were published in early numbers of the *Town Planning Review.*

33 Abercrombie, et. al., *Dublin of The Future: The. New Town Plan*, op. cit., p. 3.

34 *Ibid.*

35 I believe that we are somewhat in the dark as to how the Competition entry and the published report compare. There are various allusions as to additional maps and revisions due to destruction during the Dublin "wars". What we are looking at is the 1922 report published after the original competition.

36 *Report of Housing Inquiry*, *op. cit.*, Vol. 1.

37 Abercrombie et. al., *op. cit.*, p. 5. There is no substantive basis for these figures and Abercrombie's subsequent 1941 Sketch Plan worked on the basis of a population of approximately 750,000 with city centre housing to be largely middle class and non-manual.

38 Areas as suggested for development on map in *Report of Housing Inquiry, op. cit.*

39 Abercrombie, et. al., *op. cit.*, p. 31.

40 *Ibid.*

41 The idea of infilling part of Dublin Bay, which was common to most of the Competition entries, had earlier been mooted by Charles Dawson who favoured the reclamation of about 1,000 acres in the Merrion area "from the shallow ripples through which, almost for miles at full tide, children paddle" - see *Irish Architect & Craftsman*, Vol. 1 (1911), p.247.

42 S.A. Kelly, "A New Town Plan for the City of Dublin" *Journal of T.P.I.*, Vol. III (1916/17), p. 62.

43 As well as decentralising housing and placing new industries outside the centre, various hospitals, including Rotunda and Grangegorman, and several army barracks were to be gradually moved out to make room for new routes, commercial expansion and civic improvements - see p. 41. The decentralisation of institutions was reminiscent of the Garden City Movement's philosophy.

44 A somewhat similar proposal was brought forward in 1969 by the Dublin Port and Docks Board. See: E.D.J. Kruijtbosch, et. al., *Studies in the Long Term Development of Port of Dublin*, (Dublin Port and Docks Board 1972),75pp.

45 The data on derelict sites came from the 1913 work of Kaye-Parry and Ross.

46 Sutcliffe, A. (1970) *The Autumn of Central Paris; The Defeat of Town Planning, 1850-1970.* London: Edward Ardnold, 372pp

47 The gradual eastward movement of the centre was regretted by many. In his lecture to the Cities and Town Planning Exhibition in 1911, W.G. Strickland decried that the shift left derelict former areas of fashion and grandeur - (*Irish Times*, 27 May 1911).

48 In effect the centrepiece of his plan, the Traffic Centre, had been in part frustrated shortly after the Competition by the Corporation's decision to build housing on the Ormond Market site. However, Abercrombie did not abandon the idea believing that "in twenty-five years these cottages might well be removed", P. Abercrombie, "The New Town Plan for the City of Dublin" *Journal, T.P.I.*, Vol. III (1916), p.53.

49 Writing in 1929, Robertson referred to aspects of Abercrombie's plan as erring "on the side of being too drastic and expensive", see Manning Robertson, "Town Planning in Dublin" *Handbook*, (Dublin Civic Week, 1919), p. 26.

50 This point had been stressed by Geddes in his interview with the *Freeman's Journal* of 29 May 1911, repeated in his evidence to the *Housing Inquiry* and stressed in the *Adjudicators' Report of the Competition* entries, op. cit.,p.7.

51 This idea had been encouraged in the Competition guidelines.

52 The idea of zoning had been introduced from Germany to Britain in the previous decade (1904-1914) - see Mervyn Miller, "The Rational Enthusiast: Raymond Unwin and Germany's Planning Exemplar 1900-14," P.H.G. Autumn Conference on *The Example of Germany*, (1980), 34 pp.

53 Abercrombie believed that implementation of a Town Plan resembled the construction of a medieval cathedral, "an organic design continually undergoing modification as it progressed" - see Abercrombie, *op. cit.* (1916), p.52.

54 See "Housing and Town Planning in Ireland" *Garden Cities and Town Planning*, Vol 11, (1912). pp.9-11.

55 For example see "Leader" in *Irish Builder & Engineer*, Vol. LI, p. 780.

56 *Irish Architect and Craftsman*, Vol. I (1911), p. 20.

57 *Report of Housing Inquiry*, *op. cit* (1914), p. 211.

58 P. Abercrombie, *op. cit* (1916), p. 53.

59 *Ibid*, p. 56.

60 Abercrombie et. al., *op. cit* (1922), p. 6.

61 Modelled on the then existing Massachussetts Planning Commission. In his report of evaluation for the competition entries, Thomas Adams called for a special act of parliament to enable the establishment of a Greater Dublin Planning Commission, representative of the City Council, other Local Authorities and Members of Parliament.

62 Abercrombie et. al., *op. cit.*, (1922), p. 7.

63 The Central Town Planning Commission would consist of the chief officers of the Central Ministry, including a Chief Town Planning Controller and a Chief Inspector of Local Boards.

64 P. Abercrombie, *op. cit.,* (1916), p. 52.

65 Abercrombie et. aI., *op. cit.* (1922), p. x. This point was repeated by Abercrombie as late as 1933. Abercrombie, *Town and County Planning*, *op. cit.*, p. 137.

66 *Ibid.*, (1922).

67 *Irish Builder and Engineer*, Vol. LVIII (1916), pp. 463-4.

68 *Ibid.*, p. 581.

69 Even Abercrombie's friend and colleague Manning Robertson later referred to the reality that Abercrombie "erred, perhaps, on the side of being too drastic and expensive" (Civic Week, 1929) although the *Irish Builder & Engineer* welcomed the idea of a traffic centre and hoped there would be the will to implement the proposal - see Vol. LVIII. (1916), pp. 463-4.

70 G. Dix, "Little Plans and Noble Diagrams", *Town Planning Review*, Vol. 49 (1973), p. 332.

71 Abercrombie interviewed in *Irish Independent*, 19 February, 1938.

72 Professor Patrick Abercrombie, Sydney A. Kelly and Manning Robertson,s Town Planning Report / Sketch Development Plan, Borough of Dublin and Neighbourhood,1941, 62 pages.

Chapter 2

Planning in Northern Ireland - the early years

John Hendry

Introduction

This chapter examines the context in which the Northern Ireland planning system evolved, concentrating upon those local factors which have proved particularly relevant to the outcome. Over the period from 1921 to 1972 the region enjoyed a large measure of autonomy, electing twelve representatives to the United Kingdom Parliament whilst maintaining its own House of Commons and Upper House. Most government functions were devolved to this local Parliament which was free, within the bounds of overall Exchequer control, to pass its own laws, allocate grants for various services and generally run its own affairs. Jean Forbes (1970) in writing about this period expressed the problems of planners working within that framework:

> This telescoping of national and regional roles leaves Northern Ireland planners in an unusually isolated position. On the one hand, their territory is rarely included in a British level national overview of spatial planning policy ... the Irish Sea renders redundant any need to co-ordinate the regional strategies of neighbouring regions across the sea. On the other hand, Northern Ireland cannot be included in an all-Ireland 'national' overview of planning strategy.[1]

Thus, planning in Northern Ireland had to be undertaken largely without the guidance of a wider national policy framework, and the solutions to the then existing problems had almost invariably to be sought within boundaries which were created in a manner that ignored the area's natural sub-regions as might be defined according to the existing settlement pattern or other geographic features. Moreover, planning in Northern Ireland evolved against a background which did not reflect the same concern with social issues shown by the major British parties, whether in government or not. In fact, for the most part, planners in Northern Ireland worked in a hostile atmosphere because of local resistance to change which planning *per se* was seen to represent.

They could not, therefore, count upon the same degree of government support enjoyed by their British counterparts. This chapter is mainly concerned with the effects of the political response to planning issues during the life of the Northern Ireland Parliament, until it was prorogued in 1972.

Preservation and amenity

The roots of modern planning in Northern Ireland - the statutory regulation of development - evolved throughout the latter half of the 19th century and, as in the remainder of the United Kingdom, are principally concerned with the preservation of historic monuments and with the demolition of unfit housing. Since 1869 ecclesiastical buildings throughout Ireland which had fallen into disuse were placed in the care of the Commissioner of Public Works. By the beginning of the 20th century some 180 monuments were preserved in this way with £1,000 spent annually upon their upkeep. At the time of Partition this sum was divided between North and South and the Northern Ireland Government found itself awarded £117 annually to cover the cost of maintaining the seventeen monuments which were in the six northern counties. Thereafter the British Ancient Monuments Act of 1913 coloured the approach to architectural conservation for the next sixty years. The Ancient Monuments Act (NI) 1926, required the Ministry of Finance to produce a schedule of monuments - a duty which it duly carried out, listing some 200 monuments in all, of which one half were in public ownership. An Act of the same name in 1937 then permitted financial aid to owners of scheduled monuments, although in practice funds were limited to a few hundred pounds a year.

In 1953 a committee, set up under the Chairmanship of Sir Roland Nugent, recommended the listing of buildings in Northern Ireland in accordance with the British Town and Country Planning Act, but no action was taken to preserve the built environment for almost two decades. The passing of the Amenity Lands Act (NI) in 1965 actually permitted a degree of protection to be afforded to the countryside which was not available for buildings. It was in the late 1960s that the Ulster Architectural Heritage Society became active as a broadly based pressure group, claiming with some justice that Northern Ireland was fifty years behind the times in its attitude to heritage.[2] Following a campaign of intensive publicity and lobbying, provisions were finally included in the Planning Order (NI), 1972, which brought Northern Ireland generally in line with British practice regarding the listing of buildings and declaration of Conservation Areas.[3] This illustrates a pattern which was repeated time and again, and where there were unjustified delays in taking legislative action to implement the recommendations of advisory committees. Changes in legislation were consequently less frequent than elsewhere in the United Kingdom and were more marked in their effects as the legislators attempted to catch up on the changes which had meanwhile taken place in British practice.

Housing and redevelopment

Housing legislation in Northern Ireland also showed a remarkable resistance to change. For instance, until 1956 the Housing of the Working Classes Act, 1890, remained the principal enabling legislation under which slum clearance might have occurred. The British Housing Acts of the 1930s which provided for increased local authority involvement in housing were not enacted locally, and the Planning and Housing Act (NI) 1931, continued to place redevelopment at the discretion of individual local authorities and consequently was not acted upon. In its report on housing in Northern Ireland in 1944 the Planning Advisory Board commented:

> We believe it is true to say that these powers have not been used to any appreciable extent by any local authority in Northern Ireland. The reason for this was that the Acts made no provision for financial assistance by the Central Government. In Great Britain, however, after a period of house building to meet general needs, special grants were given from 1933 onwards for the provision of new houses for slum dwellers. No such grants were made available to local authorities for this purpose by the Northern Ireland Government.[4]

Housing conditions in Belfast were probably no worse at the turn of the century than those in comparable industrial cities throughout Britain. However, only 13 per cent of the housing stock in Northern Ireland was built during the interwar period compared to 27 per cent in Britain, and of this local total, 82 per cent was constructed by private developers. In Belfast 29,000 houses were built in this period, but only 2,562 (8 per cent) were provided by the local authority. Wilshere (1944) has referred obliquely to the 'so-called Housing Scandal' in Belfast, after which the Corporation withdrew entirely from the housing field.[5] The lack of profit to be made from housing development can only partly explain this lack of activity. It is certainly true that the city benefited more from commercial development and wished to see housing confined to the suburbs so that it might retain desirable central sites for highly rated development, but this was equally true of cities elsewhere in the United Kingdom. The essential difference would seem to be that housing at that time did not become a major issue between political parties as it did in Britain.

In Northern Ireland during World War Two 3,200 houses were destroyed and a further 50,000 badly damaged. Increasingly, voices were raised against low standards of housing, especially as a result of the figures revealed by the Planning Advisory Board:

> We have now for the first time a comprehensive picture of housing conditions in the Province. The survey shows that to provide decent housing conditions approximately 100,000 houses will be required. This is a tremendous task. About 50,000 houses of all types were built in the twenty years from 1919 to 1939, and it will be appreciated that the most energetic steps will have to be taken if the task is to be completed within a reasonable period of years after the end of the war.[6]

The Report concluded: "After full consideration of the alternative proposals ... it has been decided to recommend the setting up of a Housing Department in the Ministry of Health and Local Government".[7] However, local authorities were loath to relinquish their housing powers and argued that these could not be divorced from other services such as the provision of water and sewerage facilities. In fact, it was twenty-seven years later in 1971 that the alleged misuse of these powers finally gave rise to the creation of a central housing authority - the Northern Ireland Housing Executive.

The Board's comments on the need to initiate an organised slum clearance programme also had to wait twelve years before they achieved official Government support. It was the ponderously titled Housing (Miscellaneous Provisions) and Rent Restriction (Amendment) Act (NI) 1956, which finally required each local authority to estimate the number of unfit dwellings in its area and to submit proposals for dealing with them. The results, published in 1959,[8] showed that out of 376,324 dwellings in Northern Ireland, 95,364 were unfit - one quarter of the entire housing stock. In Belfast 18,440 houses out of 114,995 were found to be unfit. In 1960, proposals were finally put forward for the establishment of thirty redevelopment areas and in 1964 a further twenty areas were added, but it was not until 1966 - twenty-two years after the Planning Advisory Board's initial report - that the first programme involving 28,000 houses was actually approved.

Despite the neglect of redevelopment, the immediate post-war years marked the introduction of a series of important Housing Acts, providing subsidies for local authorities and private builders alike,[9] and setting up the Northern Ireland Housing Trust to supplement the efforts of local authorities.[10] Under these provisions the rate of house building grew from 2,500 dwellings per year between the wars to 7,500 per year between 1946 and 1971. Of the 191,960 dwellings built in this latter period, 37 per cent were provided by local authorities, 36 per cent by private enterprise and 24 per cent by the Northern Ireland Housing Trust.[11] The target of 10,000 houses a year by 1970 was virtually achieved by 1968 and reflected the emergence of a new faction within the Government at that time which recognised that good housing was required as part of the basic infrastructure necessary to attract investment into Northern Ireland.

Planning in the 1940s and 1950s

Turning from housing to the development of actual planning legislation, the Northern Ireland government was equally slow to provide the legislative and administrative structures required for either the control or promotion of development. In fact, the Planning and Housing Act (NI) 1931, remained the basic planning measure until 1972. This was similar to the 1932 Act in Britain and, being permissive in the use of its powers, it proved equally ineffective in the planning domain as in the housing sphere up to the time of World War Two. It was adopted in only Belfast and Londonderry, caused no development plans to be produced, and allowed planning to become more or less an appendage to bye-law control.[12] Attempts to attract new industry were separately introduced under the 1932 and 1937 New Industries Development Acts, as for the first time Government intervention was admitted to be necessary to promote development, but planning at a local level was solidly resisted. The tradition existed that people wishing to carry out development initially enlisted the services of their elected representatives on the local council. Thus suggestions for the approval of formal development plans were seen by councillors to undermine their function and the means by which they built up their support in the community.

Truly constructive thought on planning matters dates from 1942 when the Government, advised by W. R. Davidge (past-president of the Town Planning Institute) set up a Planning Commission and Planning Advisory Board. The Commission was comprised of the senior professional officers of the County Councils, County Boroughs and various government and semi-state bodies; the Board consisted of elected representatives of local authorities, learned institutions and various commercial and social bodies. The Government commanded and published nine reports by the Board between 1943 and 1951 and, although it did not endorse the reports, the act of setting up these bodies in itself marked the realisation that radical changes were necessary if the economy was to survive through the attraction of external investment. The reports of the Board are remarkable both for the range of their coverage and in that their recommendations form a pattern-book for the plans of the 1960s and 1970s.[13]

What then were the main recommendations which were made? The first was the need for the centralisation of authority. In the *Preliminary Report on Reconstruction and Planning*, published in 1944, the Board stressed the need for a comprehensive plan to be prepared by a central planning authority - a recommendation which was not put into effect until a five-year development programme was produced by the Government in 1970.[14] Similar recommendations were made for the provision of public services. In its report on *Problems of Water and Sewerage*, published in 1943, the Board recommended that the eighty existing authorities should be reduced to four, but that again had to await the reorganisation of local government in the early 1970s. In *Road Communications in Northern Ireland*, published in 1946, the need for a reduction in the number of road authorities was recorded, and similar comments regarding housing authorities have already been noted earlier. In all of these fields, opposition was met at a local level, and this opposition was strong enough to prevent Government action. Murie (1973) commented:

> Planning legislation has been slow to emerge and has operated within a political and administrative climate which has a direct and significant influence .... Where political survival requires the maintenance of a coalition of interests there will be great reluctance to threaten the most jealously guarded powers and claims of these groups.[15]

Apart from the need for administrative reform, the Board investigated the physical changes required for the prosperity of Northern Ireland. Basically it highlighted the imbalance of industry and population, with two-fifths of the population and three-fifths of manufacturing jobs concentrated in the Belfast area.[16] It drew attention to the need to attract industry to smaller settlements, but recognised the difficulty of supplying amenities to towns of under 15,000 population. In order to attract external investment, the Board underlined the need for improved transport facilities with a network of trunk roads and motorways, especially related to the flow of traffic to and from Belfast.[17]

Finally, two reports were prepared on Belfast itself in 1945 and 1952.[18] These both expressed the degree of concern which was already being shown about the imbalance between development taking place in the Belfast area compared to that elsewhere throughout Northern Ireland. The reports recommended the control of suburban growth, the co-ordination of all forms of transport allied to the construction of a new major road system, the diversion of new industry away from the city, the redevelopment of unfit housing, the protection of open space and the creation of a green belt around the city - in fact, all of the recommendations to be found in the subsequent *Belfast Regional Plan* prepared by Sir Robert Matthew two decades later. The review of progress in the 1952 report showed that, whilst the proposals of the 1945 report had been approved by the Belfast Corporation, "the lack of machinery to co-ordinate effort forced local authorities to confine themselves to immediate problems facing their own areas".[19] In short, the scale of necessary physical change was such that it could not be executed without the centralisation of control. After 1951 still no action was taken and the Commission and Board ceased to function.

Towards the end of World War Two it was recognised that some form of control would be needed to regulate the wave of development activity which peacetime would bring. The Interim Development Act (NI) 1944, based on the similarly-named British Act of 1943, therefore deemed all land to be subject to planning schemes and laid down a timetable for their preparation. Without the necessary staff or organisation available, this proved to be an impossible task, and so Outline Advisory Plans were substituted. These were "in most cases a general extension of existing land use zoning together with road improvement proposals. They were not related to any specific programmes of development nor in many cases to any specific population figure".[20] They were not statutory plans, nor were they based on any overall policy for the development of Northern Ireland.

So there came into being thirty-eight authorities of varying size and resources throughout Northern Ireland - consisting of the counties, county and municipal boroughs and urban districts - responsible for the administration of planning proposals set out for the first time in the form of advisory development plans. The largest was Belfast County Borough with a population of 416,000 and a penny rate producing £23,000, and the smallest was Dromore with a population of 2,115 and a penny rate product of £60.[21] Planning in Rural Districts was carried out by the County Councils. Some of the smaller Urban Districts also surrendered their powers to the Counties, whilst others employed consultants as part-time planning officers. Architects in private practice appointed in this way prepared the Outline Plans, carried out the housing work of the authorities and reviewed each others submissions for private building development. They were furthermore appointed as necessary to act as Appeal Commissioners in cases of dispute. Even in 1965 the membership of the Royal Town Planning Institute in Northern Ireland stood at only forty-six practitioners, with one-half employed full-time by local and central government and the remainder generally employed in architecture with part-time involvement in planning as consultants to local authorities or as auxiliary inspectors appointed by the Government. Planning powers at this time were not uniformly administered, being applied most strongly in the urban areas and generally applied "rather more strongly in the East than in the West".[22]

One particular barrier to the enforcement of planning control under the 1944 Act was the ambiguity regarding the right to compensation for refusals or conditional permissions to develop. This arose through the interpretation of the Government of Ireland Act 1920, which provided safeguards to individuals against the taking of their interests in land. In England any possible ambiguity regarding compensation was removed by the Town and Country Planning Act 1947, which nationalised development values, but in Northern Ireland the planning authorities operated in fear of claims which would become a charge against the local rates. This situation continued until the limitations on compensation had been clarified by legislation in Westminster and was only fully resolved by the Land Development Values (Compensation) Act

(NI) 1965, which made the then newly formed Ministry of Development responsible for all claims arising from planning decisions.

Planning in the 1960s

If the 1940s and 1950s were the decades of resistance to change, then the 1960s should be labelled the decade of ambitious plans. This seeming reversal Wiener (1975) attributes to the emergence of a new faction within the Unionist Party, headed by O'Neill, Faulkner and Bradford, promoting for the first time with real conviction the interests of new overseas investors as opposed to those of traditional locally-based commercial interests.[23] The unplanned growth of the Belfast urban area in stark contrast to the stagnation of development elsewhere eventually produced sufficient pressures for the Government to appoint Sir Robert Matthew in 1960 to prepare a plan for the Belfast region. This was in fact the first Regional Plan in Ireland. Forbes (1970) has commented:

> The Matthew plan must be judged in the context of its time. Its greater contribution may be seen, in future, to have been its ground-breaking function rather than its planning proposals as such. It was produced in an atmosphere which was decidedly anti-planning, and in a community intensely suspicious of change. The Matthew plan provoked a rigorous public debate which still continues, and this has served to bring planners to public notice in Northern Ireland.[24]

The Report, published in 1964,[25] was concerned principally with physical development, an economic plan being prepared in parallel by Professor Tom Wilson and published in 1965.[26] Sir Robert Matthew proposed to control the further development of Belfast by the application of a 'stopline', by initiating a system of radial motorways and by promoting eight growth centres outside the city. One of these was to be developed as a 'new city' of 100,000 population as a counter-magnet to Belfast, and this proposal was accorded the highest priority by the Government as noted by Aitken (1967):

> An important and encouraging two-day debate took place at Stormont in May 1963 .... The mood was to get on with it at all possible speed. Acting on this 'blessing' of the House, a start was made on the recruitment of a team for the new city and the drafting of a New Towns Bill.[27]

Unionist support was solidified by naming the new town Craigavon - after Sir James Craig, Northern Ireland's first Prime Minister, who took the title Lord Craigavon in 1927. Conversely, this alienated the opposition whose support was required in both the administration and settlement of the new city. In retrospect, the proposal for the development of a new city can be viewed as an attempt to emulate in Northern Ireland the apparent success of the British New Towns, without duly considering the nature of the local problem. Murie (1970) has commented:

> Fundamentally there was little attempt to assess whether the importation of the British new town settlement system was appropriate to the Irish tradition of dispersed rural settlement ... The Matthew Report did not take sufficient consideration of trends in residential and industrial location patterns which cast doubts on the relevance of the British new town model of twenty years earlier.[28]

Sir Robert Matthew saw that the imposition of a stop-line around Belfast, allied to the full-scale renewal of its inner areas, would give rise to an overspill in the order of some 36,000 people. This he saw as producing a counter-movement to the traditional pattern of urban migration. However, the full implications were not worked out and in consequence the necessary administrative support was not provided. Again Forbes (1970) opined "A weakness of the planning machinery has, however, undermined part of the Matthew design. There is no formal organisation for resettling overspill population".[29] Some incentives were later added, but displaced families showed a marked preference to move to the inner growth centres of Bangor and Newtownards, commuting daily to work and thus swelling still further the growth of the Belfast region. The radiating motorway system, intended to lure industry westward beyond the Belfast region, in fact increased accessibility to the centre and extended the commuting range of workers. The outer ring of growth centres were not notably successful in attracting outside investment but, by offering conditions which compared favourably with those of the surrounding countryside, tended to draw population from the very areas where development was seen to be most needed.

Thus, the more recent history of planning in Northern Ireland was "marked by the adoption of prestigious plans or projects which change their character and impact by a process of erosion through failure to implement the whole or by changes in parts without altering or reconsidering related parts".[30] Those who commissioned the plans had been bound to act upon the main proposals - if only to justify their choice of consultants and the cost of the reports. Being then able to lay claim to have initiated a new city or a motorway system, there was subsequently a lesser inclination to proceed with the further implementation of the plans - especially where this might invoke political debate in sensitive subject areas. Again as Murie has pointed out, "Area Plans for the growth centres ... departed from the Matthew recommendations ... without any public discussion of the effects on other parts of the plan".[31] Another over-ambitious plan which was never implemented was that for the Belfast Urban Motorway. This was originally chosen by the Belfast Corporation as the prestige solution to the city's transportation problem. "The brief for the traffic consultants, Travers Morgan, clearly specified that an urban motorway should be part of their design".[32] Although the abandonment of the motorway proposal was claimed to stem from citizen protest after the public inquiry in 1972,[33] even this may be seen as a face-saving excuse for relinquishing a solution which in practice constituted an impossible economic burden in a deteriorating economic climate and which had by then been shown to have disastrous consequences elsewhere.

Apart from its physical proposals, the Matthew plan called for the formation of a centralised planning administration to replace the thirty-four local authorities in the Belfast region (of which nineteen were planning authorities, thirty responsible for housing and twenty-two for roads), within the overall control of a Ministry of Planning and Development - thus effectively repeating the recommendations of the Planning Board in the 1940s. In 1964 a White Paper was produced on *The Administration of Town and Country Planning in Northern Ireland* with the main proposal of setting up a central planning authority to prepare a Regional Plan for the whole of Northern Ireland and Area Plans to outline development in broad-brush terms. Local authority participation was to be by way of "Action Plans" but it was proposed that development control would become a function of central government:

> Public reaction was disappointingly thin, although generally favourable .... The reactions of local authorities, on the other hand, were quite strong and, in the main, unfavourable .... Where the strongest opposition came was in the matter of development control by the central authority. It was apparent this was the strongest focus of local interest for councils and councillors.[34]

The proposal was fiercely debated within the Cabinet, with O'Neill's more radical supporters facing strong resistance from the more reactionary members who saw the centralisation of power undermining their own local support. Allen (1981) in fact alludes that "only by a coup, whilst other ministers were on vacation, did he (O'Neill) establish such a ministry".[35] So a Ministry of Development came into being with overall responsibility for planning, housing, roads, transport, water, sewerage and local government, although local authorities were permitted to retain many of their powers - in the case of planning including development control. O'Neill immediately appointed his Chief Whip, William Craig, as Minister and, with Brian Faulkner as Minister of Commerce, the new Unionist group appeared set to bring about at least a modest economic revival in Northern Ireland. However, the O'Neill Government was soon to fall and other members of his Cabinet subsequently passed out of the mainstream of politics. In 1970 the McCrory Commission recommended that Government services should be placed entirely under the direct control of the Ministries concerned.[36] This was largely influenced by the 'troubles' which flared up in 1968, and the allegations of the misuse of local powers, especially in the fields of housing and planning. This reorganisation took place on 1 October 1973 when the Ministry of Development, subsequently restyled the Department of the Environment, became the sole planning authority for Northern Ireland. Similar steps were taken to centralise road services, water and sewage disposal; at last the recommendation of the Planning Board of the 1940s had been implemented in full. Local authorities were reorganised under twenty-six district councils which were left with responsibilities largely only for environmental health, building control and the provision of community facilities. These governance arrangements for planning are still in place at the time of writing (September 2014), but a new and different era is about to commence with the scheduled implementation of the reform of public administration in Northern Ireland in April 2015. That will be a story for the future and one can only hope that prospect does not borrow heavily from the retrospect of this chapter.

Acknowledgement
This chapter draws on research previously published in, Hendry, J. (1989) The control of development and the origins of planning in Northern Ireland, in Bannon, M., Nowlan, K., Hendry, J. and Mawhinney, K. (eds.) *Planning: the Irish experience 1920-1988*. Dublin: Wolfhound Press, pp. 105-121.

Endnotes

1 Forbes, J. (1970) 'Towns and Planning in Ireland' in N. Stephens, and R. E. Glascock, (eds), *Irish Geographical Studies*. Belfast: Queen's University Belfast, p.292.

2 Ulster Architectural Heritage Society (1968) *What's left of Ulster*. Belfast.

3 For a full account, see Hendry, J. (1977) 'Conservation in Northern Ireland', *Town Planning Review*, Vol. 48, No. 4, pp.373-88.

4 Planning Advisory Board (1944) *Housing In Northern Ireland.* Belfast: HMSO. p.14.

5 Wilshere, R.S. (1944) 'Town Planning in Northern Ireland' in *Town Planning in Ireland* Dublin: The Irish Association. p.23.

6 Planning Advisory Board, *op. cit.*, p.7.

7 *Ibid.*, p.30.

8 *Proposals for Dealing with Unfit Houses* (1959). Belfast: HMSO. Cmd. 398.

9 Housing (No. 2) Act (NI), 1946.

10 Housing Act (NI), 1945.

11 The history of the Northern Ireland Housing Trust has never been recorded and this is a serious omission, for the quality of its products and the efficiency of its organisation were of the highest order. A brief account of the work of the Trust is given in Brett, C. (1986) *Housing a Divided Community*. Dublin: Institute of Public Administration. pp. 27-31.

12 Newman, C.F.S. (1965) 'A Short History of Planning in Northern Ireland', *Journal of the Town Planning Institute*, Vol. 52, No. 2, p.48.

13 Newman, C.F.S. *op. cit.*, provides a brief account of the main proposals contained in each of the Board's reports.

14 Matthew, R.H. *et. al.*, (1970) *Northern Ireland Development Programme 1970- 75*, Belfast: HMSO.

15 Murie, A. (1973) 'Planning in Northern Ireland: A Survey', *Town Planning Review*, Vol. 44, No. 4, pp.351 and 355.

16 *Location of Industry in Northern Ireland* (1944) Belfast: HMSO. Cmd. 225.

17 *Road Communications in Northern Ireland* (1946) Belfast: HMSO. Cmd.241.

18 *Planning Proposals for the Belfast Area* (1945) Cmd. 227, and *Second Report on Planning Proposals for the Belfast Area* (1952) Cmd. 302.

19 Building Design Partnership (1969) *Belfast Urban Area Plan*, Vol. 2, p.22.

20 Newman, C.F.S. *op. cit.*, p.51.

21 *Ibid.*, p.51.

22 Aitken, J.M. (1967) 'Regional Planning in Northern Ireland' in *Report of Town and Country Planning Summer School*, p.6.

23 Wiener, R. (1975) *The Rape and Plunder of the Shankill,* pp.37-38.

24 Forbes, J. *op. cit.*, p.296.

25 Matthew, R.H. (1964) *Belfast Regional Survey and Plan*, 1962. Belfast: HMSO, 326pp + maps.

26 *Economic Development in Northern Ireland* (1965) Belfast: HMSO, 153pp.

27 Aitken, J.M. *op. cit.*, p.9.

28 Murie, A. *op. cit.*, p.342.

29 Forbes, J. *op. cit.,* p.295.

30 Murie, A. *op. cit.*, p.356.

31 *Ibid.*, p.345.

32 Wiener, R. *op. cit.*, p.33.

33 An account of the evidence is assembled in *'Sandy Row at the Public Enquiry'* by the Sandy Row Development Association, Belfast, 1972.

34 Aitken, J.M. *op. cit.*, pp.12-13.

35 Allen, L.A. (1981) 'New Towns and the Troubles', *Town and Country Planning* November/December, p.284.

36 *Report of the Review Body on Local Government in Northern Ireland* (1970) Belfast: HMSO, Cmd. 546, 337pp.

Chapter 3

Alliance and institutional reform

Rick Wilford

Malachy's (and Sally's) commitment to the Alliance Party places him squarely on the side of political reform. Whilst endorsing the 1998 Belfast Agreement, Alliance interpreted it not as an end in itself, but rather as a means to pursue its integrationist philosophy. In that respect, the Alliance Party understood the consociational design of the Agreement—popularly abbreviated as power-sharing— as an interim *via media* within a society divided over mutually exclusive constitutional futures.

Itself agnostic, some would say neutral, on the medium to long-term future of Northern Ireland's constitutional status, Alliance's support for the 1998 Agreement did not then translate into unalloyed advocacy of consociationalism. Rather, the devolved architecture created by the Agreement offered the opportunity for an alternative politics to develop, one that prizes individual not communal rights and which promotes pluralism, diversity and difference. In that respect, Alliance seeks to transcend the zero-sum politics of communal division, signalled not least by its self-designation as 'Other' in the Northern Ireland Assembly.

Whilst this invites the unreflective charge that Alliance is neither fish nor fowl, 'otherness' instead signifies the open-textured nature of the Party's beliefs: members can and do hold differing constitutional aspirations, attesting to Alliance's liberalism and its related celebration of individualism and tolerance. Moreover, it practises the politics of recognition rather than identity politics: that is, it articulates a politics of *identities* in all its diversity and equivalence, rather than the 'either-or ism' that dominates Northern Ireland's political discourse.

Tolerance, liberalism and individualism, allied with a commitment to both rational discourse and equal rights, epitomise the Party's—and Malachy's—character: they are, in short, well-matched. In addition, both are reform-minded. Thus, whilst Alliance continues to inhabit the architecture of the Belfast Agreement, and its subsequent embellishment by the St Andrews and Hillsborough Agreements of 2006 and 2010 respectively, it does so as a critical friend of the current status quo.

Alliance is not, of course, alone in seeking to adapt the institutions and procedures bequeathed in 1998, but it has been among the more developed blueprints for such change. Whilst the opportunity to voice its reform agenda is most obviously supplied during election campaigns, its range was expanded by the Assembly's recent attempt to effect change *via* the Assembly and Executive Review Committee's (AERC) review of the 'Strand One' institutions (the Assembly and Executive) delineated in the Belfast Agreement.

The more immediate trigger for the review was the 2006 St Andrews Agreement which provided for an 'Institutional Review Committee' charged to examine the operational aspects of the Strand One institutions, an undertaking that first appeared in the 2004 Comprehensive Agreement authored by the UK and Irish Governments. The latter Agreement, itself intended primarily to usher in a new phase of devolution, also encompassed an agenda of prospective institutional reform which in some measure structured the terms of reference for the proposed Institutional Review Committee which, in the event, was designated as the AERC in the wake of the restoration of devolution in 2007. It comprised eleven members: four DUP, three Sinn Féin, two UUP and one each from the SDLP and Alliance Party, its composition reflecting the broadly proportional seat strengths of the Assembly's parties.

The chair and deputy chair of the Committee—like all such committee roles—were allocated by means of the d'Hondt formula, in this case to, respectively, the DUP and SF. Having been established, the Committee did not, however, enjoy a blank sheet on which to devise proposed reforms. The Comprehensive Agreement had itself outlined a number of possible changes to the operation of both the Assembly and the Executive including: the reform of the Office of the First and Deputy First Minister (OFMDFM)—essentially, hollowing out the Office by transferring functions to other Departments; limiting the change of community designation by an Assembly member to occasions where s/he changed her/his party membership; amending the procedure for appointing Ministers by providing for a cross-community Assembly vote endorsing the whole Executive, not just the nominees for First Minister (FM) and deputy First Minister (dFM) as was the case in the Belfast Agreement; and changing the status of the extant 'Committee of the Centre' that scrutinized OFMDFM from a standing to a statutory committee.

A number of these and other proposals were, in the event, addressed by the AERC, as were those emanating from the fully inclusive Preparation for Government Committee (PfGC) that had been created during the Transitional Assembly of 2006 by means of the Northern Ireland Act of the same year.

Like the Comprehensive Agreement, authored by the UK and Irish Governments, the PfGC recognised the need to address the operation of the devolved institutions, thereby suggesting a preparedness to entertain change rather than merely the restore the *status quo ante*. Its report, published shortly before the St Andrews talks and the related Agreement of 16 October 2006, identified a number of agreed proposals including: the retention of the cross-community voting procedure for the election of the Speaker (a post occupied to that date by two Alliance Members, namely, John Alderdice and Eileen Bell) and three Deputy Speakers; the retention of the Petition of Concern mechanism, whereby 30 MLAs are enabled to trigger a cross-community vote in the chamber; the change in the status of the standing Committee of the Centre (subsequently the Committee for OFMDFM) to a statutory committee; the retention of PR STV for Assembly elections; the need to place some aspects of the Ministerial Code on a statutory footing, including measures designed to promote collectivism within the Executive; and providing both that chairs and chief executives of cross-border bodies should present annual reports to the Assembly and that certain (unspecified) public appointments should be endorsed by the full Executive.

The Committee also agreed to refer a number of matters to the devolved Assembly for review by a committee charged to undertake an institutional review of operational aspects of the Strand One structures and procedures. These encompassed the phasing out of multiple mandates; a review by OFMDFM of both the number of devolved Departments and associated Ministerial responsibilities and of the means by which the Assembly engaged with civic society. In addition, the Committee agreed to refer for further discussion both the number and roles of the North-South implementation bodies (a Strand Two matter) and provision for an overarching 'Council of the Isles' (Strand Three), the former favoured by the SDLP and SF, the latter by the DUP and UUP—a clear instance of political bargaining among the major parties.

There were also a number of other issues identified by at least one party as requiring resolution prior to the restoration of devolution. Namely, the mode of electing/appointing the First and deputy First Ministers; accountability between the Executive and Assembly; those elements of the Ministerial Code to be given statutory effect; and the accountability of Ministers to the Assembly on North-South Ministerial Council affairs. Each of these issues, together with the key question concerning the conditions under which the devolution of criminal justice and policing (agreed in principle by all parties) could occur, structured the talks at St Andrews. And this latter matter was to turn on the preparedness of Alliance to assume the role of Justice Minister, all other things being equal.

The PfGC reconvened in the wake of St Andrews to address a number of the institutional and procedural changes proposed in the St Andrews Agreement, including those over which there was no agreement. For instance, whilst there was all-party consensus on the need to place the Ministerial Code on a statutory footing, the parties differed over the substance of the Code. The SDLP chafed at its proposed scope and, together with Alliance, expressed concern that its suggested breadth risked recourse to legal challenges on matters that were better resolved politically. Furthermore, the SDLP signalled opposition to the proposal that the FM and dFM should enjoy unfettered discretion in agreeing which significant or controversial issues that lay outwith an agreed Programme for Government should be tabled at the Executive. It argued that such a blanket provision would override the authority of other Ministers and was joined by the UUP in opposing the proposal. Their implied view, one later to be articulated by Alliance, was that it threatened a political carve-up by the DUP and SF of Executive business, which pushed the SDLP and UUP into a position whereby they defended departmentalism as a means of bridling the authority of OFMDFM.

Underlying the matter of a statutory Ministerial Code was a concern to promote collective responsibility within the Executive, an issue of particular but by no means unique concern to the DUP. But, at the behest of the party, a new operating procedure was proposed in the St Andrew Agreement enabling three Ministers to trigger a cross-community vote at the Executive over issues that failed to achieve consensus. This blunt device provided an assurance that solo policy runs by a Minister could be blocked, though it is subject to a number of interpretations: a means of managing dissensus, of engineering consensus or, more bleakly, of creating Executive gridlock—the view of the UUP which opposed the proposal.

The DUP, concerned to demonstrate to its voters that St Andrews represented a new Agreement and not merely a tweaked version of its 1998 predecessor, also insisted that provision be made for Assembly referral to the Executive of ministerial decisions that concerned an issue of public importance: in effect it was a means of buttressing the Petition of Concern procedure which, together with the proposal for a cross-community vote at the Executive, enabled it to propagate that representation of St Andrews for wider electoral and operational purposes.

To achieve inter-communal balance, the St Andrews Agreement incorporated SF's demand that the Northern Ireland Act 2000 which enabled the UK Government to suspend devolution be repealed. In addition, while it provided for a review group to examine the efficiency and value-for-money of existing cross-border bodies (a Unionist objective) it also enabled the group to evaluate the case for expanding the number of such bodies where mutual benefit to Northern Ireland and the Republic of Ireland would be derived, an objective sought both by SF and the SDLP. However, this proposed review group has yet to be established.

The paper trail of potential reform leading from the 2004 Comprehensive Agreement to St Andrews, *via* the PfGC, was extended to a second round of inter-party negotiations within the latter against the backdrop of the passage of the St Andrews Bill at Westminster. A particular difficulty emerged when the Bill was published concerning the procedure by which the First and deputy First Ministers were nominated and endorsed.

The St Andrews Agreement had proposed that, as between 1999 and 2002 (when devolution was suspended) that the nominating officer of the largest party (measured by the number of Assembly seats it had won) in the largest designation (Unionist, Nationalist or Other) would nominate the First Minister and the nominating officer of the largest party in the second largest designation the deputy First Minister. However, unlike the first Assembly, the Agreement omitted the provision requiring the nominees, on a joint-ticket, to be subject to a cross-community vote by the MLAs as a means of ratifying their nomination: in effect, St Andrews defined a procedure akin to a joint coronation.

This matter was referred to the reconvened PfGC which proved incapable of reaching agreement. The SDLP, UUP, Alliance and, at this stage, SF expressed a preference for retaining the method established by the 1998 Agreement, whereas the DUP endorsed the new procedure set out in the St Andrews Agreement. The DUP's opposition to the 1998 procedure was that it could not, indeed would not, countenance a process that required its MLAs to vote on a joint ticket for a SF candidate as deputy First Minister together with the nominee for First Minister, a role it prized and one which, on the basis of both polling and electoral evidence, it would secure at the planned 2007 Assembly election.

During the negotiations at the renewed PfGC, Sinn Féin had observed that the St Andrews proposal meant that only the nominee of the largest party in the largest designation could secure the First Minister role. It pressed this observation to effect during the legislative process in private discussions with the UK Government: when the St Andrews Bill (subsequently enacted) was tabled, it provided that the largest party (in terms of seats won) would nominate its candidate for First Minister in the circumstance where the largest party of the largest designation was not the largest party overall.

The inclusion of this clause in the Bill (Section 16 (C) (6) took the other Northern Ireland parties by surprise, not least the DUP which was not privy either to the SF-Government discussions or the latter's decision, *ie* it had no forewarning of the outcome of those discussions. During a subsequent interview with the author, Peter Robinson confirmed that the change had occurred at the bidding of SF and that the DUP had had to decide whether its provision was sufficient 'to allow the whole thing' (ie St Andrews) 'to go down. At that stage we put the Government on notice that from our point of view, they could put this through in legislation but whenever it came to it, we wouldn't operate the system'. It meant that should SF emerge from an Assembly election as the largest party, the DUP would refuse to nominate one of its MLAs as deputy First Minister, thereby blocking the joint-nomination procedure and hence imperilling the formation of an Executive: in short, this would trigger a political crisis.

In choosing not to press the issue during the passage of the Bill the DUP calculated that it could live with change in the sure knowledge that, if the circumstance arose, it would frustrate its implementation. Whilst this may be interpreted as supplying a muted single cheer for the politics of accommodation, it equally demarcated the tight boundary of accommodatory politics. It is evident from Peter Robinson's remarks (and those of other DUP politicians interviewed by the author) that his party could not countenance the prospect of a SF First Minister. This became apparent during the ensuing 2007 Assembly election when the DUP sought to render the contest as a plebiscite on which party would be in a position to assume the role. As its manifesto stated: only the DUP 'is realistically capable of winning more seats than Sinn Féin to stop them (sic) being nominated for the post of First Minister'. Though such a stark pronouncement was absent from its 2011 manifesto, in the run-up to the election and in response to a proposal from Martin McGuinness that, should SF emerge as the largest party, he and the DUP leader could share the title of First Minister, Peter Robinson was dismissive: 'I have no doubt there are people who don't want to see a Sinn Féin First Minister and will lend us their votes to avoid that happening..I want the DUP to be coming out on top' (BBC News Online, 22 March 2011).

The DUP's decision not to view the change as a 'deal breaker' enabled the election and the process of Executive formation to proceed provided, that is, SF did not emerge as the largest party. It also facilitated the creation of the AERC which was tasked with the review of the Strand One issues and to address those matters left unresolved by the PfGC, albeit that this process was itself delayed by the Committee's preoccupation with the planned devolution of policing and criminal justice which eventually took place in 2010 following inter-party talks at Hillsborough Castle. The successful outcome of those latter talks hinged on the vexed matter of the party identity of the prospective Justice Minister which meant that a *modus vivendi* had to be reached by the DUP and SF, neither of which could contemplate a nominee from among their rival party blocs. A compromise was reached whereby the nominee, alone among the post 2007 Ministers, would be subject to a cross-community vote within the Assembly, and had to be drawn from a party acceptable to both which, in effect, meant Alliance.

In the event, Alliance's leader, David Ford, secured the nomination with support from both the DUP and SF, albeit that each of the parties went through the motion of nominating one of their number in the full and certain knowledge that they would not succeed. Whether this device is understood as evidence of the politics of accommodation or, conversely, as the product of constraint fuelled by mistrust and suspicion, is moot. The operative point, however, is that the method of appointment represented a departure from the d'Hondt process employed to nominate all other Ministers. As such, it breached both the letter and the spirit of the 1998 Agreement, much to the annoyance of the SDLP which had a defensible claim to the role given its relative seat strength and the serial application of the d'Hondt rule based on the outcome of the 2007 Assembly election. As such, one may question the decision of Alliance to accept the nomination in these rather singular circumstances, though it is plausible to argue that, without its preparedness to take on the role, the political process could have hit the buffers.

Be that as it may, the bargain over the Justice Minister did demonstrate a certain suppleness between the DUP and SF, but this was not sustained when, at last, the AERC turned its fuller attention to the review of the Strand One institutions.

The Committee was obliged to report to the Secretary of State for Northern Ireland no later than 1 May 2015 on the procedures and institutions relating to the functioning, in particular, of the Assembly and Executive: it was, in fact, inheriting the agenda bequeathed by the PfGC, but one that could be extended by the Assembly itself. The legislative prompt for the review was the stated intention of the then Secretary of State, Owen Paterson, to table a Northern Ireland Bill in the third session of the 2010-2015 Parliament, a primary purpose of which was to effect changes relating to the disclosure of donations to Northern Ireland's political parties. But, in addition, it offered a primary legislative means to reform the devolved institutions where 'broad support' could be achieved among the parties.

The review was staged over a number of phases, the first of which focused on the number of both MLAs and Departments, and which also addressed how, if there was to be a reduction in the number of Members, the efficiency and effectiveness of plenary sessions and the committee system may be affected. In addition, it also decided to address whether or not to decouple the Assembly and Westminster constituencies, a step taken in both the devolved Wales and Scotland.

A backdrop to the review of the number of MLAs was the ill-fated, as it turned out, Parliamentary Voting System and Constituencies Act (2011) which, had it been implemented, would have reduced Northern Ireland's Westminster constituencies from 18 to 16 and, thereby, assuming each was to continue to return six MLAs, the total would fall to 96. There was no consensus among the parties on this matter: the UUP and SDLP favoured a 96 seat Assembly (*ie* each revised constituency returning six members), the DUP and Alliance advocated an 80-strong chamber (16x5), whilst SF adopted a more gnomic position, viz that it was 'committed to adequate representation for all groups and communities', observing that 'reductions in representation could potentially marginalize smaller parties and independents'. On the matter of the co-terminosity of Assembly and Westminster constituencies, SF and the SDLP favoured decoupling, the DUP and UUP sought to retain the link, while Alliance expressed its open-mindedness on the issue, whilst acknowledging that decoupling would enable the Assembly—like the Scottish Parliament and the National Assembly for Wales—to control the Assembly's constituency boundaries into the future.

In relation to the number of devolved Departments, Alliance elaborated an eight departmental model complete with re-allocated functions, the UUP advocated a nine-strong reconfiguration, the DUP indicated a preference for six to eight departments, the SDLP opted for the status quo, ie 12 departments, whilst SF limited itself to stating that it would not be opposed to a reduction in the total number. Though there was no considered agreement about the precise structure of a redesigned Executive, given that the weight of opinion favoured a reduction the AERC was able to identify 'areas of commonality' that suggested the outline of a remodelled Executive. It embraced the retention of three Departments (Health, Justice and Education), three new ones (Economy, Agriculture and Environment and Rural Development) and either a department for Urban and Social Development or Community/Communities and Social Welfare/Community, Housing and Local Government. This signalled a readiness to revisit the existing structure, which if effected would yield seven Departments plus OFMDFM.

On OFMDFM itself, the AERC agreed that it required revision and reform but could not achieve consensus on the nature and extent of such an exercise. Such diffidence rested on the fact that the DUP and SF hold conflicting views about the role of the Office. The DUP is inclined towards a more minimalist model by hollowing out the Office such that it becomes more of a strategic policy hub, whereas SF adopts a position that is wedded to the retention of its current responsibilities. During an interview with the author, Martin McGuinness stated: 'If you strip out many functions then you will be cutting down on the number of public engagements [we] undertake: [we] need to be seen working together in the community. Take that away and what you have are Ministers who are hidden, who are not seen because their responsibilities are being dealt with by other Departments. OFMDFM would become two people sitting in an ivory tower'.

The proposition that the two incumbents could slough off a number of functions and focus on steering the Executive rather than rowing a heavily freighted Office found favour with the DUP but not SF, which implies that the AERC's suggested review and revise exercise will founder between two contrasting perceptions of OFMDFM's role.

Although at odds over their own domain, Messrs Robinson and McGuinness were less inhibited in relation to another Department. In the midst of the AERC's review they issued a statement proposing the summary abolition of the Department of Employment and Learning, one of the two Departments headed by Alliance Ministers. Its demise was predicated on its functions being reallocated to two existing departments, one headed by the DUP the other by SF. Neither the DEL Minister, Stephen Farry nor his Permanent Secretary was apprised of the announcement. David Ford, Alliance leader and Justice Minister responded in blunt terms: 'We see what is apparently a carve up...besides being malicious towards the Alliance Party it is extremely bad government not to keep the economy departments together but to further fragment them'.

In the event and in the face of widespread criticism – not least because it was ill-timed and ill-judged given the AERC's continuing review – the announcement was withdrawn. What is evident from this episode is that the DUP and SF were prepared to adopt a piecemeal rather than a holistic approach to Executive reform: so much for any lingering thoughts about joined-up government, let alone joined-up thinking. Moreover, the summary announcement belied the principle of inclusiveness vaunted, not least by SF, as a cardinal feature of Northern Ireland's devolved polity.

The final phase of the AERC's review addressed the d'Hondt mechanism as the formula for allocating the Executive portfolio and committee chairs and deputy chairs; community designation in the Assembly; and the vexed matter of provision for an Official Opposition. This phase came to nought. The Committee failed to agree an alternative to d'Hondt, to the abandonment of community designation in favour of weighted majority votes (Alliance's preference) and provision for an Official Opposition. The Committee did agree to undertake a *closed inquiry* into the use/misuse of the Petition of Concern procedure, the outcome of which was to retain the status quo. In addition, AERC commissioned a delegated review of the Assembly's committee system (there had been such a review in 2008). A Committee Review Group (CRG) was established, comprising five committee chairs (one from each of the Executive parties), two advisers and the Clerk of the Assembly tasked to improve the capacity and effectiveness of committees in delivering their manifold roles, including scrutiny. However, though the remit was generous, the Committee failed to take full advantage of the opportunity given the existing uncertainties about the total number of MLAs and the (perhaps receding) prospect of a redesigned Executive, recommending that the issues should be further reviewed in 2015.

Whilst the CRG shied away from any fundamental changes it did agree a number of matters, including: the retention of the link between each Department and a single statutory committee; to retain the size of each statutory committee at 11 MLAs, subject to any reduction in their total number and the number of Departments; and that the Assembly should identify core tasks for each committee, thereby following the example of Westminster's select committees.

The outcomes of the CRG review were extremely modest, as was the case with the wider review undertaken by the AERC. Validation of that assessment is provided by the Northern Ireland (Miscellaneous Provisions) Act of 2014, the prospective legislative vehicle for institutional reform signalled by Owen Paterson. It ended dual mandates in relation to the Assembly, the House of Commons and the Dáil (a decision supported by all parties), extended the term of the 2011 Assembly by one year to 2016, thereby putting it on a par with the Welsh Assembly and Scottish Parliament and permits the Assembly to reduce the total number of MLAs to 90, ie five per constituency. There were no other agreed changes, other than concurrence about the case for a reduced number of Departments, a weighted majority (SF excluded) in favour of hollowing-out OFMDFM and a general disposition to reduce the total number of MLAs: all other matters addressed by AERC either failed to achieve consensus or were deferred until the next Assembly mandate, ie in 2016, nine years after the restoration of devolution.

The relative inertia of the AERC is not explicable in terms of the reluctance of all parties to embark on a path of reform: SF excepted, the other Executive parties were and remain much more receptive to institutional and procedural change. In that respect, Alliance, the DUP, UUP and SDLP are less corseted by the 1998 model, whereas SF is much more cautious, concerned that alterations to the original design could exert unintended consequences that might impair the stability of the devolved institutions. But responsibility for the relative modesty of the reform package is a shared one: it is, in short, a failure of parliamentarianism.

One characteristic of parliamentarians should be their preparedness to exert at least a degree of independent-mindedness, but too often the representatives of the major parties in the AERC, especially the DUP and SF, tended to defer to their respective leaderships. This attitude was encapsulated by Gregory Campbell (DUP) during the course of the AERC review. In the wake of a meeting between the Committee's deputy chair and the First and deputy First Ministers, he reminded his committee colleagues that 'in the end [reform] is a political matter for the party leaders', and reinforced the point a week later: reform 'is going to be decided in another room'. Such a limp attitude suggests a stunted understanding of the role of a parliamentarian, all the more surprising perhaps given that it is voiced by an MP. It recalls Burke's rhetorical admonition: 'what sort of reason is that in which the determination precedes the discussions; in which one sett (sic) of men deliberate, and another decide?'

Such a culture of obeisance stems in large measure from the fact that in Northern Ireland party loyalty is co-terminous with loyalty to one's community. Alliance aside, each of the other Executive parties is prey to this nexus. Seeking to transcend the communal divide and promote an integrationist philosophy, Alliance alone of the larger parties seems to occupy a political space that in principle can test the constraints of the rigid consociational model so painfully arrived at in 1998, whether in respect of policy matters or institutional reform.

Chapter 4

Meaning what we say: the vocabulary of Planning in contested societies

Frank Gaffikin

Introduction

It has been well-stated that Planning is beset with a lexicon that suffers from 'fuzzy concepts' (Markusen, 2003), referring to the vague, though comforting, terms to which it shows fond indulgence. Examples abound: *sustainable*; *smart*; *connected*; *permeable*; *accessible*; *resilient*; and *participative*, to name just some. In jest, some would even speculate that if deprived of this clichéd vocabulary whether many planners would be rendered almost speechless. Admittedly, this problem is not peculiar to planners. In discourse analysis, it is acknowledged that deliberative engagement in many social arenas can be debilitated by careless recourse to 'empty signifiers', insipid words that can mean whatever is in the eye of the beholder, and whose ambiguity is revealed whenever an attempt is made to translate aspiration into operation.

However, in planning, this obscurity can be injurious to both place-making and space mediation - the two central purposes of the profession. It can raise development ambition in a commendable manner, dissent to which many find difficult to express. Yet, when it comes to decoding generalized laudable objectives into planning guidance for material consideration when development proposals are being assessed for compliance, the ineffectual vacuity is exposed. If this encumbrance is evident in typical planning processes, it is even more manifest when it comes to addressing contested space in deeply divided societies.

Accordingly, this chapter examines key aspects of this dilemma, particularly those derived from the objective of creating 'shared space' in cities scarred by legacies of violent conflict centred on disputed territory and identity. The substance of the argument presented derives from four decades of research into the predicament of twinning regeneration with reconciliation in such places as Chicago, Belfast, Nicosia, and Jerusalem (Gaffikin and Morrissey, 2011). These cities are characterised by pronounced segregation between people with historic adversarial attachments, whether based on race, ethnicity, or rival sovereignties. They illustrate a discordant urbanism, in which the ethnic is privileged over the civic. Here, the normal spatial fragmentations, attributable to social polarity or infrastructural insensitivity, are accentuated by deliberate sectarian geography.

Beginning with an acknowledgement of Planning's failure to defy the forces of sectarianism by means of hiding behind narrow definition of its remit, the chapter proceeds to explore how such flinching inclines unintentionally to reproduce conditions of spatial separatism. Taking the example of urban policy towards disadvantaged communities in divided cities, it then illustrates how institutional amnesia in urban planning and policy agencies tends to result in them applying similar interventions over the decades with negligible impact, while deploying changing terminology to infer continuous innovative advancement. At this point, the chapter examines the challenge involved in adopting more exact language, before finally outlining a different planning agenda for divided cities, based on *'meaning what we say'*.

Planning's failure

Content analysis of planning documents in deeply divided cities reveals a tendency 'not to mention the war', as if air-brushing out the conflict absolves planners from addressing its relevance to space. This erasure of terms can be as bad as feeble resort to bland terms. Alongside this convenient denial, reasons that Planning to date has not helped deliver a more united society in deeply divided places, include its:

1. tendency to refute the pertinence of division and segregation to the planning process, as if such contentious issues are beyond the sphere and aptitude of planners. This tapered definition of responsibility serves to blind planners to an obvious connection: these conflicts are centrally about the contest of space and resource; planning is about social ordering of space and related resource allocation, and, as such, it cannot forsake its role in the former;
2. assumption that a 'neutral' approach to planning is the best guarantor of even-handedness in an antagonistic context. Yet, the term 'neutral' does not confer automatic impartiality. To be neutral in the face of inequity, for example, is to be compliant with its continued iniquity;
3. limited capacity to challenge the 'diseconomies of conflict' that often facilitate profligate and ineffective duplication of services and amenities within each sectarian bloc. This relates to a failure to define 'need' with greater precision and acumen, and to distinguish it from other terms, such as 'wish' or 'preference';
4. restricted scope for considering the wider social facet, due to its focus on 'land use planning' – a term that implies technical concern about

zoning and regulating particular development activity - with a coupled focus on the *physical* aspects of infrastructure and environment;

5. limited facility for nesting neighbourhood planning and regeneration strategies within a statutory and strategic planning framework, without which, such local schemes lack appropriate command and resource. This, in turn, is linked to the language that is adopted for this purpose. Should plans for locality be *'consistent with'* wider strategic planning, or simply have to *'pay regard to'* them? - each idiom holding very different obligation;
6. reluctance to recognize openly and define precisely the difference among types of space - for instance, ethnic, neutral, shared, dead, and cosmopolitan - in a conflict-ridden society. Such clear designation would offer a starting point to strategic targeting that amplified the scope of some of these types over that of others less supportive of urban welfare;
7. unintentional concession to major sectarian blocs to use planning to carve up 'spheres of influence', thereby forestalling a more joined together and mutual society. As will be elaborated later, in part, this capitulation is linked to problematic definitions of 'community' and 'rights' ;
8. failure to achieve all-encompassing participatory plan-making, that embraces diverse voices beyond 'tick box' categories of sectarian identity, gender, ethnicity, disability, and age;
9. deficiency in embedding planning overtly in a comprehensive programme of reconciliation, which goes beyond the collusions and 'carve-ups' involved in 'deal-making' and 'back-scratching', terms that better delineate what can pass for negotiated compromise in deeply conflictive circumstance. Often, these processes can appease sectarian gatekeepers, rather than challenge the underlying rationale for, and moral codes of, sectarianism; and
10. proclivity for euphemism and 'constructive ambiguity' in phraseology so as not to upset a fragile concord, without recognising the scope this timidity offers protagonists to pursue their enmity through other means, such as 'culture wars', or the deployment of 'equality' as a 'Trojan horse' for partisan political strategy. Terms such as 'ethnic cleansing'; 'collateral damage'; and, indeed, 'peace walls', are indicative of this depreciation towards innocuous expression to conceal offensive reality. Such shortcomings have tended to entrap planning in a series of unintended consequences that can accentuate rather than ameliorate the partitions of a split society. The remaining parts of the chapter concentrate on the example of Belfast's difficulty in these regards.

Reproducing division

Addressing the problems of this kind of contested urbanism demands radical reappraisal of intervention. Taking Belfast as a case in point, many deficiencies have debilitated city regeneration effort. For sake of brevity, some examples will suffice:

1. they tend to be based on very flimsy evaluation. Policy moves from one programme to another, without really testing what worked and what didn't in the previous programme, or indeed programmes from elsewhere. In this circuitous policy route, the underpinning concepts vary over time, giving delusionary impression of innovation and progress: *participation* becomes *partnership*; *poverty* becomes *social exclusion*; *multiple deprivation* becomes *multi-dimensionality*; *linkage* becomes *connectedness*; etc. It is almost as if because we cannot change the problem, we change the label instead. As civil servants come and go, institutional amnesia takes hold, and thereby wheels are inadvertently re-invented, because no basis exists for learning from the past. No precision of terms permits continuity of appraisal. For instance, having spent five years on intensive and comprehensive engagement around re-imagining a united Belfast in a major cross-sectoral City Visioning process in the mid-1990s, what happened? The resulting concept plan was set aside, for the whole process to be started again by a new set of public officials;

2. the spatial scale and model of intervention keeps changing. No clear and consistent decision can be reached about the appropriate policy or territorial focus. For instance, *Making Belfast Work* eventually went for big geographies in their sizeable area partnerships, most of which embraced the two main communities, and offered suitable scale and scope demanded by sensible strategies for long-term and deep-rooted regeneration. Then, along comes *Neighbourhood Renewal*, involving retreat into small, and often sectarian-enclaved, areas. The former was an organic home-grown intervention, while the latter was one simply cloned from the English model. No rationale was offered for this switch in emphasis, and no evaluation was conducted into its effect on good relations across the traditional divide;

3. there has been a tendency to not distinguish between development *in* a place, and development *of* a place. The former tends to focus on physical-led development, while the latter concentrates on people-centred development, enhancing the skills and capacities of residents. Both are needed. But, the latter is the more difficult and long-term. Anybody can erect a building. But, building community is more daunting. Nurturing neighbourliness, friendships, trust, respect, and cooperation - this is the 'soft infrastructure' that is the indispensible scaffolding of effective place. A classic example of this flawed thinking is found in the plan to build a 'community hub' in the highly contentious space in a difficult part of North Belfast, known as Girdwood, long before there is any prospect of an actual coherent 'community';

4. there has been little connection between the urban programmes for deprived areas and the wider city regeneration. This lies at the heart of the whole predicament. The token response to poverty areas embodied in early urban strategies since the 1970s gave way to more serious investment, through Urban Development Grant and other significant funding, in the City Centre and Waterfront, balanced a little by later programmes in the deprived areas, such as *Making Belfast Work*. But, the overall tendency has been to *parcel* the city into distinctive development zones; *parse* the various publics that are accordingly targeted: commercial business people; commuters; the disadvantaged; the professional class in anchor institutions, such as universities and hospitals; etc; and *portion* the investment in ways that favour the more privileged and powerful. This intrinsic tendency to parcel, parse and portion is not made explicit, and its differential impact across the divide is thereby shielded from inspection and accountability.

In the context of a city already fractured and fragmented by socio-spatial polarisations caused by increased social inequality and enduring conflict, this divisive approach merits conversion to a 3S policy of *stitch*, *scale*, and *scope*: *stitching* the city together as one coherent entity to be planned and developed as a unit, as recommended by the Forum for an Alternative Belfast; *scaling* investment proportionately in both funding level and time-frame to the challenge being addressed, while re-drawing the geographies of 'local community' to embrace cross-class and inter-denominational populations; and *scoping* the basis of all development strategy to include both the social needs and assets in an area, while drawing in all funding sources (public, private, and voluntary) behind a common vision and purpose for the city, so that, for instance, philanthropy money is complementing, rather than duplicating or substituting for, public money.

Unfortunately, the latest schemes for the city, such as the Belfast Masterplan, are still yielding to the conventional 'zoning' approach, whereby it ear-marks a development axis from Queen's University through to the city centre and the new University of Ulster campus out to the Harbour and Titanic quarter. While speaking the language of integrated development, anchor institutions, and the role of neighbourhood, it is still given to fragmenting the urban frame into the digital city, the learning city, the centre city, etc., when instead of such multiple cities, a more strategically coherent ONE CITY could be patterned (Belfast Local Strategy Partnership Board, 2004);

5. there has been scant and inconsistent concern about quality. Targeting has its virtues. But, one problem with the culture of targeting is that it tends to focus on the easily measurable, thereby reducing most appraisals to tick-box audits. There may be quality design invested in the central core, though visitors to the new Titanic quarter might query that claim, given much of its bleakness, blandness, and disconnectedness. But, whatever quality consideration is so invested, it is not rolled out to city neighbourhoods in a coherent quality design framework for the whole city. Thereby, the term 'quality' is de-valued, since it is a currency, whose exchange value seems to operate mainly in the exclusive zones of downtown and waterfront.

6. the urban prospectus is not underpinned by robust analysis. What is happening to the contemporary city derives from substantial structural and cultural changes over the last half century, including: economic re-structuring, in particular, de-industrialisation; related urban-rural shifts; growing social inequality, also reflected spatially in greater social segregation; the re-configuration of 'community' in the context of changing family formations and household structures, wider social networking, decline of religious observance, immigration, etc. These and other societal processes make for new urban complexities that are not reducible to old-style planning, based on simple categories or 'predict and provide' calculation. Put simply, this is a less predictable world, whose scale and pace of change demand meticulous analysis;

7. there has been under-appreciation of how rewarding bad behaviour can encourage more bad behaviour. Too often, there has been inclination to throw money after violence in effort to curb the prospect of further disturbance. However well-intended such intercession, perilous consequence may follow allocation of investment based on degree of violent feuding. Indeed, the multi-layering of such impulsive initiatives over existing policy may only promote a confusing maze of partnerships and plans, when what is really required is clear, consistent, and carefully conceived intervention;

8. there has been a problem with delivery. Proliferation of plans seems to generate a law of diminishing returns. The more we have, the less we seem to use. As alluded to earlier, one aspect of this problem is the lack of clarity about the hierarchy of authority accorded various plans, and how precisely they tally with each other, and how they will fit with the proposed Community Plan and Spatial Plan process. At least in the case of the former, there is emphasis on building into the plan itself precise delivery mechanisms: when it is to happen; what agencies are responsible; where the money is coming from; who it is to effect and how? etc. Again, such precise designation offers prospect of designed outcome (Gaffikin, McEldowney, and Sterrett, 2010).

But, more is possible. New planning frameworks can bring on board the range of sectors and funding bodies that can make a difference to the city, so that all such energies and resources are working in potential synergy rather than pointless rivalry. That means that the substantial public spend from the mainstream departments, such as Education and Health, together with the important role of Foundation funders, together with the voluntary and community input, are brought more cohesively together to work in optimum collaboration to address a consistent agenda of city development, while acknowledging real difference in power and perspective.

This is not about the false conviviality of a contrived consensus. Cities are inherently places of contest around allocation of scarce resources such as land and finance. Imprecise definitions of 'collaborative planning' ignore agonistic dimensions of the politics of planning in a deeply unequal society. Notwithstanding this important proviso, Belfast City Council, as the body which is set to hold primary authority for much of urban planning and regeneration, can nurture a multi-disciplinary team that traverses current silos of Development, Community Development, Good Relations, Leisure and Public Parks, etc. Such a team can bring together planners, architects, urban designers, community developers, economic developers, educationalists, conflict resolvers, etc. from a formative stage in the planning process, recognising themselves in the common vernacular of 'urbanists', engaging together to forward a visionary, strategic, inclusive, and proactive plan, with built-in delivery. But, such steps can benefit from thorough reflection on past practice, particularly in respect of the gap between the tongue of loose promise and the touch of actual impact.

Learning lessons

Einstein's famed definition of insanity involves doing the same thing repeatedly, while irrationally expecting that the next time will magically produce different results. When it comes to tackling deprivation and the linked issue of good relations between the contending tribes in Belfast, that is exactly what has been happening for over four decades. Evidence of limited impact over a considerable time-frame suggests the efficacy of fundamental re-appraisal. The intractable persistence of urban poverty, social and religious residential segregation, and related territorial contests, confirm this proposition.

To appreciate how much policy has been going round in circles on this issue, it is useful to trace some recent history. Following Boal's study of socio-spatial patterns of deprivation in Belfast in 1976, a new urban compensatory programme was launched by the name of **Belfast Areas of Need** (BAN). In essence, it offered modest extra public funding for the worst-off wards in the city, and its remaining relics include a few of our current leisure centres. Inherent in some of these early investments seemed to be the simplistic notion that if you built leisure and community facilities in some of the most disadvantaged and troubled areas that this would induce at least some of the riotous youth off the streets into more productive activity. This faint-hearted initiative was followed by the more substantial **Belfast Action Team** programme (BAT) in the early 1980s. At least this time, the 'geographies' of intervention were drawn wider to include both Protestant and Catholic areas into each BAT team locality -- for instance, Lower Shankill and Falls; New Lodge and Tiger's Bay, etc. Nevertheless, the scale and type of intervention was not proportionate to the problem addressed, and the distinctive role of community conflict in partly generating and sustaining the disadvantage was not competently analysed and incorporated into the intervention.

Meanwhile, the real action in terms of urban regeneration was starting to take shape, in terms of rehabilitating a rundown city centre that had become victim to the Provisional IRA bombing campaign. Reflected in the signature building of Castle Court, this emphasis on Downtown was then extended to Laganside, an ambitious waterfront development, designed to turn the city to the river and to optimise the re-valorisation of mature industrial spaces and brownfield sites, as dockland had moved upstream under new technologies of containerisation. The logic of this strategy of facilitating the development priorities of the most active sectors of an increasingly service-based economy was endorsed in the **1989 Belfast Urban Plan**, with its emphasis on office and retail expansion, and its notable failure to identify the dynamics of economic and political change driving the de-population, de-industrialisation, deepening segregation, and durable poverty be-setting the viability of many of the poorest areas.

This concentration on the commercial urban core to the relative neglect of the city's impoverished neighbourhoods provoked a persistent critique, and prompted a modest up-scaling of intervention, under the first **Making Belfast Work** programme in the late 1980s, progressing to its second more substantial stage by the mid-1990s. By then, it was operating, across the city, five area partnerships - inter-sectoral bodies that were encouraged to engage in long-term strategic thinking about the multi-dimensional aspects of their areas' decline and prospective resuscitation. As the name of the programme suggested, it was the first serious attempt to connect the problems of poverty and under-development to the changing urban economy. In turn, this was followed by **Neighbourhood Renewal** in the 2000s, and most recently complemented by the **Social Investment** initiative. Alongside these mainstream government programmes, there have been myriad other schemes such as URBAN, Integrated Operations, and POVERTY 1 and 2, funded under the EU; a host of community projects funded by IFI, Atlantic Philanthropy, Co-operation Ireland, Community Foundation for Northern Ireland, and most recently by the Big Lottery. Added together, this spending has not been inconsiderable. And yet, results have been dispiriting.

In terms of measuring multiple deprivation, we have had a range of indices: Boal in the 1970s; Townsend in the 1980s; Robson in the 1990s; and over recent decades, the Noble Index. They all come out much the same. Even taking it over the last 20 odd years, the same wards, in almost the same ranking, remain stubbornly the most deprived. It could be taken all the way back to the 1970s, and the picture would be similar. Even though the *populations* have changed to some extent in these wards over that period with demographic churning, the same *places* show up persistently as the most disadvantaged, as if poverty was imprinted into their very DNA. So, this calls either for resignation to 'the poor being always with us', or for concession that urban regeneration has not been working for all.

These patterns possess a long pedigree, and an historical appreciation of Belfast's overall development is useful to determine the origins of its contemporary form, if a new planning in a divided city is to be conceived. Indeed, these and related lessons can be drawn not just from Belfast's experience. They are supported by analysis of urban regeneration elsewhere (see for example, Beauregard, 1993). Initiatives undertaken in Belfast derived from earlier interventions in Britain. To take an example of one city, Liverpool: it has had virtually every intervention going, tracing back to the Educational Priority Area scheme in 1968, to the Community Development Project in 1969, to Inner Area Studies and Inner City Partnerships in the 1970s, to the Thatcher agenda of Enterprise Zones and Urban Development Corporations in the 1980s, to Major's Single Regeneration Budget in the 1990s, to Blair's Urban Priority Areas and Neighbourhood Renewal, and so on to the present. Yet, Liverpool remains a stricken city, according to many indicators of health and education performance, rates of workless households, etc. The experience demonstrates not only the limits of area-based interventions to redress disadvantage, but also the problematic of 'community' as a spatial unit of analysis and change in the context of fundamental urban problems (Ferguson and Dickens, eds., 1999).

Similarly, many of the urban strategies in Britain themselves derive from earlier policies in the USA. So, for instance, the War on Poverty there in the mid-sixties cradled a lot of these subsequent initiatives. Apparently, Ronald Reagan liked to joke that *'we fought a war against poverty, and poverty won'*. But, there has been a radical re-think in many American cities in recent decades against continual compensatory programmes into the concentrated spaces of poverty and race. Instead, cities like Chicago have been demolishing their notorious ghettos like Robert Taylor Homes and Cabrini Green with the intention of replacing these grim complexes with mixed income, mixed race communities in quality mixed tenure housing. The policy is not without many problems, not least for those former residents, now displaced and prevented from returning to the new developments. For some, it is not much more than another form of gentrification. For others, it is seen as providing a new start, combining physical improvement with social schemes of support and expected responsibility targeted at residents in need.

Such comparative analysis demands careful attention, and a re-visiting of long accepted terms such as 'gentrification', 'need', 'segregation', etc. for greater forensic interrogation and implication.

A new Planning?

Any hope of developing a coherent regeneration strategy for Belfast has to address explicitly its long-standing sectarian division. Planning is not some apolitical, technical activity. It is misdirected, if it disregards the underlying social processes which shape space. In this context, as indicated in the earlier narrative, three key processes uniquely combined to create Belfast's current patterns of de-population and deep segregation:

1. Following the Matthew Plan, 1963, the decision was taken to de-magnetise Belfast, in terms of both investment and population, and to transfer many former residents to satellite towns, such as Antrim and Craigavon, as part of an economic modernisation, based on attracting transnational capital to new greenfield-sited industrial estates, a strategy enshrined in the 1969 Belfast Urban Plan.
2. The other key aspect of this strategy related to comprehensive redevelopment of inner city Belfast at the same time, and the lower density housing and new roads infrastructure that accompanied this 'slum clearance' demanded that many former inner city residents be 'decanted' elsewhere. Again, the language is instructive.
3. These intended two major 'pull' factors in population were unexpectedly supplemented by the 'push' factor caused by the emerging Troubles at exactly the same time, inducing some to leave a city that quickly became the primary location for violent conflict. By the same token, many of those remaining, particularly in the most troubled areas, moved into tighter ghetto communities of their co-religionists for greater security, accentuating the long-standing pattern of city segregation.

Given the 'sprawl' effect of some of this de-centralisation, some 140,000 commuters come into Belfast every day, around half of the city's total resident number. It can be asked whether there are many of the important aspects of city-region planning, like office development, roads infrastructure and city parking, which are essentially designed with the commuter interest in mind. Many of these commuters take up the most skilled jobs in the city, which on a comparative basis with similar cities in Britain produces a high GDP per head. So, a city that has been doing quite well economically in the recent past is also one where a substantial section of its residents is failing to share fully in that success, producing a 'tale of two cities' effect. This social fragmentation is augmented by the ethno-national division. While there is no simple causal relationship between segregation and deprivation, there is an interactive relationship. Moreover, the continued inter-communal contest in relation to territory and identity contributes to the damaging fragmentation of the city, and thereby to its under-development. In policy terms, it makes it difficult to achieve symmetry between interventions around inclusion and those around cohesion. Proposals to tackle inequalities embedded in the former problem, can generate sectarian squabbles about which religious 'community' is getting most resource, resentment that, in turn, aggravates the very hostility that hampers effort for greater cross-community harmony (Gaffikin and Morrissey, 2011b).

As with interventions around deprivation, we have had a series of 'good relations' initiatives over the decades. Starting in 1969, the newly formed Community Relations Commission quickly decided that their ideal intervention in contested areas around bridge-building community relations was unfeasible, given the intensity of rancour. Instead, they shifted to a strategy of community development, working within each community bloc, and trusting that the common issues of deprivation that would emerge from this focus would in time present opportunities for cross-community contact and collaboration. To a modest degree, it did. But, this critical decision to prioritise single-identity work ultimately accorded legitimacy to such separatism, and the corollary was that the integrated development that should have been embedded in public investment in these areas became aspirational rather than normative. From this flawed genesis, a whole structure and culture of 'community development' formed, inherently endorsing the sectarian geographies of many 'local communities' as an unfortunate inevitability of an ethno-nationalist contest, rather than calling it what it is: a narrow ghettoization, which locked these areas into constricted spaces and visions, and encouraged rivalries over the allocation of urban resources. While this can be wrapped in plausible theories of social capital - how 'bonding capital' has to be nourished as a precursor platform to 'bridging capital', and such like - the practice is that it reinforces a deformed concept of 'community' in contested cities like Belfast that is ultimately supportive of segregation and division.

Accordingly, as the demography of places like Belfast changes to a more 50-50 share between the two traditional communities, contests over spaces are likely to intensify rather than abate. In such circumstance, a set of principles to guide the use of, and access to, the city may be beneficial. Primarily, it would challenge the proposition that any group can claim part of the city as 'their territory' that other citizens can only access by compliance with their approval criteria. Such 'balkanisation' denies a view of the whole city as everyone's neighbourhood. To work at its best, contemporary urbanism needs to be open, pliable, porous, mixed, welcoming, approachable – a pluralist place for a pluralist people. In this more dialogic 'space', disputes about contested territory can be joined more agonistically and candidly. Invariably, attempts at adjudication will throw up the complexity of language, to which Planning is inevitably tied. For instance, the concept of 'rights' is problematic rather than incontrovertible. People have a right to free assembly, including protest and marching. But, people also have a right to be free from sectarian harassment. This *'freedom to'* and *'freedom from'* can often be in conflict in a contested society. In settling such wrangles, as with all other spatial issues confronting Planning in such rancorous context, the more precise the language of engagement, the more definite the means of resolution can become.

However, such principles can only take root in a shift from the politics of coercion to the politics of persuasion, ingrained in democratic *smart pluralism*. In the case of Northern Ireland, Unionists cannot rely any longer on the authority and sway of a secure majority. If they want to retain a UK-based sovereignty, they have to reach out beyond their core constituency to win the blessing, or at least voluntary acquiescence, from a section of those with a Catholic community background. Similarly, since their signing up to the principle of consent involves discarding their physical-force tradition, mainstream Republicanism cannot attain their goal of a united Ireland without earning the willing endorsement of a section of the current Unionist community. In this way, a changed political landscape can become congruent with changing the urban landscape of contested cities like Belfast.

This requires an approach to problem-solving that identifies and discards terminology that serves to blur rather than clarify. While accepting that many terms have nuances of meaning, and that meaning itself is socially arbitrated in interactive and interpretative processes, greater use of specification, qualification, and differentiation is likely to bestow more clarity and rigour to analysis.

This 'subjecting' to analysis applies to the various parties involved in the conflict, since the relativist position of accepting groups and their standpoints only on terms of the groups' own perception is a recipe for affirming sectarian outlook. Just as viable Planning options for deeply contested places can be best based on testing, substantiated by evidence, propositions from all contesting agencies in a conflict are best examined for validity on the same scrupulous basis.

Taking this standard, it seems counter-intuitive to look for this process in vision planning. The name itself connotes a hazy imagining that sacrifices exactitude for woolly sanguinity. Yet, as mentioned earlier, at the onset of the current 'peace process', Belfast undertook a major visioning exercise in 1995 about its long-term future, involving the establishment of a representative City Partnership Board, which engaged in widespread consultation across the city's diverse constituencies, in a series of workshops, forums and seminars, lasting just over five years. Unlike many previous policy and planning processes, the contentious issue of division was not sidelined. As expressed in the preliminary vision statement, the Board projected a city that put people above claims of territory or identity, in a process designed to move its political culture beyond the habit of hate. In similar vein, the final plan (Belfast City Vision Partnership Board, 2000) spoke of a city belonging to all its citizens, and shaped by mutual civic support and respect. Yet, despite appealing consensual language, the actual translation into practical development was limited (Gaffikin and Sterrett, 2006).

Importantly, the Board identified a rubric to facilitate the integration of all dimensions affecting prosperity, equity and quality. Guided by the core messages from its consultations, it adopted the concept of a *Mutual City*, taken to be one that encouraged links and collaboration amongst all sections and areas, while opening the city up to the wider world. But, after all of this protracted effort, and even after successfully reaching a broadly consensual conclusion about the way forward for the city, implementation of its action proposals came unstuck, when it became evident that constituent partners were unwilling to set aside their own priorities, corporate objectives, or interests in favour of strategic collaboration. In part, this impasse was related to the untidy problem of moving from cosy concord to definite decision. In part, it reflected distinctive dilemmas faced by deeply divided cities in pursuing a viable urbanism. For instance, all cities are being encouraged to plan for compact form that promotes sustainability and efficiently optimises use of brownfield land. But, in Belfast, much brownfield land is in or near Protestant areas, a surplus supply related to the relative population decline in that community. Yet, new housing supply on many of these sites would likely invite Catholic occupancy, given the higher Catholic need for housing in many parts. Such patterns, in turn, are likely to be viewed by some Protestant communities, which feel most under threat of extinction, as territorial encroachment.

It would help to have an agreed citywide framework, within which local negotiations about such re-definitions of space could be conducted. Just as it helped to open up the Northern Ireland conflict to a more global reference, so it is useful to ease the intensiveness of very micro conflicts about contested land distribution by framing them within an agreed set of principles that can be consistently and transparently applied. But a real shared city has to embrace also the issue of socio-spatial segregation. Recent city developments have risked the relative marginalisation of large parts of North and West Belfast, which has long lacked a vibrant economic base, and remains scarred by 'peace' walls. A sustained strategic approach to the creation of a new development axis for this area is intrinsic to any serious objective to build a shared city. Alongside this, there is a difficult discussion about how the spatial concentrations of multiple deprivation can give way to more socially mixed communities without the negative externalities associated with gentrification.

A dynamic and differentiated interpretation of 'space' illustrates the problematic pursuit of shared space in a contested city. Is the notion of 'shared space' to be taken as inherently benign and its alternative of ethnic space to be regarded as universally malign? Conversely, is not the objective to create more 'shared space' in Belfast itself disputable? For instance, does it imply that the whole city should comprise shared space, whereby success would be calibrated in terms of the diminution of ethnic space? If a 'shared city' means an 'agreed city' and the latter embodies agreement to disagree, and thereby a high degree of separate living in a manner that is mutually respectful and non-threatening, that is one thing. But if it means a significant increase in integrated social interaction and inter-communal collaboration, rooted in values of inclusion, diversity, equity, and interdependence, that is a much more ambitious project. How can this be accorded spatial form in a city whose sectarian signature is a predominantly Catholic/Nationalist West and a predominantly Protestant/Unionist East, fragmented from each other by both the natural environment of the river Lagan, and the built environment of major infrastructure?

The market has become an increasingly important instrument for change in Belfast in the recent past, with some commentators complimenting its nonpartisan capacity to shape a more cosmopolitan outlook for the city. However, the new apartment building around the city, seen by some as creating shared spaces in terms of the sectarian geography, is at the same time creating a new social geography. Yet, would the city trade off more social segregation for less sectarian segregation? Would it avoid social housing in its new non-sectarian spaces, since such estates are deemed by some to have an association with high levels of segregation? How would such an agenda square with declared Planning values about creating balanced, socially mixed, 'sustainable' communities? Should all types of 'community' be regarded as similarly worthy for sustainability? In any case, can Planning set itself in contest with a contemporary political dynamic that shows tendency to 'neoliberalizing space' (Peck and Tickell, 2002)?

No blueprint exists for easy answer to these thorny questions. Rather, such 'wicked problems' provide an agenda that can be opened up for greater civic understanding, and critical debate that accommodates contrarian argument, supported by investment in civic literacy and capacity. Ideological rectitude and tamed discourse, promoted by deformed political correctness, are inimical to such precarious encounter. While blunt language can be seen as threatening to the fragile tranquillity of contemporary Belfast, without robust straight talking, historical evidence presented here suggests that patterns of hostility embodied in spatial separatism will likely persist, and from this debility, the poorest communities on both sides of the traditional divide will suffer most.

References

Belfast City Vision Partnership Board (2000) *Belfast City Vision: Our City, Our Future, Our Vision*. Belfast: Belfast City Vision.

Belfast Local Strategy Partnership (BLSP) (2004) *Helping to Build a Sustainable City at Peace With Itself: Strategy Statement.* Belfast: BLSP.

Beauregard, R. (1993) *Voices of Decline: the post-war fate of US cities*. Oxford: Blackwell.

Ferguson, R. and Dickens, W. (Eds.) (1999) *Urban Problems and Community Development*. Washington: Brookings Institution Press.

Gaffikin, F. and Morrissey, M. (2011) *Planning in Divided Cities: collaborative shaping of contested cities*. Oxford: Wiley-Blackwell.

Gaffikin, F. and Morrissey, M. (2011b) Community Cohesion and Social Inclusion: Unravelling a Complex Relationship. *Urban Studies,* 48, pp. 1089-1118.

Gaffikin, F., McEldowney, M. and Sterrett, K. (2010) Creating Shared Public Space in the Contested City: The Role of Urban Design. *Journal of Urban Design,* 15(4), pp. 493-513.

Gaffikin, F. and Sterrett, K. (2006) New Visions for Old Cities: The Role of Visioning in Planning. *Planning Theory and Practice,* 7(2), pp. 159-178.

Markusen, A. (2003) Fuzzy Concepts, Scanty Evidence, Policy Distance: The Case for Rigour and Policy Relevance in Critical Regional Studies. *Regional Studies*, 37(6), pp. 701-717.

Peck, J. and Tickell, A. (2002) Neoliberalizing Space. *Antipode,* 34(3), pp. 380-404.

Chapter 5

The legacy of Planning in Belfast and some of the challenges ahead

Ken Sterrett, Mark Hackett and Jayne Bassett

Introduction

The so-called 'peacewalls' across Belfast are probably the most visible manifestations of division in the city. Indeed many have become the iconic images of sustained separation between the 'two' communities. Arguably too, it is the visibility of these structures that has prompted the focused ambition in TBUC (Together Building a United Community) – for them to be removed by 2022. Yet, when we look at how the spatial environment of Belfast has been purposefully or unintentionally manipulated, we can see barriers of various shapes and forms. Roads, car parks, blighted land, gates, fences, buffer buildings and other bulwarks all contribute to sustaining an ethnically and socially divided city. This chapter explores the legacy of planning in Belfast, and particularly its impact on the city's urban structure and form. It also suggests some possible 'solutions' to the development challenges that lie ahead.

Urban structure and form

The physical configuration of Belfast is, in many respects, similar to other cities. It nestles in a valley between hills to the west and east; it has a starfish arrangement of radial roads stretching out from the city centre; and it has a commercial core that has expanded along the 'reclaimed' river (Laganside) and into the former shipyard/docks area (Titanic Quarter). However, this urban structure needs further analysis and understanding. The layout of the city has been planned and designed, at different times during its relatively recent history, to meet what we might call 'social' objectives. Again, many of these social objectives were common in other cities. Examples here, include, the redesign of the city to accommodate the car and the redevelopment of nineteenth century inner city housing. However, in Belfast many of these planning initiatives were undertaken during the period of the conflict, and have, in many respects, contributed to a problematic city layout and urban structure. In addition, it is now becoming evident that many developments in the city were deliberately employed to create barriers between communities in conflict or to manipulate the spatial environment to exclude problematic community areas.

In North Belfast, for example, two areas were deliberately planned as 'buffer zones' between communities in conflict. The business park on the north side of Duncairn Gardens was planned and designed as an 'environmental' response to a very violent interface between the New Lodge area and Tiger's Bay (Photograph 5.1). A decline in the demand for housing in Tiger's Bay helped 'facilitate' the process. Around 200 houses and a church were demolished to create a site for 'neutral' businesses. Similarly, the Hillview 'Enterprise Zone' was planned as another buffer between Oldpark and Ardoyne.

Photograph 5.1 St Barnabus's Church, Duncairn Gardens demolished to make way for a business park buffer zone

Source: www.belfastforumco.uk

However, a core issue that permeated a range of spatial reconfigurations was the protection, enhancement and fortification of the central commercial city. This started in the late 1960s /early 1970s with the urban motorway, 'downgraded' to the Westlink and then purposively developed in the 1980s as a strategy to demonstrate a vibrant commercial core. The decanting of civil servants to offices in the centre together with massive subsidies to new commercial development (Castle Court) was designed to create a retail recovery as well as the symbolism of defiance against the IRA bombing campaign. This deliberate strategy of creating a protected node of commercial activity was further supported by a range of developments that reinforced the insularity of the centre. These include buildings such as Castle Court that turn their back to north and west Belfast; the Gasworks that is sealed off from and disconnected from the Markets and Lower Ormeau and, of course Laganside and Titanic Quarter which are socially and physically 'detached'. Equally important, the commercial viability of the centre depended on car commuters and this, in turn, needed cheap car parking and a supportive road network. Interestingly, in the original documentations even the aesthetics of the proposed motorway experience were considered: "In the twilight areas 'facial cosmetics' of buildings beside the motorway which are left may be necessary so that a good front is presented to the motorway". And of course, to complement this, car parking was to become a major feature for the new modern city: "There will need to be large car parks associated with the road to receive the increasing number of cars which will visit the city" (Building Design Partnership *et al*, 1968). Of course, the contemporary spatial consequences of all of this is a core city effectively disconnected from the surrounding inner city neighbourhoods but highly connected for the 100,000+ car commuters who use the city every day.

The devastation of the inner city through the remodelling of urban space for the car had a major impact on inner north Belfast (Figure 5.1). The historical grid layout which connected streets to the main arterial thoroughfares and to the centre was largely replaced by the 'Westlink' and 'inner box' roads surrounded by a sea of fractured developments and spaces. All of this affected the general mobility of communities and, as importantly, it reinforced their isolation, both physically and psychologically, from the rest of the city. This breakdown in the structure and layout of the inner city and the spatial privilege given to the car has had widespread consequences (Figure 5.2).

Figure 5.1 Car impact map for inner Belfast

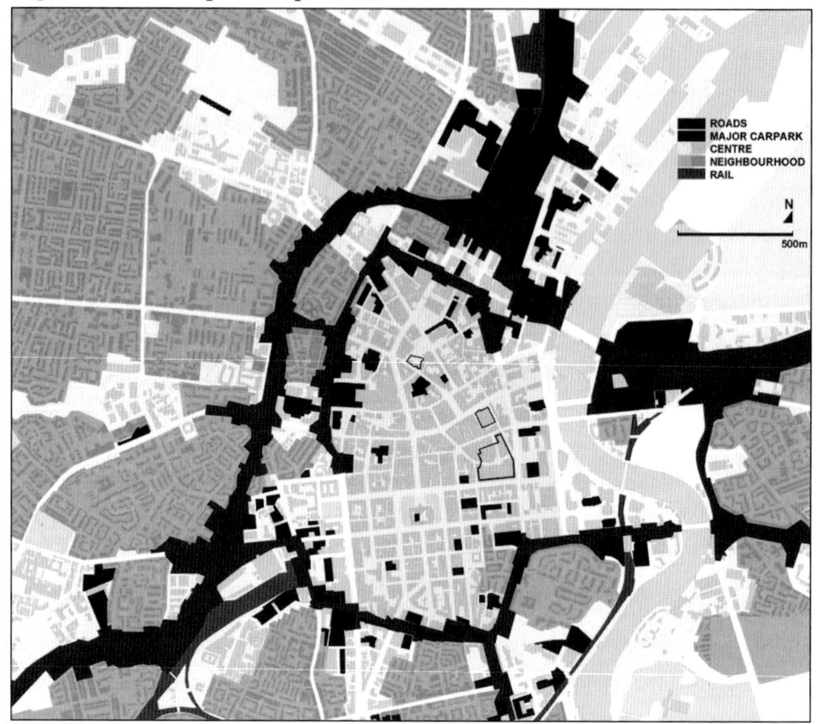

Source: Mark Hackett, Forum for Alternative Belfast.

(The dark tones indicate blighted areas of new motorways, Westlink, M2, M3, and inner ring road widening with associated major car parks. The inner city neighbourhoods affected by all of this are in a light grey tone)

Figure 5.2 The fragmentation of urban form in Belfast: figure-ground maps of inner north Belfast, 1960 and 2011

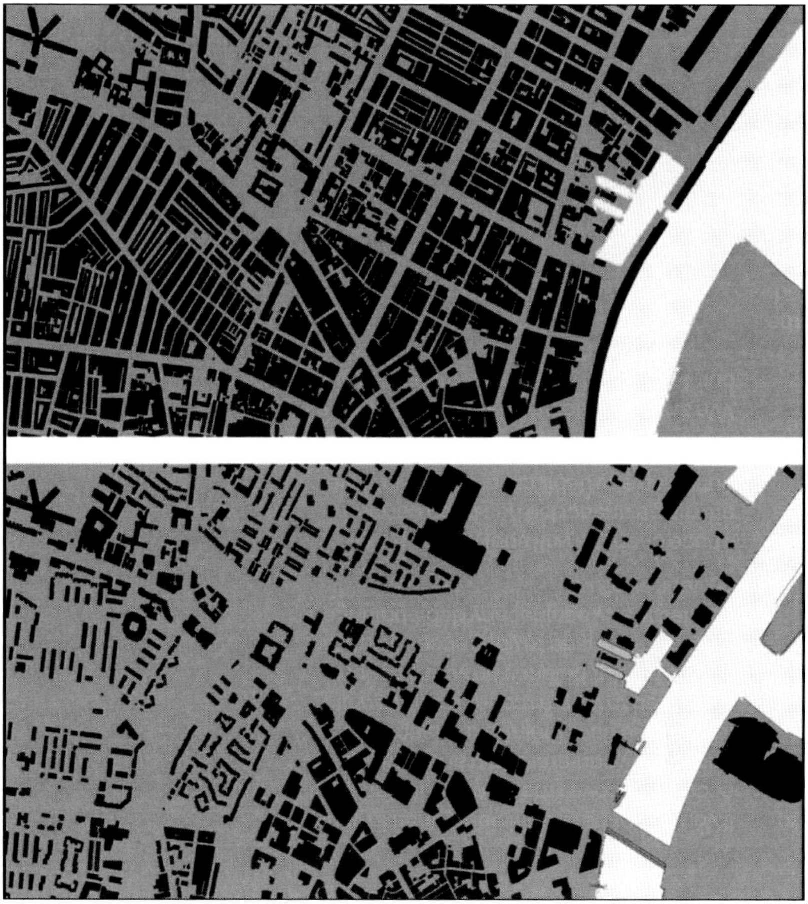

Source: Chris Duffy, QUB

Indeed, it is possible to suggest that there are two distinctive patterns of movement within the city. One, referred to as 'urban bubbling' by Atkinson and Flint (2004) captures the way in which the middle classes use the entire city and its environment as their neighbourhood. Of course the key to this level of access is the car or 'the bubble'. Working, shopping, pursuing leisure and so on around the city is very much the middle class lifestyle. And, as noted above, the city has been largely designed, developed and managed to facilitate this.

For working class neighbourhoods, on the other hand, movement is largely limited to walking and public transport. Local facilities are therefore more important, as are safe walking environments that allow access to other parts of the city. However, in inner city Belfast there is a 'double bind'.

Firstly, these single identity communities are largely territorialised. During 'the conflict', these communities tended to become very insular and self-reliant. While this offered a degree of safety and protection, it also reduced contact with the rest of the city and between communities. Moreover, new facilities were often located in the heart of a community area, and, of course, this inevitably excluded their use by 'others'. Arguably too, the remodelled layout of the physical environment during redevelopment in the 1980s helped to reinforce this insularity. The traditional grid street pattern that characterised Belfast's inner city since the nineteenth century offered a permeability which facilitated wider social interactions and connections to services and employment (Figure 5.3). In contrast, much inner city redevelopment employed cul-de-sac layouts that reduced connectivity, lowered densities and created large swathes of hard-standing. And in addition, of course, the overall process saw the loss of over 60% of the inner city's population. The Shankill area, for example, saw a decline in population of over 70% (1971-2001).

Figure 5.3 Reconfigured inner west Belfast, 1960 and 2011

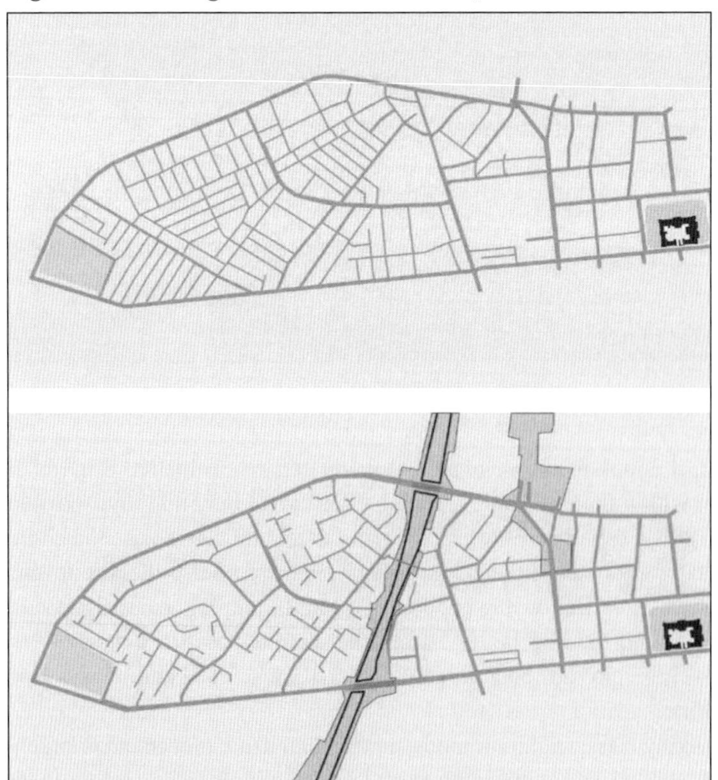

Source: Mark Hackett, Forum for Alternative Belfast.

Secondly, it is also important to note that patterns of movement in Belfast, particularly in and around the segregated residential areas, have a certain peculiarity. An ongoing legacy of 'the troubles' is what might be termed an 'inbuilt psyche' of knowing how to traverse the city (Brand, 2009). The arterial routes, for example, are carefully navigated by inner city residents to avoid passing through, or by, 'the other's' community territory. In the north and west of the city the pedestrian spaces along the arterial routes are almost exclusively used by one community or the other. While this sensitivity to community geography is also evident in how communities use public transport, it does not overly affect the behaviour of commuting car traffic. Of course, the real and psychological constraints of territory and how this plays out in terms of movement and access is made worse by a car dominated environment. While the comfort of territory has been important for communities, particularly during 'the conflict', it should not distract from the need to open up the city to local neighbourhoods and to encourage the development of a shared urban environment.

In the early 1960s Jane Jacobs was making the same point about American cities. She argued that the notion of 'neighbourhood' was a somewhat sentimental concept which was ultimately 'harmful to city planning'. For her the city is the neighbourhood, offering its citizens "wide choice and rich opportunities ….. whatever city neighborhoods may be, or may not be, and whatever usefulness they may have, or may be coaxed into having, their qualities cannot work at cross-purposes to thoroughgoing city mobility and fluidity of use, without economically weakening the city of which they are part".

Connectivity and exclusion

Belfast city centre, together with its extension into inner south, Laganside and Titanic Quarter, provide a range of services and facilities that are at the heart of the city's economy. Indeed, this is recognised in the Belfast Metropolitan Area Plan, 'The promotion of Belfast City Centre and the development opportunities within Belfast Harbour will support the provision of new job opportunities in central locations accessible to all sections of the community.' Moreover, much of the planning and regeneration emphasis over the last thirty years has been on these areas because they function as neutral, if not shared, spaces. However, as research has pointed out, many of these areas are not socially inclusive and are often seen by traditional communities as inaccessible and unwelcoming. There is no doubt, that at least in part, this is because these 'neutral' spaces and events are consumption-oriented. Genuine civic spaces that offer public amenity are very limited in number and in scope.

All of this suggests that, at the very least, facilitating good quality and direct access to key areas of the city should be a planning and regeneration priority. A study by Queen's University students showed that the city centre and Titanic Quarter were, potentially, within 5-10 minutes walking distance of Duncairn Gardens in the heart of inner north Belfast. However, the route to the city centre is frustrated by road barriers and poor quality frontage environments, while the route to Titanic Quarter is circuitous by both bus and foot. Titanic Quarter is, of course, similarly cut off from the adjacent East Belfast neighbourhoods. Good urban design practice which seeks to promote connectivity and therefore accessibility has not been a feature of planning and regeneration in Belfast. Rather, single function planning such as roads development together with site focused investment has largely ignored the broader spatial needs of the city. The underpinning assumption is that the private market will generate activity and, in turn, that activity will bring economic benefit to the city.

The problem here for planning is the exclusion this brings. Celebrating the value of individual, site particular projects sidesteps the civic and collective needs of the city. Such needs are so important in a context where exclusive ethnic and social space often triumphs over the civic. Good city form and structure is not just about aesthetics, rather it is about creating a place that everyone can share and have access to. It is also about creating spaces that have civic value rather than ethnic or commercial value. Every major development decision contributes to this. A key question for city planners, therefore, is to consider how all major development proposals can respond to and address the fractured and divided city. More than this, prioritising a re-stitching agenda would allow the development of a vision for the city that recognises that spatial fracture and disconnection helps sustain social and ethno-religious fracture and disconnection.

Major regeneration projects such as the City Centre, Laganside and Titanic Quarter have largely ignored these broader civic needs. Rather, they have relied on the neo-liberal theory that the market will solve the problems of a divided city through the generation of economic benefits that trickle down to all communities. However, this scenario implies that if new training facilities exist in Titanic Quarter or if job opportunities are available in Laganside, then it is up to individuals to overcome any access difficulties. In other words, the focus is on the individual rather than any collective concerns.

As noted earlier, issues of division take various spatial forms. The spatial legacy of the conflict together with over forty years of planning and regeneration has delivered a city that is fractured, disjointed and poorly managed. Importantly too, single identity ethno-religious neighbourhoods are being joined increasingly by mixed identity social neighbourhoods. While the former are often characterised by peace-walls, the latter are often branded by gates and fencing. As noted elsewhere in this report, areas with high levels of deprivation are often co-terminus with single identity neighbourhoods. On the other hand, the new gated communities are co-terminus with an ethnic mix and high levels of educational attainment. A survey of city centre apartments conducted by QUB as part of a study for the Northern Ireland Community Relations Council found that the majority of residents of the new apartments were not born in Northern Ireland. Moreover, they were relatively young, highly educated and transitory; and very interestingly, the majority of them didn't know their neighbours or knew only a few (Gaffikin, et al, 2008).

All of this confirms the emergence of new, non-place based communities, but it also suggests that the issue about creating and developing shared space and shared services is not limited to the traditional divisions. A number of the new gated communities sit adjacent to longstanding, single identity, working class communities who are recorded as having the highest level of educational underachievement in Northern Ireland. In this context, the issue of division is not about peace-walls but about the sort of environment that the city wants to create. The regulatory planning system that has prevailed over the last 40 years, largely ignored the 'traditional' geography of division and the evidence would suggest that it is also side-stepping these emerging new divisions.

While acknowledging that dysfunctional city form and structure is only one dimension of a deeper set of problems, it is, nevertheless, a significant issue. Creating the potential for shared space and services requires thoughtful street design and layout; it requires good walkable, safe and interesting connections. New or revitalised streets offer opportunities to locate services that can be accessed by both sides of the community and all classes. The so-called neutrality of the city centre has the potential to be expanded along arterial routes and 'new' connecting streets. The work of the Forum for Alternative Belfast largely focuses on this. The Six Links project in inner North Belfast together with proposals that emerged from the 2011 Summer School for inner south Belfast, offer opportunities to both strengthen connections as well as expanding shared streets and services.

This sort of analysis and agenda setting is not peculiar to Belfast. At an international level, there is growing recognition of the role that 'infrastructure' of various sorts can play in cementing division. In the United States, for example, Detroit (also known as Motor City) is beginning to acknowledge the impact that an extensive network of freeways have had on the city. Recent comments by the city's mayor, Mike Duggan, acknowledged that the freeways that encircle Metro Detroit have had a negative impact on the city and have contributed significantly to Detroit's steep economic decline. In his view, 'Freeways cut off and isolate neighborhoods (and) … we are still trying to recover from that.'

(http://grist.org/cities/even-detroit-is-hatin-on-freeways-now/?utm_content=buffere58a4&utm_medium=social&utm_source=twitter.com&utm_campaign=buffer)

Similarly, a major ESRC research project 'Conflict in Cities' (CinC), concluded that social and political divisions can be 'exacerbated' by a range of long term physical barriers:
'walls, buffer zones, checkpoints, urban enclaves, and even large roads, tramways and motorways – continue to play a major role in dividing cities … Mobility, or lack of it, is often used as a tool of conflict. Interventions in the physical environment can overtly further the interests of certain groups, whilst seemingly well-intentioned and apparently benign encroachments on the landscape can create or sustain inequalities in ways that are hard to reverse'. http://www.urbanconflicts.arct.cam.ac.uk/downloads/briefing-paper-2

A fresh way of looking at planning and regeneration in the city is to acknowledge that all planning, regeneration and design has a social purpose. However, for the most part, this is not made explicit or, at least, it is not openly discussed. It is important, therefore, to acknowledge firstly, the now widely held view that cities are shaped and re-shaped by social forces. Any understanding of socio-economic change and of the needs of social groups has to be factored into the analysis. This includes not only the power of capital, in all its forms, but also the distinctive political and administrative forces that mediate this in a place like Belfast.

Secondly, some of these distinctive political forces are in contest with each other, but also interestingly, are together, in conflict with the state. In relation to the former, the issue of housing land and territory remains a 'wicked issue'; in relation to the latter, the two communities have been co-operating with the Forum for Alternative Belfast on common built environment and connectivity issues (through the Belfast Conflict Resolution Consortium http://www.charterni.com/projects/belfast-conflict-resolution-consortium).

Thirdly, there is the ongoing issue of fragmented governance. Although the Northern Ireland Assembly is now relatively stable, its responsibilities for the built environment are spread across at least three government departments, each of which is headed-up by opposing political parties. Some hope lies in the shift of planning and regeneration responsibilities to the new eleven local authorities. Although there are no immediate plans to devolve transport or housing powers from central government, nevertheless, good spatial planning practice together with the new 'community planning' function, can allow many of the challenges raised above to be addressed.

These challenges are, of course, interwoven and they permeate almost all the major built environment issues facing the city. Moreover, the damage already done to Belfast's central area and the inner city by roads infrastructure and market led planning is substantial and is not easily repaired. However, this together with the other infrastructure barriers that have effectively cemented divisions need to be given as much political priority as the so-called 'peacewalls'. All of this requires a degree of small 'p' political pragmatism. Uniting conflicting communities around common interests such as disconnection from the city centre allows trust to build that may in time foster a more productive dialogue about the 'wicked issues'. Similarly, working with Ministers, councillors and officials in central and local government on individual schemes, such as the York Street Interchange and the 'Six Links' proposal, demonstrates the value of taking a more holistic and integrated approach to the development of the city. Jan Gehl makes the significant point that it took forty years, using what he calls a 'gradual approach', to get Copenhagen from a car-dominated to a people-oriented city (Gehl, J. 2008).

Conclusion

A new agenda for Planning in Belfast is emerging. It is an agenda that needs to be opened up for greater civic understanding and debate, and this task is the first thing that needs to be deliberately undertaken, supported by an investment in civic literacy and capacity. A new approach to planning involves not simply a new system in a new context, but also a shared vision for the sort of city that is properly shared. The idea of a 'shared' city has so many meanings to different people, in various contexts, that these multiple meanings must be framed in one common code that is recognisable, and achievable, not only within the Planning framework but also within a collaborative form of city governance. The market has been the dominant instrument for change in Belfast in the recent past, with some commentators complimenting its nonpartisan capacity to shape a more cosmopolitan outlook for the city. However, the new apartment building around the city, seen by some as creating shared spaces in terms of the sectarian geography, is at the same time creating a new social geography. Yet, would the city trade off more social segregation for less sectarian segregation? Would it avoid social housing in its new non-sectarian spaces and city centre regeneration, since such housing is deemed by some to have an association with high levels of segregation? How would such an agenda square with declared planning values about creating balanced, socially mixed, sustainable communities?

In terms of urban structure, there is an urgent need to recognise, and then deal with, the fragmented and disconnected city. Re-stitching the city is not just about creating a more coherent urban form, but rather it is about putting in place an urban layout that facilitates equal access to all parts of the city for all citizens irrespective of their social or ethno-religious standing. It is also about creating a city that values its civic spaces over its ethnic spaces and that this celebrates the vision of a new Belfast that is a city of equals.

References

Atkinson, J. and Flint, J. (2004) Fortress UK? Gated communities, the spatial revolt of the elites and time–space trajectories of segregation, *Housing Studies*, 19(6), pp. 875–892.

Building Design Partnership in association with Derek Lovejoy and Associates, and R. Travers Morgan (1968) *City of Belfast; Planning Aspects of the Belfast Urban Motorway*. Belfast: BDP.

Brand, R. (2009) Written and Unwritten Building Conventions in a Contested City: The Case of Belfast, *Urban Studies*, 46(12), pp. 2669–2689.

Gaffikin, F., Sterrett, K., McEldowney, M., Morrissey, M. and Hardy, M. (2008) *Planning Shared Space for a Shared Future*. Belfast: The Community Relations Council Northern Ireland.

Gehl, J. (2008) *Life Between Buildings: Using Public Space*. Copenhagen: The Danish Architectural Press.

Jacobs, J. (1993) *The Death and Life of Great American Cities*. New York: Modern Library.

Chapter 6

The Belfast waterfront: prospects for the 21st century

Jenny Muir, John Brontë and Philip Boland

Introduction

The city of Belfast has always had a special relationship with its waterfront. Indeed, the development of the Belfast waterfront has a rich history which may be traced back almost as far as the origins of the city itself. The waterfront has increased in importance over the past 25 years, as Belfast has sought to develop an inclusive, post-troubles urban environment. This reflects an international phenomenon. Where waterfronts were once viewed as belonging to a bygone era, they have re-emerged on a similar scale of importance to that they shared during their heyday as powerhouses of industrial and economic might.

Yet there is debate surrounding who benefits from these changes. This chapter seeks to unpack and inform such debate, with the aim of generating prospects and possibilities for the Belfast waterfront in the 21st century. Using material from recent research (Brontë, 2012; Muir *et al,* 2014), we examine the importance of waterfront development for the modern competitive city within neoliberal urbanism, followed by reflections on how the 'competitive waterfront' impacts upon public benefit and the public interest. We then consider the particular example of Belfast's Laganside and Titanic Quarter developments, and ask whether the economic downturn is creating an environment in which greater public benefit can be obtained despite the continuing focus on added value and competitiveness. All of this is of abiding interest to academics working in the fields of planning and urban design, notably Malachy McEldowney.

Neoliberal urbanism, the competitive city and the 'competitive waterfront'

The urban waterfront is defined as 'the water's edge in cities and towns of all sizes' (Breen and Rigby, 1994: 10). Yet through time, the purpose and characteristics of waterfronts have evolved in response to changing economic, technological and social conditions. Hoyle (1988; 2000) developed a six phase typology of waterfront development to assess historical changes in the relationship between a city and its waterfront, using port function as the key determinant. Until the nineteenth century, cities grew up around the port and the trade link was important for prosperity. Rapid growth from the nineteenth to the early twentieth century then caused ports to develop beyond the city. However the continued growth of industrial functions and the need for more space (for example, for container ships and larger ferries) led to a greater separation of the port from the city during the mid-twentieth century. This trend continued in the period from the 1960s into the 1980s, labelled by Hoyle as 'the retreat from the waterfront', in which both port and industrial use developed in more peripheral areas. The gradual move outwards left derelict sites closer to the city: sites which, from the 1970s onwards, were the target of urban renewal, a process that became more widespread from the 1980s onwards and led to a greater re-integration between these older port areas and the rest of the city.

Hoyle's typology has been examined and extended in our recent research (Muir *et al*, 2014), in which we propose a new phase of waterfront development, the 'competitive waterfront'. Here, waterfront *functions* are converging with those of the rest of the city under the common ideological banner of neoliberal urbanism and city competitiveness. However, the *type* of development remains somewhat different in waterfront areas due to greater land availability, and spatial separation remains an issue, with poor connectivity hampering the ability of some waterfronts to realise their full potential. Our model of the 'competitive waterfront' is divided into four parts: the ideological context, governance, land use and connectivity. They are described briefly below.

Oakley (2011: 234) argues that, increasingly, 'waterfront renewal is being driven by a neoliberal competitive city paradigm'. Neoliberalism is a globally dominant approach to political economy which promotes the superiority of market mechanisms through governance, political strategy, and ideological discourse (Peck and Tickell, 2002; Harvey, 2005). The ideology was not weakened by the 2008 financial crisis (Meyer and Künkel, 2012). Within this framework, entrepreneurial governance 'has led national, regional and local policy-makers to focus upon competitiveness as a key economic tool' (Boland 2007:1021; see also Turok, 2004; Bristow, 2005). Cities compete to attract private sector investment through offering financial inducements and by marketing the attractiveness of the urban environment. Thus the city becomes a 'brand', promoted through activities such as advertising campaigns, flagship projects and the staging of prestigious cultural and sporting events (Boland, 2013). The redevelopment of decaying docklands and waterfront zones represents one of the most widespread and significant opportunities for commodified urban renewal (Bruttomesso, 2001; Rubin, 2011). Consequently, cities have increasingly seen their waterfronts as potentially transformative spaces (Sandercock and Dovey, 2002), as the convergence of cultural, tourist, retail and residential functions testifies to a city's vitality and attainment of world-class status (Kokot, 2008; Chang and Huang, 2011).

The need to compete for mobile capital and labour has changed the nature of urban governance, from being providers and guarantors of welfare provision and supporting infrastructure to being enablers, intermediaries and change agents in pursuit of economic advantage (Harvey, 1989). These processes involve 'network governance' - a mix of state, civil society and market actors - and include public-private partnerships, flagship projects, aggressive marketing and consumption orientated development (Brontë, 2012; Boland, 2014). Although networked governance is often presented as creating opportunities for community involvement, outcomes usually reflect the interests of the most powerful actors (Davies, 2011) and the depoliticisation of decision-making (Haughton *et al*, 2013). The governance of waterfronts has long been associated with arms-length agencies and public-private partnerships, such as the UK's Urban Development Corporations of the 1980s (Imrie and Thomas, 1999) and similar approaches in other countries (e.g. Galland and Hansen, 2012; Moore, 2008; Heeg, 2011). Large amounts of public subsidy are a feature of waterfront developments, and the role and activity of local communities in the governance of waterfront regeneration is generally marginal (Lehrer and Laidley, 2008; Scharenberg and Bader, 2009).

The third and fourth aspects of the competitive waterfront are land use and connectivity. The availability of large sites, historic buildings and water frontage sets the scene for long-term mixed use projects (e.g. Carmona, 2009; Shaw, 2013). It is a paradox of waterfront redevelopment that cities market themselves as unique whilst following a common model of development including high value apartments, technological industries, signature buildings and commodified leisure spaces (Ward, 2011). Large sites lead to the development of 'flagship' projects, regarded as vital to city marketing (Doucet *et al*, 2011). There is an emphasis on investment return, leading to, for example, luxury apartments rather than social housing (Cowen and Bunce, 2006). However, public walkways, art, free events and access to leisure facilities are available in order to create a high quality built environment. These elements are often publicly funded, although access may be constrained by admission charges and gating of some areas.

Finally, connectivity is the Achilles Heel of waterfronts. Visits to waterfront sites often show that there is poor quality linkage with the rest of the city, especially in the early years of a development. Other aspects of connectivity include: functions under mixed use redevelopment; marketing when waterfronts are included in a city branding plan; technology, such as high speed broadband; and a final category of connectivity related to public perception. If the city's population regards the area as a distant destination, the waterfront may become a globalised enclave populated by tourists and transient workers, and its integration into the rest of the city will ultimately fail. The 'competitive waterfront' model may include different aspects of the characteristics we have described, but all point towards a framing of the waterfront as a city district rather than as a place apart. It now remains to ask: who benefits from the competitive waterfront?

While the competitive waterfront emerges as a key urban asset and strategic showcase for the 21st century city, it remains to be seen whether its regeneration is really for the good of all its inhabitants. It is important to ask: whose interests are shaping waterfront redevelopment? As McGovern (2008: 285) argues, 'the key question is not whether to develop urban waterfronts, but how they should be developed. For what purpose? For whose benefit?'

Increasingly, urban waterfront projects market a particular concept of place identity through their physical layout and landscaping, the diversity of design and density of residential complexes, and the way public space is supplemented with retail, restaurants, designer bars, retail and leisure facilities, and creative industries such as film production. It has been argued that this has led to intensified forms of privatisation and exclusion, with the waterfront becoming a colonised space of privileged 'up market' consumption (Oakley, 2011). Similarly, Cowen and Bunce (2006) suggest that redevelopment through the creation of high-income residential communities serves as a way to 'recolonise' and 'secure' waterfront spaces, and that public subsidy is often facilitating the extension of primarily elite spaces.

Deregulated planning policy assists with this 'reterritorialisation' of urban waterfronts (Bunce and Desfor, 2007: 255). Planning policy is meant to act in the public interest, and in the UK this is enshrined in statute and policy guidance. Yet planning is contained within and constrained by urban governance based on entrepreneurialism, with profound implications for the spatial planning agenda (Sandercock and Dovey, 2002). Indeed, the concept of public benefit may be changing. Oakley notes how market-oriented waterfront governance is causing 'a shift away from collective benefits to a more individual form of public benefit' (Oakley 2011: 222). This leaves the way open to argue that, for example, the construction of expensive apartment blocks on previously derelict grounds is a public benefit because purchasers experience the benefits of a new home as well as the general improvement to the environment. It also dilutes the focus of public benefit away from those in most need of it. Without very specific structural and ideological commitment, the concept of collective public benefit disappears from waterfront development. This has been experienced, for example, in Toronto (Lehrer and Laidley, 2008) and Portland, Oregon (Hagerman, 2007).

The literature leads us to believe that the wider public, especially those without economic power, may benefit least from 21st century waterfront development, and that private sector interests will be facilitated as a priority in order to maximise financial gain. Community interests may well be manipulated although small gains may also be made. However, these model conclusions need to be assessed in any individual case. Four questions have been generated for that purpose:

1. ***Conceptualisation:*** What is the understanding of 'public benefit'?
2. ***Type:*** How does the public benefit?
3. ***Role:*** Who is responsible for the delivery of public benefit?
4. ***Distribution:*** Which groups benefit most and least?

Armed with these questions, we now turn our attention to Belfast's own waterfront. The discussion draws on evidence obtained from a series of semi-structured interviews with key informants within this development arena.

The Belfast waterfront

Belfast's waterfront was important to the city from the mid-17th century onwards, although the River Lagan was unsuitable for the docking of large ships until the 1840s, due to sand banks. Goods and people had to disembark into smaller vessels in the Pool of Garmoyle further down the Lough (Sweetnam, 1988; see also an interesting fictional representation in Patterson, 2013). The Corporation for Preserving and Improving the Port of Belfast (the 'Ballast Board') was founded in 1785 and its powers expanded in 1847 when it became the Belfast Harbour Commissioners, which still owns the harbour lands today. These bodies oversaw the dredging and straightening of the river to construct the Victoria Channel, opened in 1849, and constructed new shipyards and dry docks (McCreary, 2011). The first shipyard opened in 1791 but the 'golden age' of shipbuilding lasted from 1880 – 1914 (Lynch, 2001) which included the construction of the Titanic, launched (and sunk) in 1912.

The waterfront suffered in the 1930s Depression and was bombed heavily in 1941. Investment during the 1960s and 1970s included new facilities for ferries, a new dry dock and the Samson and Goliath cranes, which are now protected structures. Harland & Wolff launched its last ship in 2003 and now operates on a reduced scale, repairing ships and oil rigs, and making wind turbines; the port functions and ferry terminal also remain (McCreary, 2011). The decline of shipbuilding and the closure of the Belfast Gasworks led to dereliction in areas closer to Belfast City Centre by the end of the 1980s, which is when the regeneration of Belfast's waterfront began in earnest.

Laganside

Belfast's Laganside Urban Development Corporation (UDC) operated from 1989 – 2007 and was a far-sighted initiative which began in the unprepossessing investment environment of the Northern Ireland 'troubles' and a property market recession. Laganside's original 140-hectare programme was largely concerned with improving infrastructure, attracting private investment and building apartments for the private market (Fitzsimons, 1995). Laganside received large amounts of public funding: by 1998, £55m from regional government, £29m from the European Regional Development Fund (ERDF), £40m for Belfast's Millennium Project (the Odyssey Arena) and additional sums from Lottery and EU PEACE funds (OECD, 2000):

> "We had access to European funding and we took the decision to maximise and secure as much funding as we could….. so the significance of this infrastructure led strategy was that people saw tangible changes happening along the river." (interview 4, private sector)

Projects supported included the Hilton Hotel, the Waterfront Hall, Custom House Square and the Odyssey. Private investment was sluggish initially, but picked up after the 1994 paramilitary ceasefires and the 1998 Good Friday Agreement (Neill *et al*, 2014). By the end of 2007, an investment leverage ratio of 1:5 was predicted (Laganside Corporation, 2007). The original redevelopment area was expanded to include the old Gasworks site and, in 1997, the Cathedral Quarter (McManus and Carruthers, 2014). The Laganside area has been managed by the Department for Social Development since 2007.

Laganside's aim was to regenerate the area 'to the stage where private sector development and investment will continue without major public intervention' (Laganside Corporation, 2007: 2). As such, initially it had little to offer nearby disadvantaged communities (Neill, 1995), although in later years a Community Strategy was produced, and the Gasworks Trust and the Belfast Gasworks Employment Matching Service (GEMS) were supported (Hemphill *et al*, 2006). However, community benefit remained a small part of the organisation's remit and some regarded Laganside's ability to relate to issues of equality and social need as 'far from clear' (Sterrett *et al*, 2005: 382).

Titanic Quarter

The 75-hectare Titanic Quarter (TQ) development continued the regeneration of Belfast's waterfront from 2001. Following the 1998 Good Friday Agreement the development was part of promoting a renewed sense of optimism for the city, depicted through the advertising slogan 'A Renaissance for Belfast' (Bairner 2006):

> The relaunch of the Titanic brand… nests within a broader representational logic of urban intervention wrapped as it is inside an urban renaissance agenda and the linked and shared project of building the 'post-conflict' city. (Neill, 2011: p.73)

The private sector led, mixed-use development was heralded as a neutral and shared space capable of promoting Belfast globally, while fostering a new era for a city scarred with a history of division, segregation and ethno-sectarian enmity. TQ has been at the forefront of official efforts to 'normalise' the city through attracting inward investment and cultural regeneration, thus encouraging cosmopolitan notions of inclusive civic identity and a new confident, neutral urban culture:

> "...we have said it is something new and positive and forward looking and open for business and that is the message that we are putting out more particularly to the world out there that we hope will invest in it." (interview 2, private sector)

In 2005 the TQ site lease was transferred from Olsen Shipping, owners of Harland & Wolff, to Harcourt Developments and the site is now managed by its subsidiary Titanic Quarter Ltd. The freehold is owned by the Belfast Harbour Commissioners, who continue their historic role of promoting harbour development. Phase One of the development, built between 2007 and 2011, included 475 apartments, offices, a further education college, an hotel and a new site for the Public Records Office of Northern Ireland (Turley Associates, 2005). In addition, a Science Park had opened in 2002 to provide office space for small high tech businesses on 10 further hectares outwith TQ, adjacent to the Thompson Graving Dock and Pump House which have

Photograph 6.1 Titanic Belfast funding partners

become major tourist attractions. TQ's Phase One was completed during the post-2008 global economic downturn, which had a severe impact on cash flow and hence the speed of development (Muir, 2013). Phase Two as planned, which included more apartments and other mixed uses, has largely failed to materialise, the exception being the very successful 'Titanic Belfast' museum which opened in April 2012. Instead, a more ad hoc approach has been adopted.

A considerable amount of public funding has been made available (Photograph 6.1), most notably almost £60m for Titanic Belfast (Ramsey, 2013). £2.7m was provided from regional government for the Thompson Graving Dock and Pump House and £2.3m from the EU PEACE III programme towards refurbishment of the 'Nomadic' ferry. In 2013, £5m was awarded from the Heritage Lottery Fund to assist with the conversion of the Harland & Wolff Headquarters into a hotel, with public access to the historic Drawing Office and Board Room (and original staircase, Photograph 6.2).

Figure 6.2 The staircase in the derelict Harland & Wolff Headquarters

Other examples of non-market usage in TQ include the construction of two public sector facilities, a campus for Belfast Metropolitan College and the Public Record Office of Northern Ireland, and the social economy business T13 Urban Sports Academy, which opened in 2011. The Titanic Slipway, adjacent to Titanic Belfast, has become a popular site for large-scale public entertainment such as concerts, firework displays and sports events, much of which is subsidised by the public sector. However, one unplanned private sector initiative has been a great success: the transformation of the old Paint Hall (where ship panels were painted) into Titanic Studios for film and television production:

> "... we stored fertiliser in it for a while and that got some level of return and then the rates people came down and said that's a massive building we are going to charge you serious rates... So were we going to tumble this building or keep it open for some unspecified use? And then the next thing we knew Tom Hanks' production company were knocking the door... and this is where the serendipity comes in, it was something that nobody had planned or foreseen and suddenly they were over and on the back of that we've had Universal Studios, Game of Thrones and all the rest." (interview 4, private sector)

In 2014 planning permission was granted for an extension to the studios, along with new office space next to the College, an indication that prospects for private investment may be improving:

> "... the lack of liquidity has a big impact in terms of the next phase of growth but has it undermined what we plan to do – no. It does mean that we have to readjust and think through... so yes big problem but are we seeing the beginning of the recession disappearing – undeniably." (interview 2, private sector)

Does Belfast have a 'competitive waterfront?

We have summarised the main characteristic of the 'competitive waterfront' as the convergence of waterfront *functions* with the rest of the city although the type of development remains different (Muir *et al*, 2014). Looking at the model in greater detail, we can conclude that Belfast's waterfront largely fits the model, although with some caveats. First, it is clear from our research and from the literature (Neill, 2011; Brontë, 2012, Coyles, 2013; Ramsey, 2013; Muir, 2013; Neill *et al*, 2014) that both Laganside and TQ have followed the principles of neoliberal urbanism and city competitiveness:

> "...it certainly has allowed us to present Belfast as a modern, growing city which has got significant potential for the future..... you've got Game of

> Thrones one of the biggest blockbusting shows in the USA being filmed there; you've got Titanic signature building world class, really iconic building with real brand value..." (interview 1, public sector)

The wider context for this is the rise of the 'twin-speed city' (Murtagh, 2011) in which differences of class and wealth are layered onto previous sectarian differences and where city competitiveness sits alongside state management of disadvantaged areas (see Boland, 2014 and Muir, 2014 for respective examples). The governance of TQ and Laganside provides a clear example of network governance including the private sector (Harcourt), arms-length agencies (Harbour Commissioners), the charitable sector (Titanic Foundation, which manages Titanic Belfast) and central and local government departments (Ramsey, 2013). Community involvement in governance has been minimal. Public subsidy has been crucial to the development. Finally, the often identified problem with connectivity does apply to TQ (less so to Laganside) even though it is not far from the city centre (see also Coyle, 2013):

> "I think one of the big issues that really needs to be addressed if we're going to see TQ and those areas being seen as an integral part of the city is having proper high quality rapid transit access into those areas because the transport connections are really poor." (interview 1, public sector)

We also found that public perception of distance from the city centre remains a problem; however, the area has proved very popular with tourists and a planned rapid transit system should improve access. Therefore we conclude that the Belfast waterfront shows many of the features of the 'competitive waterfront'. We now turn to our assessment of who benefits.

Who benefits from the Belfast waterfront?

We now return to our four questions and relate them to the Belfast waterfront:

1. Conceptualisation: What is the understanding of 'public benefit'?
2. Type: How do the public benefit?
3. Role: Who is responsible for the delivery of public benefit?
4. Distribution: Which groups benefit most and least?

Conceptualising public benefit

It is important to note that the primary purpose of waterfront developments is not to provide the kind of targeted social and economic benefits found in other types of area-based regeneration such as the refurbishment of social housing estates. Despite the large amount of public subsidy received by waterfronts (and other property-based regeneration), it is very clear that their primary purpose is to attract investment. This has been noted previously in relation to

Laganside, and TQ's vision is to achieve 'a high profile European waterfront development firmly rooted in the history and character of Belfast, acting as a driver for high quality investment and development in the city' (Turley Associates, 2005: 1).

Therefore, it is not surprising that the idea of 'public benefit' was treated somewhat ambiguously in interviews, and used interchangeably with other terms such as 'public interest', 'public good' and 'community gain'. Part of the reason for this confusion may also have been because there has been no overall evaluation of the benefits of Belfast's waterfront since the winding up of Laganside UDC. Although there was a general consensus that waterfront redevelopment does indeed contribute to a public benefit, often this was thought of as a quite superficial gain such as leisure activity or the quality of the surrounding environment. A common response was that the regeneration was better than the derelict land which it replaced:

> "75 hectares of former industrial land, close to the city centre obviously perfect for redevelopment and very good for the city of Belfast, there's no doubt about that." (interview 5, private sector)

> "Out of a wasteland it is creating something attractive, something people can enjoy." (interview 3, private sector)

Converting a large brownfield site from an urban liability to an urban asset was therefore seen to represent a general public benefit in itself, which was intertwined with the benefit of increasing global competitiveness and which was supported on the basis that it was for the overall good of the city. It follows, then, that for one participant, "I would see the benefits more in terms of investment and the trickle down from that" (interview 7, private sector). As Ramsey (2013: p.176) observes: 'TQ is cast as a prime example of how private economic development, with the support of private finance, can supposedly benefit the whole of the economy and, by extension, the people of NI'.

Types of public benefit

Here we consider four different types of potential public benefit: employment, housing, leisure and public realm, and tourism. In each case we found reliable statistics hard to come by. First, the creation of new employment opportunities has been a crucial element of both Laganside and TQ. Being an industrial city, de-industrialisation and decline in port activity hit Belfast hard. Generating investment and subsequent employment was the major driving force behind Laganside:

> "... our focus in those days [Laganside, early 1990s] was primarily on the physical and economic regeneration ...what we wanted to do was show that

> we could generate employment and by the trickledown effect that was a real way of transforming an area.... It's not that we ignored community but our main focus in those days was the physical and economic transformation of the waterfront and we were unashamedly focused on that because without that working everything else was just hot air." (interview 4, private sector)

Laganside estimated that some 14,700 jobs were created by the UDC (Laganside Corporation, 2007). Titanic Quarter's web site suggests that over 4,000 jobs have also been created in Titanic Quarter to date (Titanic Quarter, 2014a), of which around 300 are at the Titanic Belfast signature project (Titanic Foundation, 2014). However, it is unclear whether local people have been able to access employment to any significant extent given the focus on attracting the educated, professional and creative classes. This is especially important given that the waterfront borders some of the most deprived wards of the city (Ramsey, 2013). The Memorandum of Understanding, signed between TQ and Belfast City Council with the aim of delivering benefits to local communities from Titanic Belfast, was criticised for its lack of action in regard to local employment (Brontë 2012) and did not deliver the intended outputs (Muir, 2013).

The housing gains have proved even more elusive. The traditional model of regeneration includes high value private sector apartments which provide an important source of cash flow within mixed use schemes. Due to the lack of 'planning gain' legislation in Northern Ireland there was no social housing in Laganside although over 700 housing units were built (Laganside Corporation, 2007); neither were there social or affordable housing units in TQ's Phase 1. Phase 2 will include 15% social or affordable housing as a condition of Belfast City Council's Memorandum of Understanding, but given the state of the market there are currently no plans to continue with residential development on the site. It is therefore a good time to examine the place of housing provision within Belfast's waterfront, both in terms of tenure and household type - a subject in which the public and private sectors, as well as civil society, have an interest.

Thirdly, the provision of high quality public realm and space for leisure and entertainment were commonly identified as a public benefit, with walkways, squares and public art helping to counter the investment-driven focus of the waterfront:

> "...look out around here and look at it ten years ago and surely it is a better place for people to enjoy." (interview 3, private sector)

It is apparent that the public realm is also being used to foster a new, neutral urban culture, albeit one that sidesteps the area's sectarian history as well as the city's remaining present-day tensions (Neill, 2011; Coyles, 2013). Various public events held at TQ make the waterfront a central space in Belfast's aspiration to become an inclusive, post-conflict city:

> "There's no point hiding from it, I suppose Titanic Quarter is seen as a relatively 'neither one side or the other' sort of location.... All of the events, concerts down there push it as a neutral location." (interview 7, private sector)

Wide accessibility to the benefits of an improved public realm and leisure space is more questionable. Not all events are free, and car parking can be expensive. Public transport links remain poor at the present time. While it was envisaged that this will improve with the introduction of rapid transit, there is concern regarding spatial disconnection and potential for inter-city competition between TQ and the city centre in relation to leisure activities for Belfast residents.

Tourism has become a major focus on Belfast's waterfront, in large part due to the Titanic Belfast signature building and exhibition which opened in 2012, on the centenary of the ship's sinking. Titanic Belfast was supported by the state due to its status as a global attraction capable of being a standard bearer for the post-conflict city:

> "... the strategy at that stage was looking at where we had a competitive advantage over other destinations and they felt that industrial, maritime heritage gave us that competitive edge over other cities." (interview 3, voluntary sector)

Belfast's maritime history has, therefore, developed into a powerful mechanism through which to promote and market Belfast's transformation. Yet there is a view that it has been used selectively, disregarding the shipyard's unsavoury past in terms of discrimination, the sectarian labour market and poor working conditions (Neill, 2011). Similarly it has been found that people from West Belfast have minimal connection to the redevelopment and do not see themselves benefitting from it (Brontë, 2012).

Titanic Belfast is the largest maritime attraction on the Belfast waterfront, but others include the Nomadic tugboat, the Thompson Graving Dock and the Pump House, to be joined in future by public access to the Harland & Wolff Drawing Office. Of course all these attractions are also open to Belfast residents. However, there are admission charges and a day out in TQ can become expensive, thus limiting repeat visits. But there is no argument that Titanic Belfast has been extremely successful, with more than 700,000 visitors in its first year, from 128 different countries (Titanic Foundation, 2014).

Delivery and distribution of public benefit

As has been noted earlier, waterfront regeneration is delivered by partnerships rooted in network governance: private agencies lead on delivery and private finance, public agencies provide subsidy, and the third/ community sector, although often marginalised, is able to lobby for gains. In Belfast's waterfront, public benefit has been delivered primarily by non-market agencies. Third sector projects include the GEMs project in Laganside (which is still in operation), the T13 Urban Sports Academy, and Titanic Belfast itself, which is run by the Titanic Foundation, a charitable trust. In future, it will be pressure from Belfast City Council, along with planning policy, which will deliver social housing in TQ. Public sector-led projects include the Belfast Metropolitan College and the Public Record Office of Northern Ireland, both of which are replacement sites rather than new provision, paid for through Public Private Partnerships. The facility with the most potential to deliver sustained public benefit is the College, currently with 5,000 full-time and around 10,000 part-time students (Titanic Quarter, 2014b). Its arrival has also led to improved bus services and the opening of a local convenience store. The primacy of public subsidy for the delivery of public benefit leads to concerns for the future:

> "I think the big challenge in terms of the next phase of the regeneration is that the dependency on public sector funding will become more difficult in the next period of time." (interview 2, private sector)

Our final assessment concerns the distribution of public benefit, and returns to the earlier point about the purpose of property-based regeneration such as waterfront development. *These developments were never intended to benefit the less well off or people living in the immediate locality.* Both the public and private sector driven phases of Belfast's waterfront redevelopment have been driven by the determinant of generating investment for the city. This is why we have introduced the concept of the 'competitive waterfront'. As cities across the world compete for investment and global circuits of capital, their waterfronts have increasingly become spaces upon which to sell and market the city. Defining and analysing 'public' benefit along the waterfront has, as a result, proved challenging. However, there are signs that things may be changing in Belfast:

> "I think in terms of Titanic Quarter specifically, the signature building has altered the whole plan. Certainly when I looked at the masterplan originally it was very commercially led... It is still economically based but more wide in its scope in that it's aimed at tourism and the general benefits to Belfast rather than Titanic Quarter. A lack of demand for commercial use has promoted this switch

> in emphasis and certainly residential use as well...Really it was a response to changing economic circumstances." (interview 7, private sector)

This change is not as a result of a deliberate decision on the behalf of the developer; rather, it has been forced upon them by the economic downturn, perhaps creating a better governance environment:

> "... part of me thinks that it [the downturn] has not all been a bad thing. And I am sure the commercial sector will see things differently but for us...the more gradual growth in this site has brought more people on board and it has become a bit more acceptable...It's just that bit more sustainable, you have to think a bit more about what you are doing." (interview 3, voluntary sector)

Conclusion

There is now an opportunity to refocus Belfast's waterfront development in order to maximise its benefit for the city and its people. Lessons learned from Belfast and elsewhere can be used to define more carefully who are the intended beneficiaries from waterfront development and what kind of benefits are intended, within a funding package that includes both public and private elements with commensurate obligations and transparent reporting of progress. Governance structures should include both geographical communities and communities of interest to a greater extent, and the third sector should be involved in regular assessments of the development's performance and benefits. Finally, we have been very surprised by the small amount of attention paid to ecological matters in the literature and in our case study: surely, this is key to the survival of all waterfront developments. All in all, one day we hope to see the 'competitive waterfront' replaced by the 'sustainable waterfront'.

Acknowledgements

We acknowledge with thanks research assistance from Dr Martina McKnight. The project was funded by the Royal Institution of Chartered Surveyors Research Trust and the Institute of Spatial and Environmental Planning at Queen's University Belfast.

References

Bairner, A. (2006) Titanic Town: Sport, Space and the Re-imag(in)ing of Belfast, *City & Society,* 18(2), pp.159-179.

Boland, P. (2007) Unpacking the Theory-Policy Interface of Local Economic Development: An Analysis of Cardiff and Liverpool, *Urban Studies*, 44 (5-6), pp.1019-1039.

Boland, P. (2013) Sexing up the city in the international beauty contest: the performative nature of spatial planning and the factive spectacle of place branding, *Town Planning Review,* 84(2), pp.251-274.

Boland, P. (2014) Neoliberal Competitiveness and Spatial Planning: 'The Path to Economic Nirvana' or a 'Post-Political Strategy' and 'Dangerous Obsession'?, *Environment and Planning A,* 46, pp.770-787.

Breen, A. and Rigby, D. (1994) *Waterfronts: Cities Reclaim Their Edge*. New York: McGraw-Hill.

Bristow, G. (2005) Everyone's a winner: Problematising the discourse of regional competitiveness, *Journal of Economic Geography,* 5(3), pp.285-304.

Brontë, J. (2012) *Rebranding Belfast through the Titanic Quarter: Unpacking the rhetoric with reality*. Unpublished MSc dissertation, Queen's University Belfast.

Bruttomesso, R. (2001) Complexity on the urban waterfront, in Marshall, R. (ed.) *Waterfronts in post-industrial cities*. London: Spon, pp.39-49.

Bunce, S. and Desfor, G. (2007) Introduction to political ecologies of urban waterfront transformations, *Cities,* 24(2), pp.251-258.

Carmona, M. (2009) The Isle of Dogs: Four development waves, five planning models, thirty-five years, and a renaissance... of sorts, *Progress in Planning,* 71, pp.87-151.

Chang, T.C. and Huang, S. (2011) Reclaiming the City: Waterfront Development in Singapore, *Urban Studies,* 48(10), pp.2085-2100.

Cowen, D. and Bunce, S. (2006) Competitive cities and secure nations: Conflict and Convergence in Urban Waterfront Agendas after 9/11, *International Journal of Urban and Regional Research,* 30 (2), pp.427-439.

Coyles, D. (2013) Reflections on Titanic Quarter: the cultural and material legacy of an historic Belfast brand, *The Journal of Architecture,* 18(3), pp.331-363.

Davies, J. (2011) *Challenging Governance Theory: from networks to hegemony*. Bristol: The Policy Press.

Doucet, B., van Kempen, R. and van Weesep, J. (2011) Resident perceptions of flagship waterfront regeneration: The case of the Kop van Zuid in Rotterdam, *Tijdschrift voor Economische en Sociale Geografie,* 101 (2), pp.125-145.

Fitzsimons, D.S. (1995) Spearheading a new place vision: the Laganside Corporation, in Neill, W.J.V., Fitzsimons, D.S. and Murtagh, B. (eds.), *Reimaging the Pariah City: urban development in Belfast and Detroit*. Aldershot: Avebury, pp.77-112.

Galland, D. and Hansen, C.J. (2012) The Roles of Planning in Waterfront Redevelopment: From Plan-led and Market-driven Styles to Hybrid Planning?, *Planning Practice and Research,* 27 (2), pp.203-225.

Hagerman, C. (2007) Shaping neighbourhoods and nature: Urban political ecologies of urban waterfront transformations in Portland, Oregon, *Cities,* 24 (4), pp.285-297.

Harvey, D. (1989) From Managerialism to Entrepreneurialism: The Transformation in Urban Governance in Late Capitalism, *Geografiska Annaler B,* 71(1), pp.3-17.

Harvey, D. (2005) *A Brief History of Neoliberalism*. Oxford: Oxford University Press.

Haughton, G., Allmendinger, P. and Oosterlynck, S. (2013) Spaces of Neoliberal Experimentation: Soft Spaces, Post-politics and Neoliberal Governmentality, *Environment and Planning A*, 45(1), pp.217-234.

Heeg, S. (2011) Flows of Capital and Fixity of Bricks in the Built Environment of Boston, in Desfor, G., Laidley, J. and Schubert, D. (eds.) *Transforming Urban Waterfronts: Fixity and Flow.* London: Routledge, pp.274-294.

Hemphill, L., McGreal, S., Berry, J. and Watson, S. (2006) Leadership, Power and Multisector Urban Regeneration Partnerships, *Urban Studies*, 43 (1), pp. 59-80.

Hoyle, B. (1988) Development dynamics at the port-city interface, in Hoyle, B.S., Pinder, D.A. and Husain, M.S. (eds.) *Revitalising the Waterfront: International Dimensions of Dockland Development.* London: Belhaven Press, pp.3-19.

Hoyle, B. (2000) Global and Local Change on the Port – City Waterfront, *Geographical Review,* 90(3), pp. 395-417.

Imrie, R. and Thomas, H. (1999) (eds.) *British Urban Policy: An Evaluation of the Urban Development Corporations.* London: Sage.

Kokot, W. (2008) Port Cities as Areas of Transition – Comparative Ethnographic Research, in Kokot, W., Gandelsman-Trier, M., Wildner, K. and Wonneberger, A. (eds.) *Port Cities as Areas of Transition: Ethnographic Perspectives* Bielefeld: Transcript Verlag, pp.7-23.

Laganside Corporation (2007) *Regeneration Statement.* Belfast: Laganside Corporation.

Lehrer, U. and Laidley, J. (2008) Old Mega-Projects Newly Packaged? Waterfront Redevelopment in Toronto, *International Journal of Urban and Regional Research,* 32(4), pp.786-803.

Lynch, J.P. (2001) *An Unlikely Success Story: The Belfast Shipbuilding Industry 1880-1935*. Belfast: Belfast Historical Society and Ulster Historical Foundation.

McCreary, A. (2011) *Titanic Port: An illustrated history of Belfast Harbour*. Belfast: Belfast Harbour Commissioners.

McManus, C. and Carruthers, C. (2014) Cultural quarters and urban regeneration – the case of Cathedral Quarter Belfast, *International Journal of Cultural Policy,* 20(1), pp.78-98.

Magee, K. (2012) *Titanic Belfast: Will it rival Disneyland, Tate Modern and the Guggenheim?* BBC News, 29th March 2012. http://www.bbc.co.uk/news/uk-northern-ireland-17552802 Last accessed 10th October 2014.

Mayer, M. and Künkel, J. (2012) Introduction: Neoliberal Urbanism and its Contestations – Crossing Theoretical Boundaries, in Künkel, J. and Mayer, M. (eds.) *Neoliberal Urbanism and its Contestations: Crossing Theoretical Boundaries*. Basingstoke: Palgrave Macmillan, pp.3-26.

Moore, N. (2008) *Dublin Docklands Reinvented: The post-industrial regeneration of a European city quarter*. Dublin: Four Courts Press.

Muir, J. (2013) Whose Urban Regeneration? Two Belfast case studies, in Leary, M.E. and McCarthy, J. (eds.) *Routledge Companion to Urban Regeneration*. London: Routledge, pp.475-485.

Muir, J. (2014) Neoliberalising a divided society? The regeneration of Crumlin Road Gaol and Girdwood Park, North Belfast, *Local Economy,* 29 (1-2), pp.52-64.

Muir, J., Boland, B., McKnight, M. and Brontë, J. (2014) *The New Waterfront: Who Benefits?* Unpublished research report, London: RICS Research Trust.

Murtagh, B. (2011) Desegregation and Place Restructuring in the New Belfast. *Urban Studies,* 48 (6), pp. 1119-1135.

Neill, William J.V. (1995) Lipstick on the gorilla? Conflict management, urban development and image making in Belfast, in Neill, William J.V., Fitzsimons, D.S. and Murtagh, B. (eds.) *Reimaging the Pariah City: urban development in Belfast and Detroit*. Aldershot: Avebury, pp.50-76.

Neill, W.J.V. (2011) The Debasing of Myth: The Privatization of Titanic Memory in Designing the 'Post-conflict' City, *Journal of Urban Design,* 16(1), pp. 67-86.

Neill, W.J.V., Murray, M. and Grist, B. (2014) Introduction: Titanic and the New Belfast, in Neill, W.J.V., Murray, M. and Grist, B. (eds.) *Relaunching Titanic: Memory and Marketing in the New Belfast*. London: Routledge, pp.3-13.

Oakley, S. (2011) Re-imagining City Waterfronts: A Comparative Analysis of Governing Renewal in Adelaide, Darwin and Melbourne, *Urban Policy and Research,* 29(3), pp.221-238.

OECD (2000) *Urban Renaissance: Belfast's Lessons for Policy and Partnership*. Paris: Organisation for Economic Co-operation and Development.

Patterson, G. (2013) *The Mill for Grinding Old People Young*. London: Faber and Faber.

Peck, J. and Tickell, A. (2002) Neoliberalizing Space, *Antipode,* 34(3), pp.380-404.

Ramsey, P. (2013) 'A Pleasingly Blank Canvas': Urban Regeneration in Northern Ireland and the Case of Titanic Quarter, *Space and Polity,* 17(2), pp.164-179.

Rubin, J. (2011) San Francisco's Waterfront in the Age of Neoliberal Urbanism, in Desfor, G., Laidley, J. and Schubert, D. (eds.) *Transforming Urban Waterfronts: Fixity and Flow.* London: Routledge, pp.143-163.

Sandercock, L. and Dovey, K. (2002) Pleasure, Politics, and the 'Public Interest': Melbourne's Riverscape Revitalization, *Journal of the American Planning Association,* 68(2), pp.151-164.

Scharenberg, A. and Bader, I. (2009) Berlin's waterfront site struggle, *City*, 13 (2-3), pp.326-335.

Shaw, K. (2013) Docklands Dreamings: Illusions of Sustainability in the Melbourne Docks Redevelopment, *Urban Studies,* 50(11), pp.2158-2177.

Sterrett, K., Murtagh, B. and Millar, G. (2005) The social turn and urban development corporations, *Planning Practice and Research,* 20(4), pp.373-390.

Sweetnam, R. (1988) The development of the port, in Beckett, J.C. et al, *Belfast: The Making of the City 1800-1914*. Belfast: Appletree Press, pp.57-70.

Titanic Foundation (2014) *Titanic Belfast* http://www.titanic-foundation.org/TitanicBelfast Last accessed 10th October 2014.

Titanic Quarter (2014a) *TQ Work*, http://www.titanic-quarter.com/tq-work Last accessed 10th October 2014.

Titanic Quarter (2014b) *TQ Life - Learning*, http://www.titanic-quarter.com/tq-life/learning Last accessed 10th October 2014.

Turley Associates (2005) *Titanic Quarter Development Framework*. Belfast: Titanic Quarter Ltd.

Turok, I. (2004) Cities, Regions and Competitiveness, *Regional Studies*, 38(9), pp.1069-1083.

Ward, S.V. (2011) Port Cities and the Global Exchange of Planning Ideas, in Hein, C. (ed.) *Port Cities: Dynamic Landscapes and Global Networks*. London: Routledge, pp.70-85.

Chapter 7

Don't mention the culture war: beyond creative ambiguity and professional "quietism" in Northern Ireland/North of Ireland spatial planning?

William J V Neill

Introduction

The breakdown in Belfast over Christmas in 2013 of political talks dealing with how the legacy of conflict (including its spatial expression) and frictions involving symbolic spatial markers (flags, parades and commemorations) should be handled, came as no surprise to many who saw chickens (if not turkeys) coming home to roost. While these talks, facilitated by US diplomatic envoy Richard Haass, grappled with warring narratives of conflict amidst a faltering peace process, the lack of any spatial planning voice from either the Royal Town Planning Institute (RTPI) or Irish Planning Institute (IPI) in the over 600 submissions to the initiative should not go unacknowledged. As I argued 15 years ago, since at the nub of the peace process is the issue of how identities can be given agreed and officially legitimised forms of expression, the profound link between identity and place makes this issue also very much a spatial planning matter (Neill, 1999, p.273). If, as a recent critique has argued (Campbell, 2010, p. 473), the planning profession needs to be less risk averse, this Haass self-imposed exclusion must be seen as an important opportunity missed. The constraints involved, discussed below, do not, it is argued, excuse it. While discussion is focused on planning amidst conflict in Northern Ireland, the point that planners have a responsibility to stimulate spatial imaginations has more general applicability.

Constructive ambiguity

The political commentator Arthur Aughey pointed out that the Good Friday Agreement of 1998, which is the present basis of devolved government in

Northern Ireland, was launched on a sleight of hand:

> How can the agreement satisfy simultaneously the nationalist ambition to bring about the end of partition in Ireland and to establish Irish unity and the equal and opposite unionist ambition to strengthen the Union of Great Britain and Northern Ireland thereby confirming the partition of Ireland? (Aughey, 2000, p. 14)

The "constructive ambiguity was that noble lie that would, it was hoped, secure the new condition of peace" (Aughey, 2005, p. 3). Neill (2004, p. 207) welcomed the outcome in that the republican tradition was now using political and cultural salvos rather than real ones to challenge the identity of its prominent significant "other" on the island of Ireland, but regretted that in this "cultural war of position" the cultivation of a space of common civic identity remained fraught. Here analysts have noted the retrenchment from the approach of "a shared future" embodied in a document of that name introduced by direct rule ministers in 2005 that stressed reconciliation (Murtagh, 2011, p. 1125), to the replacement in 2010 by a strategy entitled "cohesion, sharing and integration" (CSI) which introduces the vague notion of mutual accommodation. Here with the Democratic Unionist Party (DUP) and Sinn Fein seeing little political investment in deconstructing their respective constituency bases (Murtagh, 2011, p. 1125), the new CSI policy has been described as amounting to "a reification of cultures which pushes change into the future and loses sight both of the positive potential and of the dangers of the present" (Todd and Ruane, 2010, p. 3). One of these dangers is described by McDowell as the problem latent in the current selling to tourists of conflict heritage landscapes in Belfast through tours, murals, festivals and so forth where narratives of the past are in sharp contrast between republican and unionist protagonists. This "reinforces territorial politics and transforms the conflict, especially for republicans, into war by other means" (McDowell, 2008, p. 407). The dangers involved in sensitive cultural identity legitimacy claims were all too apparent in 2013 with flashpoint issues involving the naming of a children's playground and commemorative events involving republican armed struggle protagonists on the one hand and, on the other, the curtailing of the previously traditional days on which the Union flag could fly on top of Belfast City Hall. The latter was to inflame ongoing unionist parading claims in Belfast involving a spatial imaginary that is roundly recognised as in need of reform not least to project an image of "normalisation" for a widely marketed "new Belfast" much hyped by city promotional agencies. However, the apex of spatial contestation in Northern Ireland in 2014 arguably remains the ongoing tension around the withdrawal of unionist consent for a "conflict transformation centre" at the site of the former Maze/Long Kesh prison on the outskirts of Belfast. While the meaning of the site is contested, it remains primarily a republican secular sacred space – the site of the deaths in the prison hospital block of hunger strikers seeking political prisoner status in the early 1980s, including Bobby Sands, (Neill, 2006, p. 116). As Graham and McDowell phrase it:

> as a heritage resource, the Maze/Long Kesh possesses a powerful resonance with an ethnocratic republican mindset ... in consequence, within the context of the hegemonic cultural politics of Northern Ireland, the republican movement is the most likely beneficiary of the site's heritage potential. (Graham and McDowell, 2007, p. 346)

It is hard not to agree with Graham and McDowell who argue that "it is difficult to see how the (prison) hospital can fail to become a shrine through repeated practices of commemoration" (2007, p. 360). Putting judgement on the efficacy of such assessments aside, what is less open to dispute is the way planners and the planning process in Northern Ireland were used to try to depoliticise what remains, nevertheless, a political hot potato. Eschewing the need for any public inquiry, planning permission for the Daniel Libeskind-designed "conflict transformation centre" was granted by the Strategic Planning Division of the Department of the Environment (N.I.) in March 2013, only three months after the application submission. The main problem identified was one of bat welfare resulting in the condition that the development:

> shall not commence until details of the location of bat boxes have been submitted to and agreed in writing with the Department. (Department of the Environment (N.I.), 2013, p. 8)

While bats also coming home to roost is undoubtedly a serious issue, it is unfortunate that spatial planning takes refuge in bat boxes to exert professional relevance on a memory site of the first order where emotions need venting and proposals need aired. While planning takes place under political direction something is lost if this is self-imposed or imposed over compliance. The visceral concerns churned up by the Maze/Long Kesh development are leached out of the bloodless planning process and its rubber-stamp conclusion however much implementing a set of statutory requirements is involved. The Maze planning decision provided a short-term fig leaf of legitimacy for a shaky cross-cultural political deal that was to implode only a few months later. It is but one manifestation of the weak professional voice of planning in the face of power in Northern Ireland when it comes to cultural identity matters. Some explanations for this are now offered and a call for greater risk-taking made in order to build a more relevant profession that is fit for purpose in an admittedly difficult context. While in the past "professionalism and bureaucratization of government have been used to insulate contested policy areas, especially planning, housing and economic development, from accusations of discrimination and bias" (Murtagh and Ellis, 2010, p. 571) the need for a more mature practice which "reappraises the knowledge and skills required in order to make a more proactive contribution to the present period of more peaceful conflict management" remains pressing (Neill, 2004, p.158).

Ethnicity and homeland

A good place to start in further explaining a supine tendency amongst the planning profession in Northern Ireland in relation to conflict is the observation of Yiftachel that current planning theories rarely address processes of ethno-spatial policies and their framing of material realities. Within the "communicative turn" of planning theory, emotive notions such as ethnicity and homeland are disciplinary blind spots, despite the fact that in most parts of the world (not least in Northern/North of Ireland) these realities are central to the production of space which engages with people's actual life and meanings (Yiftachel, 2012, pp. 540 – 541, p. 548). Going somewhat to explain this is the recent re-acknowledgement of the unclear epistemology underpinning planning as a discipline which should show how knowledge is organised and relates to reality. With a vaguely defined and diffused intellectual foundation the search continues for planners' unique competence (Davoudi and Pendlebury, 2010, p. 614). This epistemological gap has translated in the case of Northern Ireland to a lack of surety on planning's legitimate theoretical object in situations of contested space. The result has been a reluctance to engage with the big spatial practices that are at the heart of conflict and a retreat to the narrower and more comfortable "salami slicing" of space; a retreat to the bland, less controversial and creative ambiguity in policy prescription often involving the hearty endorsement of the surface neutrality of neo-liberal market values, and retreat to process concerns over spatial outcomes. These three aspects of practice are briefly considered in turn.

Ten years ago I pointed to the timidity of the planning profession in Northern Ireland in at least engaging at some level with the conflicting and interpenetrating urban imaginaries that imbue the city of Belfast. Planners, I provocatively suggested, seem more comfortable in dealing with cars on streets than marchers in sashes (Neill, 2004, p. 215). To move on to such culturally charged political terrain with suggestions, proposals and advice is of course difficult, some would say foolhardy. It should not, however, be off-limits and beyond the bounds of the conceivable with a retreat to safer professional roosting boxes which avoid any risky "epistemological leap". In terms of the management of "space on the ground" even academic discussion has tended to be preoccupied with a salami slicing approach in distinctions between ethnic space, neutral space, shared space and cosmopolitan space where difference is respectively over emphasised, co-exists together, interacts together or is transcended in some way (Spier, 2011, p. 107). While work on managing space to assist peace building on a micro scale is of course important in a city with a profusion of separating "peace walls", something is lost if the spatiality of cultural conflict in the city is treated like a block of Neapolitan ice cream which can be neatly defined and sliced. Rather, the city is like a marble cake which is shot through with competing and interpenetrating imaginaries, desires and fears with different meanings occupying the same space simultaneously. Thus 'shared space', on one interpretation in Belfast, can be presented as the right to prosecute identity claims through antagonistic parading practices (O'Dowd and Komarova, 2013, p.537) in claiming place.

A second aspect of accepted peace-building planning doctrine in Northern Ireland/North of Ireland (both terms carry competing spatial imaginaries) has been the endorsement of the broader strategy of creative ambiguity and blandness in planning visions. At one level the Regional Development Strategy for Northern Ireland published in 2001 set the tone being overly general in dealing with conflict issues, preferring to project a "feel-good haze" (Neill, 2004, p. 199). At another, the homogenising effects of standard off-the-rack building developments can be praised in Belfast by some as a way to create a modern neutral city with mediocrity in architecture and art bolstering a "banal nationalism" (Spier, 2011, p. 109). However, the recent signs are that this is not in fact a satisfactory lower cultural common denominator after all.

Process over outcomes and a culture of quietism

While the legitimacy of planning as a semi-autonomous arena where the pros and cons of development can be considered without being subject to crude political dictate has recently had to be asserted in Northern Ireland (Ellis, 2013), the response to the vulnerable state of the discipline should not be to cravenly dodge major cultural spatial issues of the day. A retreat to process concerns over spatial outcomes has, however, heightened this tendency. Here Yiftachel points out that too much of mainstream planning theory is preoccupied with "talk about the talk" with the underlying assumption that the "right kind of talk" can provide answers (2012, p. 542). The deficit in procedural skills needed in fraught conflict situations has begun to be addressed with the recent call for a more engaged understanding in Northern Ireland of situated power where ethnic space is concerned with a highlighting of "the need for a more direct political engagement with agonistic practice that challenges the technical reductionism implied in generic skills frameworks" (Murtagh and Ellis, 2010, p. 563). While this procedural exhortation is welcome it should proceed in parallel with a more imaginative approach to conjuring with spatial imaginations. In reply to any caution that this is ground on which planners should fear to tread, it is noteworthy to register that the legal profession in Northern Ireland has also recently been upbraided for embodying a "culture of quietism" during the conflict and its aftermath when there was a requirement for more moral courage. Lawyers are depicted as narrowing the focus of political struggle "onto overly legislative terrain" with "a de facto acquiescence with the status quo" (McEvoy, 2011, pp. 360, 368). While acknowledging that some 'partisan' lawyers paid with their lives while others felt obliged to preserve the "neutrality" of the profession partly to avoid sectarian division, the charge is put in uncompromising terms:

> The legal actors in Northern Ireland who staffed key institutions – including the universities - created and maintained a pervasive culture of quietism during the conflict. (McEvoy, 2011, p. 384)

When the full story is written of how the planning profession in Northern Ireland has conducted itself over the years of armed conflict, and now cultural conflict, it is likely to also document "a de facto acquiescence with the status quo". Certainly until the Good Friday Agreement in 1998 the RTPI at "national" level was to adopt a hands-off approach leaving local actors adrift to create their own culture of quietism where personal reward was seldom compatible with rocking the boat. As a matter of personal reflection, as Chair of the local Northern Irish branch of the RTPI in 1995, I found an almost total unwillingness of chartered planners to put their heads above the parapet and accompany me in giving evidence to the House of Commons Northern Ireland Committee in their inquiry into the Northern Ireland planning system.

A shared future?

In the spirit of rocking the boat but mindful that "we as planners need to focus attention on our capacities to envisage alternatives and demonstrate the possibilities for a better world" (Campbell, 2010, p. 475), I propose an alternative location for a conflict transformation centre complementing the historical assets at the Maze/Long Kesh. I take my cue from the British Prime Minister, David Cameron, who said to the Northern Ireland Assembly in June 2011:

> we cannot have a future in Northern Ireland in which everything is shared out on sectarian grounds. Northern Ireland needs a genuinely shared future, not a shared out future. (Cameron, 2011)

A difficulty remains the self-contained and unconnected cultural pillars approach to governance embedded in the Belfast/Good Friday Agreement

(Graham, 2011, p.145). While a shattering of these pillars may, Samson-like, bring down the house, nevertheless, if a sterility of thinking is to be avoided, in the words of one artist who understands the creative power of the unorthodox and the jarring of representational forms, democracy "must create inclusive conditions for a dynamic open discourse that exposes and challenges, rather than hiding and dissolving the most burning and inconvenient issues" (Wodiczko, 2009, pp. 27 – 28). This may necessitate some boldness to de-escalate the ethno-national dispute and take the sting out of Belfast's and Northern Ireland's cultural war of position. In recognition of the fact that imagination as well as logic are fundamental to the process of exploring possibility, there is sometimes merit in enabling people to consider reality in a de-familiarised way (Modena, 2011, p.64).

A counter-monument

A proposal is advanced for a Titanic counter-monument to be embodied in the materiality of the secular sacred space of the sadly neglected Titanic Drawing Offices in Belfast to counter the profanity of the commercial over-exploitation of the legacy of the doomed liner in its city of birth (Neill, 2014). New public art, which notions of a monument call to mind, is quite unchallenging in the "new Belfast". It speaks rather to the large-scale advertisement of normalisation with the lack of any critical "post-conflict" city public art practice (Jewesbury and Porter, 2010, p. 49). When property discourse and public art meets normalisation discourse, as it does in the new Titanic Quarter and its Titanic Belfast® theme park, the targeted affective response is towards a feel-good factor enhancing development value rather than deeper contemplation.

Classical monuments function as ideological signifiers and "judge and evaluate and thereby coerce viewers to adopt the normative belief systems they stand for" (Lambert and Ochsner, 2009, p.11). "Counter monuments", on the other hand, memorialise significant historical events by continuing a public conversation about those events rather than treating them as completed facts. These "memorial forms actually tend to arise in cultures that are just beginning to remember events in their history with which they have a great ambivalent relationship" (Young, 1998, p.2) As further described by Ward, "for the most part counter-monumental art and architecture are consciously positioned to become metaphorical 'stumbling blocks' against collective ignorance and forgetting" (Ward, 2009, p.148). A prominent counter-monumental form would include the Daniel Libeskind Jewish museum extension in Berlin where the power of architecture mobilises the use of rupture and void in challenging the visitor to question the meaning of the experience rather than an easy recourse to a settled interpretation.

In advancing a proposal for a Belfast Titanic counter-monument, inspiration is sought from a utopian counter-monument proposal (Saltzman, 2009, p.75) which challenges the dominant Ground Zero 9/11 memorial in New York. While Daniel Libeskind was awarded the commission of devising a master plan for the site in 2003, in trying to seek a balance between commerce and commemoration on this site of calamity, the outcome has been described as "one part Daniel Libeskind to several parts Larry Silverstein", the real estate developer who held the lease on the World Trade Center (Goldberger, 2011, p.78). The utopian counter-monument, on the other hand, is the controversial project of the artist and designer Krzysztof Wodiczko whose aim is "to create a place for a more active, critical and discursive memory of the September 11 attack examined in its historical and political context" (Wodiczko, 2009, p. 12). Of the materiality of the idea Wodiczko states:

> The architectural structure of the September 11 memorial should be easily accessible and visible to all New Yorkers. Let us envisage it as a structure to be placed not on solid ground but on water, on unstable ground, one connected through the ocean to stormy lands overseas, the lands of troubles in which we may be implicated. (Wodiczko, 2009, p 34)

The counter-monument idea proposes the construction of a memorial adrift in the waters just off Manhattan, a floating "agora" of sorts, dedicated to the exchange of ideas, the asking and provoking of questions and incorporating a conflict transformation centre. The notion is one of memory in action. The animating ethos of the memorial would be "an agonistic model of democracy, a model based not on agreement but on non-violent disagreement ... where 'adversaries' take the place of 'enemies'." (Wodiczko, 2009, p.27). To the obvious criticism that the idea is on the face of it utterly impossible of realisation, one sympathiser points out that sometimes focusing on the possible clouds our judgement of the right (Savage, 2009).

Belfast has already lost one opportunity to do something truly imaginative with the topography of Titanic. For a while, the cast iron men figures in Liverpool, constituting the public art work called "Other Place" by Anthony Gormley (renowned for his "Angel of the North" in north-east England), were available for possible installation by maritime places seeing the potential for the creative engagement of emotion with spatial form. In the event, the still controversial 100 + human forms evocatively populate the Merseyside beach just north of the city where Titanic was registered (Photograph 7.1). Their presence and the effect of what their material emotional vitalism could have been on the shores of Belfast Lough can be only wistfully contemplated in imagination.

Photograph 7.1 'Other Place': contemplation on a Merseyside beach (c. Jean Hillier)

Efforts to interrogate emotional geographies have only recently come to the fore (Smith, Davidson, Cameron and Bondi, 2009), alongside the appreciation that there is no human perception that does not have an affective tonality (Helbrecht, 2011, p. 678). At present the Titanic affective tonality in Belfast is crass. Perhaps even more imagination is needed to apply the inspiration of Wodiczko's New York counter-monument to the watery context of Titanic Belfast. The proposal is simply that the Titanic Drawing Offices be rededicated as a listed monument as a constituent part of the spatiality of a wider conflict transformation centre concept complementing the separate memory project at the former Maze/Long Kesh prison site. Daniel Libeskind, closely associated, as indicated, with the concept of counter-monuments, has been engaged by a Maze/Long Kesh development corporation to design the latter. To bring the former into a project of shared memory work would create a contemplative counter-monumental juxtaposition pointing to the dangers latent in the potentially fatal "convergence of the twain" to use Hardy's famous poetic Titanic phrase. It is surely fitting to rededicate Titanic to saving lives and not the filling of hotel beds as in the present commercial proposal on the table for the Drawing Offices where Titanic was designed by a largely unionist shipyard (Photograph 7.2).

Photograph 7.2 Harland and Wolff 'Titanic' Drawing Office on a collision course for a Titanic themed hotel (c. William J V Neill)

Titanic in Belfast should be reclaimed from the profane. The collision of memory work rather than the sharing out of memory would be the unsettling ground for a claim to counter-monument status. To the obvious criticism articulated in an interview with one senior government memory and heritage worker: "what has the Titanic to do with the Maze?" (interview, September 2010), the answer is simply everything. As expressed by Crooke, "fundamentally, the issue for Northern Ireland is not so much how to forget the past but how to put its memory to better use" (Crooke, 2005, p. 141). More recently, in talking of the challenge for post-conflict heritage work, another commentator puts it thus:

> in Northern Ireland, the challenge lies in interpreting past events openly and critically without laying blame or playing a zero-sum memory game that discounts others' perspectives in order to validate one's own. (Shea, 2010, p. 302)

Post Haass, the temptation may be to coast along with the separate spatiality of oppositional narratives about the past (Photograph 7.3), combined with more superficial commercially driven reimaging. But perhaps an imaginative re-representation of Titanic in the new Belfast can help to shatter the iceberg of the stasis in culture with a more ambitious urban imaginary. We have, as Huyssen reminds us, to live together in "an age in which globalisation produces new forms of locality that still have to find a vision of another future than that offered by neo-liberalism, market ideology and media triumphalism" (Huyssen, 2003, p. 105). As Foster has remarked "the energy of creative response to Titanic has not yet been depleted" (Foster, 2011, p. 159). And as Hillier reminds us, "cultural heritage should not be regarded as a past-presence to be 'preserved', but as a calling-towards potentiality" (Hillier, 2012, p. 1). Belfast needs to counter the hegemony of the profane, recognise and counter the reality of a still deeply divided society and show respect for the profound cultural significance of the Titanic of imagination which Belfast, albeit unknowingly, launched into the world. There may still be a chance to do the right thing as many did on that fateful night over one hundred years ago.

Photograph 7.3 Writing on the wall in Protestant West Belfast 2014 . (Photo credit : Una Sommerville)

Acknowledgement

This is a slightly revised version of an article which was published in the *Journal of Planning Theory and Practice* (2014) Vol. 15, No. 2, pp.268-275. It is reproduced here with permission.

References

Aughey, A. (2000) A dream dreamed in Belfast: The Belfast Agreement of April 10, 1998, *The Brown Journal of World Affairs*, Winter/Spring 7, pp. 13 – 25.

Aughey, A. (2005) *The politics of Northern Ireland: Beyond the Belfast Agreement.* London: Routledge.

Cameron, D. (2011) *Speech to Northern Ireland Assembly*, 2011. Retrieved June 2012, from http://www.cons ervatives.com/News/Speeches/2011/10/Paterson_Moving_Northern_Ireland_forward.aspx

Campbell, H. (2010) The idea of planning: Alive or dead-who cares? *Planning Theory and Practice*, 11, pp. 471 – 475.

Crooke, E. (2005) Dealing with the past: Museums and heritage in Northern Ireland and Cape Town, *South Africa. International Journal of Heritage Studies,* 11, pp. 131 – 142.

Davoudi, S. and Pendlebury, J. (2010) Centenary paper: The evolution of planning as an academic discipline, *Town Planning Review*, 81, pp. 613 – 646.

Department of the Environment (N.I.) (2013) *Article 31 planning application. Final development management report.* Belfast: Strategic Projects Team. S/2012/0691/F.

Ellis, G. (2013) *Stormont is planning to remove Democracy, September 25.* Belfast: Belfast Telegraph.

Foster, J. W. (2011) *Titanic: The sceptre of power*. Vancouver and Belfast: Belcouver Press, Kindle Edition.

Goldberger, P. (2011) Shaping the void: How successful is the new World Trade Center? *New Yorker,* pp. 78 – 80.

Graham, B. (2011) New spaces for the island of Ireland? Post-conflict geography, planning and politics in Northern Ireland, *Journal of Irish and Scottish Studies,* 4, pp. 131 – 147.

Graham, B. and McDowell, S. (2007) Meaning in the Maze: The heritage of Long Kesh, *Cultural Geographies*, 14, pp. 343 – 368.

Helbrecht, I. (2011) Emotion, place and culture - edited by Mick Smith, Joyce Davidson, Laura Cameron and Liz Bondi, *International Journal of Urban and Regional Research*, 35, pp. 678 – 680.

Hillier, J. (2012) *Shadows on the stock route: Theorising hot heritage as Deleuzean cultural empiricism.* Paper delivered at Association of European Schools of Planning conference, Ankara, July11 – 15.

Huyssen, A. (2003) *Present pasts. Urban palimpsests and the politics of memory.* Stanford, CA: Stanford University Press.

Jewesbury, D. and Porter, R. (2010) On Broadway, in Taru, E. (Ed.), *The centrifugal book of Europe.* Belfast: Centrifugal Press.

Lambert, L. B. and Ochsner, A. (2009) From moment to monument: Introduction in B. Lambert L.B. and Ochsner A. (Eds.), *Moment to monument: The making and unmaking of cultural significance*. Bielefield: Transcript Verlag.

McDowell, S. (2008) Selling conflict heritage through tourism in peacetime Northern Ireland: Transforming conflict or exacerbating difference? *International Journal of Heritage Studies*, 14, pp. 405 – 421.

McEvoy, K. (2011) What did the lawyers do during the "war"? Neutrality, conflict and the culture of quietism, *Modern Law Review*, 74, pp. 350 – 384.

Modena, L. (2011) *Italo Calvina's architecture of lightness: The utopian imagination in an age of urban crisis.* New York, NY: Routledge.

Murtagh, B. (2011) Desegregation and place restructuring in the New Belfast, *Urban Studies*, 48, pp. 1119 – 1135.

Murtagh, B. and Ellis, G. (2010) The skills agenda and the competencies for managing diversity and space, *Town Planning Review*, 81, pp. 563 – 583.

Neill, W. J. V. (1999) Whose city? Can a place vision for Belfast avoid the issue of identity? *European Planning Studies*, 7, pp. 269 – 281.

Neill, W. J. V. (2004) *Urban planning and cultural identity*. London: Routledge.

Neill, W. J. V. (2006) Return to Titanic and lost in the Maze: The search for representation of "post-conflict" Belfast, *Space and Polity*, 10, pp. 109 – 120.

Neill, W. J. V. (2014). Countering the hegemony of the profane: The case for a Titanic counter-monument in Belfast, in Neill, W. J. V., Murray, M. and Grist, B. (Eds.), *Relaunching Titanic: Memory and marketing in the new Be*lfast. New York, NY: Routledge.

O'Dowd, L. and Komarova, M. (2013) Three narratives in search of a city: Researching Belfast's 'post-conflict' transitions, *City*, Vol 17 (4), pp. 526-546.

Saltzman, L. (2009) Non-site, utopia, counter-memorial, in Jarzombek, M. and Widrich, M. (Eds.), *City of refuge: A 9/11 memorial*. London: Black Dog Publishing.

Savage, K. (2009) The impossible monument, in Jarzombek, M. and Widrich, M. (Eds.), *City of refuge: A 9/11memorial*. London: Black Dog Publishing.

Shea, M. (2010) Whatever you say, say something: Remembering for the future in Northern Ireland, *International Journal of Heritage* Studies, 16, pp. 289 – 304.

Smith, M., Davidson, J., Cameron, L. and Bondi, L. (2009). *Emotion place and culture*. Farnham and Burlington, VT: Ashgate.

Spier, S. (2011) Belfast und das Problem der Geschichte, in Bartels Olaf, et al. (Eds.), *Metropole: Kosmopolis*. Berlin: Jovis Verlag.

Todd, J. and Ruane, J. (2010) *A shared future to cohesion, sharing and integration.* York: Joseph Rowntree Charitable Trust.

Ward, J. (2009) Sacralized spaces and the urban remembrance of war, in Staiger, U. and Webber, A. (Eds.), *Memory culture and the contemporary city:Building sites*. Basingstoke and New York, NY: Palgrave Macmillan.

Wodiczko, K. (2009) A memorial for September 11,.in Jarzombek, M. and Widrich (Eds.), *City of refuge: A 9/11 memorial.* London: Black Dog Publishing.

Yiftachel, O. (2012) Re-engaging planning theory? Towards "South-eastern" Perspectives, in Fainstein, S and Campbell, S. (Eds.), *Readings in planning theory (3rd ed.)*. Oxford: Blackwell.

Young, J. (1998) *Interview May 24th.* Retrieved July 2012, from http://www1.yadvashem.org/odot_pdf/ Microsoft%20Word%20-%203659.pdf

Chapter 8

Community Asset Transfer and urban regeneration

Brendan Murtagh, Elaine Bennett and Lisa Copeland

Introduction

Urban planning, regeneration and making both relevant to people have been central to Malachy's research and teaching interests over the last three decades. His work in the 1980s in the Northside area of the city centre led to the development of the Cathedral Quarter as a shared space that also placed architectural heritage at the heart of the regeneration process. The area is now home to a thriving community arts scene, students and, increasingly, social enterprises, some of which have survived successive waves of redevelopment and private speculation. The Belfast Centre for the Unemployed was important for resisting Thatcherite economic ideology and creating practical alternatives for those left out of a new service economy. Today, the Centre owns the John Hewitt pub and restaurant which creates profits that are reinvested in anti-poverty programmes and community businesses have developed by buying and refurbishing assets across the area. The value of assets is that they provide a security on which further development can be based, collateral to provide business stability and a means to reinvest resources in facilities that a local community needs.

This chapter, we hope, reflects Malachy's concern for the ethics of planning and the idea that urban regeneration is not always about private profit and speculation. Specifically, it examines the scope of the social economy and community ownership of assets as an instrument in the creation of more sustainable and inclusive places. The analysis uses a series of case studies to demonstrate the potential of community asset transfer for locally based regeneration and providing communities with a degree of local economic control in the face of public service withdrawal, capital flight and market failure. The chapter concludes by identifying the critical success factors for effective community asset transfer in Northern Ireland.

Community Asset Transfer

Community Asset Transfer was introduced by the New Labour administration but gained political and policy momentum under the Coalition's *Localism* agenda. For the government this has helped to promote a 'Big Society' that enabled communities to take control over the services and facilities that affect their everyday lives (Aiken *et al*, 2011). However, for critics, it is about transferring costs and risks from the state to ill-defined communities and aims to responsibilise the local for its own social, economic and environmental crises (Sullivan, 2012). The analysis presented here suggests that neither is inevitable but that progressive transfer can be steered especially in Northern Ireland where the concept offers a meaningful approach for the type of shared, cross-community development advocated by Malachy in his political work.

Locality (responsible for asset transfer in England) defined community asset transfer as:

> Local communities' ability to acquire land and buildings, either at market value or at a discount, in order to deliver services that meet local needs. It is seen as one way in which local authorities (in particular) can support the development of social economy organisations, and thereby meet their wider strategies for renewal and improved delivery of local services (Quoted in IPPR, 2006, p.6).

The IPPR (2006) also identified three forms of ownership of rights in asset transfer:

- The right to use an asset;
- The right to appropriate returns from an asset; and
- The right to change the form and substance of an asset.

In mapping asset transfer in Northern Ireland Aiken *et al* (2011) showed that most schemes tended to be smaller projects that do not involve a full transfer of the title (a minimum of a 25 year lease). They distinguished between 3 types of projects in the UK including:

- *Stewards* which are small volunteer-run groups typical of the Northern Ireland profile;
- *Community Developers* which are medium sized organisations often with a range of assets involved in service delivery; and
- *Entrepreneurs* which are larger more professionally managed social enterprises.

Murtagh (2013) points out that without the right conditions in place, asset ownership and management can struggle to achieve benefits, especially for community groups. A clearer understanding is needed of the risks and costs involved in asset control, as assets can become liabilities that undermine the social purpose of many third sector organisations. Similarly, Aiken et al

(2011) point out that participating groups need to strike a balance between achieving financial sustainability and delivering community benefit. The opportunity for generating income to sustain a project varies considerably and new skills are required to manage assets effectively and efficiently. For success, public authorities need to be supportive, strong governance should be in place to manage the project and the asset should be in good physical condition. However, the prize of effective asset transfer and management is considerable:

> The benefits of community control of assets included: a heightened sense of identity; greater financial viability; improved levels of activity and access to services; increased opportunities for training, jobs and business development; a better physical environment; and enhanced credibility with local authorities and outside agencies. These benefits contributed to a 'social good' of local wellbeing (Aiken *et al*, 2011, p.7).

However, the wider concept of asset-based development can move beyond the use of property in order to give communities a sense of control over a range of 'hard' and 'soft' resources necessary for sustainable growth. Kretzmann and McKnight (1993) warned against a *deficit model* of local development exemplified by deprivation mapping and resource competition, not least on the attitudes and motivations of local people as they 'think of themselves and their neighbors as fundamentally deficient, victims incapable of taking charge of their lives and of their community's future'. Other consequences flow from the *power of the needs map,* not least in that it focuses on lists of demands rather than analysis of the interconnected nature of problems and it directs funding, not to residents, but to the priorities of service providers. Skills and capacities are centred on an ability to denigrate the community as much as possible, reinforcing the sense of dependency and a reliance on outsiders to sort it out. It thus minimises the critical relationships *within* the community, thereby deepening the cycle of dependence: 'problems must always be worse than last year, or more intractable than other communities, if funding is to be renewed' (Kretzmann and McKnight, 1993, p.2). Writing about post-industrial America McKnight and Kretzmann (1996) make the point that regardless of wider circumstances, the most disadvantaged areas are not likely to benefit from economic change:

> The reason for emphasizing the development of the internal assets of local urban neighborhoods is that there is very little prospect that large-scale industrial or service corporations will be locating in these neighborhoods. Nor is it likely, in spite of a prospective 'Peace Dividend,' that significant new inputs of federal money will be forthcoming soon. Therefore, it is increasingly

> futile to wait for significant help to arrive from outside the community. The hard truth is that development must start from within the community and, in most of our urban neighborhoods, there is no other choice (McKnight and Kretzmann, 1996, p.2).

Thus, social, economic and physical assets, brought under the control of the local community provide an opportunity to build local resources, circuits of wealth and prevent cash leaking out of the neighbourhood economy (NEF, 2008). However, the asset is only useful if it can be managed in sustainable and effective ways and for this, the development of social enterprise models and bespoke forms of finance are critical. Social enterprises trade goods or services for profit but distribute the surplus to community stakeholders not shareholders and this in turn is guided by democratic and locally accountable forms of governance (Bridge *et al*, 2014). Scaling and replicating asset based social enterprises as with any form of business, also require capital and the skills to use it. For Iona *et al* (2011), the priorities for community asset transfer are:

- To stimulate demand for finance by building awareness, marketing products and developing a preliminary understanding of the grant-loan relationship;
- Developing the capacity of investees to help them become investment ready, improve their financial literacy and ability to scale up or replicate successful business models;
- Processing demand and supply by supporting intermediaries to generate bankable deals. It is important to ensure that the market is not over stimulated creating a shortage of processing capacity among intermediaries.
- Developing financial products that appeal to investors as well as investees.

IPPR (2006, p.5) defines two types of risks linked to asset transfer including 'accountability' to a wider set of stakeholders and 'capture' whereby unrepresentative groups can secure important and often expensive assets. Effective regimes for asset transfer emphasise the need for the following:

1. Setting objectives that clarify the outcomes from the ownership, use and management of the asset.
2. Robust governance systems that impose a degree of rigour on decision making, internal supervision, accounts, audit and reporting regulations with the Charity Commission.
3. A strong and qualified management team.

4. Independent board members with a good skills mix.
5. Robust mechanisms for independent audit.

Successful asset transfer, therefore, requires a mix of finance, capacities, viable schemes, local willingness and support from government. In Britain, the policy environment has changed considerably in the last decade providing the enabling mechanisms to roll out projects in sustainable ways. The political motivation for such encouragement is not always benign, but policies simply enable communities to make choices, work assets in their own interests, refuse those that cannot work and ultimately build fairer local economies.

Policy context in Britain

The recent drive to promote asset transfer began with the report of the Quirk Review, *Making Assets Work*, published in May 2007. This explored the barriers and incentives affecting the transfer of public assets to both community management and ownership. Following the Review, New Labour set up the Asset Transfer Unit, the Advancing Assets Programme operated by *Locality* and a £30m Community Assets Programme delivered by the Big Lottery Fund. This was further developed by the Coalition government who introduced the *Localism Act (2011)* and which included three important provisions:

- The *General Power of Competence* that gives local authorities the freedom to act in the interests of voters, not dissimilar to the 'power of wellbeing' proposed for Community Planning in the new Councils in Northern Ireland;
- The *Community Right to Challenge,* which gives community groups an interest in taking over a failing local service or facility; and
- The *Community Right to Buy* that requires local authorities to maintain a list of assets of community value, which groups and individuals will be able to bid for, and ultimately buy, for a community use (Hostick-Boakye and Hothi, 2011).

This ability to bid enables community organisations and parish councils to nominate an asset to be included on a 'list of assets of community value' which the local authority is required to maintain. The nomination needs to be validated by the Council and the owner can challenge the listing. If the owner assents and then wants to sell the asset, a six month moratorium period will be triggered during which the asset cannot be sold. This period gives community groups time to develop a proposal and raise the required capital to bid for the property when it comes onto the open market at the end of the moratorium period.

One significant legislative support in England underpinning the new Act has been the *General Disposal Consent* set out in *Circular (06/03): Local Government Act 1972 General Disposal Consent (England) 2003* which enables disposal of land for less than the best consideration that can reasonably be obtained. This provides a facility that enables the local authority to transfer an asset at below market value where it contributes to community wellbeing and the specified circumstances are:

a) the local authority considers that the purpose for which the land is to be disposed is likely to contribute to the achievement of any one or more of the following objects in respect of the whole or any part of its area, or of all or any persons resident or present in its area;
   i) the promotion or improvement of economic well-being;
   ii) the promotion or improvement of social well-being;
   iii) the promotion or improvement of environmental well-being; and
d) the difference between the unrestricted value of the land to be disposed of and the consideration for the disposal does not exceed £2,000,000.

In 2003, the Scottish Executive introduced the *Land Reform Act* providing a Community Right to Buy for rural communities, essentially giving the community first refusal if land comes on to the market for sale. Holmes (2010) pointed out, however, that since its introduction, only 9 schemes have been completed. The Big Lottery Fund established the *Scottish Land Fund* to further support the Act and in 2006 a £50m *Growing Community Assets* investment programme was introduced. Moreover, the Scottish government is proposing to extend its provisions within urban as well as rural areas. In Wales, a £13m *Community Asset Transfer Fund* was established with the assistance of the Big Lottery and the 2005 *Social Enterprise Strategy* for Wales also prioritised community transfers, especially linked to area regeneration programmes.

The Department for Social Development (DSD, 2014) has now published the *Community Asset Transfer in Northern Ireland* policy, which aims to strengthen asset transfer across government Departments and agencies. It has funded the establishment of the Development Trust Association (NI) to support projects although there is no new legislation, spending programmes or social finance instruments of the type that have supported policy delivery in Britain. The document is remarkable for its lack of substantive content, empty signification and spurious claims and statements especially about the limits of legislation. Yet, there is case study evidence that where schemes have been implemented in Northern Ireland they have generated significant social, economic and environmental benefit both for the sponsor and the user. The next section looks at examples that illustrate the multiple and sustainable effects of specific schemes and makes the explicit case for more progressive legislation, capital and skills development.

Case study analysis

This section examines four community asset transfer schemes that illustrate the diversity of effects, challenges, opportunities and needs in the creation of more sustainable local models. Indeed, progressive approaches, such as that pursued by the Housing Executive show that these projects can reach significant scale, albeit as an isolated example of what is possible. The Housing Executive transferred to the community: 320 houses for tenant organisations; 34 commercial properties; and 24 land deals. Most of the houses are on short-term lease or license but have had a significant impact on regeneration, community development and environmental renewal. Only 10% of Community Asset Transfer projects in England are in deprived areas but 54% of community houses are in the top 20% of disadvantaged wards in Northern Ireland (QUB, 2012). Moreover, the spatial distribution of projects is comparatively even between Protestant and Catholic estates and they have provided a basis for community relations and cross-community contact schemes. The Housing Executive points out that their role as a 'wholesaler' both enables and frees local groups to get on with the task of delivering services. An audit of schemes show that they have: created local environmental resources including community allotments, improved the financial resilience of groups, provided jobs and training opportunities and enabled cross-community work in some of the most divided housing estates in Northern Ireland (QUB, 2012). This is especially the case in St. Columbs Park House in Derry/Londonderry.

Assets in a divided society: St Columbs Park House

St Columb's Park House (SCPH) is a community relations group named after the 18th Century Manor House in which it is based (in the Waterside area of Derry/Londonderry). Derry City Council (DCC) originally leased the house to the group on a long lease at a peppercorn rent. SCPH has full responsibility for the maintenance and running of the House, which has two main components. First, there is a community business offering conference and residential facilities and second is the Reconciliation Trust dedicated to community relations work but with an emphasis on the Protestant minority in the city. The business cross-subsidises the charity and has ensured a measure of stability given reducing budgets for community relations work. Their Gateways to Protestant Participation programme works with 36 groups mainly in the Waterside to support engagement between the community and statutory sector, strengthen capacity and research local needs.

The initial refurbishment of the House cost £500,000, which came mainly from the International Fund for Ireland, the Council and DSD. The SCPH has then secured £1m for a major refurbishment, which aims to develop conference facilities that will be let on a more commercial basis. SCPH is run by a voluntary management board of 12 people and there are currently 10 people employed on a full-time or part-time basis. About 15,000 people use the programmes on an annual basis and the House provides one of the few neutral spaces, especially for community groups, to meet on a cross-identity basis. SCPH is still highly grant dependant and not commercially profitable highlighting a key tension between social and economic activity as explained by the Director:

> Our main aspiration is that we become sustainable and be less dependent on government funding. We aspire to run and fund our programmes as a charitable non-profit making business without external help whilst maintaining our main ethos of community relations. But there is a danger that our activities become about making money and not about community relations. We want to make sure we can get this balance right. The social economy is just a means to an end. Once we go down the economic route we don't want to get away from the core values and mission about good relations and reconciliation work which is first and foremost our priority.

Sweating assets: The Shaftesbury Recreation Centre, south Belfast

The Shaftsbury centre is located in the lower Ormeau area of south Belfast and exemplifies transfer of management responsibilities (rather than the full property), which was to the Lower Ormeau Resident's Action Group (LORAG) in 2000. Following the lease agreement, LORAG redesigned services and facilities enabling space for community events and a training suit and a function room. Prior to the transfer the facility was open for only 30 hours a week and cost £200,000 pa whereas it is now open 7 days a week from 9.00am to 7.00pm. The centre employs 17 full-time staff, all of whom are local residents.

Currently, social enterprise activities account for approximately 40% of staff salaries and 80% of all running costs. Sport NI provided £1.7m to the outdoor 3G football pitch, a new fitness suite and changing rooms as well as £155,000 for five years to fund a Sports Development Officer. The centre receives health referrals from local GPs and associated payments on average of £60 per person for a 12 week programme on healthy eating, stopping smoking and general fitness. Approximately 550 people use the centre per day and the organisation has proposals to develop water based sports activities on the river Lagan. LORAG emphasises the role of a competent board who have a clear understanding of the need to commercialise services including charging local groups at near commercial prices.

Healthy places: the Maureen Sheehan Healthy Living Centre

A local community partnership came together in west Belfast in 1998 in response to social and health problems and to discuss the development of a new centre that would integrate health, social and community services. They formed a new group to take forward the Healthy Living Centre proposal on a site owned by the Northern Ireland Housing Executive. They initially signed an agreement with the Health and Social Care Trust (HSC) that if they secured funding to build the centre the Trust would fund the fit out and pay an element of running costs. The Housing Executive transferred the site to the HSC in 2002 under the proviso that they would lease it to the community group at a peppercorn rent. Maintenance and running costs are now fully covered by the Trust but the community group has control of the building and its uses.

The complex now includes buildings. Building 1 is a Community Managed Health Centre and is occupied by the HEART Project, Sure Start and a pharmacy. There is also a Health Information Point, the HABIT Suite (Intelligent gym) and the LOAF Café. Building 2 is a Health Centre and is occupied by a GPs Practice and a variety of social care services provided by the Trust. The total cost of the development was approximately £1.25m and this was funded through the Belfast Development Office, the Community Fund and the HSC. The project revenue is funded through the Big Lottery Fund and the Public Health Agency and additional funding is secured from rents from tenants in the centre and the pharmacy, Sure Start centre and the Loaf Café (£30,000 per annum). The Café operates as a social enterprise and provides training and employment for people with learning disabilities and is now financially sustainable.

Community finance: the Ashton Trust

The Ashton Trust in North Belfast is one of the largest social enterprises in Northern Ireland and started with a *Community Share* scheme, offering 720 shares valued at £35 per share, all to the local community. This enabled pump-prime funding, gave the community a material stake in the organisation and showed commitment and self-confidence to resource further developments. The shares had both material and symbolic value and allowed Ashton to raise additional funding in order to build scale and financial robustness in a volatile property and funding market.

Over time, the organisation built a new multi-purpose facility that integrated childcare, commercial and community uses and was constructed on DSD owned land. With the help of *Community Places* the land was sold at 'community value' rather than the original commercial value set by the government's Land and Property Services making the project financially viable. Grant aid from the EU URBAN II Programme core funded the facility which is fully let and yields a sustainable income stream. Now, the Ashton Trust is in a position to develop a government transferred youth club, which was struggling to attract numbers and finance. Here, the organisation feels that because it is so embedded in the community it can build volume and offer a range of more flexible programmes to operate the centre profitably. Ashton now generates a turnover of £3m per annum, employs nearly 200 people and has reinvested surpluses in a range of social and educational programmes including peace building initiatives that support victims and survivors of the Northern Ireland conflict. The integration of property collateral, social enterprise models, community finance and social reinvestment demonstrate the potential to create alternative economic models based on locally controlled and owned assets.

Critical success factors

These limited case studies illustrate the everyday tensions and challenges in community asset transfer. But the analysis also shows that to be sustainable and effective the critical success factors include:

- The transfer is just the start of the process and the best examples are linked to functioning community organisations with a clear business case, viable uses, market prices for services and revenue funding in place to sustain the facility.
- Grant investment is also important to refurbish or reequip the asset and incubate businesses capable of producing a revenue stream at the point of transfer.
- Progressive policy makers and an entrepreneurial attitude have helped to support responsible forms of asset transfer, trust and effective working relationships between partners.
- Skilled leaders and competent managers capable of developing the potential of the asset are also critical and many of the most successful schemes are associated with charismatic individuals, although this is risky if succession planning is not put in place.
- Relevance to local needs is essential and the best schemes offer a range of services and mechanisms to keep local people on board, including community financing and share options.
- As with any facility the need to avoid unnecessary competition with other community based services is essential to ensure that each transfer adds value and minimises displacement in the neighbourhood.

Conclusions

Community Asset Transfer has risks but also considerable potential, especially for communities that can build a property portfolio, accumulate reserves and deliver better local services. They reflect the type of concern that Malachy McEldowney has for responsible, ethical and locally controlled planning. But Northern Ireland is significantly behind the rest of the UK and the DSD policy document is remarkable for its lack of content, specific commitments and especially resources to deliver change. This is especially the case with legislation on disposal consent and right to buy, the need for new forms of social finance and for a different skill set, both for the community and the statutory sectors. The Housing Executive approach demonstrates what is possible but it is an exception and without a permissive enabling environment, risk-adverse public officials are unlikely to adopt the practices necessary for progressive asset transfer.

Three points are significant. First, legislation makes it easier, efficient, gives certainty to officials and might even help to reconceptualise property rights around community value not private speculation. Second, as the Ashton Trust case study demonstrates, groups are capable of generating social finance in order to own rather than rent property, support community businesses and deliver social programmes. However, social finance remains poorly developed especially compared with other regions where it has supported the financial and political independence of community groups. Finally, skills need to be supported around strengthening the social economy, social enterprise models and how to create community businesses that are relevant to the neighbourhood and not just for the convenience of the state. A more financially resilient community sector is in a better position to resist government and market ideologies, create opportunities for more radical politics and help build more sustainable local economies.

References

Aiken, M., Cairns, B., Taylor, M. and Moran, R. (2011) *Community Organisations Controlling Assets: A Better Understanding.* York: JRF.

Bridge, S., Murtagh, B. and O'Neill, K. (2014) *Understanding the Social Economy and the Third Sector.* Basingstoke: Palgrave.

Department for Social Development (DSD) (2014) *Community Asset Transfer in Northern Ireland.* Belfast: *DSD.*

Holmes, H. (2010) *Providing Opportunities for Rural Communities in Scotland: The Community Right to Buy in Scotland.* York: JRF.

Hostick-Boakye, S. and Hothi, M. (2011) *Grow Your Own: How Local Authorities Can Assist Social Enterprises.* London: The Young Foundation.

Iona, J, L., de Las Casas, L. and Rickey, B. (2011) *Understanding the Demand for and Supply of Social Finance.* London: NESTA.

IPPR (2006) *Community Asset Transfer: Overcoming Challenges of Governance and Accountability.* London: Adventure Capital Fund.

Kretzmann, J. and McKnight, J. (1993) *Building Communities from inside out: A Path toward Finding and Mobilizing a Community's Assets.* Evanston, IL: Institute for Policy Research, ACTA Publications.

McKnight, J. and Kretzmann, J. (1996) *Mapping Community Capacity*, Chicago. Institute for Policy Research, Chicago: Northwestern University.

Murtagh, B. (2013) Community asset transfer in Northern Ireland, *Policy and Politics*, available online September 19, 2013, http://dx.doi.org/10.1332/030557312X655837

New Economics Foundation (NEF) (2008) *Plugging the Leaks: Making The Most of Every Pound That Enters Your Local Economy.* London: NEF.

Queens University Belfast (2012) *Asset Transfer and Social Housing: Building On Delivery.* Belfast: The BRIC Project.

Sullivan, H. (2012) A big society needs an active state, *Policy and Politics*, 40(1), pp.145-48.

Chapter 9

Recent migrants to Northern Ireland: understanding new configurations of 'community'

Ruth McAreavey

Introduction

It is traditional to describe Northern Ireland in terms of two communities, Protestants and Catholics. That simple binary is no longer sufficient to describe a situation where the arrival of new migrant communities has significantly changed the way in which inter-community relations are played out. This chapter will examine recent migration to Northern Ireland and the challenges that arise. It draws upon research the author has been involved in since 2005, and is based on a series of interviews and focus groups with migrants themselves and the support agencies that work with them. The chapter commences with an overview of modern migration patterns before moving on to provide a brief history of migration to Northern Ireland. The analysis then examines the policy framework and interventions. The emergence of new configurations of community within the peculiar context of Northern Ireland is considered before concluding with final comments.

Modern processes of migration

Modern economies rely on migrants to ensure basic levels of economic growth (OECD, 2011) and so it is the case that migration remains a fact of our modern, global life (Vertovec, 2009; Goldin *et al*., 2011). Across the globe traditional immigrant gateways continue to experience the largest absolute growth in immigrant population. Migrants' pathways in these areas have been well documented (see for instance Portes and Zhou, 1992; Alba and Nee, 2003). However a growing body of literature has identified the arrival of migrants to 'new' destinations in the USA, Australia and Europe (Kandel and Cromartie, 2004; Jentsch and Simard, 2009; Luck *et al*., 2011). Communities in these areas previously had little immigration experience. Although absolute migrant numbers in many of these locations may remain small, research shows how these arrivals have transformed their small towns and rural communities (Kasimis et al., 2003; Parra and Pfeffer, 2006; Jenson and Yang, 2009; Rye and Andrzejewska, 2010; Wallace *et al*., 2013).

The extent to which these changes are felt varies significantly depending on contextual factors like migration history, racial/ethnic boundaries and institutions (Alba, 2005; Crul and Mollenkopf, 2012). Some areas demonstrate local resistance through negative attitudes and other areas provide a relatively warm reception. In these areas local communities are known to respond to migrants' needs in an *ad hoc* way, at least until incoming migrant flows become established and expected; such responses may be due to resource constraints, ambivalence, or risk-aversion even if outright resistance is lacking (Popke, 2011; Lichter, 2013). Miraftab and McConnell argue that 'the existing formal structures of decision making are ill-equipped to deal constructively with newly arrived ethnic and racial heterogeneity' (2008, p. 345). This is relevant across a range of social contexts. Even in areas where there is little obvious resistance to migrants, institutional and social structures can work against their positive social and economic integration. For instance migrants can find themselves segmented within a particular employment sector that is characterised by low pay, low skills and little security (Hoggart and Mendoza, 1999). Meanwhile the development of cultural competences within individual healthcare organisations may be ineffective given an uneven application across the sector overall with varied institutional goals and organizational ethos (Betancourt *et al*., 2005). Existing services may be framed in a way that excludes those whose cultural background and value system are different from the majority population: language accommodation often presupposes that the way in which a service is delivered is appropriate and 'simply' needs to be translated into another language (Martin and Phelan, 2010; Alexander *et al*., 2004). This lack of attention to cultural competence can ignore subtle difference, emphasising the otherisation of certain social groups (Papadopoulos and Lees, 2002). It fails to acknowledge how different cultures may come together to identify commonalities, thus impeding more deep-seated change within a society.

It is broadly recognised that strong community support facilitates positive integration (Broadway, 2007; Miraftab and McConnell, 2008; Pfeffer and Parra, 2009). More precisely, civic society organisations, employers and friends become important support systems by helping to reduce isolation and inequalities within migrant communities, providing information on support systems and by offering access to pathways towards employment (Parra and Pfeffer, 2006; Iosifides *et al*., 2007; Jeanetta *et al*., 2009; Jentsch and Simard, 2009; Validivia and Dannerbeck, 2009; Irwin *et al*., 2014; McAreavey, 2012). New destination areas may lack comprehensive support structures that helped past waves of urban migrants to settle. The particular history of migration to Northern Ireland is briefly presented below to highlight the context of migration to this new destination.

Migration to Northern Ireland

Recent theoretical developments in migration emphasise concepts such as 'transnationalism' (Castles, 2007, p.353) to suggest that the idea of 'home' is a complex one for the individual migrant. In the world of transnational labour markets 'common people...have created communities that sit astride political borders and that, in a very real sense, are 'neither here nor there, but in both places simultaneously' (Portes, 1997:3). To succeed in the new place, whether for a short stay or for a longer period, requires the cultural knowledge necessary for individuals to participate across a range of social domains and to operate within a particular legislative framework.

For a long time Northern Ireland was known as a place of emigration, although there are some longstanding and settled minority ethnic groups living there including German Jews and communities from China, India and Bangladesh. Global trends at the turn of the 20th Century resulted in the arrival of migrants from Portugal and South East Asia, notably the Philippines. They filled vacancies predominantly within the food processing and the health and social care sectors respectively. Subsequently and following the removal of barriers to economic mobility within the EU in 2004, significant changes to the rate of migration were experienced in Northern Ireland. Here, along with other parts of the UK, Sweden, and Ireland, unprecedented numbers of economic migrants arrived seeking work as those countries did not impose the types of additional restrictions found in France and Germany (O'Brennan, 2012). In Northern Ireland 25 per cent more Accession 8 citizens registered with the Worker Registration Scheme (WRS) compared to other parts of the UK. In particular many migrants moved from Poland and Lithuania.

Statistics reflect these major trends. It is estimated that over the ten-year period from 2000, 122,000 international long-term migrants arrived in Northern Ireland, while 97,000 left (Russell, 2012). Census 2011 shows that during that time the white population decreased from 99.2% of the population to 98.2%, with ethnic minority groups accounting for 1.8% (an increase of 1%). Meanwhile country of birth shows that in 2001 1.5% of the population was born outside the UK and Ireland. This figure rises to 4.5% in 2011.

Some migrants settled in urban centres including Belfast and Derry and significant numbers chose to live in communities throughout Northern Ireland. Dungannon was recorded as having the highest proportion of people born in EU accession countries (6.8%); within this district council area the Ballysaggart ward includes 825 people or 30% of the population who are EU and other migrants. Figure 9.1 illustrates the spread:

Figure 9.1 A8 Migration - Northern Ireland: Rural or Urban?

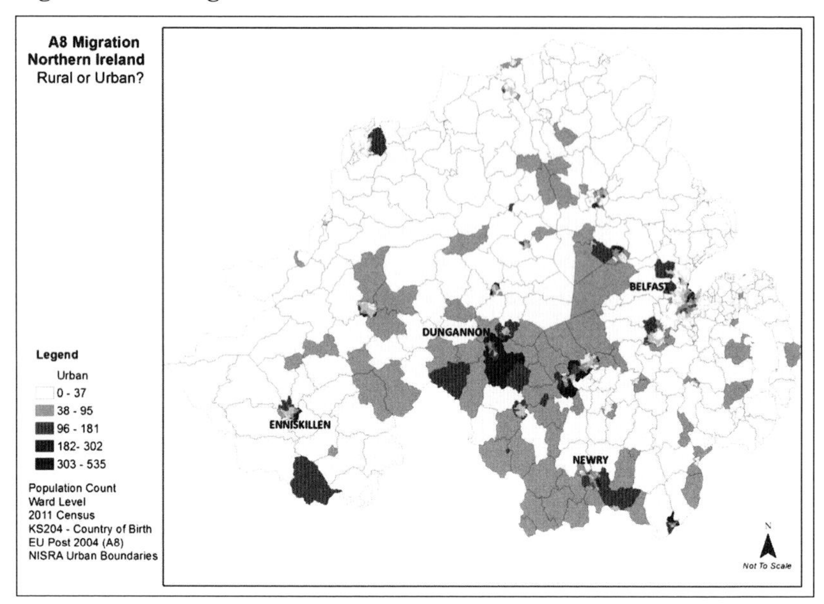

The upward trajectory of demand for Northern Ireland Health and Social Care Interpreting Services is indicative of the increased rate and pace of change: interpreter requests rose from 823 in 2004 to 84,622 in 2013. Forty-one different languages were requested during that period, the top six languages being Polish, Lithuanian, Portuguese, Chinese-Mandarin, Slovak and Tetum (in decreasing order) (Northern Ireland Health Service, 2014). Demand for interpretation continues to increase: during the first three months of 2013-14 there were 24,158 interpreter requests. As is typical of migrant housing patterns in the UK (Perry, 2012), they are over-represented within private sector housing in Northern Ireland (Census, 2011). This confines their housing choices and has resulted in ethnic clusters visible as localized migrant residences such as Polish streets and so raises the possibility of migrant ghettos (Doyle and McAreavey, 2014).

Community and identity in Northern Ireland

Despite this increasingly diverse mix of groups, an enduring essentialist interpretation of society prevails relating to the two majority groups of Protestants and Catholics. Rather than recognition as a 'new' destination, Northern Ireland has received much attention due to the on-going peace process that emerged from nearly four decades of social and political disorder that arose due to disputes over identity, territory and politics (McGarry and O'Leary, 1995). A legacy of entrenched views is evident at the neighbourhood level where a strong association between identity and space exists and with the reinforcement of real and virtual community boundaries, including separate schools, physical 'peace' walls, and social networks (Boal, 2002; Shuttleworth and Lloyd, 2009; Shuttleworth and Lloyd, 2013; Nolan, 2014). Shifting demographies of the two majority communities mean that for the first time, recent records indicate that Belfast is a predominantly Catholic city (NISRA, 2012). This has resulted in shifting power relations and consequential tense community relations between the majority groups, as witnessed following proposals to reduce the number of days during which the Union Jack flag is flown from City Hall. These changes have not been welcomed by Protestant Unionists, who perceive them as a threat to their connections with Britain and also to their identity (BBC, 2012).

Layered onto these traditional and complex ethno-religious community relations are issues of cohesion arising from increased population diversity. In 2014 the UK's only Chinese-born locally elected official was the victim of serious racial abuse (McDonald, 2014). At the time of writing the most recent figures indicate an increase in hate crime (PSNI, 2014). This prevalence of race hate crime and the belief that it is under-reported, led to the establishment of a dedicated phone-line for reporting incidences (http://www.psni.police.uk/general__operation_reiner_hate_crime_update).

Social attitudes

Statistics can hide the complex dynamics of inter-communal relations by assigning people to notional 'communities' that are then described in ways that suggest they are internally homogenous and static. For instance not all working class areas offer a hostile welcome to migrants as shown in 2007 in a loyalist working-class estate following assaults on migrants. Community leaders advocated that instead of being attacked, migrants should be supported and welcomed into the community (McDonald, 2007). It is of little surprise that attitudes to migrants in Northern Ireland are often contradictory. McDermott (2013) found that over a five-year period there was a decrease in acceptance of a marriage to an Eastern European among the majority communities, such resistance contradicting overall support for the principle of increased diversity.

Policy challenges

The arrival of 21st Century migrants, therefore, complicates an already complex picture. Policy makers in Northern Ireland struggle to find a way to incorporate the longer standing challenges with more recent aspects of equality and regarding the interests of new ethnic groups. Long-standing issues of equality between the two majority groups were addressed in the 1998 Northern Ireland Good Friday Agreement. Despite this focus it had an all-encompassing vision of the future, paying attention to 'The achievement of reconciliation, tolerance, and mutual trust, and to the protection and vindication of the human rights of all' (p.2). Thus the accompanying equality legislation that is Section 75, although borne out of traditional political and religious tensions between Protestant and Catholics, places positive duties on public authorities to have due regard for the promotion of equality of opportunity more broadly. Significantly this includes fostering good relations between different racial groups. This mainstreaming approach attempts to address institutional forms of discrimination. But the broad vision set out in the Good Friday Agreement was not followed by operational plans. In 2005 the policy document *A Shared Future* set clear targets for the improvement of relations between Protestants and Catholics. Minority community interests are addressed through the accompanying and less specific, but nonetheless helpful *Racial Equality Strategy*. Subsequently, in 2013 *Together- Building a United Community* mapped out the new good relations strategy and many expected it to incorporate a racial equality strategy (the latter being due for renewal back in 2010), but this did not happen. Instead a new Racial Equality Strategy *A sense of Belonging*, was issued for consultation in 2014. Underpinned by International human rights instruments, it sets out six shared aims including the elimination of racial inequality and combating racism and hate crime. Among the proposed measures and activities is the reform of the Race Relations legislation. Although these good relations and the racial equality strategies actively acknowledge linkages, they remain two distinct areas of policy responsibility. This reflects a historical side-lining of race and ethnicity in Northern Ireland (Connolly and Keenan, 2002). Nevertheless the emerging Racial Equality Strategy provides a very real opportunity for the creation of a diverse and vibrant society.

It is notable that other policy domains such as employment, housing and education impact on migrants' pathways. This chapter proceeds by using empirical data to examine some of those challenges before concluding with suggestions for addressing the emerging shortcomings. It uses research that the author of this chapter has been conducting in Northern Ireland since 2005.

Services and employment

Seemingly innocuous issues such as migrants' lack of familiarity with the system or poor English language skills can result in a series of negative outcomes:

> *'The problem is the work conditions, nobody checks the farms. They work long hours and they have climbed big heights to pick the mushrooms and nobody cares about them and people are afraid to talk because they are afraid to lose their jobs. Psychologically they are struggling a lot and they don't have the courage to ask for holidays. If they receive holidays nobody will pay for them. They don't have the courage to ask for a contract'* (I Advocacy worker, 20.06.13).

Lack of knowledge is not one-dimensional: one advocacy support worker described how insufficient knowledge among officials had resulted in negative outcomes including failure to access appropriate housing and delays in benefits claims. But this is not just anecdotal; such was the degree of blockages in these support systems that an Emergency Fund was issued by OFMDFM to alleviate the plight of migrants facing particular hardships including destitution. It is telling that nearly 20% of the funds were actually used to provide a stop-gap due to major delays to welfare payments (McCann and McKittrick, 2012).

The complexity of support systems can result in further exclusion of already vulnerable individuals. While this is known to happen to individuals from the majority communities, it has added significance for migrants for a range of reasons that include their limited knowledge of the safety and legal framework; reliance on a single family income and associated precariousness due to job loss (and possibly home if connected to employment); and reliance on co-ethnic networks for financial or other support due to limited family support structures:

> *'the Somalian community is very closely-knit and they help each other out a lot…they lend each other money while their case is being assessed and they are seeking asylum…most of the women indicated that they have helped recent arrivals by lending money where possible or by helping them find out how to get access to information'* (FG Somalian F, 20.02.12).

Meanwhile, the role of individual attitudes and behaviour cannot be underestimated. For migrants this can result in less than satisfactory access to services if front-line staff are able to obstruct access to those services. There were reports of a 'chill factor' where some officials performed within their role and so were technically doing their job but did not address particular needs to migrant satisfaction (I Advocacy worker, 20.06.13). In other circumstances blatant discrimination was evident:

> *'My GP sent a letter but the lady who took the letter didn't even look at the letter, this is racism and discrimination, because someone is sick and she didn't even think about her health. The place that they gave me was a smelly dump, it was not fit for a human'* (FG Congolese F 15.06.13).

Migrants' mobility is further hampered in Northern Ireland due to their inability to fully access services such as healthcare (McAreavey, 2010) and regarding access to the full labour market (Irwin *et al*. 2014). Even where government and other support institutions recognise the gaps in policy instruments and service delivery, there is no guarantee that remedial measures are always effective. In certain situations well-meaning attempts to support migrants can in fact render them powerless to achieve their true aspirations (McAreavey and Swindal, 2014). For instance the known lack of recognition of overseas qualifications is addressed through a government led scheme to provide equivalences, but this is not widely used or recognised (Irwin *et al.* 2014). Migrants' contributions to the labour market are thus severely curtailed (McAreavey and Swindal, 2014).

Emerging identities

Even though social structures require individuals to assert a single nationality through forms of citizenship, this does not accurately reflect the way in which modern migrants transcend boundaries and live a transnational existence. Proactive interactions between social actors are known to help shift perspectives, beliefs and attitudes (McAreavey, 2014). Furthermore, just as there are differences within the majority Protestant and Catholic communities, there is diversity and sometimes strife within and between migrant groups.

> *'...there are people that I know that I have helped and I know they are talking behind my back. And the reason for that is well, there are maybe 50 of those (migrants from Poland) that have really made it, they are really outstanding. These people have done well and are working hard...but these other people don't like those that are doing well because they have got more'* (I, Polish M 01.04.09).

Consequently individual expectations of a new society differ, as does the way in which migrants and other social groups perceive their own and others' culture. Ultimately this affects migrants' pathways and experiences of life in a particular place. The degree to which individuals choose to make connections in the new destination varies according to particular circumstances as this Lithuanian migrant illustrates, describing that he was

> *'working all of the hours that God sends...last job I was working in [a toy superstore] in [XX] shopping centre...And I was working from 7 to 7, that's 12 hour shifts and travelling to and from work (laughs). So you were getting up leaving to go to work your shift and coming home, going to bed, getting up and doing it all over again?*
> *That's right.*
> *What 5, 6 days a week?*
> *Seven!'*
>
> (I, Lithuanian M 01.04.09).

He regularly sent money to his parents and his wife who, at the time of the interview, were all still living in Lithuania. He explained how he planned to work in Northern Ireland for a few years so that he could save money before moving back home more permanently. One support worker described how aspirations to return to the home country are often tinted with nostalgia and rooted in imagined notions of a place that was left behind. Nonetheless as a purely economic migrant, this man's needs differed considerably from many of those who had moved with partners and children. Indeed such economic migrants' needs are in danger of falling outside of normal support structures as agencies are compelled to prioritise scarce resources towards migrants who are planning to remain for a longer period:

> *'it depends very much what your expectations are when you come over here, if you are going to be staying for 3-6 months well really they don't see it necessary to integrate and we don't see it necessary to spend a lot of time with them'* (FG Health Professional Stakeholder 18.05.09).

With a physical presence in Northern Ireland, many migrants retain daily personal ties to their home country through various means including telephone, email and Skype. Meanwhile television ensures connections with culture, language and popular media. Alongside these links, many forge new ones in the host country, such as with local churches or civic society organisations. Following from Hall (1993), some migrants could be described as 'hybrids':

> *'You make the decision yourself. This is why whenever I decide to stay here, I am aware of the fact that my child was born here, but she is Polish. We have Polish roots and our own culture etc. but I can see myself living here. And I'll be happy if my child wants to stay here too.'* (FG Polish F 19.01.10).

Hall describes 'hybrids' as individuals who do not expect to return 'home' as that journey would uncover a place transformed by modernity (1993:362), something that is not unnoticed by migrants:

> *'I left Poland. Of course I miss them very much. But even if I came back to Poland it wouldn't be the same. The connection would never be the same as it used to be'* (FG Polish F 19.01.10).

In this way they are experiencing a transformation of culture, values and ideas about society. This transcendence between two countries contributes to the accumulation of multiple identities. Of course identity is not static, it shifts according to many other factors including an individual's experiences, expectations and socio-economic status; qualifications; and culture (Barnard and Turner, 2011). Simply 'by dint of living in one area or another, and sending their children to local schools, they can become 'accidental 'Protestants or Catholics' (Nolan, 2013, p.141). Equally Geoghegan (2010) documents how the framework of division in Northern Ireland, where social events such as multicultural celebrations are defined in terms of 'otherness' to sectarian festivals, influences migrants' identity. The way in which migrants manipulate these categories is shaped by the peculiar context of division that prevails in Northern Ireland. Clearly, migrant use of sectarian identity is not necessarily a matter of straightforward adoption (Kempny, 2013). One community worker powerfully articulates this:

> *'...So at home they watch Portuguese TV and they speak Portuguese and their parents are quite comfortable with that environment. But once they move out of the house those kids become local, they change their identity, it's like a mask.... []...we're working with a group of young people now they were part of the flag protests and the police identified them and ... I went along and met with them and discovered there was a Latvian, Lithuanian and someone from Portugal; they were part of the group who lived in a Protestant area, they claimed to be British....*[explaining that] *their flag they were defending and on the way home from the flag protest they egged BME houses. Try to unravel that...[] we are finding as we go along young people are just picking up the local culture and just taking on our story as their story...'(I* Advocacy worker, 20.06.13).

Final thoughts and conclusions

Like many other rural and regional areas absolute migration flows to Northern Ireland remain small. But the impact on some communities is immense with large proportionate changes to their overall population. The peculiar context of Northern Ireland provides a challenging backdrop to this recent migration phenomenon. Many of these challenges associated with its status as a new migration destination prevail. It is likely that new ones will emerge. Indeed some difficult questions remain unanswered, such as the degree to which existing social structures in Northern Ireland are appropriate for the 21st century. Furthermore, there is a danger that new ethnic communities will exist in parallel – spatially, socially and economically - to the majority communities, with untold consequences from such division.

At the very least, the degree to which positive interactions between the traditional majority communities and new ethnic groups will ensue is fluid; it remains an unfolding story. Their inclusion in a society that claims to nurture good relations, despite fragmentation in some quarters, is critical. At a minimum this will require dedication from political leaders, policy-makers and society to create a truly inclusive and diverse society. Countless social, cultural and economic benefits will surely follow.

References

Alba, R. (2005) Bright vs. blurred boundaries: second-generation assimilation and exclusion in France, Germany, and the United States, *Ethnic and Racial Studies,* 128 (1), pp. 20–49.

Alba, R. and V. Nee (2003). *Remaking the American Mainstream: Assimilation and the New Immigration.* Cambridge, MA: Harvard University Press.

Alexander, C., Edwards, R. and Temple, B. with Kanani, U., Zhuang, L., Miah, M. and Sam, A. (2004) *Using interpreters to access services: user views*. York: Joseph Rowntree Foundation.

Barnard, H. and Turner C. (2011) *Poverty and Ethnicity: A review of evidence*. York: Joseph Rowntree Foundation.

BBC 'Q&A Northern Ireland Flag protests', BBC News (8 December 2012).

Betancourt, J. R., Green, A. R., Carrillo, J. E. and Park, E. R. (2005) Cultural competence and health care disparities: key perspectives and trends – among stakeholders in managed care, government, and academe, cultural competence is emerging as an important strategy to address health care disparities, *Health Affairs,* 24(2), pp.499–505.

Boal, F. W. (2002) Belfast: Walls within, *Political Geography*, 21(5), pp. 687–94.

Broadway, M. (2007) Meatpacking and the transformation of rural communities: a comparison of Brooks, Alberta and Garden city, Kansas, *Rural Sociology*, 72 (4), pp. 560–582.

Castles, S. (2007) Twenty-first century migration as a challenge to sociology, *Journal of Ethnic and Migration Studies*, 33(3), pp. 351-371.

Connolly, P. and Keenan, M. (2002) *Tackling Racial Inequalities in Northern Ireland: Structures and strategies*. Belfast: Northern Ireland Statistics and Research Agency.

Crul, M. and Mollenkopf, J. (2012) *The Changing Face of World Cities.* New York: Russell Sage Foundation.

Doyle, C. and McAreavey, R. (forthcoming 2015) Patterns and processes of recent migration to Northern Ireland, *Irish Geography*.

Geoghegan, P. (2010) *A Difficult Difference: Race, Religion and the New Northern Ireland.* Dublin: Irish Academic Press.

Goldin, I., Cameron, G. and Balarajan, M. (2011) *Exceptional People: How migration shaped our world and will define our future*. Princeton, New Jersey: Princeton University Press.

Hall, S. (1993) Culture, Community, Nation, *Cultural Studies,* Vol. 7 (3), pp.349-363.

Hoggart, K. and Mendoza, C. (1999) African immigrant workers in Spanish agriculture, *Sociologia Ruralis,* 37(4), pp. 538–563.

Iosifides, T., Lavrentiadou, M., Petracou, E. and Kontis, A. (2007) Forms of Social Capital and the Incorporation of Albanian Immigrants in Greece, *Journal of Ethnic and Migration Studies,* 33(8), pp. 1343-1361.

Irwin, J., McAreavey, R. and Murphy, N. (2014) *The Social and Economic Mobility of Ethnic Minority Communities in Northern Ireland.* York: Joseph Rowntree Foundation.

Jeanetta, S.C., Martinez, D. Valdivia, C. Flores, L.Y. and Dozi, P. (2009) Latinos in the midwest: newcomers assets, expectations and integration policies, *Presented at the Julian Samora Research Institute 20th Anniversary Conference: Latino(a) Communities in the Midwest. East Lansing, Michigan. November. Growth and Change in Arkansas' Hispanic Population.* Arkansas: University of Arkansas Cooperative Extension Service Printing Services, available online at: http://www.jsri.msu.edu/pdfs/20th/JeanettaMartinezPPP.pdf, accessed 12 September 2012.

Jenson, L. and Yang, T. (2009) Taken by surprise: new immigrants in the rural United States. in B. Jentsch and M. Simard (eds), *International migration and rural areas, cross-national comparative perspectives.* Farnham: Ashgate, pp. 17–42.

Jentsch, B., Simard, M. (2009) International migration and rural areas: cross-national comparative perspectives. Ashgate Publishing, Ltd. Migration Letters, 8(2), pp. 173 – 184.

Kasimis, C.A., Papadopoulos, G. and Zacopoulou E. (2003) Migrants in rural Greece, *Sociologia Ruralis,* 43(2), pp. 167–184.

Kempny, M. (2013) Tales From the Borderlands Polish Migrants' Representations of the Northern Irish Conflict in Belfast, *Space and Culture,* 16(4), pp. 435–46.

Lichter, D. (2013) Integration or Fragmentation? Racial Diversity and the American Future, *Demography*, 50(2), pp. 359-391.

Luck, G. W., Race, D. and Black, R. (2011) *Demographic change in Australia's rural landscapes: implications for society and the environment.* Collingwood, Australia: CSIRO and Dordrecht, the Netherlands: Springer.

Martin, M.C. and Phelan, M. (2010) Interpreters and Cultural Mediators –

Different but Complementary Roles, *Translocations: Migration and Social Change,* 6(1), ISSN 2009-0420.

McAreavey, R. (2010) Transcending cultural differences: the role of language in social integration, *Translocations: Migration and Social Change*, 6(2), pp.596-601.

McAreavey, R. (2012) Resistance or Resilience? Tracing the Pathway of Recent Arrivals to a 'New' Rural Destination, *Sociologia Ruralis,* 52(4), pp. 488-507.

McAreavey, R. (forthcoming 2015) Minority and majority community integration in Northern Ireland: a spectrum of tolerance in Honohan, I. and Rougier, N. (eds) *Tolerance and Diversity in Ireland, North and South.* Manchester: Manchester University Press.

McAreavey, R. and Swindal, M. (2014) The Uneven Geography of Mobility: Comparative Research on Migrants and their Host Communities in the United States and United Kingdom, *presented at Trans-Atlantic Rural Research Network annual conference*, Newcastle, UK.

McCann, J. and McKittrick, N. (2012) *OFMDFM Emergency Fund – Pilot.* Belfast: The Community Foundation for Northern Ireland and the British Red Cross.

McDermott, P. (2013) A 'Shared Society?' Attitudes on immigration and Diversity. *ARK Research Update* No. 86. Belfast: ARK, University of Ulster and Queen's University Belfast.

McDonald, H. (2007) The Observer - Loyalists make Catholic Poles welcome (18 February 2007) *The Guardian* (http://www.theguardian.com/uk/2007/feb/18/politics.northernireland, last accessed 21.10.13)

McDonald, H. (2014) Only Chinese-Born Parliamentarian in UK to Quit Politics over Racist Abuse. *The Guardian*, (29 May 2014).

McGarry, J. and O'Leary, B. (1995) *Explaining Northern Ireland.* Oxford: Blackwell.

Miraftab, F. and McConnell, E.D.D. (2008) Multiculturalizing Rural Towns Insights for Inclusive Planning,[My Copy] *International Planning Studies*, 13(4), pp. 343-360.

Nolan, P. (2013) *Northern Ireland Peace Monitoring Report Number 2.* Belfast: Community Relations Council.

Nolan, P. (2014) *Northern Ireland Peace Monitoring Report Number 3.* Belfast: Community Relations Council.

Northern Ireland Health and Social Care Interpreting Statistics (2014) *Translation Statistics* April to June 2014, Belfast: Belfast Health and Social Care Trust.

Northern Ireland Statistics and Research Agency (NISRA) (2012) *Census 2011: Key statistics for Northern Ireland.* NISRA, 11 December 2012.

O'Brennan, J. (2012) The success of the eastern EU enlargement debunks current fears. The Guardian, Saturday 19 January 2013, http://www.theguardian.com/commentisfree/2013/jan/19/success-eastern-eu-enlargement-debunks-fears, last accessed 23 August 2013.

OECD (2011) *International Migration Outlook.* Paris: OECD.

Papadopoulos, I. and Lees, S. (2002) Developing culturally competent researchers, *Issues and Innovations in Nursing Educatio*n, 37(3), 258–264.

Parra, P. and Pfeffer, M.J. (2006) New immigrants in rural communities: The challenge of integration, *Social Text*, 24(3), pp. 81–98.

Perry, J. (2012) UK migrants and the private rented sector. A policy and practice report from the Housing and Migration Network. York: Joseph Rowntree Foundation.

Pfeffer, M.J. and Parra, P. (2009) Strong Ties, Weak Ties, and Human Capital: Latino Immigrant Employment Outside the Enclave, *Rural Sociology*, 74(2), pp. 241-269.

Police Service of Northern Ireland (PSNI) (2014) *PSNI Statistical Reports*: 1st April 2013- 21st March 2014. PSNI: Belfast.

Popke, J. (2011) Latino Migration and Neoliberalism in the U.S. South: Notes toward a Rural Cosmopolitanism, *Southeastern Geographer*, 51(2), pp. 242–59.

Portes, A. (1997) Immigration theory for a new century: some problems and opportunities, *International Migration Review,* 31(4), pp. 799-825.

Portes, A. and Zhou, M. (1992) Gaining the Upper Hand: Economic Mobility Among Immigrant and Domestic Minorities, *Ethnic and Racial Studies* 15(4), pp.491-522.

Russell, R. (2012) *Migration in Northern Ireland: An update. A Research and Information Service Research Paper*. Belfast: Northern Ireland Assembly.

Rye, J.F. and Andrzejewska, J. (2010) The structural disempowerment of Eastern European migrant farm workers in Norwegian agriculture, *Journal of Rural Studies* 26(1), pp. 41–51.

Shuttleworth, I. G. and Lloyd C. D. (2009) Are Northern Ireland's Communities Dividing? Evidence from Geographically Consistent Census of Population Data, 1971-2001, *Environment and Planning A,* 41(1), pp. 213.

Shuttleworth, I.G. and Lloyd, C.D. (2013) Moving Apart or Moving Together? A Snapshot of Residential Segregation from the 2011 Census. *Shared Space: A research journal on peace, conflict and community relations in Northern Ireland*, Issue 16, pp. 51-70.

Vertovec, S. (2009) *Transnationalism.* London: Routledge.

Wallace, A., McAreavey, R. and Atkin, K. (2013) Poverty and Ethnicity In Northern Ireland: An Evidence Review. York: The Joseph Rowntree Foundation.

Chapter 10

Thoughts on a Rational Comprehensive paradox

Pat Braniff

Introduction

Where does Planning stand? Those of us who are concerned with Planning as a profession would profit from attempting to answer this question. The old clear vision is gone. The original vision of the planner as a professional person possessing a toolkit of insights, skills and concepts to be deployed in the useful and honourable task of making the hardware within an environment fit the functions to be performed within that environment has dimmed.

The Rational Comprehensive procedural model of Planning is the approach that best reflects the traditional vision of planning. In the exercise of their professional skills, few planners would seek to be less than rational or less than comprehensive. Yet the Rational Comprehensive model contains an inconvenient truth at its heart. The nature of the planner's task is such that he, or she, must strive for comprehensiveness and rationality. Yet the more comprehensive we become in our consideration of reality, the more difficult it becomes to be truly rational in our approach. Conversely, the more tightly the planner binds himself or herself into a rational straitjacket the more difficult it becomes to grapple with the vast scope and complexity of reality. This chapter constitutes an attempt to consider these difficult problems, from the standpoint of one who has espoused the cause of Rational Comprehensive planning throughout his professional life.

The very phrase "Rational Comprehensive" can be seen almost as a contradiction in terms. Reality is so vast, life is so short, our perceptions so blunt and our intellect so limited that the ideal of rationality will usually remain just that - an ideal. Rationality is more of an approach than an achievement. Comprehensiveness is also hugely problematic, simply because of the immense extent of the "broad reality" with which planners must deal.

On the other hand, planners owe it to their clients to strive for a rational and comprehensive approach. Indeed, if they do not do so, they can be accused of negligence. In the real world of planning practice, planners can find themselves being questioned in a formal public forum. They will wish to be seen as responsible and thorough. They will be asked basic questions such as: "Did you visit the site?" or "What surveys did you undertake?" In the public forum, and particularly within the context of our adversarial system, if the planner has not followed sensible procedures - like Survey, Analysis and Plan - he or she can be made to look like a negligent charlatan. That is not to say that the planner should ignore other perspectives. However, I believe that, whatever garb planners choose to wear, their ornate socio- political/theoretical belt should be supplemented by a stout pair of Rational Comprehensive braces.

Over the last four or five decades, procedural planning theory discussed a wide range of approaches to planning including Disjointed Incrementalism, Mixed Scanning, Transactive Planning, Participatory Planning and Advocacy Planning. Tremendous influence was exerted by the Planning theorists who advanced this wide range of procedural planning theories. Unfortunately, this influence was often used to oppose the Rational Comprehensive approach. As a consequence, the host of methodologies associated with the various components of the Rational Comprehensive approach was accorded less emphasis than it merited. As a result of this, many Planning schools began to produce graduates very capable of discussing policies, but less well versed in the techniques and skills needed to implement those policies. There appears to have been a general flight from numeracy.

In the early years of the last century, planners knew a lot less about the environment than they do today. Nevertheless, guided by Geddes and others, they had a clearer view of how they should apply forethought to the guidance of environmental change. They looked at the functions to be accommodated and they considered how they could make the hardware fit the functions. They dealt with surveys involving cases, variables and values. They established facts. They examined the relevance of these facts in relation to existing and future functions.

Traditionally, planners have relied upon structured and well planned surveys in their efforts to establish facts. They have tried to measure what is measurable, to categorise what is categorisable and to rank what is rankable. They have surveyed a range of topics, they have analysed the results for each topic and they have endeavoured to produce proposals to remedy the problems and capitalise upon the opportunities highlighted by these analyses. Realising that there were complex interactions between such topics as employment, education, transportation etc., planners have attempted to make their analyses more comprehensive by developing techniques such as the Facts Functions Implications Matrix technique. Such techniques seek to make analysis, not only more comprehensive but also more integrated. This technique acknowledged that most of the facts established by survey impacted upon more than one function, either positively or negatively. It drew facts and functions together in a structured manner which aided the identification of problems and led towards the development of goals (Braniff and Reid, 1983).

Planners then began to generate investment and policy proposals designed to achieve these goals. They went on to develop techniques for the examination of the interactions between proposals with a view to the maximisation of synergy (Braniff, 1991).

There are, of course, different levels of data accuracy and different levels of fact certainty. The less accurately we can measure and the more non scalar the variable measurement, the more does rationality require modification at the hands of comprehensiveness. This is not to say that the ideal of rationality is to be abandoned. Nevertheless, it requires the development of methods which can deal with the complexities and immeasurabilities of "broad reality" (that is the most all encompassing reality perceivable by planners). To make significant progress, planners should set themselves the task of updating, refining and developing the Rational Comprehensive approach so that it can offer a useful way forward.

Our opponents

In looking at this, we should recognise that there are many who oppose this vision of Planning - firstly, the politicians. The fact that they have been elected gives them legitimacy but it does not necessarily guarantee that they will behave with fairness or wisdom. Adopting and adapting Clemenceau's maxim "*War is too important to be left to the generals*", many politicians have long realised that rational procedures were a threat to their power. Inevitably, there have always been legions of administrative courtiers well prepared to tell the politicians what they wanted to hear and totally convinced that any other policy was terminally naive.

In truth, the development of rationality in Planning did pose a threat to existing power structures in both central and local government. Speaking about Planning Programming Budgeting Systems Frank Amos (Liverpool's Chief Planning Officer - from the late 1960s to the early 1970s) had this to say: "It is no more than a system for dealing with the complex issues which arise in local government based on commonsense practices. It is a trail which makes it possible to use common sense when faced with confusing information. It merits special attention because it facilitates comprehensive local government, and I emphasise that word comprehensive" (Amos, 1970). Amos was right in his search for comprehensiveness in local government. However, his approach, like other such approaches, placed Planning too close to the centres of power. It, therefore, provoked the hostility of those who felt that their power was threatened. Rational Comprehensive Planning was resented both because of its rationality and its comprehensiveness. Its rationality made its arguments too irresistible, while its comprehensiveness ensured that it trod on the toes of powerful political interests.

Apart from the politicians, there have been other opponents - some of them embedded in the ranks of those entrusted with planning education. A number of academics have denied the feasibility of effectively implementing the Rational Comprehensive approach to Planning. Their profoundly damaging slogan "*If Planning is Everything, Maybe it's Nothing*" has subtly undermined the confidence of the profession (Wildavsky, 1973). A well stated, and succinct, example of this is type of criticism is provided by Walker (1999):

> "But rational-comprehensive decision making has been sharply criticised both on technical and normative grounds. Technically, it is paralysed if full data is not available; in that case, any decision reached must be incomplete and in all probability suboptimal. Data, of course, is costly, and imposes costs for gathering and evaluation. But worse, environmental data can never be final, because of scientific uncertainty. Thus no rational-comprehensive decision dependent on it can be final, nor is there any guarantee that it is optimal. And that is not all. Most decisions having a social impact involve making a choice between one group and another, and environmental decisions may involve choices between humans and other species. The rational-comprehensive model gives no guidance for such choices."

This quote is a prime example of a declaration which is true but useless. It points out some of the difficulties associated with the Rational Comprehensive approach but fails to recognise that planners will always be forced to plan in situations of imperfect knowledge - welcome to the real world! While contemplative approaches have their uses, they should never be allowed to demoralise the planner. A planner too timid to prescribe ceases to be a planner. Once the planner has committed to the preparation of planning proposals, he or she has to say farewell to illusions of infallibility. He has to recognise that the best can be the enemy of the good. If he allows himself to be paralysed by imperfections in the available data, then he will not plan and, if he does not plan, then he ceases to be a planner.

The most unkind, and naive, criticism of Planning methodology in its more limited sense, is that offered by Taylor in his dismissal of the Geddesian procedural model of "*Survey, Analysis, Plan*" as being no more than a crudely positivistic view of scientific method (Taylor, 1980). Faludi is all too ready to join in the attack on the target identified by Taylor, "Also, I agree wholeheartedly with the conclusion drawn by Taylor: '..that planners should not seek to gain knowledge by first doing surveys in the hope of discovering empirical proofs (as the method of 'survey analysis plan' suggests), but rather they should begin by formulating their ideas and assumptions about a given problem situation.." (Faludi, 1986, p.39). Similarly, Healey (1989) implicitly downgrades Planning techniques in her rejection of there being any distinction between planners (as dealing in facts) and clients (as dealing in values). In this schema, planners are seen not as technologists but rather as purveyors of value laden advice. She is partly right in this in that planners cannot avoid having values.

Overall, there has been a divorce between theory and practice to the extent that theory is now seen by many non theoreticians as irrelevant. The relevance and applicability of the early theoreticians was easily seen and judged. Those interested in Owen could view and judge the fruit of his philosophy by visiting New Lanark. Those seeking the influence of Geddes could inspect his work from Edinburgh to India. Those wishing to assess the value of Abercrombie's theories could judge their concrete worth by visiting urban centres from Dublin to Doncaster. Unfortunately, most of today's leading theoreticians have left little in the way of physical concretisation of their theoretical constructs. This makes it difficult to arrive at a fair assessment of their worth. Some among their own number seem to entertain doubts, Scott and Roweis have this to say: ".. mainstream theory appears not so much to be incorrect as it is simply trivially true" (Scott and Roweis, 1977).

Where theoreticians have sown the seeds of doubt and demoralization has been in their treatment of procedural planning theory. For too long it has been fashionable to attack the Rational Comprehensive approach on the basis that its effective implementation was impossible. It has been alleged that the information demands, and the information handling demands, of the Rational Comprehensive approach are impossible to fulfil and that hence the approach should be discarded. Nothing could be more damaging to professional morale. Some writers even appear to suggest that, in important areas of his work, technical knowledge and skill are not essential to the modern planner:

> "Even planners themselves doubt whether they have the developmental and financial training for the jobs they now see as relevant. Where their work involves policy issues, there are doubts about whether there is any role for technical knowledge and skill." (Healey, McDonald and Thomas, 1982, p.14)

In over forty years as a planner (encompassing service in consultancy, public service and teaching) I have never known a time when the gap between academia and practice was as great as it is today. This has been largely caused by the aforementioned developments in Planning theory over the last forty years. During this period, a split has developed between theoreticians, who developed novel approaches in academia and practitioners who adhered to the traditional Rational Comprehensive approach. Sadly, the theoreticians seem to have been victorious. Of course, the current situation is also the result of many other policies and pressures. In the present government-dictated policy for university education, great emphasis is placed on research, on publications and on money brought in as grants. As a result, teaching has been de-emphasised.

It would be unfair to place all the blame on the academics. They are forced to live within the environment created by those who form the policy adopted by government. The broad thrust of policy does not favour teaching. To be a good teacher one must be an unselfish teacher and to be an unselfish teacher one must be a secure teacher. Few lecturers feel secure and those who do may be deluded. The staff appraisal regime under which the modern academic now lives measures some things but not others. Time spent with students cannot be effectively measured and, consequently, teaching is often devalued. Likewise, the pressures on academic staff seem to have resulted in many of them withdrawing from professional Institute activity. In former times, the majority of Planning academics were RTPI members. That this is no longer the case, is testimony to a lessening in overall cohesiveness in the profession.

Turning to the world of Planning practice, where most planners find employment, the situation is very different. Here there seems to be a vast difference between the working situation in the public sector and the private consultancy sector. Generally, in consultancy, the planner tries to approach his, or her, job with a toolkit of skills and insights related to the tasks in hand. A planner without some sort of a toolkit is of little practical use to a client. On the other hand, many public sector planners find themselves working as development control administrators mechanically applying Planning Policy Statements to the consideration of planning applications. In such circumstances, the planner often runs the risk of degenerating into a pseudo generalist box ticking administrator. Within the public sector, there seems to have been a general lessening of commitment to the maintenance of Planning as a skilled profession. For example, Human Resource Departments in the public sector seem to delight in moving staff just as they are beginning to develop expertise in a specialist field - retail planning for example. It seems simpler for the Human Resource administrator to take the view that a planner is a planner and can be moved from post to post regardless of expertise.

The gulf between the work situation of planners in the three main sectors seems to be widening. After a few years, the planner employed in consultancy is unlikely to transfer to the public sector - because of pension arrangements (particularly in recessionary times). Few public sector planners would leave a secure and pensionable post for the risky world of consultancy. Neither private sector nor public sector planners are likely to successfully apply for a post in academia - they simply cannot compete with the hordes of young graduates who have made their way up through the research assistant route - with dozens of publications in journals that no practicing planner would ever read.

The principal professional body which regulates and encourages Planning is, of course, the Royal Town Planning Institute (RTPI). The Institute has had a profound influence on how the profession managed itself, particularly in the field of education. Over the early 1970s period the RTPI engaged in a consultation with its membership with the objective of determining the identity and charting the future of the profession. (RTPI, 1971) The outcome of the consultations was that the Institute focussed on Environmental Planning as its general identity - with a number of specialisms being encouraged within this broad identity. In 1982, the Institute's New Educational Guidelines were published and in 1986, these Guidelines were made more specific - requiring Planning schools to respond to "the varying planning needs of specific groups, including women, ethnic minorities, the elderly and the disabled." The schools responded to this new agenda. However, this increased emphasis on issues was bound to lessen the attention paid to the development of Planning techniques and skills, an area which had previously been considered to be of prime importance to the development of the profession. These early decisions have had a profound influence on what is taught in Planning schools today.

I believe that Planning, as a professional activity, has almost dissolved. It has become so generalist, so populist, so political, so focussed on transient issues and so administrative that it has almost merged with non professional administration. Does the mechanical application of broad brush Planning Policy Statements in a development control arena, without any significant input of professional judgement really count as Planning? Wildavsky's slogan "*If Planning is Everything, Maybe it's Nothing*" may well be replaced with another "*If Planners abandon Planning Maybe they are no longer Planners.*" If we are to reverse these trends and re-arm ourselves with a modernised and extended approach to our job we must begin with Planning education.

The paradox

If we are prepared to consider the necessary changes in Planning education, we must recognise that there is a paradox which lies at the heart of the Rational Comprehensive approach. This paradox can best be described as follows.

Some types of data are amenable to scalar measurement. Other data are amenable to ordinal or categorical comparison. There are even data types, related to identity and prejudice for example, which are beyond measurement or categorisation. The reality of the Planning situation is that we must grapple with a wide range of data. We must extract meaningful facts from a variety of data types and we must endeavour to comprehend the interactions between these facts. When dealing with data amenable to scalar measurement and analysis, we must use all applicable statistical techniques and produce results which are as accurate as possible. When dealing with other kinds of data, less amenable to accurate quantification, we must augment strict rationality with other ways of thinking. Our overall objective must be to ensure that we capture all relevant data, of whatever type. We must then extract from that data all of the facts that are useful for our purpose. Inevitably some of these facts will be more rationally justifiable than others. As we expand our data set, we will inevitably include more and more non-scalar, non-ordinal and even more non-categorical data. For the Rational Comprehensive planner, dealing with such data is mandatory. Yet the more of such data we include (in our effort to be comprehensive) the more difficult it becomes to sustain rationality.

Dealing with the paradox

This is the paradox. How can this paradox be dealt with? Much is heard today about Evidence-based Planning, Spatial Planning etc. I would like to make a plea for Understanding-based Planning on the basis that the planner's remit is so wide and the territory covered is so complex that an approach capable of dealing with "broad reality" is essential. I also believe that data without context is almost useless. Properly organised data can generate information. Individual items of information can be brought together and integrated. Properly integrated information can lead to understanding. It is on the basis of this understanding that the planners can proceed to intervene in existing systems so that improvements can be made.

Integrated Planning demands that the process itself should be integrated and that each phase of the process should contribute to this integration. We should start off with an integrated survey then proceed to integrated analysis with the aim of producing a set of integrated proposals. In relation to the survey and analysis phase, care should be taken to ensure that direct compatibility is achieved. Very often it will be beneficial to use the "where" component as a hinge around which the various data sets can be arranged. In this respect, Geographic Information Systems have proved their usefulness. Of course it would also be beneficial for Planning education itself to be integrated. The traditional Geddesian framework provides a robust skeleton upon which the muscles and sinews of Planning education can grow. Each component of the Geddesian vision (Survey, Analysis, Plan) provides an opportunity to develop a range of relevant skills and insights which can be integrated into an education which gives the student a thirst for understanding and the skills to generate this understanding. All too often the Planning process has been fragmented into stand-alone components. For example, housing has been surveyed then analysed and finally stand-alone solutions to the identified problems have been brought forward. Often, education, employment, transportation and other topics have been dealt with in a similar manner. Even worse, some of the topics have been dealt with by outside consultants whose work (though often excellent) is poorly integrated with the work done by the permanent planning staff.

Quite obviously this situation can be improved upon by designing a system which allows the planner to preside over all phases of the process in a manner which ensures that thoughts and ideas are integrated and broad understanding is achieved. To use a medical analogy, the planner is rather like the general practitioner of the environment. In medicine, early practitioners were non-systems empiricists but when systems were identified (circulatory, digestive, nervous etc.), specialisms developed but so also did the concept of the general practitioner who could preside over and coordinate the efforts of the specialists while using his or her broad understanding of the patient as a whole. Such is the role of the planner in relation to the environment. The systems with which he or she deals include transportation systems, communication systems land-use systems and, of course, the interactions between these and other systems.

Another essential characteristic of the technically competent planner is his inclination to look at a situation from various points of view. In our society, in our legal proceedings and in our public dialogue we all too often adopt an adversarial stance. One individual or party declaims his or her vision of reality from his or her own point of view. Others with different ideas propound another vision from a different point of view. What is all too often forgotten is that a point of view not only makes perception possible but also limits that perception to those elements of reality which can be seen from that particular viewpoint. If we seek that broad understanding which will enable us to plan comprehensively, we must view things from a wide range of points of view. Only by doing this can we rise above partisanship and serve the overall public interest. However, though striving to increase the range of perspectives available to the planner extends the rational discourse, it still fails to get to grips with the emotional and identity related dimensions of broad reality. For that, we need empathy.

By its very nature, understanding must be comprehensive. The planner who seeks understanding cannot neglect any aspect of the situation. Understanding presupposes a comprehensive approach. Comprehensiveness is a necessary though not sufficient condition for understanding. It would, theoretically, be possible to be comprehensive, in an intellectual way, without achieving full understanding. The missing component is empathy - the ability to understand and share the feelings of others.

Suggested changes to Planning education

What can we say about the necessary changes to Planning education? How can Planning education respond to the demands of this enlarged concept of the Rational Comprehensive approach? This is a very large and important question because Planning education should itself be planned. It is obviously essential that Planning educators should have a clear understanding of the Planning process in which they have chosen to believe. It is also obviously essential that they should then institute educational programmes designed to give the students a complete understanding of that process. The required educational program must obviously tackle each of the components of the enlarged Rational Comprehensive approach. Beginning with survey, continuing with analysis, dealing with the generation of individual proposals and finally considering the interactions between proposals from a range of viewpoints is a very large order. Even more demanding is the further need to explore means of generating empathy between planners and the various social and economic groups for whom they plan. This work presents a challenging agenda.

The generation of empathy depends upon a number of factors. Firstly, the planner seeking empathy must be open-minded. Prejudice is the enemy of empathy. Secondly, the planner must make a determined effort to see the situation from a range of different points of view. In common parlance, he or she must deliberately wear different hats, assume different identities and extend his sympathies to a range of actors in the developmental drama. If Planning education can begin to address the problem of empathy generation, it will make a contribution extending well beyond Planning itself. Planning demands teamwork. Even at the level of student projects, co-operation and democratic discussion is the essential operational mode. This could well be complemented by the introduction of techniques and approaches designed to make students aware of the importance of empathy and how it may be generated. For example, student projects should include exercises designed to help students to be more communicative - exercises to challenge prejudices and question stereotypes - role playing exercises designed to enable students to learn what it feels like to be a member of a section of society different from their own. Planning students may well find it useful to adopt and defend the positions of developers, tenants, retailers and other actors in the urban drama. This can be a powerful educational tool. Dialogue with residents associations and special interest groups can yield not only useful information but also insights and feelings of empathy. Above all, attentive listening and imaginative consideration of the position of others should be valued as an alternative to the self assertion and individualism currently considered to be the mark of a good student. The very fact that group projects play such a large part in Planning education gives grounds for hope. Planning projects differ fundamentally from architectural projects in their breadth of scope and their co-operative nature. It has been said "*The architect is taught to compete - the planner is taught to contribute.*" This is broadly true and it implies that the planner's working situation is more generally predisposed to the generation of empathy than the more individualistic working situation of many other disciplines. Empathy generating techniques should be developed and stitched into the Rational Comprehensive approach at all stages of its implementation. This will have implications for Survey (what to survey), Analysis (using qualitative as well as quantitative techniques), Plan (type of projects etc.) and Programme Appraisal (appraisal from differing perspectives).

Essentially, my plea is for the development of a modernised and extended approach to the Rational Comprehensive model of Planning practice. The development of such an approach would place increased emphasis on understanding and empathy so that a wider reality could be dealt with in the Planning process. The challenge would be considerable. Nevertheless, the successful development of such an approach would yield substantial benefits to Planning - both in terms of effectiveness and credibility.

References

Amos, F. J. C. (1970) Systematic Local Government (Some Implications of Programme Planning and Budgeting Systems for Local Government). *Public Works and Municipal Services Congress.*

Braniff, P. L.(1991) *Integrated Planning Methodology,* PhD Thesis. Dublin: National University of Ireland (UCD).

Braniff, P.L. and Reid, J. (1983) Facts, Functions and Implications, *Irish Journal of Environmental Science*, 2(2), pp.57-59.

Faludi, A. (1986) *Critical Rationalism and Planning Methodology.* London: Pion Limited, p.39.

Healey, P. (1989) *Planning for the 1990s.* (Working Paper No 7). Newcastle: Department of Town and Country Planning, University of Newcastle Upon Tyne.

Healey, P. McDougall, G. and Thomas, M.J.(1982) Planning Theory Prospects for the 1980s. *Selected papers from a conference held in Oxford, 24 April 1981.* Oxford: Pergamon, p.14.

RTPI (1971) *Town Planners and their Future, Consultation Paper.* London: RTPI.

Scott, A.J. and Roweis, S.T. (1977) Urban Planning Theory and Practice: A Reappraisal. *Environment and Planning A 9*, pp.1097 1119.

Taylor, N. (1980) Planning Theory and the Philosophy of Planning, *Urban Studies,* (17) 2, pp.159172.

Walker, K. J. (1999) Environmental Policy in the Gloomy 1990s, *Australian Environmental Policy 2*, Sydney: UNSW Press, pp. 224-247.

Wildavsky, A. (1973) If Planning is Everything, Maybe it's Nothing, *Policy Sciences 4*, pp. 127-153.

Chapter 11

Northern Ireland's golden age of retail investment: the experience of the planning system in Northern Ireland

Anthony Quinn

Introduction

The impetus for the preparation of this chapter stemmed from the unprecedented level of interest shown by British retail chains in opening stores in Northern Ireland (NI) since 1994. The exceptional volume and size of the retail proposals submitted post 1994, together with their implications for the existing retail economy, guaranteed much media coverage. This attention was heightened by the scale of some of the company take-overs involved and the perception by many politicians and senior civil servants that the retail proposals constituted a form of peace dividend, capable of providing NI with state-of-the-art shopping provision. In attempting to plan for this influx, the regulatory function of the NI planning system, as discharged by both the then Planning Service and the Planning Appeals Commission, came under unparalleled pressure and scrutiny. In particular, the technical methodology deployed to assess this change became the focus of increasing attention. By casting light on the efficacy of one of the tools of technical evaluation, namely retail impact assessment and its integral requirement to assess the capacity to absorb new shopping facilities, this chapter implicitly appraises the performance of the planning system at a unique period in its history. This was a time when its capabilities and proficiency were tested to the extreme.

Accordingly, this chapter provides a temporal insight into the relationship between land use planning and retail development during one of the most significant and transformative periods in the history of Northern Ireland, namely the golden age of post-conflict commercial investment between 1994 and 2001. It begins by attempting to quantify the actual scale of change which took place during this period. It then proceeds to demonstrate how, in spite of the vagaries and dynamism of the market place, an element of generalized quantitative retail analysis could have performed a key role in planning for this retail influx. In this regard, it is asserted that the planning authority, namely the Planning Service of Northern Ireland, had the technical wherewithal with which to inject a degree of strategic retail planning into the decision-making process. However, this opportunity was either missed or passed over. The chapter concludes by attempting to understand the broader context and wider influences underpinning decision-making at this time.

The retail influx

This part of the chapter details with the scale and location of new shopping provision earmarked for NI during the 1994-2001 period, and asks the question: was there capacity for this influx?

Scale of change

On the basis of data extrapolated from the Schedule of Major Retail Applications it can be deduced that retail proposals totalling almost one million gross sq. m. (or roughly 10 million sq. ft.) were submitted to the Planning Service in Northern Ireland over a 7 year period between 1994 and 2001 (Department of the Environment (Northern Ireland), 2001). At that time, this level of shopping floorspace approximated to seven times the size of the retail floor area found in the retail core of Belfast City Centre (Valuation and Lands Agency and the School of the Built Environment, 1997). Viewed another way, it equated to 60 per cent of all new shopping floorspace built in Scotland over a timeframe twice as long, between the years 1983 and 1998 (Slipper, 1998).

In order to comprehend the magnitude of this addition to the established retail sector in NI it was first necessary to estimate the amount of shopping provision existing in 1994. In the absence of a total retail floorspace figure for NI as a whole, an inference had to made from up-to-date baseline information which existed for certain local authorities. This related to retail figures that were available for four of the twenty-six Local Government Districts in NI. Building upon this information it was then possible to arrive at an average floorspace per capita index for the whole of Northern Ireland.

Data for the four aforementioned Districts comprised Craigavon (Area Plan Research Team, 1994), Derry/Londonderry (Department of the Environment, 1996a), Larne (Department of the Environment, 1996b) and Carrickfergus (Department of the Environment, 1997). In broad terms, their location could be considered representative of the wider local government profile of Northern Ireland. Craigavon was reflective of Mid-Ulster districts. Carrickfergus and Larne were representative of the eastern part of the province, while Derry/Londonderry characterised those districts in the west. Ideally, retail floorspace data for districts in the extreme north and south of NI would have completed the picture, but unfortunately no such information could be retrieved.

Notwithstanding the above shortcoming, it can be seen in Table 11.1 that net retail floorspace provision per capita across the four districts ranged between 0.38 sq. m. and 0.90 sq. m. The low recording for Carrickfergus (0.38 sq. m. per head) can be explained by its close proximity to shopping facilities in Belfast and Newtownabbey, together with its primary function as a commuter settlement within the greater Belfast area.

Table 11.1 Retail floorspace provision in 4 Districts in Northern Ireland, 1994

	Craigavon District	**Carrickfergus District**	**Larne District**	**Derry District**	**Northern Ireland***
Total net sq. m.	58,460	13,154	25,324	89,770	
Population	76,701	34,618	30,127	100,296	1,638,274
Total net sq. m. per capita	0.76	0.38	0.84	0.90	0.72*

** mean per capita index for NI based on 4 Local Government Districts shown*

Source: Technical Supplements accompanying Development Plans for Districts

Table 11.2 Increase in retail floorspace in Northern Ireland, 1994-2001

	Gross sq. m.	**Net sq. m.**	**Population 2001**	**Net sq. m. per capita**	**Cumulative % Increase**
Existing 1994	N/K	N/K	1,638,274	0.72*	
Open/Being built 2001	410,684	266,945	1,685,267	0.16	22.0%
Approved 2001	382,967	248,929	1,685,267	0.15	42.5%
Pending 2001	195,199	126,879	1,685,267	0.08	53.0%

** 1994 per capita figure is an average of the four local government districts listed in Table 11.1*

Source: Information extrapolated from the Schedule of Major Retail Developments and from Table 11.1 above.

Based on the statistical mean of these four per capita figures, it was calculated that the average net retail floorspace in Northern Ireland stood at 0.72 sq. m. per head of population in 1994. Using this index as the baseline position, it was then possible to calculate the quantum of retail floorspace increase in the province between the years 1994 and 2001. Taking no account of store closures precipitated by the new arrivals, it was estimated that, between the years 1994 and 2001, the level of retail floorspace in Northern Ireland increased by 22 per cent - see Table 11.2.

Although it is too simplistic to equate such a figure with a corresponding level of retail impact on existing retailers, it is worth noting that some traders have commented that diversion of trade by 10-15 per cent may be sufficient to eradicate the profit margins of existing stores (McGettigan, 1999). Furthermore, if implemented, approved retail applications at this time could have increased this level of new retail floorspace provision by 42.5 per cent. This glut of planning approvals for shopping development is not surprising when it is considered that the Planning Service chose to refuse less than 5 per cent of applications during this period. Even if it is accepted that there was scope to appreciably augment the retail base in NI from the mid-1990s, statutory approval to increase the stock by 42.5 per cent over the space of seven years raises serious questions about the ability or desire of the planning system '*... to regulate the development and use of land in the public interest*' (Department of the Environment, 1998). As recognised in Planning Policy Statement 1, which outlines the General Principles governing planning in Northern Ireland, this is a fundamental tenet of the profession. Certainly, based on sheer numbers alone, the rate of approvals would seem to run contrary to the inherent principle of promoting orderly development.

Location of the retail influx

Despite the expressed objective of retail policy to direct retail investment to town centres, the majority of retail development in NI after 1994 occurred in out of centre locations. For example, between 1995 and 1997, only a quarter of the proposals submitted were approved for locations within or close to town centres (Boomer, 1999). This contrasts markedly with the experience in Britain at the time, when, in 2001, it was reported that 90 per cent of all major retail developments was earmarked for the town centre (Planning, 2001).

Was there capacity for this influx?

Given the scale of the invasion outlined above, it is perfectly reasonable to question whether or not NI had the capacity, in terms of available shopper expenditure, to absorb the new arrivals without adversely affecting existing businesses. While it is acknowledged that retail analysis is not an exact science, the thrust of this chapter maintains that some form of technical strategic guidance at the regional level was indeed possible. Working on the assumption that NI could be regarded as an identifiable catchment with a defined level of available expenditure, it is contended that a simple, robust capacity assessment could have performed a role in advising decision-makers during this period. This is best illustrated by means of the worked example below.

A worked example

A relatively straightforward supply and demand analysis can be carried out to test the capacity of NI to absorb cross channel superstore proposals between the years 1994 and 2001. Typically, when assessing the requirement for additional retail floorspace, there are a number of key indices to be considered. These relate to changes in population, retail expenditure, turnover and floorspace levels. Accordingly, the following statistics and informed assumptions underpinned this technical assessment:

- the Planning Service population projection increase for NI between the years 1994 and 2001, which approximated to 98,000 persons (Department of the Environment, 2000). As it transpired, census recordings revealed that the actual population increase was half this amount (Northern Ireland Statistics and Research Agency;
- an increase in convenience goods spending of 0.75 per cent per annum, which was in keeping with the optimistic predictions adopted by the Planning Service for these years (Department of the Environment, 1997);
- the estimation that approximately 70 per cent of the growth in consumer expenditure on convenience goods would have been spent specifically in food superstores. This was known as bulk food expenditure and the proportion was based on a rule of thumb accepted at public inquiries into major shopping applications in NI (Planning Appeals Commission, 1997);
- the average turnover for a superstore in NI in the mid to late 1990s of around £8,611 per sales sq. m. This figure was based on published accounts recorded for Sainsbury's (Unit for Retail Planning Information, 1993);
- the average convenience sales area of a superstore in NI at that time was 2,500 net sq. m. Again, this was based on the approximate sales space of a Sainsbury's superstore (Planning Appeals Commission, 1996).

Taking into account the above considerations and further assuming that existing retailers were not entitled to a share of the increase in bulk food spend between 1994 and 2001, which was estimated at £160 million, it can be hypothesised that such growth could have sustained 7 new Sainsbury's superstores during this period (see Table 11.3).

Table 11.3 Capacity to build new food superstores in Northern Ireland during 1994 - 2001 based on projected expenditure and population growth

	Year		Projected Change	
	1994	2001	1994-2001	Calculations
N.I. projected population	1,641,700	1,739,491	97,791	A
N.I. projected expenditure on convenience goods	£1,981,507,275	£2,210,999,985	£229,492,710	B
Proportion of above expenditure spent in food superstores (estimated at 70%)			£160,644,897	C=Bx70%
Convenience sq. m. required based on a store turnover of £8,611 per net sq. m.			18,656	D=C/8,611
No. of superstores required (assuming a shopfloor area of 2,500 net sq.m. for sale of convenience goods)			7	E=D/2,500

However, as it transpired, Sainsbury's succeeded in opening 8 new superstores throughout Northern Ireland. These included superstore development at Ballymena, Galwally (South Belfast), Craigavon, Armagh, Coleraine, Newry, Derry/Londonderry and Armagh. In addition to these, Tesco, Safeway and the Co-op likewise built 6 new stores between them during the same period. Clearly, therefore, it would seem that the capacity of NI to accommodate new retail development during this period had been singularly met by the development programme of one retail organisation alone, namely Sainsbury's. The inference here is that the trade captured by all other newcomers must have been diverted from existing businesses. Moreover, with the benefit of hindsight, perusal of the 2001 census results indicates that Planning Service considerably overestimated population growth across NI by approximately 50,000 people. A re-run of the above analysis on the basis of this reduced population growth reveals that the province could only have sustained 5 new superstores as opposed to the 14 that were actually built.

The merits of capacity assessment

Taking into account the above assessment it is clear that, despite being a unitary planning authority and despite having access to centralised regional floorspace figures from the Valuation and Lands Agency (NI), Planning Service declined to undertake a strategic approach to the assessment of retail applications. Instead, each application was treated as locationally unique and was evaluated separately. The only time that a semblance of strategic appraisal featured in the planning process wasat those public inquiries that were jointly held for retail applications located close to one another.

This was most unlike the approach adopted for planning new housing development throughout NI, whereby the allocation of housing in each Local Government District had to conform to Housing Growth Indicators (HGIs) specified in the NI Regional Development Strategy. These HGIs were essentially forecasts of new dwelling numbers required over a given timeframe – typically five year intervals. They were based on a combination of factors including population growth, declining household size, the spatial development strategy of the RDS and the capacity of settlements to accommodate new housing having regard to their infrastructure. While heavily criticised by developers at the time as an unwanted intervention in the market place, compliance with these HGIs actually ensured that NI is not now confronted with the 'Ghost Estates' that plague the Republic of Ireland.

If Planning Service had chosen to strategically evaluate major retail applications at the District level in a similar co-ordinated manner it is possible that this may have helped to prevent the high rate of shop vacancies that currently persist in the town centres of NI. Clearly, such a sweeping assertion ignores the impact of internet shopping and changing shopper trends. Nevertheless, the fact that town centre vacancies in NI are now more than double those in the rest of the UK tends to vindicate the view that little protection was afforded to existing retailers during this period. This failure or refusal of the planning system to strategically assess quantitative retail need for the whole of NI may point to a distinct political reluctance to do so. Perhaps there was too much of a risk that the findings would be interpreted as a quota or constraint on investment.

Nonetheless, it is evident from the worked example that capacity assessment, which forms only one half of retail impact assessment (the other being the estimation of retail impact itself) can make a worthwhile contribution to the evaluation of retail proposals. It can act as a starting point for the detailed consideration of individual proposals, or, at the very least, it can equip planning authorities with basic information that avoids them "*making decisions completely in the dark*" (Jeffreys and Knee, 1962). The fundamentals of the technique are best applied at the regional or subregional level, or, in areas where the catchment population can be estimated with a fair degree of reliability, such as in rural locations. If it is based on comparatively dependable indices, quantitative retail analysis at this level can yield a fairly robust estimation of the capacity of an area to absorb additional shopping facilities. In this respect, it would appear that, despite its mechanistic and deterministic leanings, this mathematical technique of instrumental rationality still has a contribution to make to retail planning in postmodern times. However, its intrinsic value can only be realised if there is a political will to do so.

More than just a numbers game

Certain commentators argue that planning is only a tool, the use of which is determined by the climate of opinion existing at a given time (Schiller, 1985). As occurred in Britain in the boom years of the 1980s, NI experienced a similar change in the climate of control towards new retail investment in the 1990s. This was related to the advent of more peaceful times and improved prospects for economic growth, conditions which engendered a sympathetic response from the planning system to applications for shopping development. In this regard, proposals were adjudged to be economic expressions of the new found peace. Having regard to the push-pull factors ascribed to retail globalisation by Clarke and Rimmer (1997), it is interesting to note that two pieces of opposing retail policy were extremely influential in encouraging retail development in NI at this time – the lenient Planning Policy Statement 5 (PPS 5) titled 'Retailing and Town Centres' (Department of the Environment, 1996c) and the restrictive Planning Policy Guidance Note (PPG 6) in England and Wales (Department of the Environment (England and Wales), 1996).

Cross channel retailers were attracted to NI by the introduction, in 1996, of the investor friendly PPS 5. While the thrust of its policy objectives ostensibly provided for the promotion of town centre retailing it became patently evident during the years following its introduction that disproportionate weight was being attached to the third objective, which placed emphasis on maintaining a competitive and innovative retail sector. At the same time as PPS 5 was in force in NI, restrictions on out of centre retail development in Britain were being strengthened via a revised PPG 6. This amended policy attached increased importance to the identification of a quantitative need for additional retail floorspace. As a measure of its effectiveness, it had the knock on effect of encouraging UK national chains to explore opportunities in other countries, including America and the Far East. In some respects, therefore, the incidence of British chains entering the NI market can be likened to a much earlier episode in the 1970s, when French hypermarkets had cause to expand into Spain in order to escape the restrictive locational policies connected with the Royer Law (Knee and Walters, 1985).

In NI, a parallel can also be drawn between the post-ceasefire era of the 1990s and the period of non-investment in the 1970s, when, as Brown duly noted, applications for retail build were '.... *scrutinised somewhat less carefully*' (Brown, 1984). During these decades, an almost blanket approval rate applied to all new retail applications and the ship of retail planning was steered less by the captains of regulation and more by the stormy seas of change in politics and society. In other words, just as retail proposals were lauded as beacons of economic investment during the tumultuous years of the 1970s, at a time when town centres were directly under attack, the onset of peace in the 1990s equally encouraged planners to be receptive to new investment in order to demonstrate the advantages of political stability. The warm reception given to shopping proposals was also underwritten by a perception among planners that they were only giving the people what they wanted. In other words, they were reacting to the hegemonic force of public choice in demanding such facilities. Gamble's adage of free economy, strong state also rings true for this period, when the cloud of positive political interference from the highest levels seemed to hang over the decision-making machinations of the planning system (Gamble, 1988). Political influence, in this regard, was greatly aided by the direct rule framework in NI and the unique ability it conferred upon ministers to pursue an agenda of extreme neo-liberal economics.

From a much broader perspective, the uneasy relationship between planning and retail development during these years may only be episodic testimony to the impact of macro economic factors. Deference to market forces, as manifested in the globalisation of businesses and deregulation of services, has significantly dampened aspirations to embrace the totalitarianism of strategic retail planning. As a result, planning control in NI during this time operated at a level that was, to borrow Allmendinger's words, '*....ephemeral, contingent, local, immediate and attuned to matters of detail*' (Allmendinger, 2001, p.116). Mindful of the same commentator's views, this is perfectly understandable given that

> "Planning, as a system, set of processes and individuals, is deeply embedded in the power game and is used as a rational barrier behind which political decisions that favour certain powerful interests are made." (Allmendinger *ibid*, p.97)

Indeed, based on the performance of the planning system in NI during this period, planning could be described as a '*post-hoc rationalistic exercise' or 'marginal adjustment mechanism'* (Flyvberg, 1998, pp. 109-112). That is, the planning process only served to validate a predetermined political agenda. Viewed in this light, public inquiries may be construed as little more than cathartic release valves through which to channel and control local opposition rather than as fora for wider public engagement in the decision-making process.

Conclusion

As for the current situation in NI, the Department of the Environment is in the process of strengthening its retail policy via the formulation of its Strategic Planning Policy Statement for NI. In draft form, it proposes a strict application of the town centre first approach to all major retail proposals. This is exactly what happened in England and Wales, when the Government introduced a revised PPG 6 in 1996 in response to out of centre retail developments in the 1980s. However, with an average vacancy rate of 20 per cent in town centres across NI, many local retailers are entitled to feel that the storm has effectively passed and that this tightening of policy has arrived far too late to have any positive effect.

References

Allmendinger, P. (2001) *Planning in Postmodern Times.* London and New York: Routledge, pp.97-116.

Area Plan Research Team (1994) *Craigavon Area Plan 2001. Technical Supplement on Commerce.* Department of Environment (NI): Craigavon Divisional Planning Office.

Boomer, C. (1999) Competitive town centres. *Chairman's opening address, Conference proceedings of the Royal Town Planning Institute, November 11.* Belfast: RTPI.

Brown, S. (1984) *Retail location and Retail Change in Belfast City Centre 1984, Unpublished Ph.D. thesis.* Belfast: Queen's University, p.180.

Clarke, I. and Rimmer, P. (1997) The anatomy of retail internationalisation: Daimaru's decision to invest in Melbourne, Australia. *Services Industries Journal*, 17, pp. 361-82.

Department of the Environment (1996a) *Technical Supplement on Economic & Social Base, Volume 1 of 3, Derry Area Plan 2011.* Londonderry Divisional Planning Office, pp.11-16.

Department of the Environment (1996b) *Technical Supplement on Retailing, Offices, Transport, Tourism and Leisure, Larne Area Draft Plan 2010.* Ballymena: Ballymena Divisional Planning Office, pp.59-63.

Department of the Environment (1996c) *Retailing and Town Centres. Planning Policy Statement 5 [PPS 5].* Belfast: Northern Ireland Planning Service, p.3.

Department of the Environment (England and Wales) (2001) *Town Centres and Retail Developments: Planning Policy Guidance Note 6 [PPG 6].* Revised Version. http://www.planning.odpm.gov.uk/ppg/ppg 6/index.htm.

Department of the Environment (1997) *Carrickfergus Area Draft Plan 2001. Technical Supplement.* Ballymena: Ballymena Divisional Planning Office, pp.40-60.

Department of the Environment (1997) *Carrickfergus Area Draft Plan 2001. Technical Supplement.* Ballymena: Ballymena Divisional Planning Office, pp.40-60.

Department of the Environment (1998) *General Principles. Planning Policy Statement 1 [PPS 1],* Belfast: Northern Ireland Planning Service, p.4.

Department of the Environment (2000) *Mid-year population estimates by Local Government District 1981-1998.* Belfast: Planning Service Headquarters.

Department of the Environment (Northern Ireland) (2001) *Schedule of Major Retail Applications 1973 to date, January edition.* Belfast: Planning Service Headquarters.

Flyvberg, B. (1998) Rationality and Power. Chicago: University of Chicago Press, in Allmendinger, P. (2001) *Planning in Postmodern Times*. London and New York: Routledge, pp.109-112.

Gamble, A. (1988) *The Free Economy and the Strong State.* London: Macmillan, p.8.

Jefferys, J.B. and Knee, D. (1962) *Retailing in Europe: Present Structure & Future Trends,* London: MacMillan and Co Ltd, p.6.

Knee, D. and Walters, D. (1985) *Strategy in Retailing: Theory & Application.* Oxford: Philip Allan Publishers Ltd, p.146.

McGettigan, E. (1999) Retailers Response to the Out-of-town Retailing Challenge, in Competitive town centres: *Conference proceedings of the Royal Town Planning Institute, November 11*. Belfast.

Northern Ireland Statistics and Research Agency (2003) *Northern Ireland Census 2001 Standard Tables.* Belfast: The Stationery Office.

Planning (2001) Retail Projects favour towns. *Journal of the Royal Town Planning Institute*, August 17, p.1.

Planning Appeals Commission (1996) *Report to the Commission of a Public Inquiry into an application for outline planning permission by J Sainsbury PLC at Strand Road, Londonderry, PAC Ref. No. C18/1995*. Belfast: Planning Service Headquarters, pp.215-216.

Planning Appeals Commission (1997) *Report to the Commission of Public Local Inquiry into Tesco Shopping Proposal at Knocknagoney, PAC Ref. No. C24/1995.* Belfast: Planning Service Headquarters, p.242.

Schiller, R. (1985) Land use controls on U.K. shopping centres, in Dawson, J.A. and Lord, D. J. (eds.) (1985) *Shopping Centre Development: Policies & Prospects.* London and Sydney: Croom Helm, p.40.

Slipper, R. (1998) Retailing in the Millennium, *Conference proceedings of Royal Town Planning Institute, August 27.* Glasgow: Strathclyde Graduate Business School .

Unit for Retail Planning Information (1993) *Turnover to Floorspace Ratios of Selected Retail Companies, Information Brief 93/6.* Reading: Unit for Retail Planning Information.

Valuation and Lands Agency and the School of the Built Environment (1997) *Retail Market in Belfast City.* Belfast: Valuation and Lands Agency and University of Ulster.

Chapter 12

Progression in Planning: regression in enforcement?

Stephen McKay

Introduction

The operational planning system has three key components, forward planning, development management (formerly known as development control) and planning enforcement. As all three are mutually reinforcing and interdependent, the consequence of the ineffective application of any strand inevitably undermines the legitimacy of the entire planning system (Millichap, 1998). Unfortunately, it is apparent that this has often been the case with enforcement and it is no surprise that, through time, it has come to be referred to as the Cinderella of planning (Department of the Environment, 1975).

The enforcement system is a failsafe in that its purpose is to bring unauthorised activity under control, remedy undesirable effects of unauthorised development and, where appropriate, take action against those who are in breach of the regulations (Department of the Environment, 2000). The planning enforcement equation is a complex one comprising many strands, all of which are underpinned by the need for provision of a robust legislative framework which can act as a deterrent to those who cause environmental damage. By necessity, however, the remedy to poor levels of regulatory compliance must be coupled with an understanding of the need for synergy between the legal tools and the knowledge, skills and attitudes of those who employ them. Anything less than optimal performance inevitably impacts detrimentally on the efficacy of operational practice.

As the jurisdiction of Northern Ireland progresses towards the transfer of increased planning powers to local authorities, the purpose of this chapter is to investigate not only if the existing legal toolkit is fit for purpose but also whether there are deeper structural issues which require attention. In the first instance, therefore, a review of the evolution of planning enforcement will be conducted. The rationale for this is that lessons from the past may be helpful, firstly, in identifying remedies to deal with contemporary problems and, secondly, the analysis will provide a platform for the scrutiny of operational practice. Issues emerge regarding the efficacy of the system and serious concerns are raised over the ethics and legitimacy of the actions of policymakers and legislators.

The evolution of planning enforcement law

The history of planning law in Northern Ireland reflects developments in other areas of legislation in that, for the most part, it tracks events in England and Wales (Dowling, 1995). In effect, it is imported piecemeal across the Irish Sea at a later date (Hendry, 1989) and although the rationale for this is that transposition can reflect the best aspects of practice, it will become apparent that Northern Ireland has sometimes failed to learn useful lessons from experiences in the neighbouring jurisdictions.

Whilst planning legislation *per se* can be traced from the Housing Town Planning etc Act 1909, the modern planning system evolved after the end of World War II. In this context, the 1947 Town and Country Planning Act established the basis for the contemporary planning system in England and Wales and many of the provisions contained therein form the central plank of the planning enforcement system in the different planning jurisdictions of the United Kingdom today. Before scrutinising the evolution of enforcement it is, however, important to understand the concept of development which is established in law as follows: "The carrying out of building, engineering, mining or other operations in, on, over or under land, or the making of any material change in the use of any buildings or other land" (The Planning Act (Northern Ireland) 2011, Section 23 (1)).

The modern definition is, therefore, clearly divided into two key components, *operational development* and *material change of use*. Importantly, the rationale for this segmentation will become apparent as contentious issues are identified later in the chapter.

Three key principles, in particular, emerged from the 1947 Act, discretion, time limitation and the enforcement notice. With regard to the former, the local planning authority was given licence to serve an enforcement notice wherever a breach of planning control had taken place and it was deemed expedient to do so, having regard to the development plan and any other material considerations or, alternatively, it could let matters rest as they were (Brand, 1988). The decision to take enforcement action was, therefore, a matter at the discretion of the planning authority and there was no criminal liability for a breach of control in the first instance. For the most part this remains the case today. The rationale for this approach was that the margins between lawful and unlawful development were not considered to be sufficiently clear cut to justify grounds for a criminal offence. Specifically, if someone carried out development activity unwittingly it would be unfair if they were convicted and provided with a criminal record. Deeper scrutiny of this matter later will demonstrate that there is limited justification for this affirmation. Secondly, the concept of time limitation, which has subsequently become problematic, was also introduced, whereby the time limit for enforcement action was four years from the date of the breach. Interestingly, however, there was one exception to this which, as will be seen, could provide useful insights for legislators today. In the case of minerals development, the four year period ran from the date of discovery. Thirdly, if the planning authority did decide to serve an enforcement notice the recipient had 3 options. He or she could comply with the notice; apply for retrospective permission; or appeal to the Magistrates Court. If the requirements stipulated by the planning authority were not met, a criminal offence was deemed to have occurred.

A key issue of concern, which resonates with the problems of today, emerged subsequent to the enactment of the 1947 legislation: specifically, difficulties associated with the Magistrates Court. Since the inception of the system two matters in particular have been problematic. Firstly, the technicality and vagaries of planning are such that the Magistrates Court has perennially been considered by many to be an unsuitable arena for dealing with the complexities of planning law. Secondly, the Magistrates Court has frequently been accused of adopting a judicial attitude which is highly protective of private property rights. Evidence to support these criticisms has been periodically presented, yet little action has been taken to remedy the situation (Mc Kay and Ellis, 2005).

The impact of these difficulties has been manifested in enforcement notices being dismissed by the courts on minor technicalities and, even in the event of successful prosecution, low level sanctions imposed which failed to act as a deterrent (Carnwath, 1989; Carnwath *et al*, 1990). Despite landmark case law, for example, Mansi v Elstree UDC (1964) and Miller-Mead Ltd. V Minister of Housing and Local Government (1963) which established precedents for the drafting of enforcement notices and enabling notices with minor defects to be amended (*varied*), the problems continue to permeate the system. With these issues in mind attention turns to evidence emerging through time, lessons learnt and new questions arising.

Lessons for legitimacy?

For the most part, developments in planning enforcement legislation have been systematic and reactionary rather than radical, as evidence of extant failings emerged. Notwithstanding, substantive knowledge has been gleaned which is helpful in terms of crafting remedies for current practice. With this in mind attention turns to three issues which have been constantly in the spotlight, time limitation, criminalisation and the activities of the Magistrates Court.

Time limitation

One of the most important developments in the evolution of enforcement law resulted from cognisance that there was a significant difference between *operational development* and *material change of use* as set out in the Planning Act (Northern Ireland) 2011. As highlighted above, the 1947 legislation provided immunity to *all* development through the four year time limitation regulation. However, it quickly became apparent that there was a need to differentiate between the two forms of development. In the case of operational development the structure is visible and relatively easy to detect but a change of use is notoriously difficult to spot (Humphreys, 2011). Potentially, a use may commence within a structure without being visible but can, by degrees, intensify, or morph into a new use without being detected until such time as it has become immune from enforcement action. In effect, not only were these difficulties the impetus for the current legal definition of development, but the realisation that four years is not enough time to justify immunity for a material change of use. The net effect was to change the limitation period for use.

The current status in the planning jurisdiction of England and Wales is that, whilst the four year rule remains for operational development, there is a ten year rule for material change of use. The only exception to this is for material change of use to a single residential dwelling, where the four year time limitation applies. Interestingly, the same situation prevailed in Northern Ireland until the commencement of the first provisions of the 2011 Act and here it is important to scrutinise the rationale for legislative change.

As part of the programme for the devolved system of local government, new planning legislation is required. In this context, an extensive consultation process took place where questions were asked regarding the content of the new Planning Act. Specifically, what was wrong with the existing system and how might this be remedied (Department of the Environment, 2009). Subsequently, a consultation paper, coupled with responses by the Department to comments received, was published to take forward legislative change. Though the issue of 4 and 10 year rules was raised, no suggestion was made to introduce change. It was, therefore, no surprise that when the Planning Bill 2010, the precursor to the 2011 Act, was published Section 131(1) dealt with time limitation and provided that for operational development the time limitation period for immunity would, as previously, be four years. Similarly, Section 131(3) indicated that, as previously, immunity for material change of use would be 10 years. What followed, however, has been cause for major concern. When the Planning Act (Northern Ireland) 2011 was subsequently published, Section 132 (3) specified that in the case of any material change of use "no enforcement action may be taken after the end of the 5 years beginning with the date of the breach" (page 84). In effect, the four year rule for operational development and the ten year rule for material change of use had been changed to a uniform five year rule for both *operational development* and *material change of use*.

It is a matter of concern that, in the absence of any supporting evidence, this change has been implemented, particularly when post 1947 legislation has continuously seen differentiation between the two classes of development as a necessity. Indeed, all evidence presented since has been to the contrary, with most pointing to a need to expand the 10 year limitation period. Recent work in England by Richard Humphreys QC (2011) has, for example, suggested that the 10 year rule should be doubled to 20 years. The Law Society, however, whilst at variance with this opinion, explained how the difficulties presented by the 10 year rule could be remedied. It suggested that the provisions of the Localism Act 2011 may go some way towards remedying concealment (Law Society, 2011). Section 124 of the Act allows enforcement action to be taken within the 6 months, beginning with the date on which evidence of the apparent breach of planning control came to the authority's knowledge. To understand how this development originated it is important to consider two judgements: firstly, *Robert Fidler v SoSCLG and Reigate and Banstead DC* and, secondly, *Welwyn Hatfield DC v SSCLG and Beesley.*

In both Fiddler and Beesley the defendants had concealed residential buildings, waited until the immunity period expired and then applied for Certificates of Lawful Use. In the case of the former (Fiddler), the defendant built his house beneath a haystack covered by a tarpaulin, without planning permission. Having been refused a Certificate of Lawful Use, the court ordered that the building be demolished because the straw bales and tarpaulin were, in the eyes of the law, necessary parts of the building operation. Importantly, however, the judge ruled that concealment did not in itself provide a legitimate basis for the enforcement to succeed, as something hiding something does not take away the lawful rights that accrue due to the passage of time. This was considered by many to be an unsatisfactory ruling. In the Beesley case, a farm building for agricultural purposes was given consent but was then used purely for residential purposes for a period of in excess of four years. Subsequently, the Beesleys applied for a Certificate of Lawful Use for residential purposes. Again the application was refused and the case went all the way to the Supreme Court which ruled that not to take action against such concealed development would be unthinkable.

> It would damage public confidence in planning legislation and any law abiding citizen would be astonished to suppose that the [owner's] dishonest scheme, once discovered, would not be enforced against, but rather crowned with success, thereby undermining the maxim *volenti non fit injuria* that 'one cannot profit from one's own wrongdoing '(Welwyn Hatfield BC v. Secretary of State for Communities and Local Government & Beesley [2011] 2 WLR 905).

It is significant to note that whilst the remedy implemented was essentially identified back in 1947, when it was applied to mineral development, its wider value was not appreciated for 64 years. Importantly, the evidence from the courts, compounded with the provisions of the Localism Act 2011, demonstrates not only Northern Ireland's failure to learn from good practice but suggests perversity in the adoption of an approach which precipitates the problems which have haunted the system for decades. Time limitation, however, is not the only issue of concern.

Criminalisation

The theme of criminalisation has been revisited on a number of occasions over the last fifty years but on each occasion the decision not to introduce the provision has been dismissed. Whilst initially, the rationale was that unwitting offenders should not be in receipt of a criminal record, the arguments against are more substantive. Before scrutinising the cases for and against, it is important to point out the differences between criminal and non-criminal systems. In the former, the principle of strict liability applies (mala prohibita). For example, if someone breaks the speed limit in a motor vehicle ignorance cannot be used as a defence. However, there is little substance in the argument that in Planning law unwitting offenders would always be convicted of a criminal offence. The key point is that in a criminalised system there remains an element of discretion in that a decision can be made not to take forward a prosecution. Hence, in a criminalised or non-criminalised planning system, if someone committed a minor offence prosecution could be avoided, or, in more serious cases unwitting offenders would be informed of the gravity of their actions and told how to remedy them to avoid prosecution. In many cases, therefore, before prosecution, the offender would be fully cognisant of the offence and would have failed to remedy the situation.

A more substantive problem regarding applying criminalisation to planning would be *the test of evidence.* In a criminalised system the test of evidence is beyond all reasonable doubt, where the burden of proof is placed upon the prosecution to pass this test. In discretionary systems, such as planning, the standard of proof is based upon the balance of probabilities as established in Thrasyvoulou versus Secretary of State for the Environment [1984] and the onus of proof lies with the defendant, as set out in Nelsovil Limited versus the Secretary of State for the Environment [1962]. If planning authorities were faced with this operating framework, it is inevitable that difficulties would emerge. Firstly, as a result of the substantive resources which would be required to prosecute and, secondly, the difficulty of providing the level of proof required. Under the current system, the degree of evidence required to tip the balance in favour of the defendant is much lower than in the criminalised system. As established in Gabbitas versus the Secretary of State for the Environment and Newham Borough Council [1985], evidence should not be disregarded even if it is uncorroborated, especially if it is unchallenged. The key question emerging at this juncture, therefore, is: could criminalisation of the planning system ever be rationally justified?

In pursuit of a potential remedy attention turns to the Republic of Ireland where this is the case. In effect, it is a criminal offence to carry out development without planning permission. Section 151 of the Planning and Development Act 2000 states,

> Any person who has carried out or is carrying out unauthorised development shall be guilty of an offence (The Planning and Development Act 2011, Section 151).

A significant development has, however, been accommodated within the legislation under Section 156(6), which reverses the burden of proof, placing the onus upon the defendant to prove their innocence beyond reasonable doubt. The corollary of this is that it should, in theory, increase pressure on defendants to remedy unauthorised development problems if they believe that they will have to pass such a difficult test. Whilst limited research has been conducted into its effectiveness, there is a rationale for the approach which is perhaps worthy of deeper investigation. However, even if the introduction of such a legislative mechanism has merit, there is little point unless appropriate sanctions are imposed which act as a deterrent to serious offenders. It is with this in mind that attention turns to the final area of investigation, the Magistrates Court.

The Magistrates Court

Perhaps, the area which is most frequently targeted for criticism in discussions of the failings of planning enforcement is the Magistrates Court which normally determines the most appropriate sanction to be applied to convicted offenders. The findings of Rush et al (2012) regarding the imposition of derisory penalties mirrors the findings of Grekos (2008) who found that offenders actually accrue benefit from compliance-deficit. Evidence which resonates with this accrues from the scrutiny of a number of recent cases. Firstly, the unauthorised demolition of Harrymount House which was a listed building in Warringstown. This was successfully prosecuted and a £50,000 fine imposed, the highest ever levied in Northern Ireland. However, on appeal the £15,000 fine imposed on each of the two owners was reduced to £500 and the fine of £20,000 imposed upon the contractor was reduced to the derisory sum of just £100. Secondly, at Piney Ridge which is just off the Malone Road in Belfast the offender was fined £150 and the company of which he was a Director fined £200, again for the unauthorised demolition of a listed building.

One of the most high profile breaches of planning control has been the unauthorised parking of vehicles adjacent to Belfast International Airport (Department of the Environment, 2012). This is a particularly lucrative activity as many air travellers park cheaply at *fly-parking* locations (car parks without planning permission) in close proximity to the airport, from where they are bussed in for their flights and collected upon their return, generally at lower prices than those charged on site at the airport. A fine of £24,000 is the highest to have been imposed on one of the unauthorised enterprises but, on appeal, this was reduced by 50%. A fine of £22,000 was issued to another operator and, whilst at the time of writing there is still an opportunity to appeal, serious concerns have been raised over the sanction. The legislation has provision to award daily fines and fines proportionate to the crime, however the revenue from these activities is so high that these fines are proportionately de minimis and all fly-parking businesses continue to operate, apparently prepared to be taken to court, pay the fine, or in some instances, successfully appeal against the level of sanction imposed.

The key question emerging is, therefore, why are the magistrates failing to impose sanctions which act as deterrents to those who flagrantly flout planning regulations? Perhaps part of the answer is not only that, as highlighted by Dobry (Department of the Environment, 1975) and Carnwath (1989), the judiciary fails to adequately understand the complexities of planning law but are also overly protective of private property rights. In this context, the problem is therefore partly attitudinal. Work by Rush et al (2012) indicated that magistrates deal with many different types of offences and many spend limited time dealing with breaches of planning control. It was suggested that when planning is compared to more serious crime there is the danger that those imposing sanctions across the range of offences may tend to deal more leniently with planning crimes. Whether or not this is the case, the evidence suggests that breaches of planning control have not been subject to serious penalties. However, it is significant to note that in 2012 the Judicial Studies Board issued new planning guidelines which state that the minimum fine for a planning offence should be £5000. This has had immediate impact in that derisory fines, such as those used as exemplars above, have disappeared. Coupled with a high media profile provided to planning crimes led by the then Minister for the Environment, Alex Attwood, it is significant to note there has been a recent trend of much higher level sanctioning than previously. Fines in the range of £20000 are currently not uncommon and, whilst it is premature to make any assessment regarding whether or not this indicates a paradigm shift, it will be interesting to see if a new pattern is emerging in terms of the actions of the judiciary.

Conclusion

The history of enforcement in the planning jurisdictions across the United Kingdom and Ireland provides interesting insights not only into legislative mechanisms which may or may not be effective weapons in the armoury against those who breach planning regulations, but also into the ghosts in the machine (Millichap, 1989) or structural problems that continue to haunt the system.

In terms of the Magistrates Court, concerns were raised over the attitudes of the judiciary, the low levels of sanction imposed and the unsuitable nature of such a court system to deal with the complexity and technicality of planning law, particularly when cases were being dealt with in the same forum as serious non-environmental crime. Whilst studies in the past have highlighted the notion of a dedicated planning circuit court, this has been dismissed, mainly on grounds of cost. Significantly, however, at the time of writing, the Ministry of Justice in England has confirmed its intention to press ahead with criminal justice and court reform. Whilst there is no proposal for a dedicated circuit court, the intention is to create a specialist Planning Court within the High Court to deal with an estimated 400 planning cases, including problems with Nationally Significant Infrastructure Projects. It remains to be seen how this will be legislated for and how effective it will be in dealing with problems of non-compliance.

However, whilst evidence emerging from the courts has motivated legislative change in England regarding time limitation, Northern Ireland has taken little cognisance of lessons learnt. The outcomes of the Fiddler and Beesley cases have been influential in crafting new legislation which connects back to the 1947 Town and Country Planning Act; in that time limitation (albeit for minerals only) should run from the date of discovery. Specifically, section 124 of the Localism Act 2011 for England applies to deliberate cases of concealment of planning breaches. The new legal framework has been designed to tackle blatant violations of planning control where offenders have deliberately hidden development from the planning authorities to take advantage of the time limitation restrictions. The provision gives local authorities the power to apply to the courts for a "planning enforcement order" which gives them the opportunity to take enforcement action even though the usual time limit for enforcement action has expired. The new legal mechanism, therefore, has a definitive resonance with 1947 Act, though this time it applies to all forms of concealed development. In reality, however, this may not necessarily have the desired holistic impact anticipated. The wording of Section 124 is such that it deals only with *concealed forms of development* whereby the court must be satisfied, on the balance of probabilities, that the apparent breach, or any of the matters constituting the apparent breach, has (to any extent) been deliberately concealed. Hence, the legal provisions only relate to concealed development. In effect, this begs the question whether all forms of unauthorised material change of use take place through concealment? If not, then it is unlikely to satisfactorily address the perennial problems created by material change of use. In this context, therefore, perhaps there is merit in re-considering the findings of Department for Communities and Local Government (2006) and Humphreys (2011) and expanding the time limitation period from ten to fifteen or even twenty years.

However, perhaps the area of most serious concern relates to the ethics of the processes underpinning legislative development. Law making and policy development must be informed by a robust evidence base coupled with expansive consultation, otherwise questions emerge over legitimacy. Where there is a disconnect between the evidence base and the legislative mechanisms introduced there should, at the very least, be a transparent explanation for the rationale, albeit implementation of the precautionary principle. Veracity on the part of decision makers is imperative in instilling public confidence and, unfortunately, questions remain unanswered. In Northern Ireland, it is more important than ever that lessons from the past are learnt, not only in terms of planning enforcement but at the wider political level.

References

Brand, C.M. (1988) *Enforcement of planning control.* London: Longman.

Carnwath, R.(1989) *Enforcing planning control.* London: HMSO.

Carnwath, R. Hart, G. and Williams, A.(1990) *Blundell and Dobry's Planning Appeals and Inquiries*, 4th edition. London: Sweet and Maxwell.

Department for Communities and Local Government (2006) *Review of planning enforcement in England.* Wetherby: DCLG Publications.

Department of the Environment (1975) *Investigation into Planning Enforcement, The Dobry Report.* HMSO: London.

Department of the Environment (2000) *Planning Policy Statement 9: The Enforcement of Planning Control.* Belfast: DoE.

Department of the Environment (2009) *Reform of the Planning System in NI: Your Chance to Influence Change.* Belfast: DoE

Department of the Environment (2012), www.planningni.gov.uk

Dowling, A. (1995) *Northern Ireland Planning Law.* Dublin: Gill & Macmillan Ltd.

Grekos, M. (2008) Review of civil and administrative penalties for environmental offences: background and development update paper. London: Sweet and Maxwell.

Hendry, J. (1989) *The Development of Planning in Northern Ireland.* Belfast: Queen's University.

Humphreys, R. (2011) *20 years of the ten year period for enforcement: time for reform.* JPL 5, pp. 522-523.

Law Society (2011) *The ten year period for enforcement: is it really time for reform?* London: Law Society.

McKay, S. and Ellis, G. (2005) Reparation or retribution: an investigation into regulatory compliance in planning, *Environment and Planning A.* 37 (7), pp. 1249-1262.

Millichap, D. (1998) *Planning Ghosts - Past, Present and Future.* London: Linklaters.

Table of statutes

The Housing Town Planning etc. Act 1909.

The Localism Act 2011.

The Planning Act (Northern Ireland) 2011.

The Planning and Development Act 2011.

The Town and Country Planning Act 1947.

Table of cases

Gabbitas v the Secretary of State for the Environment and Newham Borough Council [1985].

Robert Fidler v SoS CLG and Reigate and Banstead DC [2004].

Mansi v Elstree RDC 16 Property & Compensation Report [1964] 153.

Miller-Mead Ltd. v Minister of Housing and Local Government [1963] 1 All England Reports 459, 473.

Nelsovil Limited v the Secretary of State for the Environment [1962].

Thrasyvoulou v Secretary of State for the Environment [1984].

Welwyn Hatfield BC v. Secretary of State for Communities and Local Government & Beesley [2011] 2 WLR 905.

Chapter 13

The walkability of Belfast

**Geraint Ellis, Michael Donnelly, Luke Kelleher,
Ruth Hunter, Mark A Tully and Frank Kee.**

Introduction

Although once the backbone of the science and art of planning, architect-planners such as Malachy McEldowney have gradually become a valuable rare breed in many UK planning schools having been crowded out by the more social science orientated geographer-planners, who themselves are now making room for a whole new range of specialists in related disciplines, including those from sociology, ecology, economics and even health, brought into the fold through the broad idea of 'spatial planning'. The different bedfellows that are now typically found in academic planning departments (like at Queen's University Belfast) illustrate, quite neatly some of the main phases of planning education seen in the UK over the last 30 years (Frank *et al*, 2014) and help explain the differentiated character of different planning schools.

The perspectives of planning offered by architecture, geography and a range of other disciplines, such as community and public health, have much to offer how we think about cities, but if we have to characterise Malachy's work, we hope he would agree that he perhaps represented the 'beautification' strand more than the others, with his interest in urban design, conservation, shared space and identity (for example Gaffikin *et al.*, 2010, Galway and McEldowney, 2006). For this reason, this chapter will focus on the idea of 'walkability' as one of the current concepts that is driving how we think about how people can better relate to the built urban form, and it will briefly discuss how this can be applied to the city in which Malachy has done much of his work, Belfast. There is also a typological neatness with this choice as 'walkability' intersects not only the urban design/beautification tradition of planning but draws on geographical analysis in assessing the walkability of environments with the aim of making urban areas more conducive to physical activity, thus reflecting a key concern of the healthy urban planning movement. It is, therefore, a topic that perhaps has relevance to three main traditions of planning that have been most dominant through Malachy's career: urban design/beautification; spatial analysis and resource management, including a systems approach; and social equity and community focussed benefits. The added bonus here is that it also includes a strong emphasis on land use-transport interactions, which is another area in which Malachy has published (McEldowney *et al.*, 2003, 2005). In this brief chapter we will, therefore, introduce the concept of walkability, explain the insights it can deliver for planners and then discuss what Belfast looks like when taking a 'walkability' perspective.

The walkability of cities

The idea of human-scale urban design that promotes personal interaction, land use diversity and neighbourhood coherence has a strong presence in many of the historical influences on town planning including the Garden City Movement, Radburn Principles, the writings of Jane Jacobs and New Urbanism, to name just a few (Moudon *et al*, 2006). In recent years specific concerns regarding peak oil and climate change, the need for more sustainable urban forms and the obesity crisis have brought this into sharper focus, with a renewed emphasis on the need to shape our cities around the opportunities for active travel – using cycling and walking as the dominant intra-urban modes, supplemented by public transport for longer journeys. This is supported by well-established and relatively simple principles of building cities where land use and transport are tightly coordinated, neighbourhoods are well connected, ample local amenities, safe streets and a hierarchy of road users that promotes walking while discouraging single occupant car use. Yet we know that while rhetorically supporting these principles, it is rare to find a planning arena (or at least in the UK and Ireland) that has managed to implement this as standard. Indeed dominant lifestyles and cultural preferences, timid or short-sighted policies and vested interests all tend to work against these objectives. Although there are many examples of European cities – and the odd municipal leader - that have led determined and inspirational campaigns to address these issues head on, including in Copenhagen, Freiburg or Groningen and some UK cities heading in the right direction (such as Bristol and London), the default path has been to offer some supportive environmental and infrastructure investment (bike lanes, the odd greenway), but leave the core fundamental planning principles untouched. As such, the long term factors that reproduce car use as an attractive modal choice are often left in place. Belfast is a very good example of this, with some of Malachy's co-authors highlighting its problems as "the UK's most car dependent city" (Cooper *et al*, 2001). Key factors here are its relatively low density[1], a limited and expensive public transport system, a historic and ongoing bias in expenditure in favour of motorised transport, continued development of out of town services and a reluctance to shape the greater regional settlement pattern in a way that could support transit-orientated development (e.g. Dittmar and Ohland, 2004).

There are of course, many ways to think about these problems, but in recent years the concept of 'walkability' has been particularly on the rise. This can be defined as "the extent to which the built environment supports and encourages walking by providing for pedestrian comfort and safety, connecting people with varied destinations within a reasonable amount of time and effort and offering visual interest in journeys throughout the network" (Southworth, 2005, p.248). The growing popularity of the idea has been linked to its ability to offer an overall concept that can contribute to a number of pressing urban and social problems. Indeed, walkability has been linked to benefits for local urban economies (Litman, 2003), air quality (Marshall *et al*, 2009), social inclusion (Boyce, 2010) and particularly levels of physical activity (Kligerman *et al.*, 2007; Saelens *et al.*, 2003a; Van Dyck *et al.*, 2010). Although they are all long standing objectives of more progressive forms of urbanism, they have gained added momentum in recent years by being able to become united under the umbrella of the Healthy Urban Planning movement (Barton, 2001).

Owen *et al.* (2004) highlight that walking is the most common form of physical activity and Ogilvie *et al.* (2007) describe it as "near perfect exercise" (p.1204) because it is popular, convenient, free and carbon neutral. The benefits of walking have been noted as including a reduced likelihood of coronary heart disease, improvements in cholesterol profile, control of hypertension, a slowing of osteoporosis, improved body strength and rehabilitation after illness (Rippe *et al.*, 1988; Morris *et al.,* 1997). There are firm grounds, therefore, to suggest that a better understanding of the way in which the built environment facilitates walking could result in wider health benefits. As a consequence, there has been a mushrooming of studies examining the relative influence of social factors, the physical environment and policies on physical activity (estimated at over 200 studies in the last decade by Bull *et al.*, 2010). This body of research strongly suggests that certain features of the built environment can encourage (or discourage) levels of physical activity (Owens *et al.*, 2004). There are a number of papers that have reviewed the specific environmental influences on walking (e.g. Owen *et al.*, 2004; Sallis *et al.*, 2009; Saelens *et al.*, 2003b). Although these studies are largely based on cross sectional observations rather those using longitudinal observations or intervention studies, there is a strong emerging consensus that the two key concepts in the walkability of the built environment are:

- *Proximity* – i.e. origins and destinations of journeys being within walking distance for different demographic groups. This includes the provision of local services (retail, public transport, health facilities, green space, etc), mixed land use and generally higher levels of residential density.

- *Connectivity* – i.e the ability to make pedestrian journeys directly and with ample route choices – essentially this is about an increased density of footpaths and a reduction in the barriers to walking such as major roads, railways, large street blocks, etc.

These are reflected in specific features of the built environment and those that are likely to have the greatest impact on physical activity appear to be (from Southworth, 2005, p.249):

- connectivity of a network of footpaths;
- linkage with public transport;
- fine grained mix of land uses, especially those supporting local services;
- safety (from crime and road accidents);
- environmental quality of the paths;
- path context within the broader urban design, such as visual interest and street design.

Indeed, a number of studies have shown that those living in areas that we would regard as being "more walkable" actually have higher levels of physical activity – for example, Saelens *et al.* (2003a) found that those living in "high walkable areas" had 70 more minutes of physical activity than those living in "low walkable areas" and had lower obesity prevalence (adjusted for individual demographics). Similarly Frank *et al.* (2005) found that while 37% of residents of 'high walkable' areas in Atlanta met physical activity guidelines, this was only 18% in 'low walkable' areas. Clearly, the relationship between individual physical activity and the built environment is not simple with a high degree of variance between actual types of physical activity, temporal variations and differential impacts according to age and other demographic categories (Bull *et al.*, 2010). Grappling with these issues has involved a range of research disciplines, each offering its own distinct contribution (Sallis, 2009). Of particular interest here is the contribution of the planning profession, which Sallis identifies as centring on the spatial analysis of land use and other influences, which thus points to the deployment of the concept of 'walkability'.

Measuring walkability

A further benefit of "walkability" is that it is capable of direct measurement through the development of a number of assessment tools that have helped to add rigour into the evaluation of urban areas and led to effective indicators that can be used in planning practice. A useful overview of these tools have been provided by Brownson *et al.* (2009), who suggest that these can be categorised into three broad approaches. The first are "perceived environment measures"; essentially self-reported "subjective" data on individuals' perceptions of the environment, stated preference techniques and mobile methods that capture the mobile experience as pedestrians use the environment. Brownson *et al.* report on more than 100 such studies from which there appeared to be positive associations between physical activity and perceptions of the presence of local services, pavements, shops, recreational facilities and road safety. The type of walkability assessment is based on "observational measures", essentially protocols for undertaking audits of actual physical environments (e.g. such as NEWS, Cerin *et al.*, 2006) which record environmental features that are assumed to influence physical activity, such as quality of pavements, street activity etc. The third category are those derived from spatial analysis of the built environment using Geographic Information Systems (GIS) – these generally deploy existing data sources to produce "objective" assessments of what can be large geographic areas. The forms of analysis used in this last category will vary according to the research question being pursued and the data that is available, but often incorporate issues includes population density, land use mix, network characteristics (roads and/or footpaths), distribution for services etc. The application of GIS has a range of benefits that include:

- rapid development of assessments of the built environment, with minimal original survey work;
- the prevalence and consistency of GIS data allow for analysis and comparability of most urban areas;
- the analytical power of GIS allows a variety of spatial data (including health, movement patterns, physical features etc.) to be combined at different geographic scales allowing a relatively rapid testing of causal relationships;
- the fact that much GIS analysis is capable of being undertaken as a desk top analysis, using technology and skills present in most municipal authorities, it also has substantial potential to be integrated as a policy tool into decision-making over land use, health interventions and transport infrastructure.
- GIS has also been used as the basis of combining the multiple indicators that encapsulate the complexities of environment-behaviour relationships to provide a single walkability index (Frank *et al.*, 2010), which again may be conducive to being used in decision-making;
- it has been noted suggested that 'objective' measures, such as GIS measures have stronger associations with walking for health when compared to 'subjective' (i.e. self-reported) measures (Lin and Moudon, 2010).

These advantages have led to the development and adoption of a recognised "Walkability Index" (Leslie *et al.*, 2007; Frank *et al.*, 2009; IPEN[2]), using the following parameters:

1. residential density;
2. a retail floor area ratio, representing the retail building floor area divided by the retail land site area;
3. land use mix, based on five categories (residential, retail, entertainment, office and institutional) and calculated using an entropy equation;
4. street connectivity, using intersection density based on road centre lines calculated as the ratio between the number of road intersections of three of more legs and the land area.

These are brought together in the following formula to give the Walkability Index:
Walkability = [(2xz-intersection density)+(z-net residential density)+(z-retail floor area ration)+(z-land use mix).

An accurate Walkability Index can provide a useful and relatively rapid assessment of the structure of cities, giving important insights into how different parts of an urban area have evolved, where specific interventions may usefully be targeted to enhance opportunities for active travel and, because of its GIS basis, can be cross tabulated with a whole range of other spatial and socio-economic data to show how the physical features of the city may interact with other aspects of urban life. The Walkability Index therefore has potential value as a tool for guiding policy and practice and has led to a range of useful insights in research, particularly in the field of assessing the influence of the built environment on levels of obesity and the impact of specific environmental interventions on physical activity behaviour. It is in this context that the walkability of Belfast has begun to be explored, as described.

Walkability of Belfast

The walkability assessment of Belfast has emerged from a joint research between the School of Planning, Architecture and Civil Engineering and the UKCRC Centre for Excellence for Public Health, at Queen's University, Belfast. The Physical Activity and the Rejuvenation of Connswater (PARC) Study (Tully *et al.*, 2013) is evaluating the public health impact of the Connswater Community Greenway (CCG), a major urban regeneration project in Belfast. The aim of the CCG is to offer enhanced opportunities for physical activity and outdoor recreation through specific environmental improvements including the construction of 19.4 km of new cycle and walkways and the provision of recreational facilities and allotments. One element of the PARC study seeks to evaluate the influence of the built environment on the health of local residents before and after the construction of the Greenway. In order to ascertain this, a baseline study was undertaken of the environmental features in the area including administrative boundaries, topography, transport features, residential addresses, postcode centroids etc. This also included mapping the complete footpath network for the area surrounding the new Greenway. Given that no network data is collected on footpaths in Northern Ireland (unlike, for example other parts of the UK[3]) this had to be mapped afresh, using the existing map base provided under a research agreement by the Land and Property Services of Northern Ireland[4] cross-checked against aerial photographs, other online sources and field visits. This provided a useful resource for both research and policy development, through which a number of local agencies became interested in extending the analysis to a city wide level. Funding for this was secured through the Knowledge Exchange Programme of the Economic and Social Research Council, and part funded by Belfast City Council, Derry-Londonderry City Council, Department for Regional Development, Department of Health and Social Services, Public Health Agency and Belfast Healthy Cities. See for example the work undertaken as part of the KESUE project: http://www.qub.ac.uk/research-centres/KnowledgeExchangeSpatialAnalysisandHealthyUrbanEnvironments/. The network is now a publicly available resource, hosted by Spatial NI (https://www.spatialni.gov.uk/).

Our Real Walkable Network ("RWN", as we have called it) is 761km in length with over 30,000 elements across Belfast, with a detail of the network shown in Figure 13.1 (Ellis *et al.*, unpublished). The value of using such 'non-motorised networks' (Tal and Handy, 2012) is significant, yet largely unexplored (Chin *et al.,* 2008) particularly when we consider the immense effort and cost taken to develop accurate traffic and public transport models. For example, it can be used to model key pedestrian barriers at a very local scale, identify precise footpath hinterlands to public facilities (i.e.'pedsheds') and using its broader potential for spatial analysis, can be used to understand the inter-relationships of a wide range of socio-demographic data with built environment effects. Indeed, once established, this network can be used as a valuable tool for a wide range of planning initiatives and decision-making processes.

Figure 13.1 The Real Walkable Network with detail showing arrangement for nodes at road crossings

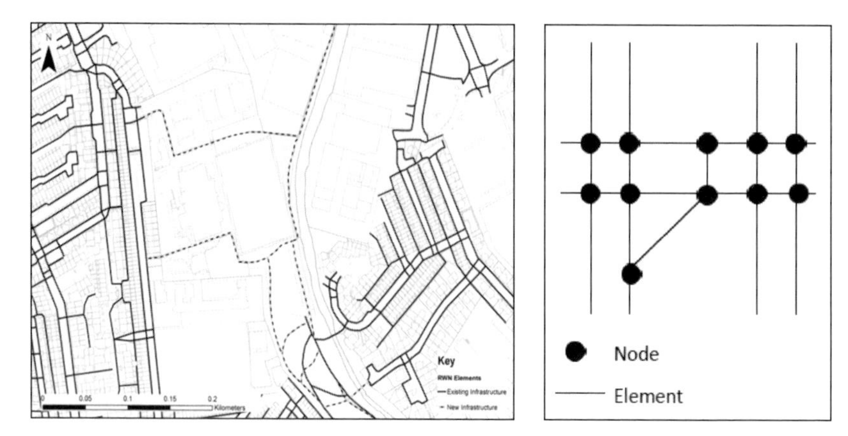

There is not space here for an extended discussion of the types of analysis that can be facilitated by this tool – such as service area mapping of health facilities, parks and the impact of slope or poor lighting on these – but we did want to very briefly indicate a city wide analysis that has been undertaken to identify the variations across Belfast of the Walkability Index, as described above. This can be computed for any geographic area for which there is availability of the component data elements – wards, postcodes, etc. In this case we have used the small area units introduced in the 2011 census. The results of this are shown in Figure 13.2, with the top and bottom scoring deciles shown in Table 13.1. This data is capable of detailed analysis, particularly if combined with broader socio-economic data or that related to deprivation, travel behaviour or the health profiles of different parts of the city. For this brief chapter, however, comments will be reserved for broad issues related to the overall structure of the city and the role of planning in reproducing the built environment over the last 60 years.

Table 13.1 Highest and lowest scoring small areas based on Walkability Index of Belfast

Woodstock_2	Upper Springfield_1
Windsor_3	Sydenham_1
Woodstock_3	Glencolin_1
New Lodge_3	Finaghy_2
Upper Malone_2	Belmont_1
Glencolin_4	Legoniel_1
Crumlin_1_Belfast	Highfield_1
Ballymacarrett_2	Stormont_2
The Mount_1	Bellevue_1
Ballymacarrett_3	Cavehill_2
The Mount_2	Finaghy_1
Botanic_4	Cherryvalley_1
Beechmount_2	Stormont_1
Ballynafeigh_3	Stranmillis_1
Woodstock_1	Cavehill_3

Figure 13.2 Walkability Index for Belfast based on the small area units of the 2011 census

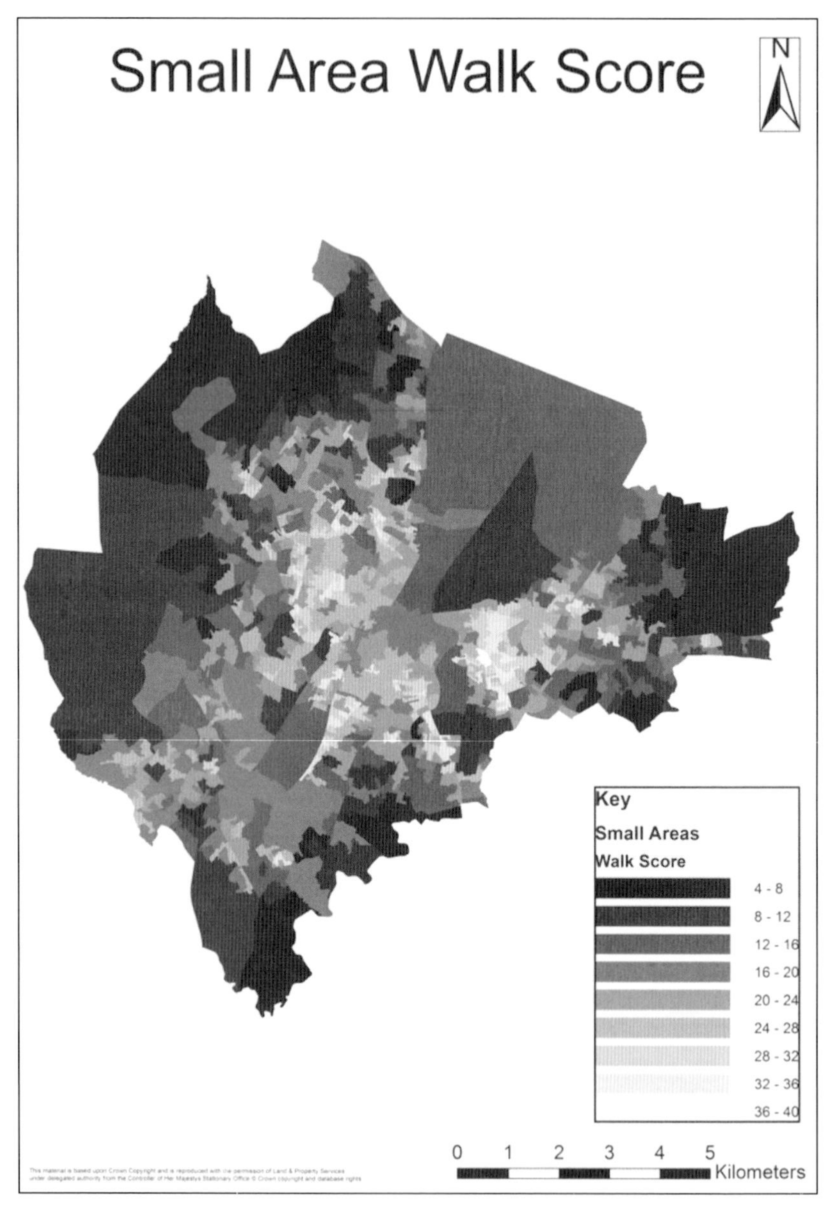

The most striking feature is that the lowest walkability scores are found in the most peripheral parts of the city. One would of course expect this as density declines in accordance with the urban bid rent curve and with it density and the provision of local services (and hence land use diversity declines). This also clearly reflects the topography of Belfast, with those areas constituting the hills around the City – beyond the former Matthew Stop Line – where only scattered housing exists, clearly having low walkability. The map also highlights those parts of the city which do host high levels of activity, yet where this is either relatively homogenous and / or results in low population density – hence relatively low walkability scores around the industrial areas of the docks and the commercial area of the Boucher Road and its surrounding industrial area.

The map does, however, show some more surprising outcomes which can be taken as a useful commentary on how the city has been developed and planned over the last century. Most clearly, one can see that, unlike many other European cities, the commercial centre of Belfast results in a low walkability score. This is derived from the segregation of the city centre during the Troubles and the low level of land use mix, particularly very low levels of housing in the central area. This has been previously recognised, although more recent efforts to lure a greater level of housing into the city centre is still struggling and recent rezoning of the few designated sites for social housing has further undermined this strategy.

One of the most distinctive patterns from this analysis, however, is a distinctive ring of walkable neighbourhoods around the city centre. These generally represent the formal villages around which the city has grown, and which retain a cluster of local services and shopping facilities. Areas such as Sandy Row, Ballyhackamore and Stranmillis fall into this category and achieve high scores on the Walkability Index due to the high density, land use mix and a street pattern - often short blocks of terraced housing, or redeveloped at similar densities and offering relatively good permeability. The development of these areas also tended to coincide with the golden age of Victorian philanthropy, so generally they are well provided for with formal open space and other common facilities. Notwithstanding that many of these areas suffer from some of the deepest levels of deprivation, the general urban form does at least offer a core framework for the development of healthy urban neighbourhoods, with the support of well-conceived urban regeneration initiatives, such as the Connswater Community Greenway.

A further observation from this analysis is what appears to be a failure of post war planning to deliver walkable environments. This is most distinctive when looking at the areas dominated by the big public sector housing schemes in West Belfast – such as Poleglass – or the big private sector suburban extensions such as Cairnshill. While these may have provided a valuable increase in the number of homes available within the urban area, the dominant planning ethic at the time, characterised by cul-de-sacs and poor provision of local services has built in a car dependency - and a tendency to lower levels of physical activity – that will continue to serve local residents poorly. Clearly the Walkability Index is not the only indicator of the quality of urban life, but this does beg the question of how well we have equipped the city and its residents to cope with future challenges.

Conclusion

This brief discussion has reviewed the idea of walkability as a way of understanding how features of the built environment combine to make an area more conducive for active lifestyles as part of a resilient approach to tackling the challenges of obesity, climate change and peak oil. The tools used to assess urban areas for these types of attributes can give a quick overview of a city and begin a process of understanding how the inherited urban fabric can lock in the challenges to improving well-being and sustainability. This represents a big challenge for us as planners - from each of the discipline's traditions – and helps us reflect on the dis-benefits of past planning approaches. Above all it also suggests that with the combined skills of urban design, spatial analysis and community development, planning can become more then simple land use regulation, but offer real benefits to society.

Endnotes

1 For example Belfast has 25.7 residents per hectare, low compared to other UK cities Glasgow (33.9), Manchester (43.5), London (52.0) and on a global scale, Hong Kong (367).

2 http://www.ipenproject.org/methods_gis.html#Measures

3 See for example, the Ordnance Survey's Urban Path Theme, http://www.ordnancesurvey.co.uk/oswebsite/products/os-mastermap/itn-layer/urban-paths.html

4 See http://www.dfpni.gov.uk/lps/index/gi.htm

References

Barton, H. (2001) *Healthy Urban Planning*. London: Routledge.

Boyce, C. (2010) Walkability, social inclusion and social isolation and street redesign, *Built Environment*, 36(4), pp. 461-473.

Brownson, R.C, Hoehner, C. M., Day, K., Forsyth, A., and Sallis, J. F. (2009) Measuring the Built Environment for Physical Activity: State of the Science, *American Journal of Preventative Medicine*, 36 (4S), pp. S99-S123.

Bull, F., Giles-Corti, B. and Wood, L. (2010) Active landscapes: the methodological challenges in developing the evidence on urban environmental and physical activity, in Ward Thompson, C, Aspinall, P and Bell, S. (Eds.) *Innovative approaches to researching landscape and health*. London: Routledge. pp. 96-116.

Cerin, E., Saelens, B.E., Sallis, J.F. and Frank, L.D. (2006) Neighbourhood Environment Walkability Scale: validity and development of a short form, *Medicine and Science in Sports and Exercise,* 38(9), pp. 1682-1691.

Chin, G.K.W., Van Niel, K.P., Giles-Corti, B., and Knuiman, M. (2008) Accessibility and connectivity in physical activity studies: The impact of missing pedestrian data, *Preventive Medicine*. 46(1), pp. 41-45.

Cooper, J., Ryley, T., and Smyth, A. (2001) Contemporary lifestyles and the implications for sustainable development policy: lessons from the UK's most car dependent city - Belfast, *Cities*, 18(2), pp. 103-113.

Dittmar, H., and Ohland, G. (Eds.) (2004) *The new transit town: best practices in transit-oriented development*. Connecticut: Island Press.

Ellis, G., Hunter, R., Tully, M., Donnelly, Kelleher, L., and Kee, F. (In press) Connectivity and Physical Activity: Using Footpath Networks to Measure the Walkability of Built Environments, *Environment and Planning B.*

Frank L.D., Schmid T.L., Sallis J.F., Chapman J., and Saelens B.E. (2005) Linking objectively measured physical activity with objectively measured urban form. Findings from SMARTRAQ, *American Journal of Preventive Medicine*, 28(2S2), pp. 117-125.

Frank, A. I., Mironowicz, I., Lourenço, J., Franchini, T., Ache, P., Finka, M. and Grams, A. (2014) Educating planners in Europe: A review of 21st century study programmes, *Progress in Planning*, 91, pp. 30-94.

Frank, L. D., Sallis, J. F., Conway, T. L., Chapman, J. E., Saelens, B. E., and Bachman, W. (2006) Many pathways from land use to health: associations between neighborhood walkability and active transportation, body mass index, and air quality, *Journal of the American Planning Association, 72*(1), pp. 75-87.

Frank, L. D., Sallis, J. F., Saelens, B. E., Leary, L., Cain, K., Conway, T. L., and Hess, P. M. (2010) The development of a walkability index: application to the Neighborhood Quality of Life Study, *British Journal of Sports Medicine*, 44(13), pp. 924-933.

Gaffikin, F., McEldowney, M., and Sterrett, K. (2010) Creating shared public space in the contested city: the role of urban design, *Journal of Urban Design*, 15(4), pp. 493-513.

Galway, N., and McEldowney, M. (2006) Place and special places: innovations in conservation practice in Northern Ireland, *Planning Theory and Practice*, 7(4), 397-420.

Kligerman, M., Sallis, J. F., Ryan, S., Frank, L. D., and Nader, P. R. (2007). Association of neighbourhood design and recreation environment variables with physical activity and body mass index in adolescents, *American Journal of Health Promotion*, 21(4), pp. 274-277.

Leslie, E., Coffee, N., Frank, L., Owen, N., Bauman, A., and Hugo, G. (2007) Walkability of local communities: using geographic information systems to objectively assess relevant environmental attributes, *Health and Place*, 13(1), pp. 111-122.

Lin, L. and Moudon, A.V. (2010) Objective versus subjective measures of the built environment, which are most effective in capturing associations with walking? *Health and Place*, 16, pp. 339-348.

Litman, T. A. (2003) Economic value of walkability, *Transportation Research Record: Journal of the Transportation Research Board*, 1828 (1), pp. 3-11.

Marshall, J. D., Brauer, M., and Frank, L. D. (2009) Healthy neighbourhoods: walkability and air pollution, *Environmental Health Perspectives*, 117(11), pp. 1752-9.

McEldowney, M., Ryley, T., Scott, M., and Smyth, A. (2005) Integrating land-use planning and transportation in Belfast: a new policy agenda for sustainable development? *Journal of Environmental Planning and management*, 48(4), pp. 507-526.

McEldowney, M., Scott, M., and Smyth, A. (2003) Integrating land-use planning and transportation-policy formulation in the Belfast metropolitan area, *Irish Geography*, 36(2), pp. 112-126.

Morris, J. and Hardman, A. (1997) Walking to health, *Sports Medicine*, 25 (3), pp.303-332.

Moudon, A. V., Lee, C., Cheadle, A. D., Garvin, C., Johnson, D., Schmid, T. L. and Lin, L. (2006) Operational definitions of walkable neighborhood: theoretical and empirical insights, *Journal of Physical Activity & Health,* 3, pp. S99-S117.

Ogilvie, D., Foster, C., Rothnie, H., Cavill, N., Hamilton, Val, Fitzsimons, C. and Mutrie, N. (2007) Interventions to promote walking; systematic review, *British Medical Journal*, 334 (7605), pp 1204- 1214.

Owen, N., Humpel, N., Leslie, E., Bauman, A., and Sallis, J. F. (2004). Understanding environmental influences on walking: review and research agenda, *American Journal of Preventive Medicine*, *27*(1), pp. 67-76..

Rippe, J.M. Ward, A, Porcari, J.P. and Freedson, P.S. (1988) Walking for Health and Fitness, *Journal of the American Medical Association,* 259 (18), pp.2720-2724.

Saelens, B. E., Sallis, J. F., Black, J. B., and Chen, D. (2003a). Neighbourhood-based differences in physical activity: an environment scale evaluation, *American Journal of Public Health*, *93*(9), pp. 1552-1558.

Saelens, B.E., Sallis, J.F. and Frank, L.D. (2003b) Environmental Correlates of Walking and Cycling: Findings From the Transportation, Urban Design, and Planning Literatures, *Annals of Behavioural Medicine*, 25 (2), pp.80-91.

Sallis, J. F., Bowles, H. R., Bauman, A., Ainsworth, B. E., Bull, F. C., Craig, C. L., and Bergman, P. (2009) Neighbourhood Environments and physical activity amongst adults in 11 countries, *American Journal of Preventive Medicine*, 36 (6), pp. 484-490.

Southworth, M. (2005) Designing the Walkable City, *Journal of Urban Planning and Development.* 131 (4), pp. 246 – 257.

Tal, G., and Handy, S. (2012) Measuring non-motorized accessibility and connectivity in a robust pedestrian network, *Transportation Research Record: Journal of the Transportation Research Board.* 2299(1), pp. 48-56.

Tully, M.A., Hunter, R.F., McAneney, H., Cupples, M.E, Donnelly, M., Ellis, G, Hutchinson, G, Prior, L, Stevenson, M, Kee, F (2013) Physical Activity and the Rejuvenation of Connswater (PARC study): protocol for a natural experiment investigating the impact of urban regeneration on public health, *BMC Public Health*, 13(1) pp. 1-9.

Van Dyck, D., Cardon, G., Deforche, B., Sallis, J. F., Owen, N., and De Bourdeaudhuij, I. (2010) Neighborhood SES and walkability are related to physical activity behaviour in Belgian adults, *Preventive Medicine*, 50, pp. S74-S79.

Chapter 14

City centre sidewalks: improving pedestrian experience through design

Urmi Sengupta

Introduction

"Sidewalks, their bordering uses, and their users, are active participants in the drama of civilization" (Jacobs, 1961, pp. 29 – 30).

Our understanding of sidewalks, pedestrian routes and public space has evolved rather slowly in recent decades. Theories of Lefebvre and Habermas have proved to be important milestones in urban design history and have altered how we view public space – to realise that space is not simply a container for action. Works by Kevin Lynch and Jane Jacobs emphasised that the urban environment shapes our behaviour, and our behaviour in turn determines the characteristics and disposition of public space. Jacob's (1961) postulation that streets are lively spaces gained prominence in the mindset of planners around the world. However, it remained a discussion within the exclusive domain of residential suburbs. Historically, the literature on public space has commanded less profile in urban design theory (Cuthbert, 2011). Loukaitou-Sideris and Ehrenfeucht (2009) attribute this relative lack of scholarly work on sidewalks to the perception that they are an undifferentiated part of the street. The sidewalk as a variant of public space has been a neglected element in urban design as opposed to urban squares, parks, streets and even underground spaces.

In the last decade or so, increased emphasis on sustainability and climate change has helped to promote the concept of walkable cities and to bring the city centre environment back into focus. A flurry of research in recent years (Ewing and Handy, 2009; Adkins et al, 2012; Lee and Talen, 2014) has been directed to defining walkability as the first step towards understanding how to plan for sidewalks and improve the pedestrian experience. Traditionally, sidewalks have been perceived as merely being pedestrian channels subjected to poor design, with improvements limited to changing their physical appearance (new paving, lighting, planters and street furniture). The interrelationship between the uses and physical features of the sidewalks and underlying aesthetics, user psychology and the inherent quality of the space, that is continually evolving, is not factored in. Cuthbert (2011) argues that public spaces are assumed rather than analysed and architectural design has clearly proceeded without appropriate knowledge. Sidewalks continue to suffer from large block sizes that are too large to permit a range of route choices; from land use patterns that are coarse with activities widely spaced and segregated by type; from over-scaled streets that dominate sidewalks; and from public officials who like to see them removed in order to reduce construction and maintenance costs. Rather than taking social production into account, sidewalks are viewed as an object of planning.

This chapter provides a critical overview on the apparent 'amnesia' in urban design and planning theory and discusses broader changes that are redefining and reshaping sidewalks and the associated urbanism. Fundamentally, the narrative aims to put sidewalks back into the context of urban design in order to truly understand it. Using a detailed case study of a popular city centre sidewalk in Belfast, the chapter argues that an urban design approach enables an effective examination of the underlying cultural change in attitudes toward walkability, aestheticism and the design of sidewalks.

Broader concepts - evolving approach

In the 1960s and 1970s planners and social geographers pursued sidewalk design with great enthusiasm though often confusing sidewalks with other types of public space. It was not until the 1990s that sidewalks became an important element of city centre urbanism. The resurgence of interest in sidewalks can be attributed partly to broader forces of city planning and design. The concept of sustainability and issues around climate change stimulated a global awareness of compact urban form and the promotion of walking in conjunction with a reduction in car use. Studies (see Kenworthy and Newman, 1989) showing a strong inverse relationship between high-density and high fuel consumption have helped build arguments that compact urban form allows users to walk more and creates healthy cities. A similar message was relayed by government-sponsored studies such as Ecotec (1993). Independent surveys that map cities' dependency on cars have gained ground. In aggregate, a distinct policy shift was observed. Planning policies turned unabashedly 'pro-city centre', promoted gentrification and discouraged car use. Residential use was formally reintroduced into city centres to infuse vibrancy and potency. The need to huddle different mixes of uses together became an essential criterion for planning approval. Approval of major schemes in central areas proceeded without any need for on-site parking arrangements.

Changes in government policies found support from the rise of New Urbanism, arguably one of the most influential planning movements since the

Garden City initiative. It adopts the twin concept of Traditional Neighbourhood Design (TND) and Transit-Oriented Development (TOD to advocate walkable neighbourhoods and to counter the growth of car-orientated suburban planning. While New Urbanism has attracted its share of criticism owing to its limitation in conceptualising aestheticism in the physical environment (Timms and Tight, 2010) and its history-centric approach (Furuseth, 1999), ultimately, it makes a convincing case for walkable neighbourhoods.

Strategic approach and regulatory framework shifts have led to an enhanced focus on walkability in recent years. Scholars have defined walkability as being a measure of the characteristics in a physical environment that facilitate walking. These include the distance between locations and the design of urban environments such as streets, pavements and buildings. A simple definition of walkability is provided by Abley (2005): “the extent to which the built environment is walking friendly” (p.3). Speck (2013) argues that four conditions must be fulfilled in order to achieve walkability:

- usefulness - aspects of daily life should be located close to each other and in a way that walking serves them;
- safety- pedestrians should be safe from vehicles as well as from crime;
- comfort - buildings and landscape should shape streets into ‘outdoor living rooms’;
- interest- streets should be lined with unique buildings, friendly faces and signs of humanity.

Collectively the scholarly view on walkability underpins the broader principle of urban design and a pragmatic response to how buildings and spaces are designed and laid out. While the efforts made to define walkability have been constructive, the formal articulation of sidewalk design has been limited rather than expansive.

At the same time, the objective of creating successful sidewalks is not without conceptual contradictions. First, sidewalk design has been influenced by the literature on public space design in general and the application of principles derived from that literature is denoted by poorly conceived or exaggerated specificity. This is attributed to our historical fascination with urban squares, civic spaces, vistas and avenues (see, for example, Whyte, 1980; Liebermann, 1984; Banerjee & Loukaitou-Sederis, 1992) often resulting in poor quality public realm at places removed from these squares and plazas. This fascination ignores the fact that the success of these squares and plazas depends on the channels feeding into them and fails to differentiate sidewalks from the associated squares and plazas. Fundamentally, as opposed to being destinations, sidewalks are a means to get to the destinations. By their very nature, destinations are static, while still advocating for diverse coexistence, fun and playfulness, an exchange of conversation, and a mix of uses (Young,

1990; Lofland, 1998; Stevens, 2007). On the other hand, sidewalks can be all of those and more due to their dynamic, constantly shifting spatial evolution. Any re-tailoring of policies to retrofit into sidewalks would result in a static environment lacking in character.

Second, sidewalks signify spaces of ethereal quality that shun permanence. Sidewalks are by their very nature kinetic. Mehorarotra (2010) defines the kinetic quality of a city or a component within it as operating in the blurred lines of contemporary urbanism and the changing roles of people and spaces in urban society. The underlying assumption of the kinetic current is that it allows for changes in the activity pattern. The distinct lack of permanence or regularity of actions makes sidewalks an antithesis to planning and thus difficult to plan. This apparent contradiction is overlooked in theories of planning and urban design.

The third contradiction relates to the issue of publicness, inclusiveness and ownership of sidewalks. Abutting businesses have been routinely encouraged by city authorities to animate sidewalks by extending their activities outdoors. This approach, branded as a 'grassroots form of urban design' (Southworth, 2014, p. 39), helps to achieve the twin objectives of livening up the space and setting up passive surveillance. However, the idea of private entities controlling access to and the use of public space has been considered regressive by some scholars. Madanipour (2009) compares the loss of public space with the loss of the idea of the city. Elsewhere, the sheer scale of businesses occupying public space has resulted in a dramatic repossession of public space. Using specific examples of the re-appropriation of public spaces in Hong Kong by Filipino maids every Sunday, Cuthbert and MeKinnell (1997) make a case for the spontaneous reassigning of uses and users. This conflict within the public realm is not strictly limited to a private versus public debate. Gaffikin *et al* (2010) argue that the conflict could also be social, religious or sectoral, thus highlighting the role of urban design in creating shared spaces and making it necessary to have a broad and balanced view. Notwithstanding the public versus private debate, in urban design terms, this approach appears counterproductive due to its excessively simplistic view and blanket approach. Far too many city centre sidewalks are littered with outdoor seating areas for cafes and pubs, which have become permanent features of the sidewalks creating visual, psychological and territorial barriers.

Such contradictions illustrate the intrinsic difficulty in defining sidewalks let alone designing or planning them. To planners and urban designers there is a drawing board challenge arising from the new understanding of sidewalks as culturally and socially significant spaces where users 'socialise' differently, often fleetingly, ephemerally and engage in what Goffmann, (1967) terms various appropriate social signalling about their presence and the presence of others. They are spaces that are used by the same person differently at different times of the day, spaces that are used to counter hegemonic expressions of squares and plazas, and spaces that simultaneously provide a stage performance and audience. On the other hand, there is a desire for old-styled public space (Southworth, 2014). So how do we plan / design for such abstractions? How do we read such qualities in sidewalks in order to enhance the pedestrian experience? At the starting point of this inquiry lies an appraisal of the role of urban design in shaping sidewalk design and pedestrian behaviours. Using standard urban design criteria such as urban grain, land use, frontage, enclosure, imageability and permeability, the next section assesses Great Victoria Street in Belfast in greater detail. This analysis focuses on the types of physical elements included, as well as the attributes measured at the micro-scale. This author conducted several walk-bys in the study area and recorded observations on activities and behaviour patterns using field notes.

An enquiry into Belfast's Great Victoria Street

Belfast is the least likely of cities to present superbly designed sidewalks. The city has a reputation as one of the most car dependent cities in Europe. Sidewalks in Belfast city centre are also a reminder of the troubled past in the form of defensive ground floor façades and controlled or easily supervised access arrangements (Gaffikin *et al*, 2010). However, they offer great potential to examine some of the concepts and contradictions discussed above. This case study uses Great Victoria Street (Figure 14.1), which is a prominent commercial street in the city centre with a large footfall due to the Europa Bus Terminus and Great Victoria Train Station. It has a mix of new and older building stock, with the Europa hotel being the most prominent landmark. The Europa Hotel also holds the distinction of being the most bombed hotel in Europe during 'the troubles'. Almost all the buildings are edging the sidewalks leaving no setbacks. The street lies just outside the primary retail core in the city centre and, therefore, consists of a combination of office entrances interspersed by restaurants and cafes. The street has been designated as both a 'Quality Walking Route' and an area of 'High Accessibility / High Density Development' by Belfast City Council.

Figure 14.1 Study area built environment structure

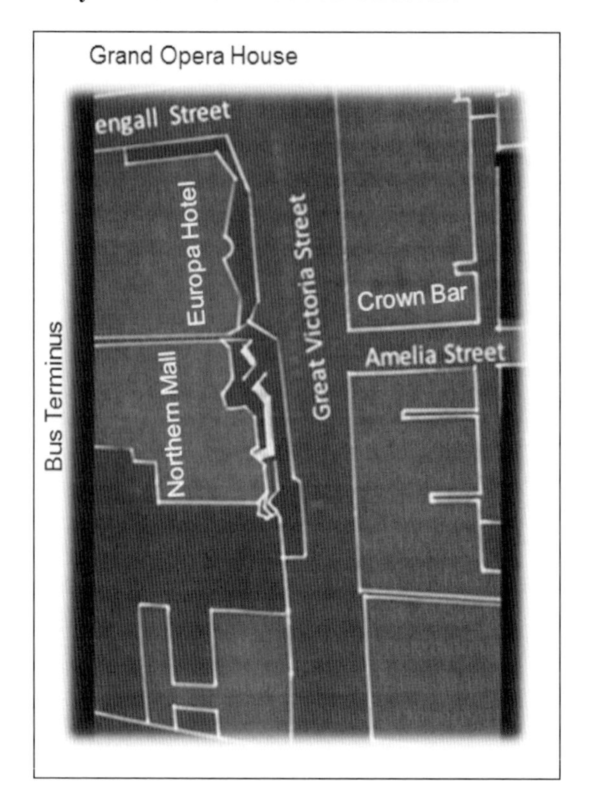

Urban grain

An examination of the ground map of a place is a crude but useful aid to understanding urban fabric. Whilst urban fabric may not be a sole determinant factor for walkability, it certainly is a starting point towards appreciating the opportunities and constraints arising from various forms and scales of development in towns and cities. A close scrutiny of the overall urban fabric of Belfast city centre suggests a clear contrast in the urban grain between the east and the west of the city centre. The dense arrangement of the buildings in the east generates a network of small connected streets which facilitates pedestrian movement, whilst restricting the movement of vehicles. It also illustrates that Great Victoria Street is essentially a severance line between car friendly development to the west and pedestrian friendly development to the east.

Land use

Sidewalks are integral to the abutting land uses. Land use is the single biggest determinant for how sidewalks are shaped. The study of land use in Great

Victoria Street shows a range of uses that help to enhance vibrancy at street level, not only by generating activities, but also by providing pedestrians with visual stimuli and psychological comfort through the mixed urban milieu. A mixed-use environment in the Europa conclave, with its retail-hotel-transport mix, creates an opportunity for diverse activities and a mix of people. The Crown Bar, the quintessential Irish pub, assimilates in the milieu as a counter-magnet to the Europa. It was possible to view people of different ethnicity and background engaged in divergent activities. A careful scrutiny of pedestrian movement showed their eyes looking for other pedestrians with similar background. Some walked slowly to let others catch up; some stood on the same side of the street; and some were observed crossing the road to meet that objective. For a city with deep-rooted social divisions that are both metaphorical and physical (Sterrett and McEldowney, 2001), a preponderance of diversity, facilitated by a mix of uses, offers people various options for engaging in different activities that share the same space. The sidewalk thus acts as a catalyst for diffusing any underlying tension and promoting shared use. However, the land uses on the upper floors of buildings along Great Victoria Street tell a rather different story. The predominance of office use, with little or no residential use in these blocks, generates specific uses and users. Overall, Great Victoria Street compares poorly with the more recently developed Victoria Square complex at the other end of the city centre, which has benefited from gentrification through high-end residential quarters on upper floors. Whilst this contrast can be explained as being reflective of the time of building, the negative effect of the dominance of a single use on walkability has been widely recognised by professional bodies (for example, American Planning Association, 2007). It promotes a particular group of pedestrians and use activity, increases footfall during the day but results in dead sidewalks during the evening. Jacobs (1961) has argued that safety in an area could be increased through natural surveillance, an approach that aims to increase the number of eyes on the street. The UK government's 'flats over shops' and 'town centre first' policies have led to a considerable rise in city centre residential populations and, as a result, mixed use city centre environments. The Northern Ireland government pursues a similar approach.

Interrelationship with building frontage and a sense of enclosure

Pedestrian behaviour has been observed to be influenced by interactions with the building frontage. Pedestrians appear to be more engaged in areas of active frontage. The nature of the building front varies along Great Victoria Street. At the street-level, the building line along the Europa conclave is set back to allow the creation of alcoves including an opportunity for storeowners to personalize these spaces. Such transitional spaces offer pedestrians the scope to see or do something on the street without entering the store, often encouraging passive or active social interaction. Pedestrians are observed to linger-on, either on their own or in small clusters. If rightly designed such semi- public / private spaces of often dubious distinction have great potential to improve the pedestrian experience. The active frontage in the Europa conclave is complemented by its articulated façade confirming Speck's (2013) view that frontages need to be both deep and porous. Depth provides opportunities for physical engagement such as sitting and shelter. Porous refers to how windows, doors and interior lighting connect the building to the outside pavement. Within the Europa conclave, Caffé Nero seating provides the opportunity for a deep and engaging frontage, whilst the Europa Hotel, with its extravagant glass façade, provides a porous frontage. Moving west, passive frontages associated with long monotonous facades and unattractive entrances abound, signifying a discord between the space and the buildings. A typical example is the BBC Blackstaff building with its defensive ground floor. As a result the footfall is significantly low on the sidewalk, suggesting pedestrian apathy to take that route. There is also a vacant site that creates dead frontage thus making the area less attractive to pedestrians.

The interrelationship of building façade and frontage leads to the creation of a sense of enclosure that provides immediate comfort to pedestrians. A sense of enclosure as an important quality of a street has been widely recognized (for example, Cullen, 1961; Alexander et al., 1977; Lynch & Hack, 1984; Jacobs, 1993). Enclosure typically is the pedestrians' perception of a three dimensional space where they associate certain activities together with spatial objects (building façade, frontage, trees and other vertical edges to the sidewalks). Enclosure becomes reality by framing the building and aesthetics in a design intervention. The Europa creates its enclosure through the seamless integration of the building, the associated space and the sculptures which become the embodiment of sensory participation. They inspire certain types of experiences and intuitions that re-orientate everyday activities such as walking and waiting to engage with the built environment in a different way. For instance, a pedestrian passing by the sculptures makes a brief visual stop with an assured nod and picks up his phone to call someone, making a distinct correlation with the enclosure and the memory of a distant someone. Enclosures found in the front of the Europa and Caffe Nero / Northern Mall (Photograph 14.1) do not repeat elsewhere on the street other than through occasional canopies across restaurant entrances.

Photograph 14. 1 Enclosure created by the Europa Hotel and Caffé Nero / Northern Mall helps to contain people and activities

Source: photographs by author

Permeability and imageability

Scholarly reflections on permeability relate to something fluid, struggling, and open-ended. Sidewalks fundamentally remain channels allowing people to flow in and out. In urban design terms impervious sidewalks are considered dead-ends that asphyxiate the pedestrian experience. Permeability in sidewalks is often systematically controlled, perhaps through property rights. The liveliest settings in the case study area are the most permeable. For instance, The Great Northern Mall provides activity and footfall, generating curiosity by pedestrians about what goes on in the buildings and the spaces along their path. Such visual and emotional stimuli provide a sense of intrigue, enhancing the pedestrian experience of walkability. Whilst it is important to achieve a high level of permeability at regular intervals, the Europa remains the only opportunity in Great Victoria Street that exhibits elements of permeability to facilitate pedestrian movement.

Linked to permeability is imageability that helps to shape the visual and spatial character of the sidewalk. Imageability, as defined by Lynch (1960), is "…that shape, color, or arrangement which facilitates the making of vividly identified, powerfully structured, highly useful mental images of the environment" (p.9). Mehta (2009) considers imageability to be the net effect of many other urban design qualities - legibility, enclosure, human scale, transparency, linkage, complexity and coherence. For the purpose of this sidewalk analysis imageability denotes all of those qualities relating to the overall aesthetics of the sidewalk. In Great Victoria Street, imageability only scores high in some pockets and this is detected by the pattern with which pedestrian movements are conducted. The flow of pedestrians across the street from the Europa with the historic Crown Bar façade and towards the Opera House appears almost instinctive to the point that, even if pedestrians wish to head in a different direction, they are naturally drawn by the invisible powers of imageability to head towards the picturesque Crown Bar. The Crown Bar also becomes a fitting background for those promoting business and distributing leaflets (Photograph 14.2). In contrast, the rest of the sidewalk (mainly to the west of the street) exhibits an insipid character and a lack of imageability which pedestrians tend to avoid.

Photograph 14.2 The aesthetically pleasing Crown Bar becomes an integral element of the sidewalk despite the street acting as a severance

Source: photographs by author

Width, street furniture and surface materials

Over the years Great Victoria Street has experienced upgrading and modification due to its importance in Belfast city centre. These improvements have helped to make the street more pedestrian-friendly. Included among the measures introduced are sidewalk widening and / or kerb extensions, improvement to the pavements with concrete slabs fitted (mainly adjacent to the Europa Hotel), tree planting, new street lighting on the sidewalks, and the provision of street furniture in some locations, and so on. However, only areas directly in front of the Europa are regarded to be conducive to both stationary and dynamic social activities and behaviours that include waiting, standing, chatting. This is attributed to the milieu created through a combination of sidewalk features such as sculptures, planters and proximity to the active frontage. The outdoor seating furniture for Caffé Nero occupies a rather large part of the public realm in the Europa conclave. The space itself works well due to its elevated profile, marking, as it does, a territorial distinction from the adjoining sidewalk and enabling an easy overlooking of the bus stop. The outdoor furniture appears to be integral to the overall ambience and it is hard to imagine what the space would be like without it. However, given the public versus private debate discussed earlier, there is certainly a case for experimenting with other forms of spatial arrangement.

A distinct lack of social interaction elsewhere on the sidewalk, despite a reasonably wide footpath, indicates discordance in what Mehta (2009) calls the behavioural environment (land uses and their management) and the physical setting (form and space characteristics). Seating space has been identified as one of the most important characteristics in retaining people in public spaces and possibly supporting social behaviour (Linday, 1978; Whyte, 1980). This has a strong interrelationship with liveliness. The distinct lack of seating spaces (benches, sidewalls, raised kerbs), excluding bus stops and the seating arrangements outside Caffé Nero, appear to inhibit any form of engagement in social activities on the street. Elsewhere, unattractive tarmac pavements, the insipid aesthetic quality of surface materials, cracks in the pavement and a large quantity of puddles reduce any motivation for lingering and engaging. The presence of trees and other greenery can increase the overall aesthetics of an area helping to form a pleasant walking environment. Likewise, the width of the sidewalk with ample space to walk is an important criterion for accommodating the movement of pedestrians on the street especially when there are stationary elements. However, the narrow width appears to have a positive correlation with activities (Photograph 14.3). Behavioural patterns suggest an attraction to narrow crowded footpaths and the avoidance of wider, rather lifeless sidewalks. This confirms the need by pedestrians for fleeting socialisation.

Photograph 14.3 Lifeless, wide footpaths are less attractive than narrow interesting footpaths

Source: photographs by author

Accessibility, safety and signage

In scholarly terms accessibility refers to user mediation on sidewalks regarding how we think with our feet in order to engage with a particular urban setting. It shows an ability by the pedestrian to be involved in potential 'other' activities while on the move. Accessibility and safety factors are also important determinants of inclusive planning. A multi-city study on walkability undertaken by the ADB (Leather *et al*, 2011) measures walkability through conflicts, crossings, and safety which mirrors Transport for London's (2004) focus on "safe, connected, accessible and pleasant activity" (p.5). A sidewalk should be designed for a variety of pedestrians including children, elderly people and those with disabilities. Dropped kerbs and ramps in the Europa conclave allow wheelchair users to access various elements of the ambiance such as the shops, cafes and to lead them into the Bus terminus. Bollards have been used to ensure a clear distinction between the sidewalk and the street. However, these safety features do not extend to the full length of the sidewalk. For instance, the driveway created around the Europa Hotel entrance acts as a deterrent to the smooth flow of the pedestrians (Photograph 14.4). Elsewhere the sidewalks also exhibit a lack of separation considerations with negative implications on walkability. The sidewalks are generally well illuminated with street lamps to give pedestrians a degree of psychological comfort of being safe. However, in the absence of active frontage, street lighting alone does not fully prevent pedestrians from feeling vulnerable. Signage is insufficient to create a positive impact on pedestrians.

Photograph 14.4 Europa Hotel access obstructing the pedestrian flow

Source: photograph by author

Conclusion

This chapter demonstrates the changes in sidewalk urbanism and the corresponding changes in pedestrian behaviour that lead sidewalks to be constructed and reconstructed. Organic and ascriptive markers such as spatial imagery and ambience are linked to pedestrian psychology both dialectically and directly, and such linkages must be explored further through in-depth analysis of the everyday functioning of sidewalks. Clearly, authorities are having to modify sidewalks to suit rapidly changing pedestrian behaviours and requirements. Simply put, technological advancement, such as the availability of 'wifi', puts a new form of space requirement for 'on the go' web browsing which may be different from sitting somewhere with a book. This conforms to the same logic that argues for removing disused phone kiosks that are still standing in public spaces. There is, therefore, an ever-increasing need to find creative ways to design and manage sidewalks. However, how we plan in a fluid situation remains an open question. Traditional methods modifying such spaces have been at best only playing a catch up. In the fast moving world of pedestrian experience, it is likely that the new space becomes obsolete as soon as it has been modified.

To conclude, this chapter suggests that it is pragmatic to continue to rely on the standard urban design approach to improve the pedestrian experience on sidewalks. Factors such as mixed use, active frontage, interesting streetscapes, positive and proportionate enclosure, permeability and imageability individually contribute to enhancing the pedestrian experience, and when put together, they are likely to make a greater contribution than the sum of all the parts. On that basis it can be argued that sidewalk design requires an interdisciplinary approach. This case study also points the way forward for contemporary solutions such as movable benches, TV screens and advertisement hoardings to suit changing pedestrian needs.

References

Abley, S. (2005) *Walkability scoping paper.* [Online]. Available from: http://www.levelofservice.com/walkability-research.pdf (Accessed 20th January 2014).

Adkins, A. *et al.* (2012) Unpacking Walkability: Testing the Influence of Urban Design Features on Perceptions of Walking Environment Attractiveness, *Journal of Urban Design*, 17(4), pp. 499-510.

Alexander, C. *et al.* (1977) *A Pattern Language: Towns, Buildings, Construction.* New York: Oxford University Press.

American Planning Association (2006) *Planning and Urban Design Standards*. New York: John Wiley & Sons.

Banerjee, T. and Loukaitou-Sederis, A. (1992) *Private Production of Downtown Public Open Spaces: Experiences of Los Angeles and San Francisco*. Los Angeles: University of Southern California.

Campaign for Better Transport (2011) *Car dependency scorecard 2011.* London: Campaign for Better Transport.

Cullen, G. N. (1961) *The Concise Townscape.* New York: Reinhold Publishing Corporation.

Cuthbert, A. (2011) *Understanding Cities: Method in Urban Design.* London: Routledge.

Cuthbert, A. and MeKinnell, G. (1997) Ambiguous space, ambiguous rights: corporate power and social control in Hong Kong, *Cities*, 14 (5), pp. 295-311.

Ewing, R. and Handy, S. (2009) Measuring the Unmeasurable: Urban Design Qualities Related to Walkability, *Journal of Urban Design*, 14(1), pp.65-84.

Forbes, D. (1996) *Asian Metropolis: Urbanisation and the Southeast Asian City*. Melbourne: Oxford University.

Gaffikin, F., McEldowney, M. and Sterrett, K. (2010) Creating Shared Public Space in the Contested City: The Role of Urban Design, *Journal of Urban Design*, 15(4), pp. 493-513.

Furuseth, O. J. (1999) New Urbanism, Pedestrianism, and Inner-city Charlotte Neighborhoods, *Southeastern Geographer*, 39(2), pp. 145-160.

Goffman, E. (1967) *Interaction Ritual: Essays in face-to-face behavior*. Chicago: Aldine.

Jacobs, J. (1961) *The Death and Life of Great American Cities*. New York: Vintage Books.

Jacobs, A. (1993) *Great Streets.* Cambridge: The MIT Press.

Leather, J., Herbert Fabian H., Sudhir Gota, S. and Mejia, M. (2011) *Walkability and Pedestrian Facilities in Asian Cities*, Working paper, Manila: ADB.

Lee, S. and Talen, E. (2014) Measuring Walkability: A Note on Auditing Methods, *Journal of Urban Design*, 19 (3), pp. 368–388.

Linday, N. (1978) It all comes down to a comfortable place to sit and watch, *Landscape Architecture*, 68(6), pp. 492 – 497.

Lofland, L. (1998) *The Public Realm: Exploring the City's Quintessential Social Territory*. New York: Aldine de Gruyter.

Loukaitou-Sideris, A. and Ehrenfeucht, R. (2009) *Sidewalks: Conflict and Negotiation Over Public Space.* Cambridge: MIT Press.

Lynch, K. (1960) *The Image of the City*. Cambridge: MIT Press.

Lynch, K. and Hack, G. (1984) *Site Planning.* Cambridge: MIT Press.

Madanipour, A. (2009) *Whose Public Space?: International Case Studies in Urban Design and Development.* New York: Routledge.

Marcus, C. and Francis, M. (1998) *People Places: Design Guidelines for Urban Open Space*. New York: Wiley.

Mehrotra, R. (2010) *Mumbai: Planning Challenges for the Compact City.* [Online].

Available from: http://src.holcimfoundation.org/dnl/238630ef-399c-4479-9fa7-5d6abe54c6cb/F13_Green_03_Mumbai_Planning_Challenges_for_the_Compact_City.pdf

Mehta, V. (2009) Look Closely and You Will See, Listen Carefully and You Will Hear: Urban Design and Social Interaction on Streets, *Journal of Urban Design,* 14(1), pp. 29-64.

Mitchell, D. (2003) *The Right to the City: Social Justice and the Fight for Public Space.* New York: The Guilford Press.

Newman, P. and Kenworthy, J. (1999) *Sustainability and Cities: Overcoming Automobile Dependence.* Washington DC: Island Press.

Southworth, M. (2014) Public Life, Public Space, and the Changing Art of City Design, *Journal of Urban Design*, 19(1), pp. 37-40.

Sorkin, M. (ed.) (1992) *Variations on a Theme Park: The New American City and the End of Public Space.* New York: Noonday Press.

Speck, J. (2013) *Walkable City: How Downtown Can Save America, One Step at a Time*. New York: Farrar, Straus and Giroux.

Sterrett, K. and McEldowney, M. (2001) Architectural ambivalence: built environment and identity, in Neill, W. J. V. and Schwedler H. U. (eds.) *Urban Planning and Cultural Inclusion*. Basingstoke: Palgrave.

Stevens, Q. (2007) *The Ludic City: Exploring the Potential of Public Spaces.* London: Routledge.

Timms, P. and Tight, M. (2010) Aesthetic aspects of walking and cycling, *Built environment*, 36(4), pp. 487-503.

Whyte, W. H. (1980) *The Social Life of Small Urban Spaces*. Washington DC: The Conservation Foundation.

Young, I. M. (1990) *Justice and the Politics of Difference*. New Jersey: Princeton University Press.

Zukin, S. (1995) *The Cultures of Cities*. Cambridge, MA: Blackwell.

Chapter 15

Reframing urban design in an era of environmental risk: urban resilience, green infrastructure and flood management

Mark Scott, Mick Lennon and Eoin O'Neill

Introduction

Our climate is changing and recent climate-related weather events across the globe have led to widespread predictions that such events will impose significant costs on society in the future. If the increases in global temperature are limited in scale, these climatic changes may provide some short-term benefits in agriculture and food production; nevertheless, negative effects upon the ecosystem generally, for water resources, and consequently for people, are expected to be more widespread should global temperature rise excessively. For example, in the context of coastal areas, sea levels are projected to rise by 3.5cm per decade which will expose some coastal areas to inundation, particularly during more frequent storm surge events, and also to coastal erosion. Environmental hazards arising from increased storminess and flooding have the potential to cause enormous damage to the built environment, housing and commercial property, critical infrastructure, and also the natural environment, imposing significant social and financial costs. They also have the potential to disrupt the supply of public services and thereby negatively impact upon societal well-being (EEA, 2008; Newbery *et al.*, 2010). Furthermore, periods of drought and longer heatwaves may also impact on our ability to provide uninterrupted supplies of drinking water, and also contribute to excess heat-related morbidity.

Addressing climate change is now a central goal within spatial planning policy and practice. For example, the UK published a Planning Policy Statement in 2007 on the role of the planning system in addressing climate change (DCLG, 2007), while recent planning legislation in Ireland identifies tackling climate change as a key statutory goal within the Irish planning system (Government of Ireland, 2010). While climate change *mitigation* measures have been increasingly mainstreamed into spatial planning systems, policy and practice in relation to climate change *adaptation* and coping with increased environmental risks are at a more formative stage. Reducing greenhouse gases (GHG) has been, of course, a central concern of planners over the last two decades. In particular, much policy attention has been given to promoting more sustainable urban forms and compact cities to address the spatial separation of home and workplace, urban sprawl and reliance on private motorcars as a means to reduce GHG emissions from transport (Banister, 1999; McEldowney *et al.*, 2005). From an urban design perspective, this agenda has been translated into designing cities to minimise resource use and pollution (Breheny, 1992), including an emphasis on brownfield sites, promoting higher densities around transport hubs and along transport corridors, mixed use development, and improving the quality of the public realm and the quality of urban life (Unsworth, 2007; Moore and Scott, 2005). Moreover, compact urban forms have the perceived advantages of promoting more efficient infrastructure provision (Burton, 2003), the revitalisation of central city areas (Heath, 2001), and conservation of the countryside and habitat protection through reduced urban sprawl (EEA, 2006).

However, climate change mitigation often appears to be a challenge beyond the scope of spatial planners and individual cities, with emissions from the energy and agricultural sectors more significant than emissions from transport. Moreover, as Donaghy (2007) highlights, climate change is a global challenge and while individual European cities may mobilise on a scale sufficient to achieve substantial reductions in GHG emissions, these savings may be offset by rapid growth in populous and coal dependent economies (such as India and China). Perhaps a more pragmatic focus for spatial planners, particularly at the city-region scale, is to promote climate change adaption measures, for while climate change is occurring globally, its impacts are experienced locally, where people live and work (Donaghy, 2007). Spatial planning has a crucial role to play in terms of reducing vulnerability and transforming the footprint of the places people live and work in to become more resilient to climate-related hazards so that they can cope with and recover more quickly from extreme disturbances such as flooding or heat stress. This will require buildings to be designed to cope with the intensity of a wider range of extreme weather events and for our critical infrastructure to be more resilient in the context of unexpected and extreme weather events (Wolsink, 2010). By influencing the location, layout and design of development, spatial planning has the capacity to adapt the built environment to climate change by delivering a more multifunctional built environment that is safe and resilient to climatic extremes.

Questions arise as to the scope of the role of spatial planning in this context given the dearth of research undertaken as to the feasibility, efficiency and cost effectiveness of various adaptation options compared with climate change mitigation (McEvoy *et al.*, 2010). Within this context, adapting urban places in the face of climate change related environmental risks may challenge the orthodoxy of compact urban form and design, as higher densities of development pose problems for urban drainage systems and urban heat island effects, while developing cities in a more ecologically sensitive approach may result in less dense urban forms, for example through enhancing multifunctional greenspaces. Nevertheless, the planning decisions taking place today in terms of urban layout and building design will determine the adaptive capacity of the urban system to climate change in the future (Lindley *et al.*, 2007).

In this chapter, we focus on flood risks as an example of how spatial planning can move centre-stage in creating more resilient places in the face of environmental risks. The next section outlines flood risk challenges and the shift from physical engineering solutions towards more holistic catchment based approaches. This is followed by a discussion surrounding the benefits of advancing an *evolutionary resilience* approach in urban design for flood risk management. It identifies and critically examines three alternative approaches and associated design philosophies in response to the problem of urban flooding. We trace the reasons why these three approaches have emerged and discuss the attributes of each. We then examine the potential of *green infrastructure* as a means to realise evolutionary resilience in designing urban environments for enhanced drainage management. The closing section contrasts the three alternative approaches to flood risk management and identifies some implications of advancing the green infrastructure concept in urban design activities. We conclude by calling for an ecological turn in urban design as a means of harnessing ecosystem services to better cope with environmental risks.

Spatial planning and flood risk

Severe flooding events in the United Kingdom and Ireland during early 2014 once again highlighted the vulnerability of urban settlements to the ever more prevalent effects of climate change. Daily news coverage for almost two months provided dramatic images of urban places and communities struggling to cope with a natural disaster. While the initial debate in the aftermath of such flooding events often centres on the immediate recovery efforts, increasingly flood risk (and the potential for increased risk from climate change impacts) raises more fundamental questions concerning how urban places should prepare or transform to cope with increased exposure to flooding events. In this chapter, we seek to position urban design as central to flood risk management strategies, advancing an evolutionary resilience framework and design principles, operationalised through green infrastructure at the urban scale.

International literature on flooding has, until recent years, tended to focus upon flood defence measures to reduce the probability of flooding; however, frequent and severe flooding events have illustrated the failure of 'hard' engineering solutions that seek to constrain rivers and channel runoff. Moreover, as Harries and Penning-Rowsell (2011) identify, institutional cultures and public perceptions formed when structural, engineered approaches were the norm tend to hamper the ability of government policies to implement a broader range of adaptation measures. However, the potential costs of flooding have driven a renewed interest in flood risk management around the globe. For example, a recent study published in *Nature Climate Change* (Jongman *et al.*, 2014), suggests that the costs of flooding throughout Europe (to homes, businesses, infrastructure etc.), are likely to rise from an annual cost of €4.5bn at present to €23bn per year by 2050 under anticipated climate change impacts and current trends in socio-economic development. Both the scale of vulnerability and the complexity of flooding causes, undermines the efficacy of traditional 'keep flood water out' approaches, suggesting that physical defences are unlikely to succeed and would be prohibitively costly given the scale of vulnerability. As a result, in many countries, flood risk management is currently undergoing a paradigm shift as it moves beyond a one-dimensional 'keep flood water out' approach, towards a more strategic, holistic and long-term approach characterised by both *mitigating* flood risk and *adaptation*, or increasing resilience to flooding events. The benefits (damages avoided) of this approach may be very large. Again, taking account of anticipated climate change impacts and current trends in socio-economic development, Feyen and Watkiss (2011) suggest the annual benefits of adaptation to river flooding across Europe will increase from about €1.3bn today to €8.3bn in the 2020s, and may be up to €50bn by the 2080s. Consequently policy emphasis on adaptation and achieving greater resilience to flooding is reflected in the enactment of EU legislation in the form of the Water Framework Directive 2000/60/EC (CEC, 2000) and the Floods Directive 2007/60/EC (CEC, 2007). Within this context, urban design has the potential to move centre stage as part of a 'whole catchment' framework to risk management, particularly relating to encouraging more ecologically sensitive development.

The causes of flooding are complex, requiring multidimensional management approaches: for example, White (2013) outlines the nature of flood risk to include not only fluvial, tidal and coastal flooding, but also exposure to flood risk from surface water including urban run-off and local drainage failure. Climate change adds a further layer of complexity, with the impact of climate change processes likely to increase flooding vulnerability, both inland and coastal – for example, caused by sea level rise and storm surges in coastal locations. Increased frequency of extreme precipitation events is expected to increase risks associated with surface, fluvial and groundwater flooding, with consequences for property, livelihoods, infrastructure, agricultural production and ecosystems (EEA, 2008). In this context, White argues that the lessons of flood risk management in England over the last decade highlight the dangers of 'false precision' when calculating flood risk and translating these risks into spatial plans. Instead, White calls for a more critical stance towards flood risk data and for empowering urban policy-makers to intervene on a more precautionary basis.

The costly and at times irreparable damage left in the wake of traditional flood defences being overwhelmed or failing highlights the lack of critical attention to 'resilience' in approaches to urban flood risk management. Here, resilience denotes a heuristic for conceptualising change management. The term has an inherent normative dimension that seeks to shift thinking towards design approaches that are more responsive to disturbance (Barr and Devine-Wright, 2012; Plieninger and Bieling, 2012). Much contemporary debate concerning the use of the concept centres on the distinction between 'equilibrium' and 'evolutionary' interpretations of resilience (Scott, 2013). The former understanding has its roots in disaster management and concerns a 'survival discourse' that focuses on the ability of a system to 'bounce back' towards 'business as usual' following a catastrophe (Shaw and Maythorne, 2013). In contrast, 'evolutionary' resilience challenges the desire for a single-state equilibrium or a 'return to normal'. Instead, it emphasises an ongoing evolutionary change process (Scott, 2013). This interpretation focuses on resilience as enabling transformation such that disturbance delivers the spur for re-invention and thereby ensures strength through continuing reflection (Erixon *et al.*, 2013). Therefore, 'evolutionary' resilience entails a more radical and optimistic perspective that embraces the opportunity to 'bounce forward' (Shaw and Maythorne, 2013). It seeks to supplant a desire for stability with the acceptance of inevitable change such that it inverts conventional modes of thought by 'assuming change and explaining stability, instead of assuming stability and explaining change' (*Folke et al.*, 2003, 352).

Designing for flood risk management

Designing for flood risk management is a complex endeavour often involving many variables, uncertainty, large temporal and spatial scales, and a multitude of agents. Nevertheless, it is possible to identify three broad approaches and the design philosophies associated with each. These approaches are characterised by different functional objectives, namely: persistence, adaptation and transformation.

Persistence

The fabric of urban areas was largely produced without much consideration for flood risk (White, 2008). Where regard was had to flooding, this most frequently involved the construction of expensive 'hard' solutions such as levees, flood barriers and the underground piping of historic drainage channels. Consequently, the accumulated legacy of design interventions has often interrupted natural flooding processes by removing vegetation, paving extensive areas with artificial impermeable surfaces, eliminating natural water storage capacity and disrupting flow paths (O'Neill, 2013). The consequence has been a divorcing of urban areas and their population from environmental constraints (White, 2008), and, compounded by the trust people place in technical experts and structural solutions (Terpstra, 2011), an embedding of urban areas with vulnerability to flood risk. Such traditional approaches to flood risk management persist. In essence, these approaches are characterised by a design philosophy focused on resisting the perceived capriciousness of nature and are typified by modes of intervention wherein the functional objective is exclusively directed at flood 'defence'. Exemplifying this established pattern of operation is the situation that persists in many municipal authorities where engineering staff work in a disciplinary 'silo' (Kambites and Owen, 2006), directing policy concerning flood risk management and perpetuating design approaches that demonstrate persistence with 'hard' solutions to urban flood problems. While this technocratic tradition has for a long time enjoyed the legitimacy afforded by specialist engineering knowledges, the enduring failure of such a 'hard' approach to effectively address urban flooding issues has undermined its authority and prompted alternative perspectives on managing flood risk. One such perspective concerns a greater focus on adapting urban environments to the inevitability of flooding.

Adaptation

The turn to adapting urban environments for flood risk management reflects broader societal concerns with the inevitability of some degree of climate change. It is a design response to a projected increase in the frequency and severity of flooding events (Bulkeley, 2013). This perspective seeks to complement rather than challenge traditional 'hard' approaches focused on flood defence through recalibrating design to facilitate a more flood adapted urban environment. In this sense, urban design initiatives focused on adaptation signal a desire to promote a 'bounce-back' form of resilience. Such an approach is characterised by a design philosophy concerned with accommodating the unavoidability of flooding events through modifications to architectural detailing and design of the public realm. For example, this approach is evident in raised plinths to 'flood proof' new developments, the allocation of attenuation areas in car parks and sequential methods of land use allocation that aim to steer developments away from identified flood plains (Roaf *et al.*, 2009; Smith, 2009). As a departure from traditional governance approaches, a focus on adaptation encompasses a broader skills set and therefore involves the cooperation of a variety of construction related disciplines. In the case of municipal authorities, this is reflected in efforts to promote greater cooperation between engineers, architects, urban designers, emergencey planners and landscape architects.

However, there is an increasing focus on moving beyond urban design adaptation. Such interest echoes wider concern with the appropriateness of current approaches to flood risk management and calls for a more profound re-evaluation of how flooding issues are considered in urban environments. For example, the European Union's Floods Directive advocates 'soft' solutions that 'make space for' water (Merz *et al.*, 2010). Accordingly, authors such as White (2008), Yu *et al.* (2008), and Berke *et al.* (2009) have sought to encourage the integration of urban design and flood risk management. In a sense, what these authors are calling for is a transformation in how flood risk is addressed in the urban environments.

Transformation

As with approaches focused on adaptation, those advocating transformative approaches to flood risk management view a measure of climate change as inevitable. However, calls for a transformation in urban design involves moving beyond a focus on construction-based interventions or simple sequential land use modes of governance aimed at flood risk 'defence' and/or 'accommodation'. Instead, it entails a holistic reassessment of the relationship between the built and non-built components of urban environments (O'Neill and Scott, 2011). In this way, a transformation demands seeing the urban environment as a hydrological unit embedded within a larger, or series of larger hydrological units[1], rather than as a collection of various built elements adversely affected by flooding. This approach advances a design philosophy focused on bio-mimicry and working with water rather than concentrating solely on controlling or avoiding it (Grant, 2012; Novotny *et al.*, 2010), reducing the hydrological impact of the built environment, thereby transforming the urban footprint of the city (O'Neill, 2013). In this sense, a transformative perspective seeks to orientate urban design towards an 'evolutionary' form of resilience thinking. In desiring greater holism in the consideration of flooding, such an approach necessitates broadening the skills base of those involved in flood risk management beyond disciplines primarily concerned with construction. Hence, it involves new working arrangements with an array of professionals not normally associated with flooding related design issues, such as ecologists, recreation and transport planners, as well as more conventional participants such as engineers, architects, urban designers, emergency planners and landscape architects. Furthermore, a transformative and holistic approach to flooding would require full collaboration in interdisciplinary partnerships as opposed to cooperation between different disciplines that remain largely isolated beyond the requirements of occasional association during flood risk design exercises (Lennon, 2014). This begs the question as to what form such a transformation in urban design could take? A reply to this may be found in the increasing popularity of the green infrastructure approach to planning, design and management.

The green infrastructure approach

The theory and application of green infrastructure (GI) has grown in depth and breadth over the past decade (Barnhill and Smardon, 2012; Comhar, 2010; Davies *et al.*, 2006; Dunn, 2010; Kilbane, 2013; Mayer *et al.*, 2012; Mell, 2013; Thomas and Littlewood, 2010; Wright, 2011). Although there remain an array of interpretations as to what exactly it entails (Cameron *et al.*, 2012; EC, 2012; Ellis, 2012), most understandings resonate with the explanation offered by Benedict and McMahon (2006, 1) as: 'an interconnected network of natural areas and other open spaces that conserves natural ecosystem values and functions…and provides a wide array of benefits for people and wildlife'. Prominent among these 'benefits' is the retention of water so that drainage into watercourses is more protracted and the peaks in flow associated with flood events are avoided. A GI approach seeks to realise such benefits by giving greater consideration to multifunctionality in the design process. In this context, GI potentially provides a holistic approach towards addressing source-pathway-receptor models applied in contemporary flood risk assessment (DEHLG/OPW, 2009; Shaw *et al.*, 2007) particularly in providing a design response focused on the receptors of flooding (people and assets) and the pathways by which flood water reaches these receptors (e.g. river channels, drainage systems etc.), by enabling water retention in the built environment through ecologically sensitive development patterns.

Attention to enhancing the multifunctional potential of sites is a key attribute differentiating the GI design philosophy from more conventional approaches focused solely on flood 'defence' or 'accommodation'. Referencing the multiple environmental, economic and community benefits that accrue from such a transformative perspective, Rouse and Bunster-Ossa (2013, 19) assert that 'these benefits derive from the multiple and overlapping functions provided across different systems – hydrology, transportation, energy, economy, and so on – that can intersect in green infrastructure'. Indeed, advocates of a GI design approach contend that the multifunctional potential of the wider urban environment can be maximised by combining the need for temporary flood storage with other ongoing functional, recreational and ecological uses (White, 2008).

The city of Portland, Oregon in the north western United States of America presents an example of how a GI design approach to flood risk management can provide an array of benefits for the local community at the site and neighbourhood scales. Prompted by an excessive burden on the city's drainage system, resulting in an average of 50 combined sewer overflows (c. 6bn gallons) to the Willamette River in 1990, Hoyer *et al.*, (2011) note how Portland's municipal authority has employed a suite of GI design initiatives to alleviate the pressure on the sewer system and reduce adverse impacts to urban watercourses. Such measures have included financial incentives for downpipe disconnection (with stormwater redirected to lawns, gardens, and infiltration into the ground), the construction of green roofs that enhance local biodiversity, and the provision of a green space recreational network that simultaneously serves to slow rainwater runoff into the Willamette River. These ongoing GI initiatives comprised part of a 20-year plan known as the Combined Sewer Overflow (CSO) Abatement Programme that provided for low-cost and small-scale GI 'Cornerstone Projects', in combination with high-cost grey infrastructure 'Big Pipe' projects (CoP, 2011). The cumulative effect of numerous local small-scale GI measures (e.g. 56,000 downpipe disconnections, 2,800 infiltration sumps and sedimentation manholes, and a green streets programme) has helped to reactivate the local hydrological cycle, thereby easing pressure on the city's combined sewer system by over 2.1bn gallons annually and consequently reducing flood events generated by under-capacity in the urban drainage system. Furthermore, these GI initiative helped reduce CSO discharges to the Willamette River by about 35% down to an average of four overflows each winter and one every third summer[2] (CoP, 2011, 2012). Importantly, this has been achieved without compromising on aesthetic appeal (Hoyer *et al.*, 2011, 43). This contrasts with the objectionable appearance of many flood defence interventions associated with traditional 'hard' engineering approaches to flood risk management, such as flood barriers (Entrix, 2010). Indeed, 'soft' design initiatives undertaken by the municipal authority to reduce the quantum of impervious surfaces in the urban area have improved the appearance and experience of the urban landscape. Such initiatives include roadside tree planting, increasing the number of publicly accessible green spaces and the construction of attractive swales and rain gardens in residential streets which are specifically designed to supplement a decentralised approach to drainage management, enhance streetscape appearance and boost local biodiversity (Hoyer *et al.*, 2011). Erickson (2006) examines similar multifunctional and local level drainage initiatives in Vancouver, Canada. Here, the municipal authority has promoted a Green Streets programme that offers local residents the opportunity to engage in urban gardening by sponsoring a roadside enhancement project. This project augments the degree of permeable surface within the city while concurrently supporting community development by encouraging a sense of ownership and pride in a neighbourhood's public realm through helping to dissolve firm delineations between public and private spaces. Photograph 15.1 outlines an alternative example from a social housing scheme in Sydney, Australia. In this case, the locality is prone to flash flooding caused by poor urban drainage during heavy precipitation events. In this context, the green space provides multiple functions: as a store for flood water during heavy rain; for urban cooling by retaining water in the locality during high summer temperatures (rather than draining away); and providing an attractive green space for local residents.

Photograph 15.1 Social housing scheme in Sydney with multifunctional greenspace (which serves as storm water sink)

Source: Mark Scott

Guildford in England offers an example of how a GI approach can be applied at the masterplanning scale. In this case, about 67 hectares of the settlement are situated within the 1 in 100 year floodplain of the River Wey, and contain approximately 620 vulnerable properties within it (GBC and EA, 2009). Moreover, almost 47 hectares of this area would normally be defined as a floodplain with a probability of flooding at 1 in 20 years or greater. In the absence of a feasible 'hard' engineering option, the challenge for Guildford has been to identify a solution to the problem of flood risk by 'using redevelopment opportunities to provide increased safety, additional floodwater storage, and improved floodwater flows, whilst making space for water and the enjoyment of the River Wey' (GBC & EA, 2009, 2). To achieve this, the municipal authority stipulates a policy whereby as local redevelopment opportunities arise, effort is directed at reducing the probability of flooding by ensuring that new building footprints are set back from the River Wey to allow greater space for floodwater. Furthermore, the municipal authority seeks to restore flood plains and flood flow paths where feasible so that natural water storage capacity is increased in the urban landscape (O'Neill, 2013).

At the city-wide scale, guidance on how a GI design approach may be advanced is provided by points based planning regulations in Berlin (Kazmierczak and Carter, 2010), Malmö (Kruuse, 2011) and Seattle (Beatley, 2010). The objective of such schemes is to increase the quantum and quality of permeable surface area in a move towards achieving water infiltration rates experienced in natural ground cover. This is promoted through increased planting to deliver a combination of reduced water runoff rates, enhanced biodiversity and an improved aesthetic experience of urban spaces. These schemes enable designers to flexibly integrate landscaping elements into developments by allowing them to propose designs that respond to the particular opportunities and constraints of a specific site. The 'Biotope Area Factor' (Berlin) and 'Green Factor' (Malmö and Seattle) operate by allocating different scores to different design elements. The developer must ensure that the proposed design exceeds a certain minimum threshold to proceed with construction on site. For example, in commercial (C) and neighbourhood commercial (NC) zones NC1, NC2, NC3, C1 and C2 in Seattle, developments must achieve a minimum Green Factor score of 0.30 under the provisions of Seattle Municipal Code 23.47A.016 - see Figure 15.1 for an extract from the Seattle Green Factor Score Sheet used in development management. The scoring mechanisms include a variety of functions and are weighted according to relative functional desirability. Prominent in these scoring mechanisms are issues concerning drainage management, ecological enhancement, recreational space provision and aesthetic benefit. In Berlin, the focus is placed on the use of planting schemes in private properties to increase on-site water retention. In Malmö, greater emphasis has been placed on improving user experience of semi-private residential courtyards through constructing new water retention areas that provide ecologically rich habitats and offer recreational opportunities for local residents. These private and semi-private space issues are also addressed in the Seattle Green Factor scheme, although here, considerable stress has also been given to public spaces. In this scheme, applicants to the municipal authority are permitted to include landscape-enhancing elements in public areas adjacent to the development site. This has increased the permeable surface cover in public areas by incentivising developers to improve the quality of the public realm through investing in the streetscape. As noted by Rouse and Bunster-Ossa (2013, 78), 'Where bare, five-by-five-foot tree pits used to be the norm, planting strips now tend to be larger and include understory planting'.

Figure 15.1 Seattle Green Factor Score Sheet

Revised 12/28/10

Green Factor Score Sheet SEATTLE×*green factor*

Project title:

enter sq ft of parcel

Parcel size *(enter this value first)* * 5,000

SCORE -

	Landscape Elements**		Totals from GF worksheet	Factor	Total
A	**Landscaped areas (select one of the following for each area)**				
1	Landscaped areas with a soil depth of less than 24"		*enter sq ft* 0	0.1	-
2	Landscaped areas with a soil depth of 24" or greater		*enter sq ft* 0	0.6	-
3	Bioretention facilities		*enter sq ft* 0	1.0	-
B	**Plantings (credit for plants in landscaped areas from Section A)**				
1	Mulch, ground covers, or other plants less than 2' tall at maturity		*enter sq ft* 0	0.1	-
2	Shrubs or perennials 2'+ at maturity - calculated at 12 sq ft per plant (typically planted no closer than 18" on center)	*enter number of plants* 0	0	0.3	-
3	Tree canopy for "small trees" or equivalent (canopy spread 8' to 15') - calculated at 75 sq ft per tree	*enter number of plants* 0	0	0.3	-
4	Tree canopy for "small/medium trees" or equivalent (canopy spread 16' to 20') - calculated at 150 sq ft per tree	*enter number of plants* 0	0	0.3	-
5	Tree canopy for "medium/large trees" or equivalent (canopy spread of 21' to 25') - calculated at 250 sq ft per tree	*enter number of plants* 0	0	0.4	-
6	Tree canopy for "large trees" or equivalent (canopy spread of 26' to 30') - calculated at 350 sq ft per tree	*enter number of plants* 0	0	0.4	-
7	Tree canopy for preservation of large existing trees with trunks 6"+ in diameter - calculated at 20 sq ft per inch diameter	*enter inches DBH* 0	0	0.8	-
C	**Green roofs**				
1	Over at least 2" and less than 4" of growth medium		*enter sq ft* 0	0.4	-
2	Over at least 4" of growth medium		*enter sq ft* 0	0.7	-
D	**Vegetated walls**		*enter sq ft* 0	0.7	-
E	**Approved water features**		*enter sq ft* 0	0.7	-
F	**Permeable paving**				
1	Permeable paving over at least 6" and less than 24" of soil or gravel		*enter sq ft* 0	0.2	-
2	Permeable paving over at least 24" of soil or gravel		*enter sq ft* 0	0.5	-
G	**Structural soil systems**		*enter sq ft* 0	0.2	-
		sub-total of sq ft =	0		
H	**Bonuses**				
1	Drought-tolerant or native plant species		*enter sq ft* 0	0.1	-
2	Landscaped areas where at least 50% of annual irrigation needs are met through the use of harvested rainwater		*enter sq ft* 0	0.2	-
3	Landscaping visible to passersby from adjacent public right of way or public open spaces		*enter sq ft* 0	0.1	-
4	Landscaping in food cultivation		*enter sq ft* 0	0.1	-
				Green Factor numerator =	-

**** Do not count public rights-of-way in parcel size calculation.***

***** You may count landscape improvements in rights-of-way contiguous with the parcel. All landscaping on private and public property must comply with the Landscape Standards Director's Rule (DR 6-2009)***

Source: http://www.seattle.gov/dpd/cityplanning/completeprojectslist/greenfactor

Successfully implementing these initiatives involves the acquisition of new design skills and knowledge concerning less interventionist, yet innovative approaches to maintenance. For example, Portland has attempted to reconcile aesthetic appeal with a low-cost approach by 'refining the planting plans for green streets to ensure they are both attractive and low-maintenance' (Hoyer *et al.*, 2011, 44). This approach has been synergised with community development initiatives by supporting local residents in helping maintain the appearance and functionality of green street initiatives. Such new design and maintenance approaches echo the achievements of Vancouver's 'Green Streets' initiative discussed above. They likewise confirm the benefits of innovative design and maintenance approaches identified by Erickson (2006, 199) regarding the 'Country Lanes' initiative in Vancouver where alleys have been retrofitted by removing impermeable surfaces and installing low-maintenance planted pervious material that can support vehicles. In this sense, city-wide GI initiatives can have a direct positive impact on urban design at a range of scales and cater for a variety of functions. At the micro scale, influencing urban development outcomes is also essential – for example, Photograph 15.2 illustrates a recent residential development in green roofs in new residential areas in Ostfildern (located in the urban periphery of Stuttgart). The primary aim of the green roofs is water retention to reduce run-off to the drainage system. However, secondary benefits include urban cooling in high summer temperatures and humid conditions experience locally and maximising biodiversity gain at the site level. These different approaches also reflect different design traditions, property rights and regulatory approaches, and environmental contexts. However, the key principle is transferable across these contexts – the enhancement, creation and the integration of multifunctional green networks and spaces into ecologically sensitive urban development. Uniting these approaches is a holistic and optimistic perspective to forging positive synergies between the complex abiotic, biotic and cultural dimensions of the urban environment (Ahern, 2013). Each of the examples outlined above thereby advances evolutionary resilience by promoting a future-orientated stance that elevates innovation through continuing reflection in a desire to 'bounce-forward' in response to an assumption of ongoing change.

Photograph 15.2 Green roofs in new residential areas in Ostfildern (located in the urban periphery of Stuttgart)

Source: Karen Foley

Conclusions

The persistence of traditional approaches to flood risk management is evident in much urban design activity. This design philosophy is manifested in projects that seek to resist, disrupt and dominate the natural hydrological cycle. These 'defence' focused design perspectives involve intensive and expensive interventions with limited function beyond the reduction of flood risk. Furthermore, such 'hard' solutions are generally inflexible and once their capacity to prevent flooding is exceeded, they can require considerable effort and cost to rebuild. Problems associated with this approach to resisting nature has prompted the emergence of design approaches focused on adapting to flood risk by advancing a form of 'bounce-back' resilience. While an improvement on traditional approaches, this chapter calls for a more profound change in how the issue of flood risk management is incorporated into the design of urban areas. As argued by Carmona (2014), the emergence of more ecologically focused 'urbanisms' (e.g. sustainable urbanism, landscape urbanism, ecological urbanism) 'seek to neatly package favoured physical forms with prescribed social and/or ecological content and philosophical meaning, but often end up in circular debates about aesthetics' (2014, 4-5). However, in this chapter we argue for a transformative understanding of the role in urban design of place-resilience. This involves attention to the multifunctional potential of sites and seeks to engender an 'evolutionary' resilience that facilitates on-going reflection on how to deliver more sustainable urban forms. The attributes characterising this progression from resistance to bounce-back and evolutionary resilience are illustrated in Table 15.1.

Table 15.1 Attributes of the resistance and resilience concepts

Guiding Concept	Approaches to Flood Risk Management	Design Philosophy	Functional Objectives	Urban Design Example
Resistance	Persistence	Dominate nature	Flood defence	Flood barriers, constructed levees
Resilience (Bounce-back)	Adaptation	Accommodate flooding	Reduce vulnerability to inevitable flooding	Raised plinths, impermeable attenuation areas
Resilience (Evolutionary)	Transformation	Biominicry and working with nature (Green Infrastructure)	Multifunctionality, responsiveness, flexibility	Rain gardens, green roofs

This chapter advances the GI approach as a means for realising evolutionary resilience in urban flood risk management. The chapter does not oppose the application of traditional or adaptation focused approaches to flooding, as these are likely to be the most appropriate modes of action in certain circumstances. However, the chapter does challenge the dominance of traditional 'hard' solutions to issues of flood risk management, while concurrently suggesting that an adaptation focused approach is often limited in scope and ambition. Thus, in seeking to complement these two approaches, this chapter advances an alternative design perspective that advocates 'working with' as opposed to 'dominating' or 'adapting to' nature. Such an approach necessitates a broader skills set than that which is currently deployed in addressing urban flooding issues. For example, a challenge arising is to advance urban design that 'works with' nature by creating a more 'permeable landscape' which provides for: water absorption and storage; habitat connectivity; recreational access; and the requirements of emergency response (legible evacuation route to safety). Consequently, it requires greater collaboration between an array of different specialisms. However, it is contended that the hard work of producing these new interdisciplinary working arrangements will ultimately result in an aesthetically and functionally enhanced urban public realm.

In this chapter, we focus on the role of green infrastructure in adapting and transforming urban places in the context of increased flood risk. In a northern European context, anticipated climate change will increase flooding risk with increased frequency of precipitation events. Within this context, a tension potentially arises between GI measures to adapt to climate change and policies designed to mitigate climate change. As discussed in the introduction to this chapter, over the last two decades urban planning orthodoxy has promoted compact urban form and higher densities to reduce energy consumption and the ecological footprint of cities (Howley et al., 2009). However, as McEvoy et al. (2006) outline, densification efforts often pose problems for urban drainage systems, while brownfield sites targeted for development may actually serve more important functions in terms of water retention, recreational uses and urban cooling. At the same time, a GI approach may undermine compact city policies through a greater emphasis on multifunctional greenspace provision and less intensive urban development patterns. Within the context of mitigation/adaptation tensions, the role of urban design is to reconcile these competing demands within the design process. For example, a GI approach may suggest promoting higher density development within key nodes or public transport corridors (reducing the need for car travel) intermeshed with multifunctional green corridors, or promoting green roofs and green walls to promote water retention within densely developed areas.

Endnotes

1 Such larger hydrological units are most commonly referred to as ‘river basins’ in the British Isles or ‘watersheds’ in North America.

2 Following its 20-year implementation, Portland’s Combined Sewer Overflow CSO Abatement Programme (green and grey infrastructure) has resulted in a 94% reduction in combined sewer overflows to the Willamette River down from about 50 overflows per year to an average of four overflows each winter and one every third summer. Implementation has enabled the City of Portland to meet regulatory standards and legal obligations (CoP, 2011, 2012).

References

Ahern, J. (2013) Urban landscape sustainability and resilience: the promise and challenges of integrating ecology with urban planning and design, *Landscape Ecology,* 28, pp. 1203-1212.

Banister, D. (1999) Planning more to travel less: land use and transport, *Town Planning Review*, 70, pp. 313-338.

Barnhill, K. and Smardon, R. (2012) Gaining Ground: Green Infrastructure Attitudes and Perceptions from Stakeholders in Syracuse, New York, *Environmental Practice,* 14**,** pp. 6-16.

Barr, S. and Devine-Wright, P. (2012) Resilient communities: sustainabilities in transition. *Local Environment,* 17**,** pp. 525-532.

Beatley, T. (2010) *Biophilic Cities: Integrating Nature Into Urban Design and Planning*. Washington: Island Press.

Benedict, M. and Mcmahon, E. (2006) *Green Infrastructure: linking landscapes and communities.* London, England, U.K.: Island Press.

Berke, P. R., Song, Y. and Stevens, M. (2009) Integrating hazard mitigation into New Urban and conventional developments, *Journal of Planning Education and Research,* 28**,** pp. 441-455.

Breheny, M. (1992) The contradictions of the compact city: a review, in M. Breheny (Ed) *Sustainable development and urban form*. London: Pion Limited.

Bulkeley, H. (2013) *Cities and climate change.* London: Routledge.

Burton, E. (2003) Housing for an urban renaissance: implications for social equity, *Housing Studies*, 18(4), pp. 537-562.

Cameron, R. W. F., Blanuša, T., Taylor, J. E., Salisbury, A., Halstead, A. J., Henricot, B. and Thompson, K. (2012) The domestic garden – Its contribution to urban green infrastructure. *Urban Forestry & Urban Greening,* 11**,** pp. 129-137.

Carmona, M. (2014) The Place-shaping Continuum: A Theory of Urban Design Process. *Journal of Urban Design,* 19**,** pp. 2-36.

CEC, (2000) *Water Framework Directive (Directive 2000/60/EC).* Brussels, Belgium: Commission of the European Communities (CEC).

CEC, (2007) *Floods Directive (Directive 2007/60/EC).* Brussels, Belgium: Commission of the European Communities (CEC).

COMHAR, (2010) *Creating Green Infrastructure for Ireland: enhancing natural capital for human well being.* Dublin, Ireland: Comhar SDC.

COP (2011) *Combined Sewer Overflow CSO Abatement Program Final Report 1991-2011,* Portland, Oregon, U.S.A.: Environmental Services, City of Portland (CoP).

COP (2012) *City of Portland's Combined Sewer Overflow Program Demonstration of ASFO Compliance Final Report.* Portland, Oregon, U.S.A.: Environmental Services, City of Portland (CoP).

Davies, C., Macfarlane, R. and Roe, M. H. (2006) *Green Infrastructure Planning Guide, 2 Volumes: Final Report and GI Planning.* Newcastle, England, U.K.: University of Northumbria, North East Community Forests, University of Newcastle, Countryside Agency, English Nature, Forestry Commission, Groundwork Trusts.

DCLG (Department of Communities and Local Government) (2007) *Planning Policy Statement: Planning and Climate Change (Supplement to Planning Policy Statement 1)*. London: TSO.

DEHLG/OPW (2009) *The Planning System and Flood Risk Assessment for Planning Authorities,* Dublin, Ireland: Department of Environment, Heritage & Local Government (DEHLG)/Office for Public Works (PW).

Donaghy, K. (2007) Climate change and planning: responding to the challenge, *Town Planning Review*, 78, pp. i-ix.

Dunn, A. D. (2010) Siting Green Infrastructure: Legal and Policy Solutions to Alleviate Urban Poverty and Promote Healthy Communities. *Pace Law Faculty Publications,* Paper 559.

EC (2012) *The Multifunctionality of Green Infrastructure.* Brussels, Belgium: European Commission.

EEA (European Environment Agency) (2008) *Impacts of Europe's changing climate: 2008 indicator based Assessment*, Joint EEA-JRC-WHO report: EEA Report No. 5/2008. Copenhagen: EEA.

EEA (2008) *Impacts of Europe's changing climate: 2008 indicator based Assessment (EEA Report No. 5/2008).* Copenhagen, Denmark: European Environment Agency (EEA)

Ellis, J. B. (2012) Sustainable surface water management and green infrastructure in UK urban catchment planning. *Journal of Environmental Planning and Management,* 56**,** pp. 24-41.

ENTRIX, (2010) *Portland's Green Infrastructure: Quantifying the Health, Energy, and Community Livability Benefits* Portland. Oregon, U.S.A.: City of Portland Bureau of Environmental Services.

Erickson, D., (2006) *Metrogreen: Connecting Open Space in North American Cities.* Washington, D.C, U.S.A.: Island Press.

Erixon, H., Borgström, S. and Andersson, E. (2013) Challenging dichotomies – exploring resilience as an integrative and operative conceptual framework for large-scale urban green structures, *Planning Theory & Practice,* 14**,** pp. 349-372.

Feyen, L. and Watkiss, P. (2011) Technical policy briefing note 3. The impacts and economic costs of river floods in Europe, and the costs and benefits of adaptation. Results from the EC RTD ClimateCost Project, in Watkiss, P. (ed.) *The Climate Cost Project. Final report.* Stockholm, Sweden: Stockholm Environment Institute.

Folke, C., Colding, J. and Berkes, F. 2003. Synthesis: Building resilience and adaptive capacity in social-ecological systems, in Berkes, F., Colding, J. and Folke, C. (eds.) *Navigating Social-Ecological Systems: Building Resilience for Complexity and Change.* Cambridge, England, U.K.: Cambridge University Press.

GBC and EA (2009) *Flood Risk Reduction Measures, a supplement to the Guildford Borough Strategic Flood Risk Assessment: Forming part of the Guildford Development Framework Evidence Base.* Guildford, England, U.K.: Guildford Borough Council and Environmental Agency.

Government of Ireland (2010) *Planning and Development (Amendment) Act.* Dublin: Government of Ireland.

Grant, G., (2012) *Ecosystem Services Come To Town: Greening Cities by Working with Nature.* Chichester, England, U.K.: John Wiley and Sons Ltd.

Harries, T. and Penning-Rowsell, E. (2011) Victim pressure, institutional inertia and climate change adaptation: The case of flood risk, *Global Environmental Change,* 21**,** pp. 188-197.

Heath, T. (2001) Revitalising cities, attitudes towards city-centre living in the United Kingdom, J*ournal of Planning Education and Research*, 20 (4), pp. 464-475.

Howley, P., Scott, M. and Redmond, D. (2009) Sustainability versus liveability: an investigation of neighbourhood satisfaction. *Journal of Environmental Planning and Management,* 52**,** pp. 847-864.

Hoyer, J., Dickhaut, W. and Weber, B. (2011) *Water Sensitive Urban Design – principles and inspiration for sustainable stormwater management in the city of the future.* Hamburg, Germany: Hafen City Universität.

Jongman, B., Hochrainer-Stigler, S., Feyen, L., Aerts, J. C. J. H., Mechler, R., Botzen, W. J. W., Bouwer, L. M., Pflug, G., Rojas, R. and Ward, P. J. (2014) Increasing stress on disaster-risk finance due to large floods. *Nature Climate Change,* doi:10.1038/nclimate2124.

Kambites, C. and Owen, S. (2006) Renewed prospects for green infrastructure in the UK. *Planning Practice and Research,* 21**,** pp. 483-496.

Kazmierczak, A. and Carter, J. (2010) *Adaptation to climate change using green and blue infrastructure. A database of case studies.* Manchester, England, U.K.: University of Manchester.

Kilbane, S. (2013) Green infrastructure: planning a national green network for Australia. *Journal of Landscape Architecture,* 8, pp. 64-73.

Kruuse, A. (2011) The Green Space Factor and Green Points. *Town & Country Planning,* 80, pp. 287-290.

Lennon, M. (2014) Green infrastructure and planning policy: a critical assessment. *Local Environment,* Available at: http://dx.doi.org/10.1080/13549839.2014.880411.

Mayer, A. L., Shuster, W. D., Beaulieu, J. J., Hopton, M. E., Rhea, L. K., Roy, A. H. and Thurston, H. W. (2012) Building green infrastructure via citizen participation: A six-year study in the Shepherd Creek (Ohio). *Environmental Practice,* 14, pp. 57-67.

McEldowney, M., Ryley, T., Scott, M. and Smyth, A. (2005) Integrating land-use planning and transportation in Belfast: a new policy agenda for sustainable development? *Journal of Environmental Planning and management*, 48(4), pp. 507-526.

McEvoy, D., Lindley, S. and Handley, J. (2006) Adaptation and mitigation in urban areas: synergies and conflicts. *In:* Proceedings of the Institution of Civil Engineers-Municipal Engineer. London: Published for the Institution of Civil Engineers by Thomas Telford Services, c1992-, 185-192.

Mell, I. C. (2013) Can you tell a green field from a cold steel rail? Examining the “green” of Green Infrastructure development. *Local Environment,* 18, pp. 152-166.

Merz, B., Hall, J., Disse, M. and Schumann, A. (2010) Fluvial flood risk management in a changing world. *Natural Hazards & Earth System Sciences,* 10, pp. 509-527.

Moore, N., and Scott, M. (Eds.) (2005) *Renewing Urban Communities: Environment, Citizenship and Sustainability in Ireland.* Ashgate: Aldershot.

Newbery, D., Echenique, M., Goddard, J., Heathwaite, L., Morris, J., Schultz, W., Swanwick, C. and Tewdwr-Jones, M. (2010) *Land Use Futures: Making the Most of Land in the 21st Century*. London: Foresight Government Office for Science.

Novotny, V., Ahern, J. and Brown, P., 2010. *Water Centric Sustainable Communities: Planning, Retrofitting and Building the Next Urban Environment.* Hoboken, New Jersey, U.S.A.: John Wiley & Sons.

O'Neill, E. (2013) Neighbourhood design considerations in flood risk management. *Planning Theory and Practice,* 14, pp. 129-134.

O'Neill, E. and Scott, M. (2011) Policy & Planning Brief. *Planning Theory and Practice,* 12, pp. 312-317.

Plieninger, T. and Bieling, C. 2012. Connecting cultural landscapes to resilience, in Plieninger, T. and Bieling, C. (eds.) *Resilience and the Cultural Landscape: Understanding and Managing Change in Human-Shaped Environments.* Cambridge, England, U.K.: Cambridge University Press.

Roaf, S., Crichton, D. and Nicol, F. (2009) *Adapting Buildings and Cities for Climate Change: A 21st Century Survival Guide.* Oxford, England, U.K.: Elsevier.

Rouse, D. C. and Bunster-Ossa, I. F. (2013) *Green Infrastructure: A Landscape Approach.* Washington, D.C., U.S.A.: American Planning Association.

Scott, M. (2013) Resilience: a Conceptual Lens for Rural Studies? *Geography Compass,* 7, pp. 597-610.

Shaw, K. and Maythorne, L. (2013) Managing for local resilience: towards a strategic approach, *Public Policy and Administration,* 28, pp. 43-65.

Shaw, R., Colley, M. and Connell, R. (2007) *Climate change adaptation by design: a guide for sustainable communities.* London, England, U.K.: TCPA.

Smith, P. F. (2009) *Building for a Changing Climate: The Challenge for Construction, Planning and Energy.* London, England, U.K.: Earthscan.

Terpstra, T. (2011) Emotions, Trust, and Perceived Risk: Affective and Cognitive Routes to Flood Preparedness Behavior, *Risk Analysis,* 31, pp. 1658-1675.

Thomas, K. and Littlewood, S. (2010) From Green Belts to Green Infrastructure? The evolution of a new concept in the emerging soft governance of spatial strategies, *Planning Practice and Research,* 25, pp. 203-222.

White, I. (2008) The absorbent city: urban form and flood risk management. *Proceedings of the ICE-Urban Design and Planning,* 161, pp. 151-161.

White, I. (2013) The more we know, the more we know we don't know: Reflections on a decade of planning, flood risk management and false precision, *Planning Theory and Practice,* 14, pp. 106-114.

Wolsink, M. (2010) Contested environmental policy infrastructure: socio-political acceptance of renewable energy, water, and waste facilities, *Environmental Impact Assessment Review*, 30, pp. 302-311.

Wright, H. (2011) Understanding green infrastructure: the development of a contested concept in England, *Local Environment,* 16, pp. 1003-1019.

Yu, K., Lei, Z. and Dihua, L. (2008) Live with water: flood adaptive landscapes in the Yellow River basin of China, *Journal of Landscape Architecture,* 3.

Chapter 16

Marine Spatial Planning: a comparison of two North American case studies

Wesley Flannery

Introduction

Marine Spatial Planning (MSP) is a relatively new management practice, promoted as a means of managing human uses of the sea in a sustainable manner and of implementing ecosystem-based marine management (Elher and Douvere, 2007). One way to develop and improve the practice of MSP is to learn from initiatives that have adopted some of its key principles. Critical assessments of key elements of MSP as implemented in these initiatives can serve to inform and enhance future MSP policy and practice. The European Commission (EC) strongly advocates MSP and has developed a set of guiding principles for its implementation, including: (a) the adoption of an ecosystem approach; (b) defining objectives to guide MSP; (c) developing MSP in a transparent manner; (d) incorporating monitoring and evaluation in the planning process; (e) coordination within Member States; (f) ensuring the legal effect of national MSP; (g) crossborder cooperation and consultation; (h) achieving coherence between terrestrial and maritime spatial planning; (i) strong data and knowledge base; (j) using MSP according to area and type of activity; and (k) stakeholder participation. Many of these principles are germane to good planning practice in general and can be found in a large number of ecosystem-based marine management initiatives.

This chapter critically examines nine of these principles[1] by assessing their applicability in two initiatives: The Channel Islands National Marine Sanctuary (CINMS); and The Eastern Scotian Shelf Integrated Management (ESSIM) Initiative. Case study methodology is described in the first instance. A discussion of the key MSP planning principles evaluated in the case studies is then presented. This is followed by an account and discussion of the case study findings. The chapter concludes with some recommendations for future MSP initiatives.

Methodology

Processes and outputs of the CINMS and ESSIM initiatives are critically examined for evidence of implementation of the MSP principles advanced by the EC. In the CINMS case study this involved a review of: the CINMS plan; its advisory council's terms and conditions; its decision-making and operational protocols; minutes of meetings; and the advisory council's work plan. Semi-structured interviews were conducted with 12 members of the CINMS Advisory Council and one member of the CINMS management team. Texts analysed for the ESSIM case study included: a number of academic papers, predominately produced by members of the ESSIM Planning office; the ESSIM Plan; the advisory council's terms of conditions, protocols, and minutes of meetings; and workshop proceedings. In-depth interviews with 11 members of the ESSIM Advisory Council were conducted. A group interview was also conducted with members from the ESSIM Planning Office. Deductive coding was performed on texts and interview transcripts. Codes related to the key MSP principles under investigation.

MSP planning principles

The EC posits that an ecosystem approach should be an overarching principle for MSP (CEC, 2008). There is, however, considerable debate about the efficacy an ecosystem approach and how it should be implemented (Kidd *et al.*, 2011). It is argued, for example, that there is a lack of sufficient scientific understanding of marine ecosystems to enable its effective implementation (Frid *et al.*, 2006; Wang, 2005). Critics argue that the transition to an ecosystem approach in policy and management spheres is out of step with scientific progress and the development of resource management tools and that, in effect, science needs to 'catch up' before it can be implemented effectively (Thrush *et al.*, 2010). Others argue that the ecosystem approach is not about science or an extension of natural resource management tools, but that it is a fundamental reframing of how we interact with nature (Gumbine, 1994) and that it can be supported, for the most part, by existing biological, oceanographic, economic and social information appropriate to the issues being managed (Murawski, 2007). Although there may be insufficient data available to answer conclusively all questions relating to the impacts of particular management choices, there is usually sufficient data to identify qualitatively the likely interactions among species and sectors and the directionality of particular human activities on biota and their socio-economic impacts (CBD, 2007).

An in-depth review of the application of the ecosystem approach revealed that despite its broad acceptance, it is still more of a concept than a practice (CBD, 2007). A review of relevant marine initiatives found that there was a disconnect between how it was conceptualised in the academic literature and how it was applied in practice (Arkema *et al*., 2006). The review found that initiatives are inclined to overlook critical ecological and human factors emphasised in the academic literature (Arkema *et al*., 2006).

The EC promotes the adoption of an objectives-based approach to MSP, with national or regional strategic objectives being implemented through operational objectives (CEC, 2008). Strategic objectives are predominately of an aspirational nature, whereas operational objectives are usually defined in terms of measurable quantities (de la Mare, 2005). In this regard, the use of SMART (Specific, Measurable, Achievable, Realistic, Time-limited) principles in designing objectives has been advocated by a number of MSP researchers and practitioners (de la Mare, 2005; Douvere and Elher, 2010). The need for transparent and comprehensible MSP processes is also stressed by the EC (CEC, 2008).

The EC argues that a single administrative entity should lead MSP processes and that it should be based on a legally binding framework. This may be achieved through existing governance structures, avoiding the need for new entities to be created. The legal framework for MSP should clearly define administrative competencies and who is to be bound by the plan, and should provide for inter-institutional cooperation (CEC, 2010). Through cross-border cooperation, states should coordinate plans for shared, transboundary ecosystems (CEC, 2008). This will require early communication, consultation and cooperation with neighbouring states. To achieve consistency in the coastal zone, states also should seek to coordinate marine and terrestrial planning processes, through, for example, the adoption of Integrated Coastal Zone Management (ICZM) processes (CEC, 2008).

Effective MSP requires current, accurate environmental and socio-economic data (CEC, 2008). Furthermore, MSP initiatives should be adaptive and flexible to react to new information. The adoption of an adaptive, flexible process will allow for evaluation findings of management strategies to be incorporated into future strategies (Lee, 1993). An adaptive approach requires regular monitoring and evaluation so that MSP initiatives can assess whether their plans are leading to anticipated outcomes and can formulae corrective strategies, if necessary (Douvere and Elher, 2010). Effective monitoring and evaluation requires that appropriate indicators are defined for all objectives early in the MSP process (CEC, 2010).

MSP principles in practice

This section presents the findings of the two case studies. Each case study includes a brief overview of the initiative and the policy and legislative framework within which it functions. Findings in relation to the EC guiding principle are presented in each case study.

CINMS case study

The CINMS was established in 1980, under the auspices of The Marine Protection, Research and Sanctuaries Act (MPRSA) (US Government, 1972), comprises approximately 1,110 square nautical miles (nmi) off the coast of Southern California, and has been highlighted as an example of a marine ecosystem-based management (EBM) initiative (Flannery and Ó Cinnéide, 2011; Douvere, 2008). A Stakeholder Advisory Council (SAC) in respect of CINMS was established in 1998. The SAC has 21 seats, 10 government seats and 11 community stakeholder seats. A review of the CINMS management plan began in 1998, with a new plan coming into effect on the 19th of March 2009. The management plan outlines the sanctuary's management objectives, related action plans and performance measures.

Ecosystem approach

The CINMS plan seeks to adopt an ecosystem approach in its management plan (US Department of Commerce, 2008). The plan integrates the management of all human activity in the sanctuary. It contains a number of action plans to address cross-sectoral issues. Two action plans in particular are highly relevant to adopting an ecosystem approach: the Water Quality Action Plan; and the Resource Protection Action Plan. Both plans seek to understand the cumulative impact of human activity within and around the sanctuary and to address these through cross-sectoral strategies (US Department of Commerce, 2008). A number of interviewees expressed concern with the adoption of an ecosystem approach in the CINMS. One interviewee believed that the adoption of such an approach will be seized upon by local environmental groups to introduce more conservation measures. Another was concerned that the 'ecosystem argument' would be used to extend the boundaries of the Sanctuary to include some of the mainland coastal zone as the current CINMS plan contains a commitment to evaluate the possibility of extending the Sanctuary boundaries. Another interviewee was not sure what an ecosystem approach would mean in practice other than 'more funding for scientists.'

Objective-based planning

The process of defining objectives and action areas for the plan began in 1999 when the CINMS held a number of scoping meetings. Issues raised at these meetings were refined by CINMS staff in conjunction with the Council. To aid this process, sanctuary staff analysed the specific threats each of these issues posed to the sanctuary. They also conducted an analysis to determine which of these issues were currently being addressed successfully through existing measures. Sanctuary staff considered the feasibility of each action as well as the availability of resources to address them, including staff expertise and potential external partners for implementation of management strategies. At the end of this process nine broad action areas were finalised and included in the management plan: a) public awareness and understanding; b) conservation science; c) boundary evaluation; d) water quality; e) emergency response; f) enforcement; g) maritime heritage; h) resource protection; i) operations; and j) performance evaluation (US Department of Commerce, 2008). A detailed action plan has been produced for each of these action areas. Each action plan contains a description of the issue at hand, the management strategies and associated objectives the CINMS will implement to address these issues, an account of strategy implementers, the status of each activity, how frequently it will occur, partners for its implementation, and estimated annual costs (US Department of Commerce, 2008). It also highlights strategies from the other action plans that are directly or indirectly linked to the overall objective. In this manner the CINMS approximates with the SMART Principles.

Coordinated governance, statutory status and crossborder coordination
To promote comprehensive protection of sanctuary resources, the CINMS has developed cooperative agreements and memoranda of understanding with several regulatory agencies holding competencies within the sanctuary. Furthermore, the MPRSA empowers the CINMS, through the Secretary of Commerce, to hold federal agencies responsible for their actions in the sanctuary. Federal agency actions that are likely to destroy, cause the loss of, or injure any sanctuary resource are subject to consultation with the Secretary of Commerce, even if it occurs outside a sanctuary (US Government, 1972). The agency, however, must only consider the Secretary's recommendations and may ignore them so long as it provides a written statement explaining why it chose to do so (US Government, 1972). However, if after ignoring the Secretary's recommendations, the agency's actions results in the destruction of a sanctuary resource, that agency must take prompt action to prevent and mitigate further damage and also restore or replace the resource by means of a way agreed to by the Secretary (US Government, 1972). A number of other management instruments focus on protecting valuable or vulnerable areas and have been developed independently of the CINMS plan. For example, a number of marine protected areas (MPAs) were implemented prior to the completion of the CINMS plan. These were developed through a separate five year multi-agency, multi-stakeholder planning process. However, the fragmented nature of marine governance in the area has inhibited their effective implementation as the portion of the MPAs in state waters were implemented four years before the portion in federal waters due to an internal dispute between two agencies in the National Oceanic and Atmospheric Administration (Crowder *et al.*, 2006). Due to its geographical location, the CINMS does not have to address cross-border issues *per se*. It does, however, cooperate and consult with other management bodies and agencies which operate in the waters contiguous to

the sanctuary. It also cooperates and consults with the neighbouring National Marine Sanctuaries. Interviewees, however, indicated that representatives of these sanctuaries rarely, if ever, attend Council meetings.

Incorporating data, knowledge, monitoring and evaluation

Due to its remit the CINMS conducts research and data collection on an ongoing basis. Research focuses on collecting data on marine resources, evaluating ecosystem health, assessing the impact of human activity in the sanctuary, implementing effective resource management strategies, and increasing understanding of the importance of the Sanctuary. A number of CINMS action plans contain commitments to undertake further research and to gather further data to aid decision-making. For example, the Water Quality Action Plan contains strategies which will see the sanctuary complete a water quality characterisation report, and compile and synthesise information on jurisdictional water quality authorities and responsibilities. It will then develop corrective actions for managing the impacts on water quality within the sanctuary. There is a lack of spatial information on the CINMS regarding the sanctuary's resources and uses. However, the plan contained a commitment to begin to address this deficit by analysing existing spatial data. The CINMS Plan contains a Performance Evaluation Action Plan which instructs sanctuary staff to conduct routine performance evaluations over the first five years of the plan. The action plan contains performance measures for all the strategies outlined in the other action plans. Sanctuary staff are required to report the findings of their evaluations and work with the Council to identify successful implementation of management strategies and to establish management strategies that need to be reformulated in order to achieve their objectives. A number of interviewees expressed frustration at the emphasis on gathering ecological data with little or no research being conducted on the socio-economic impact of planning decisions.

Transparency

Advisory Council meetings are open to the general public and time is provided at these meetings for public comment. A number of interviewees, however, raised concerns regarding the transparency of the process for selecting representatives. Representatives are chosen by the sanctuary superintendent. Those aspiring to become Council members apply directly to the sanctuary superintendent. The sanctuary superintendent then submits copies of all applications to the Council, which acts as a preliminary reviewing body. Some interviewees expressed concerns with the prevailing selection process. They argued that the selection process allowed the Council to be dominated by stakeholders who are unlikely to disagree with the actions of sanctuary management.

ESSIM case study

The ESSIM initiative was the first integrated ocean management project established under the Canada's *Oceans Act* (Foster *et al*., 2006). The *Oceans Act* mandated the Department of Fisheries and Oceans Canada (DFO) to develop and implement integrated management plans for Canada's oceans. The management of the initiative is largely overseen by the ESSIM Planning Office in conjunction with an advisory council. A strategic plan was developed for the area and contains objectives for future management (Flannery and Ó Cinnéide, 2012).

Ecosystem approach

The ecosystem approach is one of ESSIM's guiding principles (DFO, 2007). Adopting this approach, according to the ESSIM plan (DFO, 2007), means that "the management of human activities should make every effort to ensure the integrity of ecosystem components, functions and properties are maintained and/or restored at appropriate temporal and spatial scales" (p.13). To achieve this, the management plan focuses on ensuring human activity does not adversely affect biodiversity, ecosystem productivity, or marine environmental quality (DFO, 2007). The plan contains a number of strategies to implement this, such as: identifying threats and management options for biodiversity conservation; assessing and reviewing factors influencing productivity; and assessing sources and impacts of wastes and debris (DFO, 2007). To implement this principle "the ESSIM planning process considers the ecosystem and all of its users comprehensively" rather than concentrating on individual sectors (DFO, 2007). Efforts at adopting this approach, however, are ultimately undone by the ESSIM plan's weak implementation strategy which eschews coordinated action planning in favour of sectoral planning. The ESSIM Plan does not provide detailed strategies or actions plans to achieve its cross-sectoral objectives. Instead, the plan aims "to augment or enhance existing decision-making processes by linking sector planning and management to an overarching set of goals and objectives" (DFO, 2007, p.5). Action planning is left to the preserve of the various marine sectors with little or no coordination or integration of these plans. Thus, the implementation of the ESSIM initiative's ecosystem approach is largely dependent on individual sectors voluntarily adopting this principle and related objectives and strategies in their own plans.

Objectives-based planning

The goal of the ESSIM Plan is to provide an objectives-based approach to ocean management (DFO, 2007). The plan contains three overarching objectives: collaborative governance and integrated management; sustainable human use; and healthy ecosystems. These are supported by more specific objectives and strategies. In this way the ESSIM initiative attempts to develop detailed strategies to give practical effect to its aspirational objectives. However, many of these strategies are very general. For example, one strategy supporting the objective of integrated management is to: *facilitate stakeholder involvement and capacity*. The strategy contains no indication about the actions that are to be taken to facilitate this. The plan does not contain a timeframe for the implementation of these strategies, but it does envisage progress being made through a series of short-term action plans. Individual marine sectors are expected to develop action plans to implement these strategies. Such an implementation strategy is liable to inhibit coordinated implementation. A sub-committee meeting observed as part of this study discussed this issue. The role of the Council in developing and coordinating action plans was debated. However, it was generally agreed that action planning should be left to sectoral interests. To generate an overview of how the ESSIM plan was being implemented, it was suggested that each sectoral plan might be analysed by theme. Themed papers could then be generated illustrating how the ESSIM Plan's objectives were being implemented. Expressing frustration with the sector-based implementation strategy, two interviewees questioned if it truly represented integrated management. One asked:

> "are we doing integrated management now, not really, we're each doing our own plans." (ESSIM Council Member)

Statutory standing and coordinated governance

Although the 1997 *Oceans Act* assigns DFO as the lead agency for integrated marine planning process, it does not endow DFO with sufficient authority to regulate all activities within the planning areas. Thus, DFO assumes a largely coordinating role, leaving various other departments with their traditional competencies. This, however, enables government agencies and departments to effectively ignore the ESSIM plan if it does not further their own management objectives. This has impacted adversely on the manner in which some government departments participate in the ESSIM process and has inhibited efforts at developing constructive dialogue amongst stakeholders and regulators (Flannery and Ó Cinnéide, 2012).

Cross-border cooperation and consultation

The spatial boundaries of the ESSIM initiative are based on a combination of administrative and ecological considerations (Rutherford *et al.*, 2005) and have been the subject of much debate and controversy. The planning area as designated corresponds with the Northwest Atlantic Fisheries Organization (NAFO) fisheries management division 4VW. This area, however, encroaches on the jurisdictional area of the Canada-Newfoundland and Labrador Offshore

Petroleum Board, who are not party to the ESSIM process. This issue was not resolved before the development of the ESSIM Plan, with the result that the Minster of Fisheries and Oceans has refused to endorse it, which in turn has led to implementation issues and disenchantment of many stakeholders involved in the process (Flannery and Ó Cinnéide, 2012)..

Coherence with terrestrial plans

The landward boundary of the planning area has been subject to change. Although the ESSIM initiative was originally designed to have an offshore focus, it sought to incorporate coastal waters into the initiative during the planning process (Rutherford *et al.*, 2005). It then returned to its original remit with the plan focusing exclusively on offshore seas, specifically the area beyond the 12 nmi territorial sea limit, although a number of representatives from provincial and municipal planning bodies remained on the Council. This created Nova Scotia's own version of the 'West Lothian Question', as some interviewees expressed frustration at the fact that these representatives were taking part in a planning process that would not have a direct impact on their own management processes.

Monitoring and evaluation

The ESSIM plan is to be reviewed every five years. The successful implementation of the plan "requires an effective and comprehensive program for performance evaluation and reporting" that is regarded as "an integral component of the objectives-based approach and the key to the practice of adaptive management" (Rutherford *et al.*, p.63). The plan, however, does not contain indicators or performance measures for any of its objectives, strategies or actions.

Incorporating data and knowledge

DFO has undertaken a significant amount of scientific research and assessment work in support of the ESSIM initiative. This included the publication of a number of reports on the ecosystem of the planning area. As well as these technical reports, DFO has also published a number of discussion papers regarding the planning process. These include: *The Development of a Collaborative Management and Planning Process*, which was designed to stimulate and guide discussion on the structures of the collaborative planning model; *Issues, Challenges and Opportunities: A Discussion Paper prepared for the Federal-Provincial ESSIM Working Group*, which was based on the bilateral discussions between DFO and various ocean sectors and which outlined broad management issues; *A Strategic Planning Framework for the Eastern Scotian Shelf Ocean Management Plan: A Discussion Paper prepared for the ESSIM Forum*, which presented the core elements of the plan and various options for the development of a comprehensive ocean management framework; and *Eastern Scotian Shelf Integrated Management (ESSIM) Initiative: Proposed Collaborative Planning Model – A Discussion Paper*, outlining the proposed collaborative planning model (Schaefer and Barale, 2011). One interviewee commented that these discursive reports were as valuable as the scientific reports as they helped to structure the planning process. An atlas of human activity in the planning area was also produced which included spatial and temporal information about a number of activities in the planning area. All interviewees felt that sufficient data and information were made available to them.

Transparency

Council meetings are closed to the general public and one needs formal permission to attend. The ESSIM initiative has a dedicated website where it makes all its documents and reports available. There is also an online discussion forum dedicated to the ESSIM initiative. The minutes of the Council meetings are available on this forum. One interviewee questioned the transparency of the relationship between DFO and the fisheries organisations represented on the Council. At a Council meeting observed in the course of this study, a DFO officer made a presentation on behalf of the fisheries sector outlining its framework for developing an action plan. The interviewee cited this as evidence of DFO having an extremely close relationship with local fisheries. DFO officers who were interviewed for this study expressed a willingness to engage with all sectors and to help them develop action plans. Furthermore, they owned up to a special relationship with the fisheries sector and defended it on the grounds that they are its regulator. The presentation of the fisheries action plan by a DFO staff member was explained on the basis of the fisheries representative being unable to attend the Council meeting, and it was denied that this was indicative of collusion between DFO and the fisheries sector.

Discussion

These case studies suggest several useful lessons in terms of implementing MSP. The difficulty of implementing an ecosystem approach in areas with fragmented governance is demonstrated by the experience of the CINMS in implementing MPAs. It is argued that planning of MPAs should be part of the MSP processes, rather than being conducted separately, and that they should be implemented within a comprehensive place-based management plan (Young *et al.*, 2007). Adopting such an approach would enable the CINMS to link its MPAs to other management strategies.

The CINMS capacity to adopt a truly integrated management approach is greatly aided by its statutory standing and capacity to somewhat hold other agencies responsible for their actions. Its efforts at implementing an ecosystem approach can only be assessed once it completes its Water Quality and Resource Protection action plans. The objectives for these action plans, and the plan as a whole, compare favourably to those of the EBM initiatives assessed by Arkema *et al.* (2006). The broad, aspirational management objectives of the plans are to be achieved through detailed strategies that are specific and measurable and which have to be implemented within a specific timeframe. In this manner the CINMS objectives roughly approximate with the SMART principles for objective setting as advanced by some MSP theorists (Day, 2008; Douvere and Elher, 2010).

The experience of the ESSIM initiative highlights a number of key lessons. MSP lead agencies must make the transition from sectoral to ecosystem-based management and adopt new ecosystem focused operational procedures. Although the ESSIM initiative adopted an ecosystem approach as one of its guiding principles, there is little evidence of its practical implementation. Without detailed strategies and action plans, implementation remains very much an aspirational goal rather than something that is being achieved in any tangible or measurable manner. Future MSP initiatives need to consider how an ecosystem approach may be incorporated into the planning process *and* how this approach is to be implemented once planning has been finalised. Depending on sector-based plans, as ESSIM did to effect ecosystem-based management strategies, is not fruitful as it results in piecemeal, fragmented implementation. This implementation strategy is more likely to further embed a sectoral approach to marine management rather than usher in a new era of place-based management.

Implementation of the ESSIM plan is also inhibited by a lack of specificity in its objectives and strategies. The ESSIM plan contains three overarching cross-sectoral objectives which are to be achieved through more specific objectives and strategies. These lower level objectives, however, are aspirational rather than operational and, in most cases, are very general. The strategies also are imprecise and do not contain specific, measurable actions. Clear monitoring and evaluation strategies also need to be established in advance of implementation.

Conclusions and recommendations

Several lessons for MSP initiatives may be drawn from the evidence presented above. First, to expedite the transition to MSP, the place-based nature and integrated management dimensions of the ecosystem approach need to be emphasised in MSP initiatives. MSP lead agencies need to break with traditional sectoral planning and thinking and need to evolve new ecosystem focused work practices. They must adopt an ecosystem outlook and have the competence to coordinate at ecosystem level, as illustrated well by the CINMS case study. This may mean that lead agencies need to be invested with the authority to hold other agencies and regulators accountable for their actions and to compel them to comply with integrated marine plans. Second, MSP initiatives need to develop a clear understanding of how an ecosystem approach may be incorporated into the planning process and how this approach is to be implemented once planning has been finalised. The ESSIM initiative mirrored the marine projects reviewed by Arkema *et al.* (2006) insofar as it experienced considerable difficulties in progressing the ecosystem approach from abstract concept to practice. The ecosystem approach must, therefore, be clearly understood and emphasised in the objective setting phase, through the plan development stage and be fully incorporated into implementation strategies.

As demonstrated in particular by the ESSIM case study, it is vitally important that proper consideration be given to the manner in which objectives are to be achieved. It experienced difficulties in designing strategies to give practical effect to these aspirational objectives and in transitioning to plan implementation. Conversely, the CINMS illustrated the benefit of having specific, measurable objectives and detailed implementation strategies. The use of the SMART principles for objective setting may be useful in ensuring that aspirational objectives are translated into operational objectives (Day, 2008). It may also be valuable to adopt the CINMS approach of specifying implementers for each objective. The SMART principles also should be adopted in developing objectives.

Although a variety of tools can be used to effect a legally binding process (Schaefer *et al.*, 2011) the ESSIM case study demonstrates that a legal obligation to consider certain planning principles and guidelines in the decision process does not automatically result in the successful implementation of these principles. Although Canada's *Oceans Act* affords the ESSIM initiative legal status, it still experienced difficulties in implementing its plan. The Act does not imbue DFO with the competence to extract commitments from other governmental departments and agencies or to make them comply with the plan. This contrasts with the CINMS experience, where plan implementation is progressing satisfactorily due in large measure to NOAA's competency in terms of getting other agencies to comply with the CINMS Plan. Thus, MSP initiatives not only have to operate on a statutory basis but must also be empowered with sufficient authority to govern marine areas. MSP legislation needs to provide the lead agency with authority to hold other government agencies accountable for plan implementation.

Implementation of the ESSIM initiative has been frustrated due to its boundary issues. The implementation of MPAs in the CINMS was also delayed due to the complex legislative framework within which it operates. MSP legislation must streamline the complex legislative and governance framework of marine environments and strive to ensure that implementation of MSP is not hampered or undermined by fragmented governance (Young, 2002).

Endnotes

1 The evaluation of the principle of stakeholder participation in the CINMS and ESSIM initiatives has already been reported; see (Flannery and Ó Cinnéide, 2011) and (Flannery and Ó Cinnéide, 2012) respectively. The principle of deploying MSP according to area or type of activity could not be evaluated in these studies.

References

Arkema, K.K., Abramson, S.C. and Dewsbury, B.M. (2006) Marine ecosystem-based management: from characterization to implementation, *Frontiers in Ecology and the Environment*, 4, pp. 525-532.

CBD (2007) In-depth review of the application of the ecosystem approach. Barriers to the application of the ecosystem approach. *Proceedings of the 12th meeting of the subsidiary body on scientific, technical and technological advice Paris*, Paris: UNESCO.

CEC (2010) *Communication from the Commission to the European Parliament, the Council, the European Economic and Social Committee and the Committee of the Regions: Maritime spatial planning in the EU - achievements and future development*, Luxembourg: Publications Office of the European Union.

CEC (2008) *Communication from the Commission: roadmap for maritime spatial planning: achieving common principles in the EU, COM(2008) 791 final*. Brussels: CEC.

Crowder, L.B., Osherenko, G., Young, O.R., Airame, S., Norse, E.A. and Baron, N., (2006) Resolving Mismatches in US Ocean Governance, *Science*, 313, pp. 617-618.

Day, J. (2008) The need and practice of monitoring, evaluating and adapting marine planning and management--lessons from the Great Barrier Reef, *Marine Policy*, 32, pp. 823-831.

de la Mare, W.K. (2005) Marine ecosystem-based management as a hierarchical control system, *Marine Policy*, 29, pp. 57-68.

DFO (2007) *Eastern Scotian Shelf Integrated Ocean Management Plan*. Dartmouth, Nova Scotia: Oceans and Coastal Management Division, Fisheries and Oceans Canada.

Douvere, F. and Ehler, C. (2010) The importance of monitoring and evaluation in adaptive maritime spatial planning, *Journal of Coastal Conservation*, 15, pp. 305-311.

Douvere, F. (2008) The importance of marine spatial planning in advancing ecosystem-based sea use management, *Marine Policy*, 32, pp. 762-771.

Ehler, C. and Douvere F. (2007) *Visions for a seachange: report of the first international workshop on marine spatial planning*. Paris: UNESCO.

Flannery, W. and Ó Cinnéide, M. (2012) Deriving Lessons Relating to Marine Spatial Planning from Canada's Eastern Scotian Shelf Integrated Management Initiative, *Journal of Environmental Policy & Planning*, 14, pp. 97-117.

Flannery, W. and Ó Cinnéide, M. (2011) Stakeholder Participation in Marine Spatial Planning: Lessons from the Channel Islands National Marine Sanctuary, *Society & Natural Resources*, 25, pp. 727-742.

Foster, E., Haward, M. and Coffen-Smout, S. (2005) Implementing integrated oceans management: Australia's south east regional marine plan (SERMP) and Canada's eastern Scotian shelf integrated management (ESSIM) initiative, *Marine Policy*, 29, pp. 391-405.

Frid, C.L.J., Paramor, O.A.L. and Scott, C.L. (2006) Ecosystem-based management of fisheries: is science limiting? *ICES Journal of Marine Science*, 63, pp. 1567-1572.

Grumbine, R.E. (1994) What Is Ecosystem Management? *Conservation Biology*, 8, pp. 27-38.

Kidd, S., Maltby, E., Robinson, L., Barker, A. and Lumb, C. (2011) The ecosystem approach and planning and management of the marine environment. In: Kidd, S., Plater, A. and Frid, C. (Eds.), *The ecosystem approach and planning and management*, London: Earthscan; 2011. p. 1-33.

Lee, K. (1993) *Compass and gyroscope: integrating politics and science for the environment*. Washington, DC: Island Press, 1993.

Murawski, S.A. (2007) Ten myths concerning ecosystem approaches to marine resource management, *Marine Policy*, 31, pp. 681-690.

Rutherford, R.J., Herbert, G.J. and Coffen-Smout S. (2005) Integrated ocean management and the collaborative planning process: the Eastern Scotian Shelf Integrated Management (ESSIM) Initiative, *Marine Policy*, 29, pp. 75-83.

Schaefer, N. and Barale, V. (20110 Maritime spatial planning: opportunities and challenges in the framework of the EU integrated maritime policy, *Journal of Coastal Conservation*, 15, pp. 237-45.

Thrush, S.F. and Dayton, P.K. (2010) What Can Ecology Contribute to Ecosystem-Based Management? *Annual Review of Marine Scienc*e, 2, pp. 419-441.

U.S Department of Commerce. (2008) *Channel Islands National Marine Sanctuary Management plan / Final Environmental Impact Statement.* National Oceanic and Atmospheric Administration: National Marine Sanctuary Program.

US Government (1972) *Marine Protection, Research and Sanctuaries Act.* Washington DC: US Government.

Wang, H. (2005) An evaluation of the modular approach to the assessment and management of large marine ecosystems, in Hennessey, T.M. and Sutinen, J.G. (Eds.). *Large Marine Ecosystems*, London: Elsevier, pp. 335-355.

Young, O.R., Osherenko, G., Ekstrom, J., Crowder, L.B., Ogden, J. and Wilson, J.A. (2007) Solving the Crisis in Ocean Governance: Place-Based Management of Marine Ecosystems. *Environment*, 49, pp. 20-32.

Young, O.R. (2002) *The institutional dimensions of environmental change: fit, interplay, and scale*. Cambridge, MA: MIT Press.

Chapter 17

Comparing the political imperative to designate new national parks in a devolved Scotland and Northern Ireland

Jonathan Bell and Aileen Stockdale

Introduction

This chapter compares attempts to designate new national parks in Scotland and Northern Ireland and seeks to identify the relationship between these attempts and political devolution in the UK in the late 1990s. The chapter is drawn from a larger research project (Bell, 2013a) and analyses data from semi-structured interviews conducted with high ranking politicians, government officials and regional and local stakeholders. An analysis of archival documents and policy texts (research reports, media material and organisational position statements and web based information) was also undertaken. The chapter focuses on the designation of the Cairngorms National Park (CNP) in Scotland in 2003 which is now the UK's largest national park (4,528km^2) and the failed attempt to designate a Mournes National Park in Northern Ireland which remains as an Area of Outstanding Natural Beauty.

Both the Mournes and Cairngorms are multi-functional and environmentally significant landscapes comprising distinct social, economic and environmental functions. They are inhabited, predominantly privately owned landscapes with a legacy of traditional industries (agriculture, forestry and small scale quarrying), recreational activity and tourism. However, managing these often competing activities within a sustainable development (WECD, 1987; Redclift, 2006) agenda, incorporating environmental, social and economic goals, has proved difficult at times (Lambert, 2001; Gimingham, 2002a; MHT, 2007; CAAN, 2007). While national park designation offers a potential management mechanism for multi-functional landscapes, it is shown in this chapter that the underlining political circumstances can accelerate or undermine the designation process.

The chapter is organised into four sections. First, the underpinnings to the global national park concept and the historical absence compared to England and Wales of national parks in Scotland and Northern Ireland are explained. Second, the emergence of UK devolution post 1999 and the return of national parks on to the political agenda in both Scotland and Northern Ireland are discussed. Third, a series of political motives is explored and contrasted between Scotland and Northern Ireland to demonstrate the relationship between governing circumstances and the progression of national parks policy. Finally, the chapter concludes by outlining the subtle differences in the political motivations for progressing national parks and, in light of contrasting outcomes, the influence of differing governing circumstances is highlighted.

The concept of 'parks' for the 'nation' and the historical absence of National Parks in Scotland and Northern Ireland

The world's first national park designation at Yellowstone in 1872 stemmed from a report by Law Frederick Olmsted (1865) highlighting the threat that 'the rapid and gigantic expansion of private property' (Harroy et al., 1974: p.7) posed to America's natural resources. The U.S. Federal government decided to set aside land for the benefit of the "nation" as a whole. Accordingly, the term "national park" is derived from the desire to preserve "parks" for the "nation" (Harroy *et al.*, 1974).

Many of the first national parks established in North America and Australia were part of an emerging nationhood and became symbolic of post-colonial national identity re-construction. National parks, therefore, have clear political connotations linked to the construction of nation states and the expression of cultural identity. The American pre-occupation of national identity with wilderness was associated with the pursuit of a cultural identity forged out of 'natural grandeur' (Beinart and Coates, 1995: p.75), to rival the cathedrals and castles of Europe (Dilsaver, 1997).

In a UK context, the Addison Committee (1931) was the first of several government appointed committees to officially investigate the introduction of UK national parks. The Dower (1945) and Hobhouse (1947) reports prompted legislative reform in England and Wales where national parks were designated in the second half of the 20th century under the National Parks and Access to the Countryside Act 1949 (Table 17.1). The Ramsay Report (1947), which outlined similar proposals to Dower and Hobhouse, did not provoke a parallel legislative response in Scotland (Barker and Stockdale, 2008). Ramsay's proposal for land nationalisation was 'undoubtedly a serious obstacle in the eyes of a government which, although radical, was not prepared to upset landowners too much' (Shoard, 1987: p.292).

Table 17. 1 UK National Parks

National Parks	Year Designated
Peak District	1951
Lake District	1951
Snowdonia	1951
Dartmoor	1951
North York Moors	1952
Pembrokeshire Coast	1952
Exmoor	1954
Yorkshire Dales	1954
Northumberland	1956
Brecon Beacons	1957
Loch Lomond and the Trossachs	2002
Cairngorms	2003
New Forest	2005
South Downs	2009

The five Scottish national parks proposed by Ramsay in 1947 were designated as National Park Development Areas in 1951 (Gimingham, 2002a). The core area of the Cairngorms was designated as a National Nature Reserve in 1954 and was succeeded by National Scenic Area designation in 1982. However, escalating conflicts between recreation and nature conservation throughout the 1980s (Lambert, 2001; Coppock, 1980) and a perceived democratic deficit within the current structures of administration (Gimingham, 2002b), demonstrated the need for more integrated and inclusive management. The World Conservation Strategy (1980) identified the Scottish Highlands as a priority area for designating national parks and the Countryside Commission recommended:

> an announcement by government of the political will to set up national parks in certain defined areas (the Cairngorms, Loch Lomond, Ben Nevis/Glen Coe/ Black Mountain and Wester Ross). (Countryside Commission for Scotland, 1990: p.38)

Further site specific designations (SSSIs, SPAs, SACs) were applied to the Cairngorms throughout the 1980s and 1990s. However, opposition from certain interest groups, particularly landowners and the National Farmers'Union, suppressed campaigns to establish national parks (Crabtree, 1991; Warren, 2009) as opinion within Scottish Office circles 'hardened against' national park designation:

> "I had always been told [in the early 1990's] the instruction was to look at what could be done but national park is not one of the solutions we want to hear…on the whole the Conservatives were a landowners party and was never

particularly pro national park" (Former Scottish Office official) quoted in Gimingham (2002a: p.207).

The Cairngorms Working Party was created in 1991 to develop a management strategy and discuss administrative changes in the Cairngorms (Cairngorms Working Party, 1993). While international pressure mounted (IUCN, 1994), the Conservative government declared that national park designation in the Cairngorms and Loch Lomond and the Trossachs was 'not justified' (The Scottish Office, 1995: p.36); instead, the Cairngorms Partnership was established in 1994 to develop and implement an integrated management strategy for the Cairngorms (Rettie, 2001).

In the same year that Hobhouse and Ramsay had published proposals for national park designation in England / Wales and Scotland respectively, the Northern Ireland Planning Advisory Board (1947: pp.10-11) 'unanimously and urgently recommend(ed) that some areas be scheduled as National Parks' (Figure17.1).

Figure 17.1 The five areas proposed for national park designation in the Ulster Countryside Report (1947)

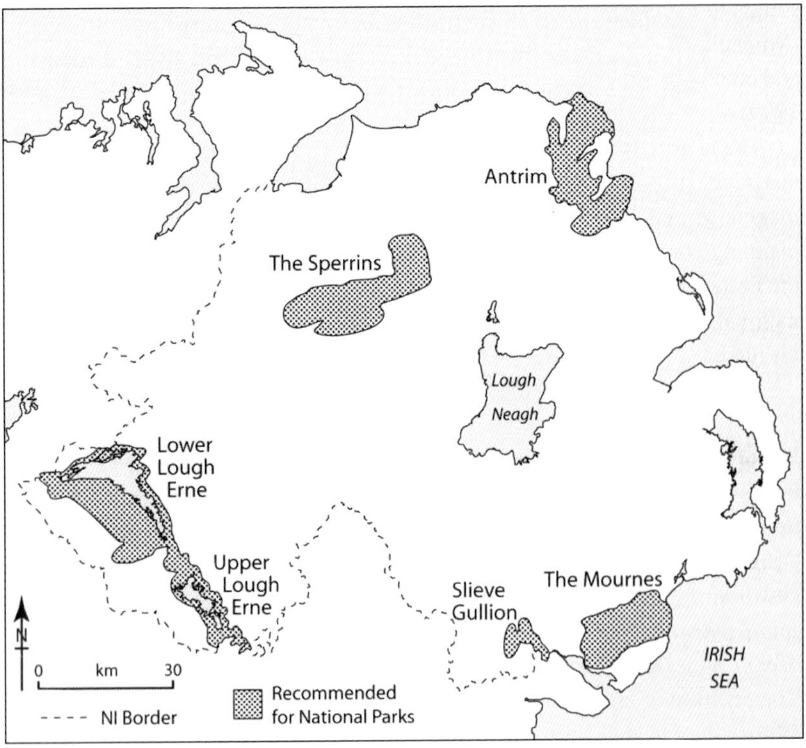

Source: Bell and Stockdale, (2009: p.8)

The proposals, however, were 'greeted with almost total silence by the government of the day' (Buchanan, 1982: p.273) before another government appointed committee called in 1960 for 'urgent action' (Buchanan, 1982: p.274). The legislative capacity for designating national parks was provided through the Amenity Lands Act (1965) and the Nature Conservation and Amenity Lands Order (1985). Despite this legislative provision, other political priorities (including dealing with civil unrest), strong landowner opposition and political lobbying from farming organisations quashed any prospects of national park designation at this time (Buchanan, 1982; Mitchell, 1999). Meanwhile, there are six National Parks in the Republic of Ireland (Killarney, Wicklow Mountains, Connemara, Glenveagh, the Burren and Ballycroy), which vary greatly from the model of national parks adopted in the UK (Bell and Stockdale, 2009).

Growing recognition of the need for integrated landscape management in Northern Ireland resulted in the creation of AONB management structures during the early 1990s. A Mourne committee (consisting of local people, politicians, user group/community representatives) and a Mourne liaison group (comprising agencies with executive powers within the AONB) were established. Together these groups constituted the Mourne Partnership which sought to achieve greater co-operation and co-ordination between stakeholders (Mitchell, 1999). The Mourne Heritage Trust (MHT) was established in 1997 and continues to provide for the management of the Mourne AONB (Mitchell, 1999).

The restoration of devolved government in 1998 transformed the political landscape of Northern Ireland offering the opportunity for key decision makers to venture 'beyond the longstanding tensions associated with rural planning control' (Greer and Murray, 2003: p.14) and look more seriously at the issue of National Park designation. The political context within which the national park issue re-emerged in both Scotland and Northern Ireland is now discussed.

Devolution and the re-emergence of national parks on the political agenda

Following the election of New Labour in 1997, devolution referendums in September 1997 paved the way for the creation of a National Assembly for Wales and a Scottish Parliament. In Scotland this was perceived to create a new politics which is 'less distant from the very communities it is supposed to serve' (Mitchell, 2000: p.138). In Northern Ireland devolution was essentially driven by a desire to bring to an end to three decades of sectarian conflict. The prospect of ending the 'troubles' in Northern Ireland grew throughout the 1990s with the announcement of paramilitary ceasefires. In 1998, the Belfast Agreement, commonly referred to as the Good Friday Agreement, was signed and with it political powers were returned to Northern Ireland in December 1999 ending nearly three decades of Direct Rule. There was a series of setbacks, political stalemates and Northern Ireland Assembly suspensions but eventually a devolved government, in all but policing and justice, was secured in 2007 following the St. Andrews Agreement. Policing and justice functions were transferred to the Assembly in May 2010 (Northern Ireland Assembly, 2010).

As well as progressing constitutional reform, the incumbent UK government signalled its intention to designate new national parks. At the 1999 Labour Party conference the then Deputy Prime Minister, John Prescott, announced:

> "50 years on, this Labour government will begin the process to create new National Parks - in the South Downs and the New Forest" (Prescott, 1999)

Even prior to devolution, Donald Dewar, the then Secretary of State for Scotland, publicly declared his wish to designate Scottish national parks (The Scottish Office, 1997a) during the first term of the new Scottish Parliament. In Northern Ireland, national parks appeared to be on the political radar before the Belfast Agreement (1998) but there were no public signs of a political intent to designate.

One interviewee described Lord Dubs, the Northern Ireland Office Environment and Agriculture Minister between May 1997 and December 1999, as being "very keen, he was an enthusiast for the environment…and when he was the Minister he plodded over the Mournes….he started talking about a national park". Lord Dubs explained during interview: "I was totally committed to it [designating a Mourne national park] and I would have done it". He explained how he had tasked a group in the Mournes to come up with *"modest"* proposals for designating national parks. However, an over-ambitious proposal, which was beyond the Minister's financial budget due to funding constraints and the imminent Belfast Agreement with its other political priorities, ensured the national park proposal never gained momentum during this period. In contrast, Donald Dewar's transition from Secretary of State to First Minister of Scotland ensured that national park designation became one of the first policy priorities in the Scottish Parliament.

Meanwhile, the Environment Minister in the Northern Ireland Executive (Dermot Nesbitt) publicly announced his intention to take forward a national park designation in the Mournes (BBC, 2002). The political motivations for pursuing national parks in Scotland can be understood by examining a series of policy documents. Interview data is relied upon to deepen understanding of what fuelled the national park agenda within Northern Ireland.

National parks for Scotland and Northern Ireland: comparing the political motives

Sustainable development (WCED, 1987) became a guiding rudder of the Scottish Parliament (The Scottish Office, 1997b). Rural economic development and tackling 'gross inequalities of wealth and power' (The Scottish Office, 1997b: 7) in rural areas were identified as Scottish Executive priorities (The Scottish Executive, 2000b). National parks were tied up in the wider Land Reform agenda reflecting the government's desire to strengthen the public interest in land:

> "they [the Scottish Labour party] used national parks to make a statement about where we stand in Scotland in relation to the public versus private land ownership interests and the balance between those two" (Andrew Thin, Chairman SNH).

'Widening the power bases' and 'devolving power as close as practicable to the local level' were deemed essential pre-requisites for 'real' sustainable development (The Scottish Office, 1997b: pp.5-7). Accordingly, the Scottish Parliament recognised the potential of national parks for facilitating rural economic development and enhancing democracy in rural areas (Scottish Executive, 2000: p.46).

Nationalist sentiment underpinned the early national parks movement in the late 1800s and since then national parks have 'featured strongly in state-building processes' (Ramutsindela, 2004: p.29). National parks represent a symbol of cultural expression and national identity in post-colonial societies. With the advent of political devolution, Scottish national parks seem to have been anchored in similar nationalist tendencies. National parks were viewed by the Scottish Labour Party as an opportunity to demonstrate a break from the past; not only a break from Conservative rule, but a move away from Westminster rule:

> "Prior to devolution there was probably only one piece of Scottish legislation in Westminster a year and national parks wouldn't have been too far up the queue' (Former Scottish Office official).

> "We had national parks in the first manifesto because it is one of the things we couldn't do before devolution...pre-devolution the landowners in Scotland in the House of Lords would have blocked national parks...the Tories represented the landed interests...we had just had a long period of Conservative government and they were implacably opposed to national parks so for us, it was a landmark piece of legislation we put through along with land reform" (Sarah Boyack, Minister for Environment, Planning and Transport (1999-2000).

One Highland councillor felt that the altered political landscape diminished the influence of landed interests at the highest level within the Scottish political system to oppose national park designation:

> "they [landowners] were pragmatic enough to know that it was going to happen, with Labour so clear and adamant they knew they could no longer oppose it at a political level".

Donald Dewar's desire to emphasise the benefits of having a Scottish Parliament was evident from the outset:

> "in its first six months [the Scottish Parliament] has already taken decisive action in key policy areas of crucial importance...the decision to introduce National Parks in Scotland" (The Scottish Office, 1997b: 1).

These sentiments suggest that, following devolution, Scottish national parks were linked to a nation-building agenda and a political desire to re-assert Scotland as a country that could once again determine its own fate. McCarthy *et al.* (2002: p.669) claimed that national park designation in Scotland represented a 'catching up with history' while Rennie (2006: p.228) argued that the National Parks (Scotland) Act 2000 became a 'flagship statement' linked to the 'post-devolution nationalist fervor'. These nationalistic tendencies and the desire to reinforce Scottish nationhood have developed considerably over the lifetime of the Scottish Parliament. The Scottish National Party (SNP) now command a Parliamentary majority. Following the 2014 referendum on Scottish independence, Scotland will remain as part of the United Kingdom with the Scottish government likely to receive further devolution of powers from Westminster (HM Government, 2014; The Scottish Government, 2014).

In Northern Ireland, devolution was considered an essential pre-condition for kick-starting the national parks policy:

> "Going back to Direct Rule, there wasn't really much chance of a national park because Direct Rule Ministers had far more important things to worry about… it only came to prominence when we had our own government…" (Mourne farmer).

Unlike in Scotland, however, the impetus for progressing national parks solely emanated from Dermot Nesbitt (a former Northern Ireland Environment Minister) rather than from the wider devolved administration:

> "It didn't come from the Civil Service…David Trimble [first Minister for Northern Ireland from July 1998 to October 2002, barring brief spells of

> resignation and Assembly suspension] and the other Ministers did not champion it, that's not to say they were against it...so by viewing no opposition, it was taken as support and therefore I ran with it" (Dermot Nesbitt).

Nesbitt linked the lack of wider political attention towards national parks with the fragile and uncertain nature of the devolution settlement:

> "Post 1998 when we were in government, up until 2002, we spent a lot of time fire- fighting; was there not going to be a continuation of government; was there [going to be arms] decommissioning. So at the time...yes we were focussed on government but there was a bigger picture still to deliver which was a stable political Northern Ireland".

Understanding of why the national park policy agenda emerged can be considered under three categories. First, influential local lobbying:

> "We [the MHT] did all the lobbying...we actually lobbied Dermot Nesbitt in the first place" (MHT representative).

> "Various local people said to me, think about that, so I thought about it, looked, examined it and said this is something Northern Ireland doesn't have" (Dermot Nesbitt).

Second, political symbolism:

> "It was [linked to] that sort of optimistic, incarnation, that bright new shiny devolved government" (Conservationist).

> "... to the extent that I tried to say yes this is a new Northern Ireland, we're bringing peace and stability..." (Dermot Nesbitt).

Third, economic priorities within government:

> "[at the time] we were all aware of the very real economic pressures and under pressure to identify new opportunities and make savings within [each] department...one of the aspects that we need[ed] to grow was the tourism... Northern Ireland doesn't have a national park, its [national park] got a brand name all around the world, we are trying to raise tourism, it [national park] ticks a lot of boxes, at least it is worthy of saying lets get it on the list [of possibilities]" (Dermot Nesbitt).

The lack of nationalistic underpinnings to the national park agenda, in contrast to Scotland, can be attributed to the complexity of dual nationalistic identities in Northern Ireland, where separate 'British' and 'Irish' nationalities are celebrated, rather than a 'Northern Irish' identity (Elliott, 2002, Bell et al., 2010). Indeed, as attempts were made to progress a Mourne national park, the process aroused geo-political and ethno-national sentiment amongst local communities (Bell, 2013a). The political desire to initiate a Northern Irish national park agenda was still however, tied up in political symbolism. Unlike in Scotland (Rennie, 2006), this symbolism was based around demonstrating post-conflict transition and less around building a sense of nationhood. Accordingly, economic priorities were at the forefront of political thinking around the potential role of a national park in Northern Ireland.

Devolution resulted in speedy progression towards designation of Scotland's first national parks. However, flaws were evident in the early stages of the policy process in Northern Ireland (Bell and Stockdale 2009; Bell, 2013a; Bell, 2013b), which have undoubtedly delayed and possibly ended any immediate prospect of national park introduction in Northern Ireland. The temporary suspension of the Assembly on 11th February 2002 was deemed by several interviewees as a direct hindrance to national park progression:

> "I view it [Assembly suspension] as damaging, the reality is we don't have a national park anywhere at this minute and it went into a very slow crawl under Direct Rule [2002-2007]" (Dermot Nesbitt).

> "Nesbitt latched onto the idea and then devolution fell so he wasn't able to see it through, it lost momentum…I think it did kill it in a way" (Conservationist).

In the Mournes a twin-track approach was adopted which involved preparing draft primary legislation alongside a formal consultation undertaken by the government appointed Mourne National Park Working Party from 1st September 2006 until 31st January 2007. However, the preparation of legislation was de-railed by a series of factors between 2002 and 2006: the diversion of resources for the Review of Public Administration (RPA); deficiencies in the research base; and a lack of agreement as to an appropriate national park model with incoming Ministers seeking to "put their own stamp on the draft legislation" (Former DoE official). For example, Jeff Rooker (Direct Rule Minister) requested legislation be prepared along the lines of the English and Welsh model:

> "I remember him [Rooker] saying that he could see no reason why we did not introduce legislation for national parks exactly as they are in England and Wales and he instructed officials to prepare legislation along those lines" (Former DoE official).

> "Rooker was hell bent on just bringing a UK style national park across the water…we had to actually stop him in his tracks. It wouldn't suit anywhere on this island" (Conservationist).

This conservationist felt that certain features of the English and Welsh model (restrictive rural housing policy and a national park authority possessing development control powers) would be widely resisted by Northern Ireland landowners. The apparent lack of understanding of the need for a national park model tailored specifically to the Mournes context, such as the distinct 'Celtic model' proposed by the MHT (Mitchell, 1999), demonstrated the insensitivity of a Direct Rule Minister to local circumstances.

In contrast to Scotland where detailed proposals and legislation in the form of the National Parks Scotland Act, 2000 were laid out prior to local consultation (SNH, 2001), ultimately in Northern Ireland the Mourne National Park consultation was launched within a legislative vacuum. Accordingly, Cairngorm and Mourne stakeholders acquired different mindsets from the outset of the respective consultation processes:

> "with the aims set out in the legislation we thought this was gonna be a good thing" (Cairngorm farmer).

> "if you go to buy a motor car and you asked them questions about the car and he couldn't answer one of them, would you buy the motor car? We didn't want to say pass the legislation and then we're snookered" (Mourne farmer).

This contrasting legislative context (a product of differing devolution trajectories) directly influenced the level and form of stakeholder engagement within the participatory arena. In the Cairngorms, stakeholders were opposed, but generally adopted a constructive stance:

> "There was strong will within the [Scottish] Executive to make this happen so rather than sit back and let them do this to us we got heavily involved to make sure it worked for us" (Business owner);

> "…we weren't going to stop it so therefore we had to get on and work with it instead of against it" (Estate manager).

Therefore, while there was undoubted opposition, it never evolved into a vociferous anti-national park campaign:

> "We were not going to die in a ditch over it" (Estate owner);

> "I can't remember a campaign against it…I never detected any absolute outright hostile opposition to it" (Former Scottish Natural Heritage official).

By contrast, some Mourne landowners chose to disrupt and protest vociferously at public meetings, rather than engage constructively in the process:

> "They [national park opponents] organised people to go to the meetings with [anti-national park] placards" (Conservationist);

> "There is a feeling that discussing in depth what a national park meant would give the impression that the mindset was, 'this is inevitable so let's get the best results we can'...the attitude here was we are not going to let this happen so why should we negotiate" (Mourne farmer).

Varying legislative contexts, amongst other issues, contributed to Cairngorm and Mourne landowners adopting differing stances during the consultation process which inevitably contributed to differing outcomes (Bell and Stockdale, 2009; Bell, 2013a; Bell, 2013b). While the Cairngorms became Scotland's second national park, the prospects of a first national park for Northern Ireland appear more remote than ever, with the Minister for the Environment announcing that national parks policy in Northern Ireland has been shelved (BBC, 2014).

Conclusion

Despite repeated recommendations, no national parks were designated in Scotland or Northern Ireland throughout the 20th century. In both regions this can be largely attributed to landowner opposition and political circumstances. With a changed political landscape in the UK in the late 1990s, this chapter has shown that political circumstances continued to play a defining role in determining whether national parks were designated in Scotland and Northern Ireland.

Due to decades of sectarian conflict and Direct Rule, devolution in Northern Ireland was highly contested and protracted compared with Scotland. While the national parks policy process was initiated in Scotland prior to devolution, national park ambitions in Northern Ireland were curtailed under Direct Rule due to funding constraints and other political priorities. However, a national park designation agenda was taken forward in both regions during the early years of devolution. Recognition of their symbolic political value and the contribution that they could make to sustainable rural development represented two factors which fuelled the national parks imperative in Scotland. In response to local lobbying and an overriding economic imperative, devolution provided the catalyst for a Northern Ireland Minister (Nesbitt) to pursue national park designation in the Mournes locality. But unlike Northern Ireland, strong support for national parks at the highest political level (First Minister) aided national park progression in Scotland. While national parks were tied up in a

Scottish nation building agenda such motives were less apparent in Northern Ireland, perhaps due to the existence of dual national identities. However, the value of national parks as a demonstrable symbol of post-conflict transition and political progress and as a potential economic generator was recognised.

As in Scotland, the onset of more proximate governing through devolution initially gave impetus to the national parks agenda in Northern Ireland. While devolution smoothed the passage towards the introduction of national parks in Scotland, the policy process stalled in Northern Ireland. The suspension of the Northern Ireland Assembly between 2002 and 2006 contributed to delaying the preparation of primary legislation and the Mourne consultation was launched within a legislative vacuum which had stark consequences for stakeholder involvement.

In light of the initial economic imperative underpinning the political motive to introduce a Mourne National Park, it is ironic to note that in the same month (November, 2013) that the Environment Minister decided to bring the long running Northern Ireland national park saga to an end, it was reported (Arup, 2013) that national parks contribute £1 billion to the Welsh economy. This disjointed and ultimately failed national parks policy process and seemingly missed economic opportunity reflect the reality of stuttering governance arrangements in Northern Ireland since 1998.

References

Arup (2013) *Valuing Wales' National* Parks. London: Arup.

Barker, A. and Stockdale, A. (2008) Out of the wilderness? Achieving sustainable development within Scottish national parks, *Journal of Environmental Management,* 88(1), pp.181-193.

Beinart, W. and Coates, P. (1995) *Environment and history: the taming of nature in the USA and South Africa.* London: Routledge.

Bell, J., Jarman, N. and Harvey, B. (2010) *Beyond Belfast: contested spaces in urban, rural and cross border settings.* Belfast: Community Relations Council.

Bell, J.P.W. (2013a) Designating national parks in contested landscapes: governance challenges and the evolving national park concept in Northern Ireland, with lessons from Scotland. (unpublished) PhD Thesis, Belfast: Queen's University Belfast.

Bell, J.P.W. (2013b) Exploring the governance challenges associated with the failed attempt to designate a national park in Northern Ireland, *International Journal of Sustainable Development and Planning,* 8(3), pp.330-347.

Bell, J.P.W and Stockdale, A. (2009) Towards a multi-purpose model for the proposed Mourne national park, *Irish Geography,* 42(3), pp.293-321.

BBC (2002) National park plan moves closer, Available at: http://news.bbc.co.uk/1/hi/northern_ireland/2282701.stm (Accessed: 6th January 2011).

BBC (2014) Environment Minister Mark H Durkan shelves national parks plan, Available at: http://www.bbc.co.uk/news/uk-northern-ireland-24903525. Accessed: 10th September 2014.

Buchanan, R.H. (1982) Landscape. The recreational use of the countryside in J.G. Cruickshank and D.N. Wilcock (eds.) *Northern Ireland. Environment and Natural Resources.* Belfast: Queen's University Belfast, pp. 265.

CAAN (2007) *Mourne Area of Outstanding Natural Beauty Access Study.* Belfast: Countryside Access and Activities Network.

Cairngorms Working Party (1993) *Common sense and sustainability. A partnership for the Cairngorms*. Edinburgh: HMSO.

CNPA (2012) Facts and figures. Available at: http://www.cairngorms.co.uk/the-park/facts-figures (Accessed: 16th July 2012).

Coppock, J.T. (1980) Price of progress, *The Geographical Magazine,* 11(6), pp.422.

Countryside Commission for Scotland (1990) *The mountain areas of Scotland: conservation and management.* Edinburgh: Countryside Commission for Scotland.

Crabtree, J. (1991) National park designation in Scotland, *Land Use Policy,* 8(3), 241.

DoE (1965) *The Amenity Lands Act (NI*). Belfast: HMSO.

Elliott, M. (2002). Religion and identity in Northern Ireland, in Elliott, M. (ed.), *The Long Road to Peace in Northern Ireland.* Liverpool: Liverpool University Press, pp.169.

Gimingham, C. (2002a) Chapter 17: The Cairngorms in the future, in Gimingham, C. (ed.), *The ecology, land use and conservation of the Cairngorms.* Chichester: Packard Publishing, pp. 200.

Gimingham, C. (2002b) Chapter 16: Towards an integrated management strategy, in Gimingham, C. (ed.), *The ecology, land use and conservation of the Cairngorms.* Chichester: Packard Publishing, pp. 185.

Govan, H., Inglis, A., Pretty, J., Harrison, M. and Wightman, A. (1998) *Best practice in community participation for national parks.* Edinburgh: Scottish Natural Heritage.

Greer, J. and Murray, M. (eds.) (2003) *Rural Planning and Development in Northern Ireland,* Dublin: Institute of Public Administration, p.14.

Harroy, J.P., Tassi, F., Pratesi, F. and Humphries, C. (1974) *National park's of the world.* London: Orbis Publishing.

HM Government (2014) *The parties' published proposals on further devolution for Scotland.* London: Crown Copyright.

IUCN (1994) *Parks for life: action for protected areas in Europe.* Gland: IUCN.

Knox, C. (2012) The reform of public administration in Northern Ireland: a squandered opportunity?, *Administration,* 60(1), pp.117-138.

Lambert, R.A. (2001) *Contested mountains: nature development and environment in the Cairngorms region of Scotland, 1880-1980.* Cambridge: White Horse Press.

McAlister, R. (2010) Putting the 'community' into community planning: assessing community inclusion in Northern Ireland, *International Journal of Urban and Regional Research,* 34(3), pp.533-547.

McCarthy, J. and Lloyd, G.I., Barbara (2002) National parks in Scotland; balancing environment and economy, *European Planning Studies,* 10(5), pp.665-670.

MHT (2007) *An introduction to the Mourne Biodiversity Action Plan - a reflection of Mourne's rich natural heritage.* Newcastle (NI): Mourne Heritage Trust.

Mitchell, A. (1999), The evolution of environmental management in Mourne, *Policies and Priorities for Ireland's Landscapes*. Co. Offaly: The Heritage Council, pp.103-117.

Mitchell, J. (2000) New parliament, new politics in Scotland, *Parliamentary Affairs,* 53(3), pp.605.

Northern Ireland Assembly (2010) *Engagement strategy for the Northern Ireland Assembly.* Belfast: Northern Ireland Assembly.

Northern Ireland Planning Advisory Board (1947) *The Ulster countryside report.* Belfast: Northern Ireland Planning Advisory Board.

Prescott, J. (1999) John Prescott's conference speech. Available at: http://news.bbc.co.uk/1/hi/uk_politics/460795.stm (Accessed: 7th December 2010).

Ramutsindela, M. (2004) *Parks and people in postcolonial societies. Experiences in Southern Africa.* London: Kluwer Academic Publishers.

Redclift, M.R. (2006) Sustainable development (1987-2005): an oxymoron comes of age, *Horizontes Antropológicos,* 12(4), pp.65-84.

Rennie, A. (2006) The importance of national parks to nation building: support for the National Parks Act (2000) in the Scottish Parliament, *Scottish Geographical Journal,* 122(3), pp.223.

Rettie, K.M. (2001) *The Report on the proposal for a national park in the Cairngorms. An independent assessment of the consultation on the proposed national park for the Cairngorms.* Edinburgh: Scottish Natural Heritage.

Shoard, M. (1987) *No space for parks; Marion Shoard explains why Scotland lacks national parks,* Geographical magazine, Surrey: Circle Publishing.

SNH (2001) *Report 1. The Report on the proposal for a national park in the Cairngorms.* Perth: Scottish Natural Heritage.

The Scottish Government (2014) *More powers for the Scottish Parliament, Scottish government proposals.* Edinburgh: Crown Copyright.

The Scottish Office (1995) *Rural Scotland - people, prosperity and partnership.* Edinburgh: HMSO.

The Scottish Office (1997a) *Scotland's Parliament.* Edinburgh: The Scottish Office.

The Scottish Office (1997b) *Towards a development strategy for rural Scotland: A discussion paper.* Edinburgh: The Stationary Office.

Warren, C. (2009) *Managing Scotland's environment,* second edn, Edinburgh: Edinburgh University Press.

WCED (1987) *Our common future.* Oxford: Oxford University Press.

Chapter 18

'Keeping the name on the land': patrilineal succession in Northern Ireland family farming

Linda Price and Rachel Conn

Introduction

This chapter engages with the issue of patrilineal succession by focussing on Northern Ireland. Across the UK and the developed world succession, it is suggested, has been naturalised as largely occurring from father to son. The word 'patrilineal' is defined by the Concise Oxford Dictionary as 'relating to, or based on relationship to the father or descent through the male line'. The culture or way of life of family farming continues to be dominated by the pre-requisite of 'keeping the name on the land' via the male name. Family farms are increasingly struggling to be viable and require the support and work of a growing number of family members, men and women. However, rather than focusing on the 'mechanics' of succession, this chapter sets out to draw on research from Northern Ireland to interrogate the enduring cultural requirement to keep the family on the land via the male line, to fulfil a sense of destiny, belonging and responsibility to past male generations. For men their identity as 'farmer' will be shown to exist in relation to that of women as 'helper'. It is suggested that it is these relational gender identities across generations that enable the farm to survive and patrilineal succession to take place. As the findings will demonstrate, it is this compulsion to 'keep the name on the land' that influences farm decisions, practices and strategies.

The chapter begins by outlining a theoretical basis for patrilineal family farming in the UK which is informed by gender theory. From here, the specific context of family farming in Northern Ireland is discussed before providing an outline of the methodological approach implemented in the research. The discussion then draws on research conducted with existing farm holders and identified successors across Northern Ireland. Here it will be shown that 'keeping the name on the land' remains important both amongst the business holders and those identified as successors. The argument will be developed, therefore, that family farming is patrilineal, that family members work to enable farm survival, thereby facilitating farm succession and that ultimately 'keeping the name on the land' is imperative.

Conceptual approach to patrilineal succession

Agricultural gender identities

It is suggested here that farm culture is underpinned by patrilineal, relational gender identities whose construction, enactment and maintenance are becoming ever more difficult to retain. Maintenance of such a culture also requires the compliance of the majority of the extended kinship that comprises the farm family (see Gasson and Errington, 1993) in order for the farm/culture to be perpetuated through the male line which continues to be the norm. Since the 1980s the economic value of women's gendered work roles within the social character of the family farm has been acknowledged (Gasson, 1992; Whatmore, 1991). Political economy perspectives have usefully explained in more detail how the reproductive and productive gender relationships of family farming are integrated in a 'domestic political economy' model. Such work usefully demonstrates the stubbornness of the social structures of family farming. Here farming women are shown to often contribute unpaid work to the farm culture both inside and outside the farm door in order that the family can avoid being subsumed within capitalist agriculture (see Shortall, 2002; Silvasti, 2003 and Alston, 2006 as Northern Irish, Finnish and Australian examples). Questions arise, however, as to 'how' such gender relations of coping with capitalist agriculture are produced and maintained within the heterosexual 'gender regime' required by the patrilineal culture (Little, 2003). Here Connell's work (2002) is useful in considering the relational nature of farming gender identities through the lens of hegemonic masculinity and emphasised femininity (Brandth, 1995; Morris and Evans, 2001). Thus dominant norms are shown to exist where the status of farm women complements rather than challenges the status of farming men. Such insights assist conceptualisation of the position of farming men and women around the dominant gender coding of farmer/helper that pervades the culture across and within generations (Price and Evans, 2005; Scott, 1996). From birth, men are usually socialised as a farmer's 'son' and have the opportunity to inherit and learn the skills of farming (Brandth, 2002). Across the developed world daughters have been shown to learn, predominantly, to be supporters of farming men as they move through the life-cycle of 'farmer's son', 'boss farmer' and 'retired farmer' (see Heather *et al.* 2005; Price, 2010a and Scott, 1996 for Canadian, UK and US insights).

Clearly post-structural approaches to understanding identities of farming individuals resist the primacy given here to the social structures of family farming and the dominant pattern of the farmer/helper dualism. Diverse identities and subjective performance clearly exist in any social setting including that of farming (Butler, 1990; O'Hara, 1998; Bennett, 2005). Clearly, not all sons will want to stay in farming (Ni Laoire, 2005). But it is the overall pattern of farming which this chapter is concerned with and this remains patrilineal. Farm individuals, therefore, are situated within a global agri-economic policy context which requires social relations of production. The experiences of such individuals are also nested within the micro, gendered emotional geographies of the farm. Ideas of hereditary belonging and 'keeping the name on the land', therefore, are clearly important to farm men and supported by the majority of women (Price, 20l0a). Despite changes in inheritance laws in countries such as Norway, women's compliance with patrilineality is evident in that it is still predominantly men who inherit, own and retain decision-making on family farms (Almas and Haugen, 1991). Internationally, women have often been shown to suppress their legal and monetary rights, effectively subsidising patrilineal survival (Price, 2006). The status of 'farmer's wife' has been shown to still provide a certain status for many rural women (Hughes, 1997). Research is also beginning to demonstrate the impact the responsibility of maintaining a farming gender identity, the farm itself and ultimately ensuring succession has on men (see Ramirez-Ferrero, 2005 and Price, 20l0b as US and UK examples). Here, through their gender identity as farmer, it is beginning to be acknowledged how repeated actions of mind and body may lead to men believing a farmer is 'who' they are. For men, as farmer, engage with animals and nature in a spatial arena where legacy, culture, belonging, home and work are intertwined and ultimately reproduced and maintained via the culture of patrilineal succession (Caralan, 2008; Harrison, 2000). Such identities form the bedrock of the culture and thus 'keeping the name on the land'.

Family farm survival

As has been demonstrated the farmer/helper dualism underpins the very existence of the family farm. In order for patrilineal succession to occur the farm must survive. However, the farm does not necessarily need to be making a profit. What is important is that the land stays in the family and can be passed down the male line. Even to maintain such survival, given current agri-econonic conditions, takes the compliance and efforts of the majority of the wider kinship circle of family farming. Thus, this chapter questions analyses of farm succession that only focus on family farming as a 'business'. As will be shown in the discussion, family farming is more than this. The land still exerts a hold that dominates family decisions on the trajectory of the farm. It is this understanding that must now, it is suggested, be incorporated into political economy approaches to explaining farm decisions, adjustment and ultimately survival. The political economy perspective became dominant, internationally, from the 1980s onwards to explain agrarian change and its uneven development within the confines of wider economic, state processes (Ilbery, 1998). The approach was subsequently modified to include investigation of the decisions of the 'business holder' in relation to changing, global agricultural reform. Here some acknowledgment of the social relations of the farm household to such development was evident (Munton *et al.* 1992). The key point here is that approaches to human agency within changing market conditions have largely been confined to a focus on the male 'farmer'. This is mainly as a result of the prevalence of men's appearance in official statistics as business-holder. Such statistics continue to exclude many farming women, sons and retired farmers (Lobley and Potter, 2004). Therefore, their influence and contributions to farm survival, decisions and succession have lacked acknowledgement (Potter and Tilzey, 2005; Price and Evans, 2006). As has already been shown, without the majority of farming men and women 'signing up' to the patrilineal culture and enacting farmer/helper relational, generational gender identities, it is unlikely that there would even be a farm. This has been underestimated by researchers developing understanding of the motives for adopting strategies which are productivist, post-productivist or multifunctional (Evans et al. 2002; Wilson, 2001, 2008). For example, decisions on the adoption of farm 'holding strategies', 'expansion' or 'constriction' are likely to be influenced by the availability of a suitable successor and thus options for retirement (Price, 2010a).

Such decisions require the support of the wider farming family. It has been clearly demonstrated that many farming women perform diverse, pluriactive roles in order to support the patrilineal farming culture, often with the wish to see their sons have the opportunity to take over the farm and carry on imprinting their 'name on the land'. Such multiple roles have been well-documented as including on-farm and off-farm work as well as work which psychologically and financially supports the farm family (Price, 2006; Price and Evans, 2006, 2009). Women have also been shown to take strategic decisions based on the overall motives of the farm culture (Farmar-Bowers, 2010). For example, as Alston (2006) outlines, during the 2006 Australian drought women were prepared to work away from the farm in order to supplement it economically and assist its survival for patrilineal succession. Often such women, as Heather *et al.* (2005) note in Canada, are well-aware that they are risking their own well-being in carrying such burdens. Farming women are clearly crucial to patrilineal farm survival including, as Gasson and Errington (1993) note, farming daughters accepting pay-offs or 'dowries' on marriage in place of being farm successors. A trend is also noticeable in farming sons often having to wait longer than ever to become farm partners as fear of divorce and farm break up worries the older generations (Price and Evans, 2006). Such complicated family dynamics form the foundations of family farm enterprises, survival and thus succession.

Keeping the name on the land has been shown to be imperative in family farming and this, it is suggested, can only be achieved by the wider kinship circle largely supporting such a way of life. This support coalesces around the farmer / helper identities that across generations farming men and women largely adopt. The context to family farming in Northern Ireland is now provided which is followed by a brief outline of the methodology adopted in the research. The findings will then draw on statistical and narrative data to reinforce how the pre-requisite of 'keeping the name on the land' remains important to existing business holders and influences the choice of successor and motivations for becoming a successor.

Patrilineal family farming in Northern Ireland

Agriculture remains important in Northern Ireland (NI) playing a major role in the economy. The Gross Value Added for Northern Ireland in 2009 was 1.1 per cent compared to 0.6 per cent in the rest of the UK (Agriculture in the Home Counties, UK Parliament Briefing Papers 2009). With Northern Ireland being the smallest country in the UK, this shows its continuing dependence on agriculture. Thus, Northern Ireland provides an ideal arena in which to outline the pull of 'keeping the name on the land' via patrilineal succession. This will be shown to be the case despite farm incomes falling over recent years reflecting the trend in the rest of the UK. According to the Department for Agriculture and Rural Development (DARD) in NI, expenditure for farm families for feedstuffs alone has almost doubled in ten years. (DARD, Aggregate Agricultural Account 1981-2010). The income received from animals requiring these feeds has not shown the same returns. Data by DARD, (DARD Farm Numbers, Farm Surveys Branch 2010) show that 75 per cent of farm businesses now focus on cattle and sheep farming, for example (DARD Farm Numbers, Farm Surveys Branch 2010).

According to Agriculture in the Home Countries, (UK Parliament Briefing Papers), 5.7 per cent of Northern Ireland's total labour force is involved in agriculture in general, which is higher than England and Scotland as a whole. The percentage of total land area of Northern Ireland used for agriculture is 73.2 per cent, higher than England which is 68.2 per cent. The average farm size in England is 41 hectares however in Northern Ireland the average is 35 hectares. According to DARD Farm Numbers, Farm Surveys Branch (2010), there are 25,264 Farm Businesses in existence. Of these 89 percent were classed as small businesses, the majority of which being very small. In 2008 there were 194 fewer farm businesses than in 2007. The downward trend in the number of farms is on average 1.7 percent per year from 2003 to 2008 and 2 per cent per year over the ten years period to 2008 (DARD, Statistical Review of Northern Ireland Agriculture 2008). What these figures demonstrate is that family farming, even with falling incomes, remains a key feature of life in

registered can be accessed online using Yell.com. The Yellow Pages is an accepted sampling frame to select respondents for farm surveys and produced 3,169 results for farms across Northern Ireland. The results were sorted into each county, with a random sample of 50 being generated in each county. This was achieved by selecting every fifth farm business from the list provided, 300 in total. The two questionnaires were placed in 300 envelopes, thus 600 questionnaires in total were posted out with two self-addressed envelopes and two covering letters. It is acknowledged that this required the existing business holder to pass the second questionnaire onto an identified successor, where one existed. One hundred and thirteen questionnaires were returned from existing business holders and 75 from successors. The overall response rate was favourable at 31.3 per cent (Mitchell, 1985),37.7 per cent returned from business holders and 25 per cent from successors.

The questionnaires were designed with a predominance of open-ended questions, with similar issues being put together, in order to derive a broad understanding of the farm businesses and plans for succession across Northern Ireland. The questionnaire for business holders largely focussed on ascertaining what plans were in place for succession, factors affecting selection of successor and conditions and characteristics necessary for succession. The one aimed at the successor focussed largely on attitudes towards being identified as successor and plans for the future.

Anonymity was crucial to the research, with the opportunity being provided to provide contact details if participants wished to be considered to take part in follow-up individual interviews. Providing two self-addressed envelopes ensured that confidentiality was ensured within both groups. Responses were numerically coded and then entered into a spreadsheet. Ordinal data was coded to reflect the order in the data. Similarly, Likert scale statements were coded so that five responded to strongly agree and one to strongly disagree statements. The reverse was used for negative statements. Qualitative data was grouped around similar comments. A grounded theoretical approach was taken where themes emerging from the coding and analysis emerged in relation to the overall objectives of the research. These themes informed the topics for discussion in the follow-up semi-structured interviews (Glaser and Straus, 1967).

Five interviewees were selected for follow-up interviews. The overriding themes to emerge from the questionnaires were that the older generation was wary of handing over a 'poisoned chalice' to the next generation who, on the whole, were better educated. However, identified successors, despite falling farm returns, articulated the same attachment and belonging to the land as that of the older generation. This attachment to 'keeping the name on the land' therefore emerged as a key finding of the research. The interviews took place at a location of the participant's choice. Permission was given to record the interviews, but only to aid transcription. Both numerical and narrative data is interspersed in the following discussion. Throughout, the argument is developed that, despite the older generation of business holders having become jaded with farming, staying on the land at whatever age retains an intense pull for farming men.

Findings: business holders' perspective (Boss Farmer)

The research was not solely aimed at men. However, it transpired that all those business holders that responded to the questionnaire and thus volunteered for interview were male. Therefore, the findings provide an interesting opportunity to focus on the perspectives of men in family farming from their identity as 'farmer'. This includes being the 'boss' farmer, farmers 'son' or retired 'farmer' as outlined in the conceptual discussion. Of the respondents, 82 per cent had inherited the farm business. As Laband and Lentiz (1983) suggest, farmers do not only have an attachment to the profession but also a desire to maintain the farm in the family as a result of feelings of responsibility to past generations of men. The farms of 32 per cent of respondents had been in the family for four generations or more, with 72 per cent considering it important that the farm remains in the family. This indicates an intense emotional attachment to the land superseding economic imperatives (Jonovic and Messick, 1989). The idea of a succession plan, however, had only been considered by 56 per cent of respondents. This indicates a much more intuitive approach to succession planning based on a feeling of 'when' or 'if' a successor is available and ready to take over. In NI 60 per cent of respondents had identified a potential successor, with 99 per cent being the farmers' son. This confirms the need to keep the name on the land via accepted cultural practices.

However, the route to handing over the reins is becoming more protracted. The majority of business holders felt that acquiring managerial competence took place over a number of years, once trust in the willingness of the successor to keep the name on the land had been assured. Thus, succession is not a single event, but often takes place incrementally over a period of time (see Price and Evans, 2006; Rosenblatt and Anderson, 1981). For 20 per cent of respondents, retirement could not be contemplated until they were 70. Thus, the age of retirement or the inability of farming men to retire completely and thus give up their identity as farmer/male is increasing (Caskie *et al.* 2002). Giving up identity as a farmer clearly troubled the older generation with age and health being stated as primary reasons for 'having' to retire. This figure is increased where no successor exists. Succession will only be considered by 66 per cent of respondent's when they are no longer able to farm. It is evident, therefore, that allowing succession is an emotional rather than rational process. Such decisions are bound up with a sense of identity, belonging and fear of loss of identity, and attachment if the farm to which that identity is attached is no longer available (Caralan, 2008; Harrison, 2000).

Changes in tax laws and agricultural policy are not shown to impact decisions to facilitate succession. The majority of respondents indicated that such issues are only engaged with 'when' succession happens. The older generation are clearly jaded and tired as a result of ever-greater efforts having been required to keep the name on the land. Falling farm incomes and numbers of farm workers have been shown to increase work burdens and isolation for farming men (Price and Evans, 2009). They worry that whilst they feel they have a responsibility to maintain the farm for the next generation, should they wish to succeed that they may indeed be handing over a poisoned chalice. Worries included: 'Will it be viable to provide a successor with a suitable income?', 'Will it be a millstone around their neck?' and 'Will they have no time off like me?' There is a growing realisation that the farm alone is unlikely to provide an adequate income. However, the majority of respondents indicated how important it is that 'the farm stays in the family', 'we hope that there's enough income to keep a young family, but keeping it in the family that's the main thing'. Existing business holders are aware, therefore, that 'keeping the name on the land' will be increasingly difficult and that it is unlikely that successors will earn a living from the farm alone. Thus, education is not seen as a route out of farming, but rather a way to supplement the farm income. None of the respondents, however, felt that their family should not be able to stay farming, rather that 'there should be funding available for young people' and that 'help should be given to farmers who are reaching retirement'. The 'way of life' of farming is taken as a given, almost a right. As one respondent noted, 'there needs to be better prices for milk and beef to encourage younger farmers to be able to pay for extra to give them a better life'. There is a dichotomy here, however, in that business holders feel that government should do more to support the farming lifestyle, but on the other hand that 'there's too much red tape and interference now'. Thus, the autonomy and independence of the lifestyle which has traditionally been valued is felt to be eroded.

What came through strongly in the interviews was that despite the increasing economic pressures on staying on the land that potential successors still value the opportunity to farm and stay on the land. As one business holder stated, 'I tried something else but didn't like it - farming was in my blood'. This sense of being part 'of' the land came across strongly in that 'my farming background would have been the main reasons for my love of animals'. The key message was that farming 'is not just a profession but a way of life'. The naturalization of men as inheritors and custodian of the land featured strongly in that one of the interviewees noted that 'our farm has been in the family for nine generations', but that 'this wouldn't have been the case if there had only been daughters'. Although issues were highlighted where there was more than one son, the findings indicate that these issues are usually resolved early on, so that plans for other siblings can be made. For example, 'it's nearly always the eldest (son) but he wasn't interested in farming, so it went to the next'. Where only daughters exist, as has been noted by Price and Evans (2006), quite often they marry neighbouring farmer's sons. The respondents noted that the likelihood is that 'they'll take the land and incorporate it with the son in laws'.

The overall vision of existing business holders was simply to 'keep going and remain fairly independent'. The younger generation appear to have similar views, discounting some analyses that indicate that younger generations in NI have a more distant relationship with the land (Moss, 1996). Neither do the findings indicate that successors will choose to be part-time farmers (Hennessy and Rehman, 2007). The pull just to 'keep going', to take over the reins and to imprint the family name even more firmly in the land, therefore, appears to be a key concern for potential successors, even if discouraged by the older generation.

Findings: successors' perspectives (Farmer's Son)

Amongst the identified successors, all of whom were male, 57 per cent indicated that they had decided they wanted to be farming before they had left school. Again, attachment to the lifestyle and the land comes through strongly in that 'I always enjoyed farming' and 'I was brought up on a farm and enjoy outdoors and animals'. This again negates the idea of farming purely as profession and confirms that given high land prices that it would be 'practically impossible to start farming without owning a farm'. Enjoyment of farming was the key reason given for wanting to be the farm successor, with 50 per cent having farming qualifications. Clearly the older generation are encouraging greater education, both within and outside of agriculture. As identified successors noted 'there's no money in it now' and 'not enough income to support future plans and family'. Clearly, therefore, just staying in farming and keeping the farm going are accepted as ever-more difficult. A question remains therefore as to 'why' the younger generation would wish to succeed in such unfavourable economic conditions. Thus, the pull of the land and lifestyle clearly supersede economic imperatives.

The theme of 'survival', clearly occupied the mind of successors who just aim to keep the farm going 'as long as possible, try to make a profit although this is becoming more of a challenge'. Clearly successors do want to be farming productively and to 'expand to allow me to survive'. The desire to 'keep the farm in the family' underlined many of the responses of the younger generation and was followed up in the interviews. The majority felt that 'we just need to keep the farming going for the next generation'. It appears that each generation feels this responsibility prior to succession. Again, however, there was no recognition that selling unprofitable farms may be an option reiterating a feeling that 'grants and more funding would help - there should be some sort of financial aid'. Government support is felt to be weak with supermarkets dictating prices when 'better prices for end produce to show the young farmer that the effort and long hours will pay off' were felt to be appropriate. Again, a sense of independence was valued but within the remit of a 'hands off' approach to government support.

Ultimately, the interviews reveal that successors want to inherit the lifestyle and that keeping the farm going, hopefully productively is one way of achieving this. It is 'staying on the land,' however, that is the greatest pull. As one identified successor noted: 'It wasn't expected or even wanted, my parents wanted me to become a doctor or a vet'. It appears, therefore, that each generation of potential successors feels a pull to maintain the lifestyle of family farming and to 'keep the name on the land'. It seems that this potential to continue the patrilineal lineage exerts a strong hold. As one interviewee indicated 'it's a great environment, great for children - town children know nothing about the like of it - it's a great start for them - it brings a bit of closeness between the children and their parent'. Having the opportunity to provide children with the experience of growing up on a farm appears important. Many of the respondents indicated that 'it's all I wanted to do- it's in your blood'. Interestingly, the older generation appear to be encouraging the younger generation away from farming, but feel a responsibility to keep it going until the opportunity to succeed is provided. One interviewee stated that 'I felt no pressure to follow my father', another that 'I was encouraged from childhood to pursue an alternate career'. Successors appreciate that 'it isn't an easy life'. It is this circle of responsibility that came through amongst both generations, to provide the 'opportunity' if the next generation should want to take it up.

The fact that the majority of successors had no major plans for the farm is interesting; merely 'we just want to keep the farm going'. This indicates the importance of lifestyle over profit. There is awareness that the farm alone will not provide an income and that part-time work and subsidization by farming women will often be required (Price, 2006). The feeling that 'they', the urban society, do not understand 'us', the rural/agricultural one, was prevalent in the responses. Successors want to stay farming, want government support, but also want the freedom to enjoy their lifestyle. As one potential successor indicated, 'farmers should be left to get on with the job they do best, feeding the country'. This desire to ensure a 'rural' upbringing for children appears to be part of the pull of 'staying on the land' against the increasing encroachment of urban society (Scott *et al.* 2007). Such a rural/agricultural culture is felt to be in jeopardy, but giving the next generation the experience to grown up on a family farm is clearly important. It is not difficult to see how this responsibility to just 'keep going' for the next generation to circulate such experiences takes hold. So, successors indicate that they will 'just keep going' and 'keep our heads above water'. Despite awareness across the generations of the increasing hardships of the lifestyle and understanding of the closeness to nature, family and history is implicitly understood. Thus, keeping 'name on the land', whilst no longer easy or even encouraged, retains a pull across existing business holders and their potential successors. The findings confirm that it is this emotional pull to keep going, to protect the lifestyle and to ensure its existence for the next generation to experience that enables patrilineal family farming to continue in its present form.

Conclusions

Two key conclusions can be drawn from the findings. Firstly, existing business holders feel a responsibility to provide the opportunity to keep the farm in existence in case their successor, usually a son, wishes to succeed them. There is clearly a conflict emerging in the emotional landscape of existing successors. When men reach their mid-fifties they often appear jaded with the lifestyle. The increased work involved with falling profits and loss of farm workers has ground down their enthusiasm. Often they are tired of the work and of having to rely on farming women, in particular, just to keep the farm going to enable succession. Education of farming sons is being encouraged but whilst the older generation often hope that their children will adopt professions outside of farming, they still feel an intense responsibility to keep the farm going in case their sons 'wish' to succeed. They do, however, wish the farm to be kept in the family and not sold, even if it does not provide an income. Increasingly, this is fulfilling their sense of responsibility to their forefathers. So, on the one hand the older generation are fed up with the lifestyle, but on the other feel that they had the opportunity and so must their sons. Keeping the name on the land is important, therefore, but the older generation would be content if the major family income did not come from agriculture. Thus, there appears to be a love/hate relationship with farming life. On one side the patrilineal opportunity is appreciated, for it is this that provides farming men with their dominant identity. On the other side there is a sense that it 'traps' older men into the identity of 'farmer'. The prospect, therefore, of leaving or retiring from farming when so much of self, mind and body feels an 'attachment', a sense of 'belonging' to the cultural and physical space of family farming appears to be a huge challenge for older farming men.

Secondly, it can be concluded that despite encouragement to move away from farming by their fathers, identified successors still appear keen to carry on the lifestyle, even when the farm cannot provide an adequate income. The respondents confirmed the same sense of belonging to the land and the family story that their fathers felt. However, whilst their fathers have often become jaded with the life it is clear that their sons still have the enthusiasm to be part of the family's 'rootedness' in the soil and of 'keeping the name on the land'. The sense of being men through whom the patrilineal line travels has, almost inadvertently, been sewn from birth. There appears to be something about growing up on the farm that leads men to often imbue a sense of pride of being born to farm, a sense of destiny, of it being in their blood. This is clearly hard to pull away from. Potential successor's feelings of pride and place in the world came through in the findings. The findings show how an affinity to the landscape, the land and nature are all important to farming men with the 'sights' and 'sounds' mingling almost unconsciously with everyday geographies and actions. This is what Raymond Williams might describe as a 'structure of feeling' (Williams, 1972). All of the male respondents felt that farming is 'in my blood'. Such intense feelings are powerful, producing lived realities. Providing the opportunity for the next generation to experience the farming lifestyle was imperative to the identified successors. These less tangible aspects of farm life have been largely ignored in research considering farm adjustment and survival strategies. It is suggested here, however, that greater focus on the historical, lifestyle aspects of family farming should be acknowledged in explaining family farm survival. As the findings demonstrate, profit is not the key motivation for wanting to take over the family farm. In a rural location, being the 'boss farmer' still provides men with a certain status. To be largely autonomous, surrounded by nature and 'fixed' by a patrilineal destiny still exerts a powerful hold for the men taking part in the Northern Irish study. Here being a 'rural farming' individual, working with the land and nature is still shown to be thought of as preferable to an urban lifestyle.

The findings are illuminating, therefore, in reinforcing the 'pull of the land'. Of course the respondents had all stayed in farming and research with those who have chosen to leave or have no inheritors is required. Farm survival and succession has been shown to be increasingly difficult to achieve and requires increasing efforts by the majority of family members. Farming women have been shown to be crucial to this enterprise, but to largely support the 'idea' of patrilineal succession. It is suggested that future work on strategies for farm survival would be enhanced by considering how 'keeping the name on the land' influences survival and management strategies of family farms. As many of the respondents said 'we just want to keep going!' It is this 'keeping going' via patrilineal succession for motivations deeper than profit that now requires greater attention.

Acknowledgement

This chapter was initially published as: Price, L. and R. Conn (2012) 'Keeping the name on the land': patrilineal succession in Northern Irish family farming, in Lobley, M., J.Baker and I. Whitehead (eds.) *Keeping it in the family - International perspectives on succession and retirement on family farms.* Farnham: Ashgate, pp.93-109. It is reproduced with kind permission from Ashgate.

References

Almas, R. and Haugen, M. (1991) Norwegian gender roles in transition: the masculinization hypothesis in the past and in the future, *Journal of Rural Studies*, 7 (1), pp. 79-83.

Alston, M. (2006) The gendered impact of drought, in Bock, B and Shortall, S. (eds) *Rural Gender Relations: Issues and Case Studies*. Wallingford: CABA, pp. 165-181.

Bennett, K. (2005) The identification of farmer's wives: research challenges in the northern fells, Cumbria, in Little, L. and Morris, C. (eds) *Critical Studies in Rural Gender Issues*. Aldershot: Ashgate, pp. 60-75.

Brandth, B. (1995) Rural masculinity in transition: gender images in tractor advertisements, *Journal of Rural Studies*, 11, pp. 123-133.

Brandth, B. (2002) Gender identity in European family farming: a literature review, *Sociologia Ruralis,* 42 (2), pp. 181-201.

Butler, L. (1990) *Gender Trouble: Feminism and the Subversion of Identity.* London: Routledge.

Caralan, M. (2008) More-than-representational knowledge/s of the countryside: how we think as bodies, *Sociologia Ruralis*, 48 (4), pp. 408-423.

Caskie, P., Davies, L. Campbell, D. and Wallace, M. (2002) *An Economic Study of Farmer Early Retirement and New Entrant Schemes for Northern Ireland.* Belfast: Queen's University Belfast.

Cassidy, M. (2004) *Tapping into the Rural Heart*, BBC News website [accessed July 2011], http://news.bbc.co.uklllhi/northern_ireland/3499S11.stm.

Connell, R. (2002) *Gender*. Cambridge: Polity Press.

Department of Agriculture and Rural Development (2008) Department of Agriculture and Rural Development, Policy and Economics Division, *Statistical Review of Northern Ireland Agriculture (2008)* [accessed April 2010], http://www.dardni.gov.uklstats-review-2008-final.pdf

Department of Agriculture and Rural Development (2011) *Department of Agriculture and Rural Development Aggregate Agricultural Account 1981-2010*, Policy and Economics Division (2011) [accessed June 2011], http://www.dardni .gov. uklindexlpublications/pubs-dard-statistics/pubs-dard-statistics-agricultural-aggregate-account.htm.

Department of Agriculture and Rural Development (2010) *Department of Agriculture and Rural Development Farm Numbers Survey Farm Census Branch 2010* [accessed April 2010], http://www.dardni.gov.uklindex/publications/pubs-dard-statistics/pubs-dard-statistics-farm-numbers.htm

Department of Agriculture and Rural Development (2010) *Review of Financial Assistance for Young Farmers (2010)* [accessed April 2010], http://www.dardni.gov.uk/full-report.pdf

Department of Agriculture and Rural Development (2010) *Farm Incomes in Northern Ireland 2008-2009*, [accessed June 2011], http://www.dardni.gov.uk/index/publications/pubs-dardstatistics/farm_incomes _in_northernireland2008-2009.htm

Department of Agriculture and Rural Development (2010) *Farm Incomes in Northern Ireland 2009-2010,* [accessed June 2011], http://www.dardni.gov.uklindex/publications/pubs-dard-statistics/farm-incomes-in-northern-ireland-2009-10.htm

Department of Agriculture and Rural Development (2011) *Agricultural Census Historical Labour data 1912-2010* [accessed June 2011], http://www.dardni.gov.uk/index/publ cations/pubs-dard-statistics/agricuitural-census-historical-labour-data-1912-to-date.htm

European Commission (2011) Aid to Farmers in Less Favoured Areas, Rural Development Policy 2007-2013, Agriculture and Rural Development. European Commission EU [accessed July 2011], http://ec.europa.eu/agricuiture/rurdev/lfalindex_en.ht

Evans, N. (2009) Adjustment strategies revisited. Agriculture change in the Welsh marches, *Journal of Rural Studies*, 25 (2), pp. 217-23.

Evans, N., Morris, C. and Winter, M. (2002) Conceptualizing agriculture: a critique of post-productivism as the new orthodoxy, *Progress in Human Geography*, 26, pp 313-332.

Farmar-Bowers, Q. (2010) Understanding the strategic decisions women make in farming families, *Journal of Rural Studies*, 26 (2), pp. 141-151.

DEFRA (2011) *Fresh Start, Food and Farming, Department for Environment Food and Rural Affairs* [accessed June 2011], http://www.Defra.gov.uklfood-farm/farm - manage/training -and -new -entrants/

Gasson, R. (1992) Farmer's wives - their contribution to the farm business, *Journal of Agricultural Economics*, 43 (1), pp. 74-87.

Gasson, R. and Errington, A. (1993) *The farm family business*. Wallingford: CAB International.

Glaser, B. and Strauss, A. (1967) T*he Discovery of Grounded Theory: Strategies for Qualitative Research*. Chicago: A1dine de Gruyter.

Harrison, P. (2000) Making sense: embodiment and the sensibilities of the everyday, *Environment and Planning D: Society and Space*, 18, pp. 497-517.

Hennessy, T. and Rehman, T. (2007). An investigation into factors affecting the occupational choices of nominated farm heirs in Ireland, *Journal of Agricultural Economics*, 58, pp. 61-75.

Hughes, A. (1997) Rurality and 'cultures of womanhood': domestic identities and moral order in village life, in Cloke, P. and Little, L. (eds.) *Contested Countryside Cultures: Otherness, Marginalisation and Rurality*. London; Routledge, pp 123-138.

Ilbery, B. (1998) *The Geography of Rural Change*. Harlow: Longman Limited.

Jonovic, D. and Messick, W. (1989) Psychological issues in planning for the farm owner, *Journal of Financial Planning*, pp. 137-141.

Laband, D. and Lentz, B. (1983) Occupational inheritance in agriculture, *American Journal of Agriculture Economics*, 65 (2), pp. 311-314.

Little,L.(2003) 'Riding the rural love train': heterosexuality and the rural community, *Sociologia Ruralis*, 43 (4), pp. 401-417.

Lobley, M. and Potter, C. (2004) Agricultural change and restructuring: recent evidence from a survey of agricultural households in England, *Journal of Rural Studies*, 20 (4), pp. 499-510.

Mitchell, T. (1985) An evaluation of the validity of correlational research conducted in organizations, *Academy of Management Review*, 10, pp. 192-205.

Morris, C. and Evans, N. 200l. Cheese makers are always women: gendered representation of farm life in the agricultural press. Gender, *Place and Culture*, 8, pp 375-390.

Moss, L. (1996) Pluriactivity and survival? A study of family farms in No*rthern Ireland, in Caruthers, S. and Miller, F. (eds)* Crisis on the Family Farm: Ethics or Economics? Reading: Centre for Agricultural Strategy.

Munton, R., Marsden, T. and Ward, N. (1992) Uneven agrarian development and the social relations of farm households, in Bowler, L.Bryant, C. and Nellis, M. (eds) *Contemporary Rural Systems in Transition: Vol 1: Agriculture and Environment.* Oxon: CAB International, pp. 61-74.

Ni Laoire, C. (2005) 'You're not a man at all!' Masculinity, responsibility, and staying on the land in contemporary Ireland, *Irish Journal of Sociology*, 14 (2), pp.94-114.

O'Hara, P. (1998). *Partners in production? Women, farm and family in Ireland.* Oxford: Berghahn Books.

Potter, C. and Tilzey, C. (2005) Agricultural policy discourses in the European post- Fordist transition: neoliberalism, neomercantisism and multifunctionality, *Progress in Human Geography*, 29 (5), pp. 581--600.

Price, L. (2006) A new farming subsidy? Women, work and family farm survival, *Royal Agricultural Society England Journal,* Warwickshire: Stoneleigh Royal Agricultural Society, pp. 49-58.

Price, L. (2010a) 'Doing it with men': feminist research practice and patriarchal inheritance practices in Welsh family farming, *Gender, Place and Culture*, 17(2), pp. 81-99.

Price, L. (2010b) The damaging impacts of patriarchy on UK male family farmers, in Winch, D. Ramsey, D. and Koster, R. (eds) *Sustainable Rural Community Change: Geographical Perspectives from North America, the British Isles, and Australia.* Washington; Eastern Washington University Press, pp. 42-62.

Price, L. and Evans, N. (2005) Work and worry: farm women's way of life, in Little, L. and Morris, C. (eds) *Critical Studies in Rural Gender Issues.* Aldershot: Ashgate, pp. 45-59.

Price, L. and Evans, N. (2006) From 'as good as gold' to 'gold diggers': farming women and the survival of British family farming, *Sociologia Ruralis*, 46(4), pp. 280-299.

Price, L. and Evans, N. (2009) From stress to distress: conceptualising the British family farming patriarchal way of life, *Journal of Rural Studies*, 25 (1), pp. 1-11.

Ramirez-Ferrero, E. (2005) *Troubled Fields: Men, Emotions and the Crisis in American Farming.* New York: Columbia University Press.

Rosenblatt, P. and Anderson, R. (1981) Interaction in farm families: tension and stress, in Coward, T. and Smith, W. (eds.) *The Family in Rural Society.* Colarado: Westview Press.

Scott, A., Gilbert, A. and Gelen, A. (2007) *The Urban Rural Divide, Myth or Reality*. Scotland: Macaulay Institute.

Scott, S. (1996) Drudges, helpers and team players: oral historical accounts of farm work in Appalachian Kentucky, *Rural Sociology*, 61(2), pp. 209-22.

Scottish Government (2011) New Entrants and Young Farmers, The Scottish Government [accessed June 2011] http://www.scotland.gov.uk/Topics/farmingrurallSRDP/RuralPriorities/Packages/NewEntrantsandYoungFarmers.

Shortall, S. (1999) *Women and Farming: Property and Power*. Basingstoke: Macmillan Press.

Shortall, S. (2002) Gendered agricultural and rural restructuring: a case study of Northern Ireland, *Sociologia Ruralis*, 42(2), pp. 160-175.

Silvasti, T. (2003) Bending borders of gendered labour division on farms: the case of Finland, *Sociologia Ruralis*, 43(2), pp. 154-167.

UK Agriculture, http://www.ukagriculture.com/uk_farming.cfm

UK Parliament (2009) *Agriculture in the Home Counties*, UK Parliament Briefing Papers 2009 [accessed June 2011], www.parliament.uklbriefing-papers/SN03994.pdf

Whatmore, S. (1991) *Farming Women: Gender, Work and the Family Enterprise*. London: Macmillan.

Williams, R. (1972) *The Country and the City*. London: Chatto and Windus.

Wilson, G. (200l) From productivism to post-productivism ... and back again? Exploring the (un)changed natural and mental landscapes of European agriculture, *Transactions of the Institute of British Geographers*, 26, pp. 77-102.

Wilson, G. (2008) From 'weak' to 'strong multi functionality: conceptualizing farm-level multi-functional transitional pathways, *Journal of Rural Studies*, 24(3), pp. 367-383.

YESS Welsh Government Farm and Scheme Information (2011) [accessed June 2011], http://wales.gov.uk/topics/environmentcountryside/farmingandcountryside/farminglyoungentrantsupportschemeyessl?lang=en

Chapter 19

Caring for the past or past caring? Challenges for the voluntary sector in conservation

Karen Latimer

Introduction

The 20th century saw a positive plethora of bodies with an interest in the protection and conservation of historic buildings come into existence. The National Trust, of course, was established in the 19th century but only just, being founded in 1895; its Scottish cousin, or sibling, followed suit in the 1930s. By the late 1950s the Georgian Group, the Victorian Society, the Society for the Protection of Ancient Buildings and the Civic Trust (re-launched in 2010 as Civic Voice) had come into existence. And on the other side of the Irish Sea we had the launch of the Irish Georgian Society, founded in 1958. It was not until 1969, however, that the first conservation pressure group appeared in Ulster.

Charles Brett (1982) noted that the "sudden surprising post-war upsurge of interest in architectural conservation, quite without precedent in history, was in fact almost a worldwide phenomenon". When he made this comment in the early 80s, he went on to question whether this was just a passing phase. Some thirty years on this question is still a difficult one to answer and indirectly led to the topic addressed here. Michael Middleton (1987) in his thought-provoking book *Man Made the Town* makes a strong case for building on the experience of the past. He also points out that renewal and conservation should not be seen as alternatives but rather as two sides of the same coin leading to a creative refashioning of our towns and cities so that they can change to meet evolving needs but still retain their essential character. Conservation, he claims, "seeks to slow down change and to bring it under more purposeful and creative control". Writing at almost exactly the same time, a group of academics based at Queen's University Belfast (including Malachy McEldowney in whose honour this Festschrift has been produced) commented that a key factor in any conservation strategy for Belfast "is that conservation policy should come to form an essential element in the wider strategy for the economic regeneration of the city" (Hendry *et al.*, 1987).

This laudable aim is one that has long been recognised by architectural conservationists in the voluntary sector and is one that continues to exercise pressure groups and conservation bodies in the 21st century. It is not an easy path to hoe, however, hence the ever-present threat of "past caring" referred to in the title. Middleton again strikes a warning note saying that planning is often perceived as "the instrument of an elitist-professional cadre, encapsulating the values and standards of middle-class pressure groups". The author Candia McWilliam (2010), discussing her father, the architectural historian Colin McWilliam, remarks that "If people mention the conservation of buildings now, they think of something almost aspirational, associated with a style of life, a type of person, a version of the past. All this could not be further from how my father thought and worked and lived. He was working to save buildings…". In the 21st century pressure groups have, by and large, shaken off this rather unflattering and, in the main, incorrect image but to do so have had to take on a wider remit and become more professional and adept at lobbying politicians and officials alike. By examining the history to date of one local pressure group, the Ulster Architectural Heritage Society (UAHS), some conclusions can be drawn about the changing remit in the role of the voluntary sector in caring for our past.

The Ulster Architectural Heritage Society

The Ulster Architectural Heritage Society, founded in 1967, is recognized well beyond these shores for its doughty campaigning over many years and in exceptionally difficult circumstances, and for its highly impressive publications list (list of publications <www.uahs.org> last accessed October 2014). Voluntary bodies in the conservation field often come into being to save a building or protect an area of particular significance; in the case of the UAHS it was a combination of these things. It was founded as a direct result of the loss of a number of important Victorian buildings in Belfast and elsewhere. Notable amongst these was the imposing Institute for the Deaf and Dumb and Blind, Lisburn Road, built in 1843-5 to the designs of Charles Lanyon, demolished in 1963. In the same year Thomas Jackson's fine Tudor Revival terrace, Queen's Elms, deliberately designed in 1859 to respond to the front elevation of the Queen's College opposite, was also demolished. Shortly after, in 1965, William Batt's decorative and historically interesting gate lodge to the Botanic Gardens of 1877 followed suit. This simple building contributed greatly to the streetscape and was a key building in the context of the Gardens and yet it was demolished for no pressing reason.

Another key concern that led to the foundation of the UAHS was the lack of legislation to protect listed buildings and areas of architectural interest in Northern Ireland. In November 1967 the UAHS was formed with Professor Estyn Evans, Ireland's first professor of geography and founder of the Ulster Folk and Transport Museum, as President; Charles Brett, a local solicitor and author of the first major work on the architecture of Belfast (Brett, 1967), as Chairman; and Desmond Hodges, a conservation architect shortly to become the first Director of the Edinburgh New Town Conservation Committee, taking on the role of honorary secretary. The inaugural meeting of the UAHS was chaired by Robert Matthew, designer of the New University of Ulster at Coleraine, future RIBA Gold Medal winner and influential figure in the reformist architectural and planning establishment in both Scotland and Northern Ireland at the time. Miles Glendinning notes in his biography of Matthew that "Perhaps most remarkable, in retrospect, in 1967 he strongly supported a new twist to the agenda of 'parity' by presiding over the founding of Northern Ireland's first preservation group, the Ulster Architectural Heritage Society" (Glendinning, 2008). The roll call of UAHS committee members over the almost fifty years of its existence is impressive indeed and reads like a *Who's Who* of Ulster conservationists.

Early successes included the restoration during European Architectural Heritage Year in 1975 of the historically highly important Palm House in the Botanic Gardens which was in a state of extreme dereliction. Another cause championed in these early years was the restoration of Frank Matcham's Grand Opera House also in 1975: the work was carried out by the conservation architect Robert McKinstry another early member of the UAHS. The main work, however, in the early years of the UAHS' existence, was campaigning for listed building protection. In 1967 there were no statutory listing, no conservation areas, no grant aid and no historic buildings record – much for the caring conservationist to fight for. In 1968 the UAHS claimed "that the approach to conservation in Ulster was fifty years behind the times" (SAVE, 2001). After five years of campaigning and significant pressure from the UAHS and others, the Planning (NI) Order 1972 came into being. It was modelled on the UK Town and Country Planning Act of 1968 and it provided a legislative basis for planning very similar to that of the rest of the UK. The Order introduced listing with conservation areas following in 1974. One of the first buildings to be listed was the handsome Ruskinian Gothic library designed by WH Lynn for the then Queen's College. That same building is currently undergoing refurbishment as a new Graduate School offering teaching, group study, social space and support accommodation. The UAHS has carefully scrutinised the planning application and has had discussions with the University about the work – *plus* ça *change, plus c'est la même chose.*

The early committee members of the UAHS recognised the importance of influencing public opinion and government representatives by holding public meetings, appearing at public enquiries and leading deputations to meet ministers. These were a regular occurrence in the early years of the Society. It soon became obvious that evidence was needed to back up claims and arguments and so the famous UAHS black and white publications were instigated with that for Queen's University being one of the first off the presses. The original edition was compiled by Charles Brett and Alistair Rowan (Rowan, 1968) and was later revised by Hugh Dixon and David Evans. The UAHS had published twenty lists between 1969 and 1972 and these formed the basis of the early statutory lists. The UAHS publications list is the envy of all other conservation societies in Ireland, the UK and beyond. In addition to numerous lists and gazetteers covering the whole geographical area of Ulster, there are publications on building types such as court houses and market houses, gate lodges, classical churches, model schools and workhouses. The work of individual architects such as Roger Mulholland and JJ McCarthy has also been covered and a new series on the work of architects of importance in Ulster and beyond is in the pipeline. Individual buildings also feature in the list – notably Belfast City Hall, Stormont and Bendhu – the unique, even eccentric, building standing sentinel on the cliff overlooking the harbour at Ballintoy. The UAHS promotes the appreciation and enjoyment of good architecture of ***all*** periods and is very conscious that the well-designed buildings of today will be the listed buildings and heritage of the future. A major publication in 2006 was *Modern Ulster* Architecture (Evans, 2006) with introductory essays by Paul Larmour, David Evans and Charles Rattray, covering Modern Movement architecture in Ulster from 1900 to the present day. The growing professionalism of the voluntary sector is essential if it is to be taken seriously by those with the power and influence to effect change – but this comes at a cost. This has an impact on publishing also. The UAHS books need to be produced to a high standard with high quality illustrations; the website needs to look good and work well and be constantly updated. All this costs money and financial support is increasingly hard to find.

Another key factor in the establishment of the UAHS was the growing awareness of the gradual erosion of the character of the small towns and villages in the Ulster countryside. Planning policy allowed a liberal number of new homes to be built in the countryside and these tended to be very different in style from the simple traditional buildings they so often replaced. An increasing number of modest dwellings, nonetheless of architectural importance, were at risk. A joint initiative on the part of the UAHS and the Northern Ireland Committee of the National Trust led to the formation in 1972 of Hearth. Charles Brett used to say that the National Trust was the heavy brigade of the conservation battlefield and the UAHS the light hussars. Perhaps Hearth equates to the foot soldiers on the front line doing the practical work. Certainly the original aim was for Hearth to be the practical wing of the UAHS restoring small but architecturally significant buildings, either listed or in conservation areas, which were at risk.

Hearth and the protection of small buildings

A brief reference to the work of Hearth is included here in the context of the work of the voluntary sector in conservation and because of the organisation's link to the UAHS. More detailed information can be found in Marcus Patton's illuminating, witty and very personal account of the history of Hearth published in the UAHS book, *Avenues to the Past* (Patton, 2003). Patton records that the setting up of Hearth was "an eleventh-hour attempt to rescue at least some remaining examples of Ulster's architectural character which are disappearing fast as a result of redevelopment and neglect. If this effort fails, and does not inspire imitators, most of the buildings which give character to the towns and villages of Northern Ireland will vanish." Further reference to particular schemes in the context of preserving the character of Ulster's towns and villages can be found in the book of essays in honour of another highly respected Queen's planning academic, John Greer (Latimer, 2005).

Hearth today consists of two sister organisations, Hearth Revolving Fund (HRF) and Hearth Housing Association (HHA). HRF was founded in 1972 with the aim of purchasing and restoring small buildings for re-sale. The aim of a revolving fund (and the clue is in the name) is for a relatively small amount of capital to be used over and over again to buy, restore and sell successive buildings thereby rescuing those of importance that might otherwise be lost. Small buildings there have been indeed, including the lockhouses at Drumbeg and Ballyskeagh, Woodbine Cottage on the Antrim Road in Belfast and houses in Glenoe and Moira; a fair smattering of larger and more challenging projects too, such as Portrush Town Hall, Turnly's tower in Cushendall, College Green House in Belfast and most recently Riddel's warehouse in Ann Street in Belfast have benefitted from the work of the Revolving Fund. HHA was formed in 1978, registered under the Housing (NI) Order 1976. It, like HRF, is non-profit-making and has charitable status and it rescues houses at risk of demolition and usually in very poor condition, putting them to a new use as social housing. It provides a wide range of housing units allocated under the Department for Social Development's Housing Selection Scheme.

Hearth has restored over one hundred buildings under its housing wing and some forty more through its revolving fund. In so doing it has provided high quality housing and contributed to the preservation of the character of many towns and villages in Northern Ireland. It has received many conservation awards in recognition of its work in saving buildings at risk. Increasingly, however, this work is becoming harder and harder to do. The challenges facing small charities and the voluntary sector are becoming increasingly difficult.

Challenges

The early years of the UAHS as described above were heady ones indeed. Once listed building protection was in place the focus gradually moved to campaigning, lobbying, engaging with government on policy, and education in the broadest sense. Rather than there being nothing left to do there seemed to be more to do than ever before and fewer people to do it, or perhaps the same number but with less time to spare. Dick Oram, one of the early DoE listers, notes in an essay on space, time and conservation that "Those who have an interest in conservation must always be vigilant, especially since government, at least in the North of Ireland, seems to be ever more content to be a processor of the law and to leave the proactive and promotional work to others" (Oram, 2003). He goes on to point out that "there is a great deal of educating to be done".

The UAHS has risen to the challenge, appointing over the last number of years a Research Officer, a Buildings at Risk Officer who maintains the online Buildings at Risk Register in partnership with the Northern Ireland Environment Agency, and for a time, an Education Officer. It has continued to publish a wide range of books on a variety of architectural topics in order to promote interest in, and an awareness of the importance of, local architecture and the built environment generally. Education is not limited to schoolchildren and the general public, however, and schemes are in hand through Hearth to work on training in traditional building skills. The recently published new online edition of the *Directory of Traditional Building Skills* draws together a wide variety of specialists in the field of conservation from architects to individual crafts practitioners and provides a general framework of guidance for working with historic buildings. Staff and volunteers regularly scan planning applications, provide advice, give talks and work tirelessly (and in the darkest hours it seems sometimes fruitlessly) to raise attention to issues.

The loss of traditional buildings is still happening, the plea for Third Party Appeals continues to fall on deaf ears forcing bodies such as the UAHS down the line of judicial review which is a difficult and expensive process, and the lack of use of Article 4 Directions, which would ensure planning permission be required for specific types of development otherwise regarded as "permitted development," remains of concern as does the not unrelated issue of delisting. The judicious use of Article 4 Directions would go a long way to solving the problem of inappropriate replacement of windows and doors proliferating in conservation areas. And although enforcement powers such as Repairs and Urgent Works notices, not available when the UAHS was founded, do now exist they seem rarely to be used. The Stables at Sion Mills recently restored by Hearth remains the only example of compulsory purchase and back-to-back restoration in Northern Ireland. It is a case study in itself of the problems facing the conservation sector – but that is for another day, another paper perhaps. The building was allowed to deteriorate into a perilous state before eventually being transferred to Hearth. By that time much valuable and original fabric had been lost and the project cost far more to restore than would have been the case if government had acted in a positive and joined–up manner to insist on holding repairs or to enable the transfer of ownership so that the building could be put to a new use.

The arguments that conservation does not cost jobs but actually creates them, that we need to cultivate a distinctive city image to attract tourism, that old buildings should be seen as assets not liabilities and that their reuse is inherently sustainable, are made over and over again in publications, letters, responses to public consultations and in face-to-face meetings. Although there may be some acceptance of these arguments, to those of us working at the coal-face little seems to have changed. Words do not seem to translate into action. Despite many fine pronouncements about re-use, embodied energy and sustainability, the emphasis, certainly in the field of social housing and even in relation to the government's own estate, still seems to be on new build.

There are other challenges, too. Lack of resources bedevil us all – amateurs and professionals alike. What is particularly difficult for small charities is the uncertain and erratic nature of the funding whether it be listed building grant aid or charitable support. There are some wonderful exceptions to this and they know who they are! A particular problem is a delay in payments often for what appear to be very minor reasons. Small charities do not have the reserves to cope with delayed payments and what might seem a trivial amount to a large organisation can cause severe cash flow problems to the minnow on the receiving end.

Indeed bureaucracy generally is a huge problem for small voluntary organisations. The level of bureaucracy is such that participating in the sector has lost much of its appeal. The workload is substantial, accountability is rightly expected but there is so much paperwork that there seems little time actually to achieve the aims that brought volunteers (and often highly skilled volunteers giving their services for no monetary reward) into the sector in the first place. Outcomes are seemingly less important than the route travelled to get there and the rules and regulations that have to be adhered to along the way are almost impossibly burdensome for a small organisation. This gives rise to the further problem of leadership in the voluntary sector and succession planning. Who will pick up the baton in the time-poor, bureaucracy-riddled 21st century? As Charlie Brett, founder member of the UAHS frequently emphasised, voluntary work has to be fun as well as fulfilling.

Conclusions

There are undoubtedly challenges facing the voluntary sector in the field of conservation in the 21st century; the question is, are they so great that the aforementioned foot soldiers are past caring about the past and how it relates to the present? Conservationists are fond of saying there are no such things as problem buildings, only problem owners. Barry Joyce, Derbyshire County Council Planning Officer, at a UAHS conference in 2000 classified such owners as follows: the eccentric, the crook, the plain unresponsive, the philistine and the incompetent (Joyce, 2000). The eccentric ranges from the stubbornly unco-operative to the clinically insane, the crook from the small-time con man to the big-time corporate swindler, the unresponsive from the couldn't-care-less individual to the totally impassive bureaucrat, the philistine from the well-meaning do-it-yourselfer to the enthusiastic defacer, and "then the dreariest of them all," the incompetent who manages to produce the most intractable problem of all by paying too much, not having a business plan, not having the property surveyed and failing to talk to the planning authority in advance of purchase. And who said there was no fun to be had by amateurs and professionals alike?

On a more serious note, there are still reasons to get involved. You get to work for the most part with talented, skilled, committed professionals. Together you can take the long-term view untrammelled by the need for political gain and help shape the environment you want to live in. There has been much debate about the importance of conserving old buildings and perhaps more critically how they should be conserved particularly when put to new use. Debate ranges across aesthetics, historical memory, economics, tourism and sustainability. For many, however, it is the Latin term *genius loci* used to describe the particular essence or spirit of a place that resonates in relation to conservation. Kate Clark from English Heritage writing about the importance of understanding historic buildings for conservation reminds us that "historic environment is a precious and irreplaceable asset – once gone it is gone forever. It is important for its memories, its familiarity, for the story it has to tell and its contribution to our communities" (Clark, 2001). The late Robert McKinstry, conservation architect par excellence and a founder member of the UAHS, said of a voluntary body that if it "continues to fulfil a real need then it flourishes and becomes strong; if in time it is no longer necessary then it simply fades away" (McKinstry, 1982). In the same forum Professor Alistair Rowan warned that the Irish are "a nation of rebuilders rather than restorers… [for whom] an old building, whatever its cultural context, is something not so much deserving repair as replacement" (Rowan, 1982). It would seem, therefore, that the need is still there.

The role of the voluntary sector in conservation continues to form part of the conservation course run so effectively for many years by Malachy McEldowney and this chapter is loosely based on the lectures given by me to students on that course. It is perhaps fitting to conclude this chapter in a book dedicated to a planner and an academic who has contributed much in the field of conservation both as a researcher and as an educator with the words once more of conservationist and author, Michael Middleton (1987): "A building, however marvellous, is but a sentence in the paragraph of the street, in the chapter of the neighbourhood or quarter, in the book that is the town."

References

Brett, C. (1967) *Buildings of Belfast 1700-1914.* London: Weidenfeld and Nicolson.

Brett, C. (1982) Our shared heritage, in *Ireland's architecture: a shared heritage*. Dublin: An Taisce, pp.2-4.

Clark, K. (2001) *Informed conservation: understanding historic buildings and their landscapes for conservation*. London: English Heritage.

Evans, D. (1980) *Historic buildings, groups of buildings, areas of architectural importance in the vicinity of the Queen's University of Belfast.* Rev. ed. Belfast: Ulster Architectural Heritage Society.

Evans, D *et al.* (2006) *Modern Ulster architecture.* Belfast: Ulster Architectural Heritage Society.

Glendinning, M. (2008) *Modern architect: the life and times of Robert Matthew*. London: RIBA Publishing. pp.353-354.

Hendry, John *et al.* (1987) *Conservation in Belfast.* Belfast: The Queen's University of Belfast.

Joyce, B. (2000) Problem owners, in *Buildings at risk: some options and solutions*. Belfast: Ulster Architectural Heritage Society, pp.18-21.

Latimer, K. (2005) Preserving character in the towns and villages of Northern Ireland, in McEldowney, M. *et al.* (eds.) *Planning in Ireland and beyond.* Belfast: School of Environmental Planning, Queen's University Belfast, pp.157-168.

McKinstry, R. (1982) Problems and achievements: north, in *Ireland's architecture: a shared heritage.* Dublin: An Taisce, pp.14-15.

McWilliam, C. (2010) *What to look for in winter.* London: Jonathan Cape.

Middleton, M. (1987) *Man made the town.* London: Bodley Head.

Oram, R. (2003) Space, time and conservation, in Reeves-Smyth, T. and Oram, R. (eds.) *Avenues to the past*. Belfast: Ulster Architectural Heritage Society, pp.253-264.

Patton, M. (2003) Conservation at the coal-face: a short history of Hearth, in Reeves-Smyth, T. and Oram, R. (eds.) *Avenues to the past*. Belfast: Ulster Architectural Heritage Society, pp.75-103.

Rowan, A. (1982). The Irishness of Irish Architecture, in *Ireland's architecture: a shared heritage*. Dublin: An Taisce. pp.4-5.

SAVE Britain's Heritage. (2001) *Blink and you'll miss it: Northern Ireland's heritage in danger*. London: SAVE.

Websites

List of publications <www.uahs.org> last accessed March 2015.

Chapter 20

From commemoration to celebration: Berlin and its housing estate World Heritage Sites

David Houston and Michael Murray

Introduction

Place making and history are inextricably linked in Berlin through narratives of memory and an attendant complex of memorialisation. The contemporary pulse of this capital city may well beat to the post 1989 reunification of Germany but constant reminders about the darkest of 20th century events are ever present. Berlin portrays itself as a city of great tragedy derived from political circumstances and human suffering and it is out of this deeply emotional past that a melancholia of commemoration is visibly expressed. The public realm abounds with physical reminders that something awful happened in the years leading up to the Second World War, during the war years, and in the aftermath of division and separation. The conservation and interpretation of particular sites (for example, the Topography of Terror on Wilhelmstrasse and the Berlin Wall Memorial on Bernauer Strasse) sit alongside recently constructed memorials with deeply symbolic significance for memory work (for example, the Memorial to the Murdered Jews of Europe close to the Brandenburg Gate). In this vein Berlin is a city for quiet contemplation and which has generated a sustained academic and planning practitioner commentary (see for example, Ladd, 1997; Heckner, 2002; Neill, 2005; Till, 2005; Webber, 2008; Colomb, 2012; Di Bella, 2012; Schlusche, 2014). Berlin is a city of painful remembrance.

But there is also a parallel Berlin where the heritage of places, buildings and personalities can be celebrated and which is gaining the traction of attention not least as a result of UNESCO World Heritage Site designations. The palaces and parks of Potsdam and Berlin along with Museum Island in the centre of the city were accorded this accolade in the 1990s and each forms a key element of the notable architectural ensemble. In 2008 six Modernist housing estates were also inscribed on the World Heritage List on the basis of their historical authenticity and innovative design. All were constructed between 1913 and 1934 and today are living communities that can be experienced as urban planning spectacle within the context of Berlin as a tourist-historic city. For the students and staff of Planning at Queen's University Belfast, who have been coming to Berlin on fieldtrips over many years, some of which have been led by Malachy McEldowney, an examination of these housing estates offers interesting perspectives on planning history, social reform and urban design. They also raise critical questions around the selection of place-based heritage in a city that arguably wishes to now move beyond the imperatives of commemoration while not disowning its troubled past. This chapter deals with these matters and is structured as follows: firstly, we introduce the background to World Heritage Site inscription and against that backcloth we examine the justification for including the six estates on the UNESCO list; secondly, we discuss the contemporary appearance of each estate and the measures in train to secure conservation and promotion; and thirdly by way of conclusion, we consider more broadly the contribution made by the existing and prospective World Heritage Site inventory of Berlin to the formation of a new commentary around urban celebration. A portfolio of Berlin estate housing colour photographs, taken by the authors in April 2014, accompanies this chapter and can be viewed at: http://www.qub.ac.uk/schools/SchoolofPlanningArchitectureandCivilEngineering/Planning/FileStore/Filetoupload,453301,en.pdf

World Heritage Site inscription

The UNESCO *Convention Concerning the Protection of the World Cultural and Natural Heritage* was adopted in November 1972 with a key aim being to prevent the deterioration or disappearance of heritage items with universal value. The Convention applies to sites, monuments and groups of buildings (Article 1), along with natural features, natural sites and geological and physiographical formations (Article 2). Properties put forward by parties to the Convention, following evaluation of their merits, would then, if approved, be inscribed on the World Heritage List. An absence of balance in the composition of the list in regard to geography and inscribed properties resulted in the publication in 1994 by UNESCO of a *Global Strategy for a Representative, Balanced and Credible World Heritage List*. This embraced a wider definition of heritage to include "demonstrations of human coexistence with the land as well as human interactions, cultural coexistence, spirituality and creative expression" (http://whc.unesco.org/en/globalstrategy/, accessed 9 June 2014). Significant developments in town planning, architecture and landscape design are included in the accompanying selection criteria. Accordingly, the description of the Berlin Modernist housing estates, as described by UNESCO in its inscription decision of July 2008, fits well with these considerations and reads as follows:

> The set of housing estates in the Berlin Modern Style provides outstanding testimony to the implementation of housing policies during the period 1910-1933 and especially during the Weimar Republic, when the city of Berlin was characterised by its political, social, cultural, and technical progressiveness. The housing estates reflect, with the highest degree of quality, the combination of urbanism, architecture, garden design and aesthetic research typical of early 20th century modernism, as well as the application of new hygienic and social standards. Some of the most prominent leading architects of German modernism were involved in the design and construction of the properties; they developed innovative urban, building and flat typologies, technical solutions and aesthetic achievements. (Decision of the World Heritage Committee, in Landesdenkmalamt Berlin im Auftrag der Senatsverwaltung für Stadtentwicklung Berlin (ed) (2009) *Siedlungen der Berliner moderne: eintragung in die welterbeliste der UNESCO*. Berlin: Verlagshaus Braun, p.283).

The political and social background mentioned above is important given the rapid growth of Berlin during the latter part of the 19th century and the early years of the 20th century. Its inhabitants increased from 932,000 in 1871 to 3.7 million in 1910 (Bodenschatz, 2010, p.13) reflecting the prominence of the city as the high-tech industrial centre of the world with a corresponding need for skilled labour (Hall, 1998). Electricity was key to economic success with large scale employment companies such as Siemens & Halske and Allgemeine Elektrizitäts Gesellschaft (AEG) at the heart of the electrical engineering sector. The corollary to prosperity was the need for urban expansion linked to major housing provision and thus the immediate solution to-hand favoured high density, tenement house construction. As observed by Becker-Cantarino (1996) "dismal, overcrowded public housing projects (the so-called *Mietskasernem*, rental barracks - multi-storey blocks constructed around a maze of small, paved courtyards, the *Hinterhöfe*" (p.3) sought to accommodate much of this population explosion. Writing in 1910 Heinrich Pudor voiced a combination of concern and ambition in regard to these conditions and which at a broader level was illustrative of the growing momentum at that time for housing policy reform. He argued, "We must not only break through the countless housing blocks here and there in order to make the network of housing as wide meshed as possible, but also create places within this tangle of houses from which elemental fresh air might rise, reinvigorating the musty, dead air of the housing quarters" (in Boyd Whyte and Frisby, 2012, p.256). A number of factors were to converge around such an agenda and pave the way for establishing new housing estates.

First was the attention being given to the creation of Garden Cities that drew on the inspiration provided by Ebenezer Howard to envision new urban forms embracing community engagement, innovative house design, and land plots with accompanying greenery. While interwar Europe witnessed the construction of numerous housing estates that drew on variations of these Howardian ideas, Berlin is cited as being located at the forefront of the European housing reform movement on the basis of its Modernist housing estates (Kafkoula, 2013). Second was the importance of local government reorganisation and which in turn sponsored city planning on the urban periphery. In 1920 eight former cities, 59 rural communities and 27 rural districts were amalgamated into the single administrative polity of *Stadtgemeinde Berlin* (Municipality of Berlin) thus facilitating a more coherent planning approach within an integrated settled area (Sonne, 2004). New building ordinances followed in regard to the zoning of industry and housing, while revised density and design regulations effectively ended the conventional courtyard format of the tenements (Boyd Whyte and Frisby, 2012, p.464). The prevailing message at the time was that expert planning to facilitate orderly cities with decent housing standards, enforced by law, would not be inconsistent with capitalist growth (Phillips, 1996). Third was the formation of new agency structures to facilitate the funding of cooperative housing in Berlin. In 1924 the *Gemeinnützige Heimstätten-Aktiengesellschaft* (GEHAG), a non-profit homes, savings and construction corporation, was established with German Trade Union support to take a lead role in delivery. This initiative was set within the context of the earlier collapse of privately financed housing construction and the incorporation into federal legislation in 1918 of housing construction as a public sector function (Henderson, 1999), with the guarantee of "a healthy home for every German". Between 1924 and 1930 some 135,000 apartments were built in Berlin within this framework of a state housing construction initiative (Senate Department for Urban Development and the Environment, accessed 9 June 2014). And fourth was the presence of a highly skilled cadre of architects and landscape architects capable of designing volume housing units in the Modernist style with accompanying green spaces. Included among their ranks was Martin Wagner who headed-up urban planning across Greater Berlin between 1926 and 1933, Walter Gropius who was a director of the Weimar and Dessau Bauhaus between 1919 and 1928, and Bruno Taut whose practice was intimately linked to the *Deutsche Gartenstadt-gesellschaft* (German garden city society). These architects collaborated within a varying geometry of leadership with publications from that period capturing the excitement of the Modernist project. Thus writing in 1930 Walter Gropius argued that: "The basic requirements for the general planning of a large residential development are: daylight; fresh air; sunshine; tranquillity; limited population density; good accessibility; rationally designed, convenient apartment interiors: pleasant overall ambience" (in Boyd Whyte and Frisby, 2012, pp.484-485). When added to the proposition of Bruno Taut in 1924 that "Housebuilding will from now on be homebuilding" (in Boyd Whyte and Frisby, 2012, p.475), the essence of housing reform is sharply defined as a humane antidote to the then extant tenement system. The justification for inscription on the World Heritage List of six housing estates in Berlin is derived from all these material considerations.

The six Modernist housing estates

As illustrated in Figure 20.1 the six Modernist housing estates are situated in the main beyond the city core and, at the time of their building and landscape design, they were able to take advantage of a rural setting on the urban periphery. It was only the planning of Carl Legien that had to respond to the immediate setting of a densely settled inner city district. Significantly, for reasons of access to employment, the estate locations were also convenient to public transport stations. The accommodation stock comprises almost 6,200 units (Table 20.1), mainly apartments, but also including some single family dwellings as in the case of Falkenberg and Britz. Four of the housing estates are in excess of 1,000 units (Britz, Carl Legien, Weisse Stadt and Siemensstadt).

Figure 20.1: The location of the six Modernist housing estates in Berlin

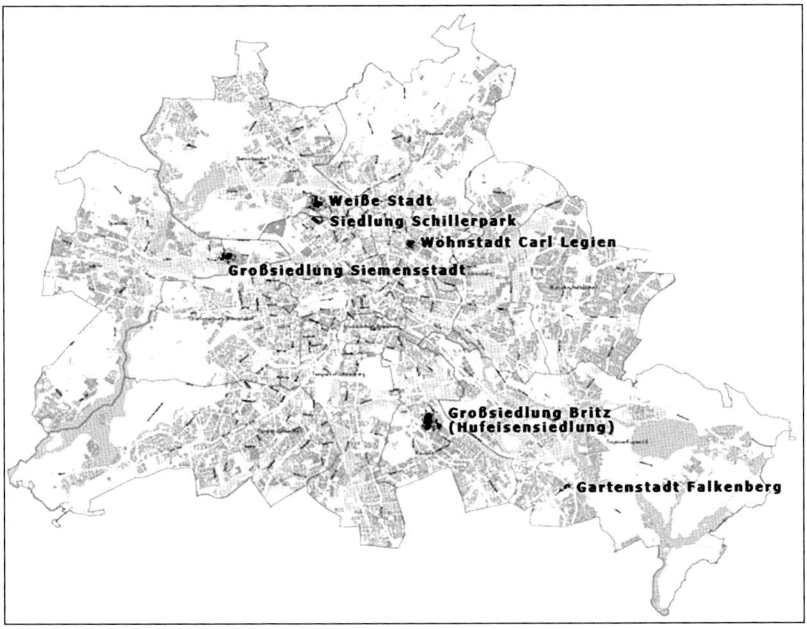

Source: Senate Department for Urban Development and the Environment (http://www.stadtentwicklung.berlin.de/denkmal/denkmale_in_berlin/en/weltkulturerbe/siedlungen/ausstellung.shtml) accessed 15 May 2014.

While there is variation in unit sizes, from 1 to 5 rooms, the design principles were informed by a desire to create housing for all income bands while at the same time ensuring an equality of amenity provision in regard to bathrooms and kitchens. The addition of balconies and loggias were incorporated to enhance daylight penetration and the enjoyment of sunshine. The landscaping elements comprise common areas of greenery between and surrounding building blocks as well as private gardens (as in the case of Falkenberg and Britz) again with the deliberate intention of strengthening the functional value of the properties and an outdoor lifestyle by residents. A brief discussion of the six housing estates can be taken forward under four headings: plan form; materials and colour; restoration and conservation; heritage interpretation and tourism.

Table 20.1: The profile of the six Modernist housing estates in Berlin

	Gartenstadt Falkenberg	Siedlung Schillerpark	Grosssiedlung Britz	Wohnstadt Carl Legien	Weisse Stadt	Grosssiedlung Siemensstadt
Construction period	1913-16	1924-30 (reconstruction in part 1951-57)	1925-30	1928-30	1929-31	1929-34
Architects	Bruno Taut, Heinrich Tessenow	Bruno Taut	Bruno Taut, Martin Wagner	Bruno Taut, Franz Hillinger	Otto Rudolf Salvisberg, Bruno Ahrends, Wilhelm Büning	Hans Scharoun, Walter Gropius, Otto Bartning, Fred Forbat, Hugo Häring, Paul Henning
Landscape architects	Ludwig Lesser	Walter Rossow, Friedrich Bauer	Leberecht Migge, Ottokar Wagler	Bruno Taut	Ludwig Lesser	Leberecht Migge
Residential units	128	303	1,963	1,149	1,268	1,370
Number of residents	Approx. 230	Approx. 740	Approx. 3,100	Approx. 1,200	Approx. 2,100	Approx. 2,800
World Heritage Site area (ha)	4.4	4.6	37.1	8.4	14.3	19.3
Buffer zone area (ha)	31.2	31.9	73.1	25.5	50.1	46.7

Source: adapted from Senate Department for Urban Development and the Environment (2012) *World heritage in Berlin: six Berlin Modernism housing estates*, Berlin.

(1) Plan form. In each case the design of the six housing estates reflected a desire to move away from the visually enclosed tenements to more open aspect developments. In Falkenberg the plan form is most evocative of two village streets with the initial phase being a short cul-de-sac of varying and mainly row houses facing each other (*Akazienhof*, Photograph 20.1), and the second being a mixture of ribbon style dwellings on each side of a road whose front gardens serve to give extra width to what resembles a winding country lane (*Gartenstadtweg*). By way of contrast the other estates comprise an essentially block-based layout, although Britz has elements of each format underscoring the particular influence of Bruno Taut as a champion of garden town living. This combination is most clearly demonstrated at Britz by the design of *Das Hufeisen* (The Horseshoe) which involves a 350m long, three storey horseshoe shaped ribbon of apartments and local shops enclosing a sunken green area with a central pond (Photograph 20.2). To the rear of this focal point in the estate there are narrow residential streets with rows of low single family houses and individual gardens. The block forms evidenced at Schillerpark (Photograph 20.3), Carl Legien (Photograph 20.4), Weisse Stadt (Photograph 20.5) and Siemensstadt enclose a series of rectangular green courtyards with openings that add emphasis to a spatial structure of intended outdoor living. Mature planting gives screening, while varied block compositions accentuate the integration of this open space into the overall

Photograph 20.1: Gartenstadt Falkenberg

Source: photograph by authors, April 2014

Photograph 20.2: Grosssiedlung Britz

Source: http://www.stadtentwicklung.berlin.de/denkmal/denkmale_in_berlin/en/weltkulturerbe/accessed 24 June 2014

Photograph 20.3: Siedlung Schillerpark

Source: photograph by authors, April 2014

Photograph 20.4: Wohnstadt Carl Legien

Source: photograph by authors, April 2014

Photograph 20.5: Weisse Stadt

Source: photograph by authors, April 2014

design, for example, sun seeking facades and balconies facing each other (at Carl Legien) or facing more wall-type frontages with doorway insertions (at Weisse Stadt and Siemensstadt). In the case of Siemensstadt there is also attention given to the insertion of a public park area within the estate; this spine of community open space (*Grüne Mitte*) provides visual separation between adjacent groups of blocks and links with the parcels of greenspace between individual blocks.

(2) Materials and colour. The use of colour in building design is a unifying theme across all the housing estates with the most dramatic finishes applied in Falkenberg. Again the contribution of Bruno Taut, dubbed the "master of colourful architecture in Berlin" (Brenne, 2013), is apparent. Different colour combinations are applied to walls, doors, windows, shutters, balconies, trellis arches and porches, while the overall warmth of the project is enhanced by the use of terracotta coloured roofing tiles. The use of colour is very powerful in Falkenberg to such a degree that, during construction, the estate earned the sobriquet "Ink-Box Estate" (*Tuschkastensiedlung*). The concept of highlighting architectural elements in this fashion has carried across to the apartment blocks with, for example, red brick being used for wall facades at Schillerpark, red paint being used to pigment plaster at Britz, and white surfaces being a dominant element at Weisse Stadt. A combination of yellow-brown bricks on balconies and beige walls at Siemensstadt serve additionally to draw attention to the design of unusual kidney-shaped balconies as extensions to the interior living space. Indeed colour is used very effectively to create visual linkages across apartment blocks, most effectively seen at Carl Legien where bands of blue and yellow paint on U-shaped blocks almost flow across the central street. In all cases entrance doors and windows are given special colour treatment to embellish the artistic contribution of these functional elements to the architectural ensemble.

(3) Restoration and conservation. At the time of their inscription on the World Heritage List all six housing estates were for the most part still in possession of their original fabric and planned density. They suffered little damage during the Second World War by virtue of their situation outside the urban core and in the case of Siemensstadt and Schillerpark, which were in proximity to industrial and military complexes, only individual housing units were affected (Landesdenkmalamt Berlin im Auftrag der Senatsverwaltung für Stadtentwicklung Berlin, 2009, p154). During the interim there has been external resurfacing, recolouring and replacement of fabric elements, including the addition of energy efficiency measures, that have been able to draw on information contained within architectural archives. The restoration work has also engaged with the greenscape of the housing estates where in the main the original path networks have survived; new trees and hedges consistent with original designs have been planted, for example, in Falkenberg and in other

estates there has been selective felling to re-open previous visual linkages, for example, in Carl Legien. The restoration work has been co-funded by federal and municipal authorities and for the period 2009-2014, some €12.3 million has been provided by the Federal Ministry of Transport, Building and Urban Development / Federal Ministry for the Environment, Nature Conservation, Building and Nuclear Safety under a dedicated "Investment Programme for National UNESCO World Heritage Sites" (www.welterbeprogramm.de, accessed 13 June 2014). The works carried out have been compliant with legislation that seeks to protect the housing estates and, while prior to 1989 there were separate statutes affecting property in east and west Berlin, all six estates are now protected by the *Denkmalschutzgesetz Berlin* (Law on Preservation of Historic Buildings and Monuments in Berlin) and are entered in the Berlin Register of Historic Places. These regulatory controls affect not only the designated World Heritage Sites but also the adjacent buffer zones (*Pufferzone*) that comprise the immediate setting of the estates.

(4) Heritage interpretation and tourism. World Heritage Site inscription carries an expectation that sites and buildings will be presented to national and international audiences and thus the Berlin Modernist housing estates have required a commitment to detailed historical and contemporary interpretation for visitors. At the same time those charged with the development of tourism have had to appreciate that these are living environments that necessitates a respectful gaze on architectural spectacle. The sites will never become populist attractions *vis a vis* other 'must see' places in Berlin and thus the interpretation available thus far speaks to specialist interest whether on information panels or within visitor information centres that have utilised vacant floorspace in local shop units, for example, in Siemensstadt (Photograph 20.6) or, as in the case of Schillerpark - a former public toilet facility. Our analysis of the six estates indicates, however, an absence of consistency in approach with some sites having information panels that specifically acknowledge the UNESCO designation (for example Falkenberg and Schillerpark), while others have visitor centres that have varied and very restricted opening hours (for example, Siemennstadt and Britz). A housing unit in Britz has been re-modelled to its original colours with period furnishings and is marketed for tourist hire but the available show apartments elsewhere are difficult to locate. Connectivity signage between nearby transit stations and the estates varies and there are no discernible routes within the sites for visitors to follow. For the most part tourists are self-reliant, notwithstanding the availability of some on-line information on the *Senatsverwaltung für Stadtentwicklung und Umwelt* web site and printed colour brochures that can be collected at the City Models of Berlin permanent exhibition centre in Am Köllnischen Park, Berlin-Mitte.

Photograph 20.6: Grosssiedlung Siemensstadt

Source: photograph by authors, April 2014

Towards a new commentary of urban celebration in Berlin

As suggested by Ashworth (2010) "people create heritage in response to their contemporary needs" (p.1269) and thus heritage can be viewed as an instrument of "ideology, power, social control and management, and economic change" (ibid, p.1270). The designation of significant sites as cultural heritage places indicates that something important has happened there; but on occasion an alternative official strategy of wishing to forget can result in the destruction of uncomfortable and perceived irrelevant sites; heritage can simply be discarded as well as created. It is interesting that in Berlin there is a contemporary effort to forge a new post-unification identity out of a past that both pre-dates the Second World War and the east-west division (see Heckner, 2002). The case of the six Modernist housing estates discussed above provides a good illustration of how urban planning and architecture are being used to signify one period in that past. The contested demolition between 2006-2008 of the *Palast der Republik*, the symbolic political and cultural centre of the former GDR, and its replacement by the emerging pastiche *Stadtschloss Berlin Humbolt-Forum* underlines this search for a new and different heritage future. However, the politics of memory have also moved towards a more contradictory engagement with built legacies from the Cold War era. In that regard the current proposal by Berlin city authorities to seek World Heritage Site designation for two major housing construction projects on Karl-Marx-Allee and in Hansaviertal represents, arguably, a more subtle reshaping of collective memory towards a celebration of the different urban planning and development trajectories from the 1950s. Both denote a spirit of competitive modernisation that drew on the particular conventions of urban design prevailing at that time in the USSR and USA respectively (Bodenschatz, 2010). A boulevard axis modelled along the lines of Soviet Classicism characterises Karl-Marx-Allee (formerly Stalinallee), whereas residential blocks set within a greenscape environment are dominant within Hansaviertal. While their varying aesthetic and functional attributes can inform the technical rationale for designation, it would seem that heritage preservation in this instance is being used to build cultural bridges that can selectively redefine the meanings of the urban landscapes. In that regard the extensive peripheral housing estates of the 1960s, notably though not exclusively in the eastern suburbs, are sidelined from mentioning.

To conclude, the designated and proposed housing estate World Heritage Sites of Berlin demonstrate significant urban planning, architectural and landscape design accomplishments. They contrast with a heritage of places that is constructed around commemoration and questioning, what Karen Till (2005) has labelled the 'haunting by the past'. The Modernist housing estates of the Weimar Republic are a material reminder of other times and when conjoined with the selected housing projects of the 1950s, they provide opportunity to fashion meanings of celebration in the present that may shift the essence of place towards an alternative appreciation that something with good intention also happened in Berlin.

References

Ashworth, G.J. (2010) Heritage is also about demolition and disinheritance: power, ideology and popular identification in decisions about *the Palast de Republik*, Berlin, in Amoeda, R. Lira, S. and Pinheiro, C. (eds) *Heritage 2010: heritage and sustainable development.* Barcelos; Green Lines Institute for Sustainable Development, pp.1269-1274.

Becker-Cantarino, B. (ed.) (1996) *Berlin in focus: cultural transformations in Germany*. Westport: Greenwood Press.

Brenne, W. (2013) *Bruno Taut: master of colourful architecture in Berlin.* Berlin: Braun Publishing AG.

Bodenschatz, H. (2010) *Berlin urban design: a brief history.* Berlin: DOM Publishers. Colomb, C. (2012) *Staging the new Berlin: place marketing and the politics of urban reinvention post-1989.* New York: Routledge.

Di Bella, M.P. (2012) Walking memory: Berlin's Holocaust Trail, *Journeys*, 13(2), pp.55-70.

Gropius, W. (1930) Large housing estates, in Boyd Whyte, I. and Frisby, D. (eds.) (2012) *Weimar and now: German cultural criticism, Volume 46: Metropolis Berlin: 1880-1940*. Berkeley: University of California Press, pp.484-486.

Hall, P. (1998) *Cities in civilisation*. London: Weidenfeld and Nicolson.

Heckner, E. (2002) Berlin remake: building memory and the politics of Capital identity, *The Germanic Review: Literature, Culture, Theory*, 77(4), pp.304-325.

Henderson, S.R. (1999) Self-help housing in the Weimar Republic: the work of Ernst May, *Housing Studies*, 14(3), pp.311-328.

Kafkoula, K. (2013) On garden-city lines: looking into social housing estates of interwar Europe, *Planning Perspectives*, 28(2), pp.171-198.

Ladd, B. (1997) *The ghosts of Berlin*. Chicago: The University of Chicago Press.

Landesdenkmalamt Berlin im Auftrag der Senatsverwaltung für Stadtentwicklung Berlin (ed) (2009)*Siedlungen der Berliner moderne: eintragung in die welterbeliste der UNESCO*. Berlin: Verlagshaus Braun.

Neill, W.J.V. (2005) Berlin Babylon: the spatiality of memory and identity in recent planning for the German capital, in McEldowney, M., Murray, M., Murtagh, B. and Sterrett, K. (eds.) *Planning in Ireland and beyond: multidisciplinary essays in honour of John V. Greer*, pp.63-88. Belfast: The Queen's University of Belfast.

Phillips, W.R.E. (1996) The German example and the professionalisation of American and British city planning at the turn of the century, *Planning Perspectives*, 11(2), pp.167-183.

Pudor, H. (1910) The people's park in Greater Berlin, in Boyd Whyte, I. and Frisby, D. (eds.) (2012) *Weimar and now: German cultural criticism, Volume 46: Metropolis Berlin: 1880-1940*. Berkeley: University of California Press, pp.256-257.

Schlusche, G. (2014) Memory work in Berlin: a comparative perspective, in Neill, W.J.V., Murray, M. and Grist, B. (eds.) (2014) *Relaunching Titanic: memory and marketing in the new Belfast*. London: Routledge, pp.109-120.

Senate Department for Urban Development and the Environment (2012) *World heritage in Berlin: six Berlin Modernism housing estates*. Berlin.

Sonne, W. (2004) Specific intentions-general realities: on the relation between urban forms and political aspirations in Berlin during the twentieth century, *Planning Perspectives*, 19(3), pp.283-310.

Taut, B. (1924) The new home: woman as creative spirit, in Boyd Whyte, I. and Frisby, D. (eds.) (2012) *Weimar and now: German cultural criticism, Volume 46: Metropolis Berlin: 1880-1940*. Berkeley: University of California Press, pp.473-475.

Till, K.E. (2005) *The new Berlin: memory, politics, place*. Minneapolis: University of Minnesota Press.

Webber, A.J. (2008) *Berlin in the 20th century: a cultural topography*. Cambridge: Cambridge University Press.

INDEX